Communism in
Eastern Europe

Communist Eastern Europe

Communism in Eastern Europe

Edited by Teresa Rakowska-Harmstone and Andrew Gyorgy

Indiana University Press
Bloomington and London

Manufactured in the United States of America

Library of Congress Cataloging in Publication Data
Main entry under title:
Communism in Eastern Europe.
Includes bibliographical references and index.
1. Communism—Europe, Eastern—Addresses, essays,
lectures.   I. Rakowska-Harmstone, Teresa.
II. Gyorgy, Andrew, 1917–
HX238.5.C65   335.43'0947   78-20402
ISBN 0-253-33791-7
ISBN 0-253-20225-6 pbk. 1 2 3 4 5 83 82 81 80 79

Contents

The success of a volume like *Communism in Eastern Europe* depends on the interplay of several factors and on the cooperation of a number of colleagues. The editors gratefully acknowledge the patience and support of their co-authors and of the publisher, Indiana University Press, who agreed from the inception of this project with the two principal underlying assumptions:

(1) That there is a need for a comprehensive, lucid, and technically accurate general textbook in the field of East European politics designed for junior-senior as well as graduate courses in the fields of politics and international affairs; and

(2) That the volume should be organized around two types and patterns of approaches, namely, individual country-by-country case-studies, buttressed by certain significant *functional* chapters illuminating the key supranational and interregional problem areas of East Central Europe.

Consequently, our book is divided into twelve chapters, eight of which are individual country studies, while four present a broad panorama of such regionally oriented subjects as the role and function of Eastern Europe in world politics; the economic development of the area; the impact of contemporary Eurocommunism; and certain key aspects of current political and leadership changes in Eastern Europe. The individual authors were asked by the editors to focus on the following key subjects: the geopolitical background of the country involved; the size and distinctive characteristics of the population; the relevant features of the nation's historic development, with particular emphasis on the turbulent interwar period of dictatorships and semidictatorships throughout the region; and various psychological and sociological forces which have helped shape the last three decades. Other factors considered were the political party structures—the dominant right-wing elements as well as the slowly emerging underground leftist groups—which set the stage for a full-fledged Communist "takeover."

Our colleagues and fellow authors were also requested to consider in some detail, as part of the structural focus of a typical "country" chapter, the current state of cultural affairs, human rights, dissenters and defectors, and—in general —issues related to the theory and practice of human rights. These important considerations lead inevitably to discussion of the scope, intensity, and overall effectiveness of political opposition in the given East European country, its chances of asserting itself and of having its voice heard. Such issues have been particularly interesting in connection with recent Hungarian and Polish developments, and probably least relevant in the German Democratic Republic and Bulgaria.

A review of the recent past and of current developments inevitably foreshadows a cautious preview of possible future events in the countries of East Central Europe, and both our individual country and functional chapters do speculate about certain contingencies broadly related to the future of the Soviet control of the eight East European countries, and their more than 150 million inhabitants. Of course, such future predictions and ideological forecasts have to be restrained and careful by definition, given the tenuous "balance-of-power" position and geopolitical character of most of Eastern Europe.

While the book considers broadly the evolution of this region since the end of World War II in 1945, it deals primarily with the events of the 1970s and with projections for the 1980s. In Soviet political terms, the stress is on post-Khrushchev developments, i.e., the 1964–79 period. Among the main themes treated are nationalism; intra-bloc political and economic integration through WTO and CMEA; Eurocommunism; and detente. It is hoped that the volume will strike a useful balance between the myriad long- and short-term issues confronting Eastern Europe, one of the world's more conflict-ridden political regions.

Because so many languages are involved in this book, diacritical and accent marks have been deleted from foreign words. The short bibliography at the end of each country chapter is intended as a guide to further reading, not as a list of sources on which the chapter is based.

T. R.-H.

A. G.

Communism in
Eastern Europe

1   Eastern Europe in World Perspective

Vernon V. Aspaturian

Until comparatively recent times, Eastern Europe did not exist as a distinct geographical, regional, or political concept; its role on the world stage was marginal. Today, Eastern Europe is recognized as one of the major geographical-political regions of the world. Before World War II and particularly before World War I, global or world politics were essentially colonial and imperial politics and the exclusive province of a handful of Great Powers, all located in Europe except for the United States and Japan. Eastern Europe, like most of the non-European world, was essentially an object of great-power politics rather than an actor on the European stage, to say nothing of the world stage. Knowledge of, not to mention contact with, the world beyond its immediate proximity was nil, except for the awareness of a vast and generous America to which millions of East Europeans migrated after 1900.

Similarly, the outside world was only dimly aware of the nations and few states of Eastern Europe that existed in the late nineteenth and early twentieth centuries. Subsumed for centuries as parts of the four great empires of the East—the German, Hapsburg, Russian, and Ottoman—the nations of Eastern Europe possessed little international or world visibility as distinctive national personalities. The region was even remote and unfamiliar to Western Europe, with the exception of Hungary, as part of the Dual Monarchy, and Poland, whose disappearance from the diplomatic scene was briefly interrupted by Napoleon's creation of the Grand Duchy of Warsaw, which helped to keep Poland alive as a submerged but nevertheless distinctive national personality. As for Czechs and Slovaks, Romanians, Croats, Slovenes, Serbs, Bosnians, Macedonians, Montenegrins, Bulgarians, Albanians, Estonians, Latvians, Lithuanians, Belorussians, and Ukrainians, to say nothing of nuances like Uniates and Hussites, Ghegs and Toscs, Ruthenians and

1

Szeklers, or Masurians and Kaschubes, they were indiscriminately perceived as Austro-Hungarians, Russians, Turks, or indeterminate Slavs by all but a handful of scholars, poets, and statesmen who knew better.

As recently as 1938, at the height of the Sudeten crisis, an exasperated and outraged Prime Minister Neville Chamberlain referred to Czechoslovakia and the Sudeten crisis in a public radio broadcast as "a quarrel in a far away country between people about whom we know nothing"; it was "horrible, fantastic, incredible," he said, that Britain should somehow be concerned.[1] And yet Czechoslovakia is the westernmost country of contemporary Eastern Europe, nestled in the center of the European continent; its control, Bismarck had assured the Germans, ensured the mastery of all Europe.

During and after World War II, the countries of Eastern Europe moved out of the mists of remoteness and were conceptually united with Western Europe as part of Europe in the cultural, as distinct from the geographic, sense. But because of Soviet occupation and control, the countries and nations of Eastern Europe were again congealed into a single gray mass, rarely disaggregated into their individual personalities. For the world beyond Europe and America, Eastern Europe was as remote and distant as were the Congo and Burma to East Europeans. As late as 1956, Eastern Europe and East Europeans were perceived even by educated Africans and Asians as an undifferentiated mass; to some degree this accounted for the relative indifference of the emerging Third World to their fate as satellites of the Soviet Union. This indifference was illustrated by the voting behavior of Third World countries in the U.N. General Assembly at the time of the Hungarian uprising in 1956.

Thus, during the past century, the status and role of Eastern Europe in the international community have passed through a number of phases, corresponding to the changing structural self-perception of its role in the world community and the reciprocal perception by the outside world. These phasal roles can be sequentially summarized as a general movement from objects of international politics, to instruments and pawns, to subjects and actors, first on the European stage and then on the world stage, in a number of capacities.

Until about 1850, Eastern Europe was largely an object over which four great empires contended; after 1850, some parts of Eastern Europe, as they became independent, were in turn instruments and pawns of the Great Powers; during the interwar period, the newly independent countries of Eastern Europe assumed the role and status of actors and subjects in the international community, an evolution that was arrested first by Nazi Germany and then by the Soviet Union after World War II. Eastern Europe as a geographical-regional concept did not make its appearance until after World War I, when the succession states were carved out of the German, Hapsburg, and Russian empires, of which most of the area was a part. The southern part of contemporary Eastern Europe was subject to the Ottoman Empire for centuries. It is ironic that this relatively less developed sector of Eastern Europe under Ottoman rule was the first to proliferate into independent states, a process that was largely completed before World War I. Ottoman Europe and its successor states in Europe, however, were generally described as part of a subregion, the Balkans, sometimes called Southeastern Europe and, before 1914, often considered part of the Near East.

After World War I the "northern tier" and the "southern tier" of Eastern Europe were united into a single geographical-regional concept. After World War II the geographical concept of Eastern Europe merged with the ideological concept to form the contemporary political-regional concept. Since about 1957, in spite of its association with the USSR and in some respects because of it, Eastern Europe has emerged as one of the major geographical-political regions of the world, whose states function in part as members of a distinct grouping or bloc and in part as individual and separate actors on the world stage. Whether as part of a group or in their individual capacities, the states of Eastern Europe are perceived by themselves and by others as actively engaged in diplomatic, political, economic, and military activities on a global scale.

The parochialism of Eastern Europe is a thing of the past. While the region does not function as a world power, either as a group of states or as individual states, it does act in a global context with a world perspective. This is true of every state in the region, even the smallest. Who would have dreamed, for example, even twenty-five years ago, that a bizarre relationship like the now defunct Peking-Tirana axis could have existed? That Albania would become aware of China is understandable, but that China would find the tiny speck that is Albania on the fringes of Eastern Europe and proclaim her a political-ideological ally against both "imperialism" and "revisionism," resulting in a wide array of economic, cultural, political, and military interaction between them, is, in its strange way, a remarkable tribute to the visibility of Eastern Europe on the world scene.

The status of Eastern Europe as one of the major geographical-political regions of the world was given quasi-official recognition by the United Nations when it was informally stipulated that at least one nonpermanent member of the Security Council should be elected from the states of this region on a rotating basis. Geographical Eastern Europe and political Eastern Europe are not perfectly congruent. For all practical purposes, Eastern Europe today means Communist Europe, except for the USSR. This conception excludes Greece, Turkish Thrace, Finland, and the European non-Russian republics of the Soviet Union, which are geographically a part of Eastern Europe, and correspondingly includes the German Democratic Republic and the former German provinces of Pomerania and Silesia (now parts of Poland), which traditionally were not considered a part of the geographical area.

Since the concept Eastern Europe has also been burdened with a cultural characteristic, some nations and states of Eastern Europe, particularly those whose history, culture, and religion were Western-oriented, resented inclusion in a broader unit that seemed to separate them from Western Europe and to associate them with Byzantine/ Ottoman Europe and the Balkans, an area that was considered backward. Thus, before World War II countries like Poland, Czechoslovakia, Hungary, and Germany (the northern tier) preferred to be identified with another subregional concept, Central Europe, separate and distinct from Eastern Europe (the Soviet Union) and Southeastern Europe (the Balkans).

In 1978 the aggregate population of Eastern Europe numbered more than 132 million and was distributed among eight states and more than a dozen distinct nationalities, whose history and tradition of mutual animosity, hostility, and conflict need not be recorded here.[2] Two major Christian religions dominate the region: Latin Christianity in the North and Byzantine Christianity in the South, with pockets of Protestant sects, Uniate Catholics, and Moslem groups. Two major alphabets, the Latin and the Cyrillic, correspond to the Catholic-Byzantine cleavage. Extensive Jewish communities once existed in Poland, Czechoslovakia, Hungary, and Romania, but as a result of the holocaust, only small residual Jewish communities can be found in Eastern Europe today. The paramount language group is Slavic, divided between West Slavic and South Slavic. Four of the states, embracing ten nations, are Slavic, whereas the remaining states each represent a distinct language grouping.[3]

Thus, in spite of the political-ideological homogeneity that characterizes contemporary Eastern Europe, it is a remarkably diverse aggregation of states and nations in terms of traditional characteristics. It has been the traditional diversities rather than the perceived homogeneities that have shaped the Eastern European past and have determined its political fate to be more often an object of the international system than a subject, individually and collectively.

Since the beginning of the nineteenth century, when the first nations of Eastern Europe emerged as independent states out of the four empires of which they were a part, they have never been capable, individually or collectively, of resisting either German or Russian encroachment on their political existence. Even as the Ottoman Empire was forced into retreat from Southeastern Europe, the emerging states and nations were quickly reduced to pawns or objects of the two great European nations—Russians and Germans—in rivalry with one another for dominance in the region. The Germans were represented not only by Prussia and its successor, the German Empire, but also by the Hapsburg Empire, which technically speaking was not *the* German state, but a German dominated state (especially before 1867), constitutionally organized as a Dual Monarchy (Austro-Hungarian) and masquerading as a multinational state.

Because of the relatively small size, inexperience, weakness, and mutual rivalries of the Eastern European nations, they were vulnerable to the manipulation and exploitation of the Germans and Russians and were forced or cajoled to gravitate into the sphere of one or the other of the two great nations. The most notable exception in the eighteenth century was Poland, which attempted to vie with both as an equally great or imperial nation, but without much success. Since Poland refused to seek the protection or patronage of either the Germans or the Russians and thus threatened both, it was Poland's fate to be dismembered. The smaller nations of Southeastern Europe that emerged later managed to preserve their formal independence by deliberately seeking or accepting the protection of the Hapsburg or Romanov empires. From 1850 to World War II, for a variety of reasons, the German influence was more dominant than the Russian. After World War I, because both Germany and Russia were weak pariah states, Eastern Europe was blessed with real autonomy under the remote and benign protection of France, but with the resurgence of German power after 1933, the countries fell one by one into the German orbit, with Poland once again subjected to partition.

EASTERN EUROPE IN WORLD DIPLOMACY BETWEEN THE WARS

During the brief interwar period, the countries of Eastern Europe functioned in the European community as *separate* actors rather than as a regional unit or part of a political grouping, and as *independent* actors rather than as subjects and pawns of larger states. Although all of the East European states were members of the League of Nations and maintained diplomatic relations with a modest spectrum of states outside Europe, their international activity was restricted largely to Europe; they played little or no role on the world or global stage, except for Poland, which became a semipermanent member of the League Council and had pretensions of being more than a parochial Eastern European state. The only non-European state with which the East European countries developed extensive contacts and relationships was the United States, not only because of President Wilson's role in determining the fate and shape of Eastern Europe, but also because millions of immigrants from the Hapsburg and Russian empires were drawn from the subject nationalities that became the new states of Eastern Europe.

With the rise of Fascism in Italy, and particularly with the advent of Hitler in Germany and the re-entry of Moscow into the general stream of European diplomacy after the completion of the First Five-Year Plan, it appears in retrospect that the countries of Eastern Europe enjoyed independence and autonomy only because the traditional great powers—Germany and Russia—had been weakened.

Unfortunately, the countries of Eastern Europe did not take the opportunity of the interwar period to submerge their differences and design ways in which to preserve their autonomy collectively against a possible resurgence of German and Russian power, which they would be unable to resist individually. Instead, irredentism, revisionism, and revanchism prevailed, as typified by the Hungarian cry "Nem, Nem Soha!" ("No, No, Never"), a reference to the Treaty of Trianon, which dismembered Hungary and reduced her to a nondescript Balkan-type state. The revisionism of the discontented East European countries (Hungary, Bulgaria, and Poland to some degree) was fueled and inflamed by the revisionist aspirations of Germany and Italy, while the restiveness of nationalities who found themselves as part of a binational or multinational state, instead of their own nation-state (Slovaks in Czechoslovakia and Croats in Yugoslavia), was also exploited and manipulated by both Hitler and Mussolini. It was an unfortunate coincidence that precisely those states that were the targets of the revisionist powers were also the ones with the most serious domestic nationality or minority problems (Czechoslovakia, Yugoslavia, and Romania).

Rivalries, animosities, and hatreds separated the winners and losers of World War I, but even among winners and losers there were serious mutual demands and claims.

The new successor states and those largely satisfied with the settle-ments after World War I (Poland, Czechoslovakia, Yugoslavia, Ro-mania, and Greece), as a rule, allied themselves with France, the most powerful state in Europe, and entered into local alliances with one another, directed against the irredentism and revisionism of Austria, Hungary, and Bulgaria. The Little Entente (Czechoslovakia, Yugo-slavia, and Romania) and the Balkan Entente (Romania, Yugoslavia, Greece, and Turkey) represented not only the independence of the East European states in their behavior but also their dependence upon France. These local alliances, furthermore, represented efforts at collec-tive action to fill the power vacuum in the area, while simultaneously reflecting the deep cleavages that separated the small countries from one another and rendered them vulnerable to penetration, manipula-tion, and control by the Great Powers.

It seemed only natural, as the *status quo* states of Eastern Europe looked to France for support and protection, that the revisionist states of Eastern Europe would increasingly rely upon Germany and Italy to support their revisionist aspirations. Within a few years after Hitler's advent to power—and particularly after the annexation of Austria—Hungary and Bulgaria gravitated toward Berlin and Rome. As France's willingness and ability to protect her East European clients diminished after the Sudeten crisis and Munich, Hitler, in effect, was given a free hand in Eastern Europe. Even *status quo* states like Romania and Yugo-slavia sought the protection of German might, not only against their local tormentors but against the Soviet Union as well. Even before the Anschluss and Munich, France's alliance with Moscow appeared to Eastern Europe to nullify whatever protection France had afforded them against the USSR, which increasingly posed a threat to all of Eastern Europe, not only in traditional territorial terms but also be-cause of the revolutionary threat to their social systems.

Thus, except for Poland, which was the immediate target of Ger-many, all of the states of Eastern Europe became client or potential client states of Germany, subject to barter and manipulation as Berlin saw fit. As the arbiter of Eastern Europe's destiny, Hitler first made an arrangement with Stalin, demarcating spheres of influence in the re-gion, with entire states and provinces bartered away to Moscow in exchange for a benign neutrality in the war between Germany and the Allied Powers. Germany then posed as an "honest broker," arbitrating disputes between her clients (most notably the division of Transyl-vania between Hungary and Romania), and dismembered Yugoslavia and Greece, redistributing their territory in 1941 among their neigh-bors. Croats and Slovaks found satisfaction in the creation of their own states under German patronage; Hungary and Bulgaria exulted in their territorial acquisitions, while the Czechs, Poles, and Serbs were deprived of their statehood.

Although Germany altered the entire political and territorial landscape of Eastern Europe, this arrangement proved to be temporary. Once Germany was defeated and the Soviet Union appeared on the scene to claim the entire area as her exclusive zone of ideological, political, economic, and military influence, Eastern Europe once again was subjected to territorial and demographic convulsions, and while the new landscape of Eastern Europe did not resemble that created by Hitler, neither did it resemble very much that of the prewar period. Three states—Latvia, Lithuania, and Estonia—disappeared into the jaws of the Soviet Union, while a new state, the German Democratic Republic, was created. Slovakia and Croatia disappeared as independent states, whereas Austria, Czechoslovakia, and Yugoslavia were reconstituted, the first, as it existed before 1938; the second, somewhat truncated by the Soviet annexation of the Carpatho-Ukraine; and the third, slightly expanded at Italy's expense. Hungary was pressed back into her 1937 frontiers, as was Bulgaria, but Poland and Romania suffered extensive territorial losses to the Soviet Union. Poland was compensated for her losses with Pomerania, Silesia, and part of East Prussia, while Romania had to be content with the restoration of all Transylvania to her control.

The Soviet Union annexed about 200,000 square miles of territory in Eastern Europe and moved its borders westward by about 200 miles, whereas the boundaries of "Eastern Europe" were now pressed beyond Central Europe and into the easternmost frontiers of Western Europe, as the western frontier of East Germany extended beyond 10 degrees longitude, west of Hamburg and little more than 150 miles east of the Rhine. More fundamental than the territorial changes were the ideological and socioeconomic convulsions that rocked the region, as Eastern Europe assumed not only a new profile but also a new identity, as an aggregated appendage of the Soviet state and an extension of the Soviet sociopolitical order and Soviet military power.

EASTERN EUROPE AS A WORLD ACTOR

Between 1945 and 1949, Eastern Europe once again became an arena of contending Great Powers, but this time the powers were the USSR and the United States, since only the latter had the power to offer itself as a protector of Eastern Europe against the territorial, ideological, sociopolitical and military onslaught from the East. But since the United States did not have any immediate, tangible vital interest in Eastern Europe, but rather an abstract ideological-political interest and an overall strategic interest in its rivalry with the Soviet Union, it was not prepared to take the risks or to make the sacrifices that Moscow was prepared to do in order to retain control over an area of traditional, vital, and immediate interest to her overall well-being. For the Soviet Union, Eastern Europe was simultaneously a defense *glacis;* a springboard for possible expansion westward; an ideological legitimization of her universal pretensions; a laboratory for the application of the Soviet model of development; a reservoir of human, natural, and economic resources to be exploited for Soviet recovery; a collection of diplomatic pawns and surrogates to be used in international politics; and a source of psychological and even quantitative comfort in international organizations and conferences, where the Soviet Union might otherwise be isolated and alone.

U.S. interest in Eastern Europe and charges of Soviet violations of the Yalta Agreement with respect to "free democratic institutions" and "free elections," when combined with an unexpected American passion for the reunification of Germany, struck Stalin and the Soviet leaders as malign and designed to deprive the Soviet Union of her just deserts, to press her back within her pre-1939 frontiers, and to deny her the global role to which she was entitled as one of the major world powers. Although anticommunist ideological goals were certainly involved, the U.S. attempt to weaken the Soviet presence in Eastern Europe was directed primarily at depriving the Soviet Union of a forward geopolitical springboard for possible invasion or intervention in Central and Western Europe. Its objective then and now has been to remove, once and for all, the direct threat of Soviet intervention in Germany and Western Europe in response either to attempted Communist uprisings or takeovers within these individual countries or to vulnerabilities and openings that might entice the Soviet Union to move its own forces directly into the area. What the United States sought was a transformation of Eastern Europe from a potential Soviet springboard into a buffer zone between Soviet power and West-Central Europe.

Whether Eastern Europe is a buffer zone, a defense *glacis,* or a springboard for expansion is in the eye of the beholder and cannot be objectively measured. If Eastern Europe could function simultaneously as a defensive zone and a springboard for the Soviet Union, it could so function for the United States and Western Europe as well. Since Stalin was aware that the East European states were too weak and fragmented to function as an independent buffer zone between the USSR and the United States, assuming they were willing to do so (which was dubious), the Soviet leader saw in the U.S. demand for "free elections" a not-so-subtle attempt to mobilize the widespread anti-Soviet and anti-Russian sentiment in most of these countries. This would effectively nullify Roosevelt's concession to Stalin that the states of Eastern Europe would have to have "friendly governments," i.e., friendly to the USSR. Stalin knew that "free elections" were incompatible with "friendly governments" and so did the Truman Administration.

Although after 1948, except for Yugoslavia, the Soviet grip on Eastern Europe tightened with a seeming permanence, the countries of Eastern Europe once again became objects of contending powers rather than independent actors on the international stage. After 1956, when U.S. credibility as a contender with the Soviet Union for Eastern Europe diminished with the quashing of the Hungarian uprising, China attempted to convert Eastern Europe into an object of ideological contention between Moscow and Peking, perceiving a possibility that the East European states might find it useful to employ China as a counterpoise against Moscow within the family of Communist states. But within the narrower confines of the Communist interstate fraternity, the East European states were allowed more latitude as subjects. They initially welcomed the usefulness of the Chinese connection, which they exploited to gain considerable autonomy "within" the Communist interstate system in return for not seeking greater autonomy outside the system.

Since 1956 and in spite of the invasion of Czechoslovakia in 1968 and the proclamation of the "Brezhnev doctrine," the international role and status of Eastern Europe as a collectivity and as individual states have increased perceptibly. It is important to recognize, however, that international visibility is not a one-dimensional phenomenon but a multidimensional one. Instead of a single role or identity in the world community developed to an intense pitch, East European activity in the world community assumed the pattern of accepting new roles and seeking several international environments in which to function. The latitude of activity for Eastern Europe as a whole and as individual states varies considerably as to both roles and environment. Each East European state has and continues to seek its own individual equilibrium with the Soviet Union and with every other East European state as well as with Eastern Europe as a whole, and this equilibrium varies considerably. Thus some East Europeans states have more roles to play than others, possess a different spectrum of identities, and function in a different set of environments.

The increasing involvement of Eastern Europe in the international community is not an unmixed blessing, as some East European countries have discovered. Eastern Europe and individual East European states find that often they are involved involuntarily in global concerns in distant corners of the world because of their Soviet connection, and seemingly must maintain a foreign policy that is not too distinct from that of a great or super power. Thus, during the Czech Spring of 1968, one Czech writer was moved to complain: "We are a small country. . . . We should have a modest foreign policy, one conforming to our possibilities. I do not understand why we have to intervene in the affairs of Madagascar, Guatemala, or Nigeria."[4]

Yet, as Yugoslavia demonstrated after 1948, expanding one's involvement and activity in the international community results in the creation and discovery of new roles, new identities, new associations and new constituencies, which can sustain and promote the interests of a small state in many dimensions. While it is true that many East European states resent being adjuncts of Soviet global concerns in the general international environment or pawns within the international Communist movement against China and other Communist heretics, in general, the expansion of Eastern Europe's international activities has on the whole been beneficial and will continue to be so. Pawns and clients do not always remain pawns and clients, as China, Yugoslavia, Albania, Romania, and even Cuba have demonstrated in different ways.

All of the states of Eastern Europe enjoy separate and independent membership in the United Nations and the general international system. This is the widest international movement in which they function as actors, but it is also an environment in which the intensity of their activity is restricted. During the Stalinist period, the East European states functioned as a bloc within the organization, never deviating from the Soviet position. They were permitted to function in U.N. agencies and activities only to the degree permitted them by Moscow and usually as surrogates of the Soviet Union on various committees and commissions. As a general rule, Eastern Europe and the Soviet Union boycotted almost all of the U.N. specialized agencies.

The overall global character of Eastern Europe's international behavior can perhaps be placed in proper perspective by comparing it with that of the behavior of all states in the international community. This comparison will take the form of examining the relative participation of individual East European countries in international organizations and in general diplomatic interaction. The data employed are somewhat dated (1963–65) and are designed to give the most general type of measurement. The aggregate data for membership in international or-

Eastern Europe in World Perspective

Table 1 Memberships in International Organizations, 1965

Country	Rank	U.N. Organizations	Other	Total
USSR	59.5	9	29	38
Poland	48.5	12	30	42
Czechoslovakia	57.5	11	28	39
Hungary	70.5	8	26	34
Bulgaria	77	9	24	33
Romania	55.5	11	29	40
Yugoslavia	27	15	35	50
Averages	56	11	29	40
GDR	119	0	5	5
Albania	115	8	9	17
Cuba	82.5	12	20	32
Mongolia	117.5	6	4	10
China	121.5	0	2	2
N. Korea	121.5	0	2	2
N. Vietnam	120	0	3	3
USA	10	16	51	67
France	1	16	91	107
TOTAL COUNTRIES	122	—	—	—
Mean	—	13	27	40
Median	—	19	24	37

Source: C. L. Taylor and M. C. Hudson, *World Handbook of Political and Social Indicators*, second edition (New Haven: Yale University Press, 1972).

ganizations in Table 1 provide the individual country's rank among the 122 states with such participation, the number of U.N. organizations to which it belongs, the number of memberships in other international organizations, and the total of all such memberships.

As would be expected, the unaffiliated Communist state, Yugoslavia, exhibited the widest degree of membership, while Albania and the Asian Communist states exhibited the most limited membership, actually ranking at the bottom of the 122 states. A point of clarification is in order here, since two of the Asian Communist states, North Korea and North Vietnam, along with East Germany, were divided nation-states and neither were members of the United Nations nor were completely accepted or assimilated into the international system in the mid-1960s. Since then China, East Germany, and a united Vietnam have been admitted to the United Nations, and their activity has naturally increased, as Table 3 demonstrates. Generally speaking, the range of participation by the other East European states was rather middling, with rankings spread from 48.5 for Poland to 77 for Bulgaria. The ranking for the Soviet Union was 59.5. France, the country with the widest membership in international organizations, belonged to 107 such organizations, whereas the spread for Eastern Europe was from 17 for Albania to 50 for Yugoslavia, with the median and mean for the 122 countries as a whole being 40 and 37, respectively. The aggregate average for total membership for Eastern Europe (excluding Albania and East Germany) was 40.

Moving on to general diplomatic interaction, measured in terms of diplomats sent, diplomats received, and number of missions abroad, out of 119 countries listed, the Soviet Union ranked eleventh. The countries of Eastern Europe, again excluding Albania and East Germany, exhibited remarkably high levels of activity for small and medium states, ranging from a rank of 19.5 for Czechoslovakia and Yugoslavia to 39 for Romania. As measured against the United States, ranking first with 100 missions abroad, the Soviet Union had 65 missions abroad, whereas Eastern European countries (with the exception of Albania and East Germany) ranged from 40 for Romania to 57 for Yugoslavia and Czechoslovakia; the mean and median for all 119 countries were 31 and 25, respectively. The aggregate average number of missions abroad for Eastern Europe (except for Albania and East Germany) was 50, giving it an average aggregate ranking of 25.

Table 2 Diplomatic Representation, 1963–64

Country	Rank	Diplomats Sent	Diplomats Received	Missions Abroad
USSR	11	1,345	732	65
Poland	21.5	386	301	55
Czechoslovakia	19.5	422	321	57
Hungary	35.5	264	209	42
Bulgaria	26.5	247	209	47
Romania	39	360	228	40
Yugoslavia	19.5	280	324	57
Average	27	327	265	50
GDR	83.5	153	186	16
Albania	85.5	56	59	15
Cuba	38	216	201	41
Mongolia	94	43	—	11
China	40.5	405	389	38
N. Korea	78	111	—	18
N. Vietnam	81	81	—	17
USA	1	2,782	1,418	100
TOTAL COUNTRIES	119	—	—	—
Mean		196	224	31
Median		102	172	25

Source: C. L. Taylor and M. C. Hudson, *World Handbook of Political and Social Indicators*, second edition (New Haven: Yale University Press, 1972).

The relatively wide disparity in activity between institutional membership (average ranking of 40) and bilateral diplomatic contacts (average ranking of 25) suggests that Moscow feels less threatened by bilateral diplomatic activity than by memberships in international organizations, and hence is more tolerant of the former than the latter. Membership in organizations involves affiliation, organizational commitment, and partial identification with noncommunist states, which may be employed as constituency support against the demands of Moscow, whereas bilateral diplomatic contact appears to be less threatening to Soviet influence, which has higher priority than any commitment that an individual East European state may have with another state. The Soviet Union is wary of any organizational commitments by its East European clients which might collide with commitments to Communist organizations or to the Soviet Union itself.

After 1956, Soviet and East European activity in the United Nations and in U.N.-associated organizations increased, and the spectrum of membership for the two, while similar, is by no means identical. Thus, as of 1974, of the major U.N.-affiliated organizations, the Soviet Union did not belong to the Food and Agricultural Organization (FAO), whereas all of the East European states except Albania belonged; the USSR did not belong to GATT (General Agreement on Tariffs and Trade), whereas Czechoslovakia, Romania, Poland, and Yugoslavia belonged. Albania belonged to the fewest such organizations, while Yugoslavia belonged to all. The remaining East European states and the USSR did not belong to the International Bank, the International Development Association, the International Monetary Fund, or the International Development Association.

The global activity of the East European states occurred, first, because they were involved and manipulated by the Soviet Union in its global concerns. Individual states were used by Moscow as foils, or as proxies in various activities. For example, Czechoslovakia funneled arms first to Israel and then to Egypt; Bulgaria represented the Soviet position in various international bodies and conferences. Above and beyond the Soviet connection, adherence to Marxism-Leninism and the activity of East European Communist parties and leaders in the world Communist movement conditioned and socialized East European Communists to think "internationally" and to behave globally once they came to power. Soviet writers, for example, even cite the world Communist movement as a sort of socialization vehicle, conditioning the behavior of Communist states: "As a rule, before a given country becomes socialist, its Marxist-Leninist party already has a system of stable ties with fraternal parties in other countries, established in the course of its activity in the world Communist movement."[5]

As Communist states become members of the general interstate community, they retain their membership in the world Communist movement, the second general international environment in which they function. In this environment, acting out their roles as Communist parties rather than as states, they interact with other Communist parties, ruling and nonruling, the latter considered to be leaders of future Communist states. With the development of Titoism, then Maoism, and now Eurocommunism, the world Communist movement has become a more doctrinally flexible environment, to the point where it can hardly be called a "movement" at all. More latitude for intensive identity-building is permissible for individual East European Communist parties in this environment because of the fragmentation or decentralization of the world Communist movement. Various groupings, including polarized aggregations, exist within this environment, whose outer parameters become more flexible, as intramovement groupings become tighter.

Aside from their identity as members of the general interstate system and the world Communist movement, Eastern Europe, as a whole or as individual states, belongs to a number of subsystems, which are subordinate to either the general interstate system or the world Communist movement, or both.

Subsystems within the international Communist environments are as follows:

1. *The World Socialist System,* made up of the 14 self-identified Marxist-Leninist states, irrespective of mutual acceptance.
2. *The Socialist Community,* consisting of all Marxist-Leninist states except Albania, China, and possibly Yugoslavia.
3. *The Warsaw Treaty Organization,* a multilateral military alliance, ostensibly open to all European states, but in fact including only the USSR and all East European states except Yugoslavia and Albania.
4. *The Council for Mutual Economic Assistance (CMEA),* an economic organization, purportedly aimed at "socialist integration" and the establishment of an "international socialist division of labor." All East European states, including Yugoslavia (as an "associate" member) but excluding Albania, belong, as do Mongolia, Vietnam, and Cuba.

Subsystems within the general international environment to which all or some East European states belong are the following:

1. *Eastern Europe,* as a geographical-political region, which by definition includes all East European Communist states.
2. *Europe,* a cultural-civilization-racial-geographical concept, with which East European states identify more and more, as Asian Communist states identify more with the Third World and with underdeveloped countries. As East European socioeconomic indicators approach those of Western Europe, the gap between East and West Europe will become narrower and the gap between European and Asian Communist states will broaden. The European identity of the East European states, including the USSR, becomes increasingly more emphatic. The Helsinki Conference on European Security, for example, was defined as a European conference, in which all East European states participated as separate members and not as part of a bloc. Romania and Yugoslavia, for example, took positions at this conference substantially at variance with the USSR.
3. *The Third World,* made up primarily of the underdeveloped countries of Asia, Africa, and Latin America, but with which Yugoslavia and Romania have established special links, making them quasi-members.
4. *The Non-Aligned World,* closely approximating the above but defined in terms of position between the two contending poles. Marshal Tito and Yugoslavia have been founders and leading members. Romania has also sought to affiliate itself with this grouping, although Romania is aligned as a member of the Warsaw Pact. Romania, however, has been a fractious and dissident member.

Thus, it is clear that East European countries, far from behaving uniformly, belong to a number of groupings, some of them overlapping in membership. Even within the narrower Soviet bloc groupings (WTO and CMEA), some variations in behavior persist. Romania, for example, remains on excellent terms with Peking, which has asserted that the other East European countries, except Yugoslavia and Albania, have reverted to being Soviet puppet states. Romania, furthermore, maintains friendly relations with Israel, departs from Soviet voting patterns in international organizations and conferences, and behaves as a maverick in a number of ways.

But Eastern Europe's role in the international community is not simply linked to the various groupings to which it belongs or the environments within which it operates. In many ways, Eastern Europe constitutes a cultural bridge between the Soviet Union and Western Europe, since some East European states and nations (Poles, Czechs, Slovenes, Croats, Hungarians, and East Germans) are more "western" than "eastern" in culture, tradition, and orientation. Eurocommunism may serve to reinforce the spiritual link between Western and Eastern Europe but within a Communist environment, just as the Helsinki movement has had the same effect outside the world of Communist states and powers.

The more identities and roles the countries of Eastern Europe develop and the more international environments they function within, the more diluted their identity as Communist states becomes and the more they tend to identify themselves as *European* and *developed* Communist states. These identities and roles are fostered by the East European economic, technical, and military assistance programs which are found in every continent. East European countries are involved in these programs in their individual capacities as developed states, as parts of international organizations, or as a function of their association with the Soviet Union. Commercial links with Western Europe, the United States, and Third World countries have steadily increased. Thousands of professional citizens of East European countries have experienced travel and work abroad in a diverse spectrum of countries. And, frequently, underdeveloped countries find it much easier to deal with small, less threatening developed Communist states than with the Soviet Union. While Moscow may view this as providing the USSR with surrogate access to areas where it might be unwelcome, it is also obvious that these links serve to strengthen the independent contacts of East European states with the outside world.

An important measure of Eastern Europe's status within the international community are the range and intensity of its associations and interactions with states in both Communist and noncommunist subgroups. Generally speaking, the more intense a country's identification with Communist subgroups and organizations and the more extensive its participation in such groups, the less likely it is to identify or participate in noncommunist interstate groupings and organizations. In other words, the more integrated an Eastern European state is in Communist groupings, the less likely it will act as an independent actor in the general international community. With respect to memberships and affiliations, Table 3 provides data which tend to support this obser-

Table 3 Membership and Affiliation of Communist States in Interstate Organizations and Groupings[a]

| Country | World Communist Environment | | | | | | | | | | General Interstate Environment | | | | | | | | | | | | | | | | | | | | GNP Per Capita 1976 |
| | | | | | | | | | | | UN and Affiliated Agencies | | | | | | | | | | | | | | | | Other Interstate Groupings | | | | |
	WCM	WSS	Socialist Community	WTO	CMEA	EJINR	IBEC	IIB	USSR Alliance	Other Alliance	United Nations	IAEA	ILO	FAO	UNESCO	WHO	BANK	IFC	IDA	FUND	ICAO	UPU	ITU	WMO	IMCO	GATT	Third World	Non-Aligned States	Eastern Europe	Helsinki Europe	
USSR	×	×	×	×	×	×	×	×		×	×	×	×	—	×	×	—	—	—	—	×	×	×	×	×	—	—	—	×	×	$3,590
Ukraine	×	×	Not Recognized as Separate Actors								×	×	×	—	×	×	—	—	—	—	—	×	×	×	—	—	—	—	NR	—	
Byelorussia	×	×									×	×	×	—	×	×	—	—	—	—	—	×	×	×	—	—	—	—	NR	—	
Poland	×	×	×	×	×	×	×	×	×	×	×	×	×	×	×	×	—	—	—	—	×	×	×	×	×	×	—	—	×	×	2,675
Czechoslovakia	×	×	×	×	×	×	×	×	×	×	×	×	×	×	×	×	—	—	—	—	×	×	×	×	×	×	—	—	×	×	3,885
GDR[b]	×	×	×	×	×	×	×	×	×	×	×	×	—	×	×	—	—	—	—	—	—	—	—	—	×	—	—	—	×	×	3,940
Hungary	×	×	×	×	×	×	×	×	×	×	×	×	×	×	×	×	—	—	—	—	×	×	×	×	×	—	—	—	×	×	2,528
Bulgaria	×	×	×	×	×	×	×	×	×	×	×	×	×	×	×	×	—	—	—	—	×	×	×	×	×	—	—	—	×	×	2,440
Romania**	×	×	×	×	×	×	×	×	×	×	×	×	×	×	×	×	×	×	—	—	×	×	×	×	×	—	×	×	×	×	2,440
Yugoslavia	×	×	—	—	d	—	—	—	e	e	×	×	×	×	×	×	×	×	×	×	×	×	×	×	×	×	×	×	×	×	1,510[c]
Albania	×	?	—	f	g	—	—	—	—	h	×	×	×	—	×	×	—	—	—	—	—	×	×	×	—	×	×	—	×	—	497[c]
Mongolia	×	×	×	—	×	—	—	—	×	—	×	×	—	—	×	×	—	—	—	—	—	×	×	×	—	—	×	—	—	—	554[c]
China	×	?	—	—	—	—	—	—	×	×	×	×	×	×	×	×	—	—	—	—	×	×	×	×	×	—	×	—	—	—	340
North Korea	×	×	?	—	—	—	—	—	×	×	—	—	×	—	—	×	—	—	—	—	—	—	—	—	—	—	×	?	—	—	388[c]
Vietnam[b]	×	×	?	—	×	—	—	—	—	—	×	—	—	—	—	—	—	—	—	—	—	—	—	—	—	—	×	—	—	—	52[c]
Cuba	×	×	×	—	×	—	—	—	—	—	×	×	×	×	×	×	—	—	—	—	×	×	×	×	×	×	×	×	—	—	633[c]

Notes:

[a] Data for UN as of September 1973
[b] Data on affiliation with UN agencies incomplete
[c] 1975
[d] Associate member since 1964
[e] Nullified, 1949
[f] Withdrew, 1968
[g] Ceased participation since 1968
[h] Expired or nullified
[i] Withdrew 1966
[j] Observer status since June 1973
NR Not recognized as separate actor
** Romania's participation in Communist organizations is substantially less intense than that of other East European states.

Legend

WCM: World Communist Movement
WSS: World Socialist System
WTO: Warsaw Treaty Organization
CMEA: Council of Mutual Economic Assistance
EJNR: Eastern Joint Institute of Nuclear Research
IBEC: International Bank of Economic Cooperation
IIB: International Investment Bank
IAEA: International Atomic Energy Association
ILO: International Labor Organization
FAO: Food and Agricultural Organization
UNESCO: UN Educational Scientific and Cultural Organization
WHO: World Health Organization
BANK: International Bank for Reconstruction and Development
IFC: International Finance Corporation
IDA: International Development Association
FUND: International Monetary Fund
ICAO: International Civil Aviation Organization
UPU: Universal Postal Union
ITU: International Telecommunications Union
WMO: World Meteorological Organization
IMCO: Inter-Governmental Maritime Consultative Organization
GATT: General Agreement on Tariffs and Trade

Sources: *Treaties and Alliances of the World* (New York: Scribners, 1974), for data on UN memberships and affiliations. Per capita GNP calculated from data in *Handbook of Economic Statistics, 1977* (Washington, D.C., 1977).

vation. The table clearly illustrates the relative behavioral uniformity of five East European states (Poland, Czechoslovakia, German Democratic Republic, Hungary, Bulgaria), which (with minor exceptions) have associational profiles virtually identical to that of the Soviet Union. At the same time, the table delineates variances from Soviet behavior and shows the correspondence between the extent of affiliations with Communist organizations and the degree of association with noncommunist organizations. The distinction between the two in this analysis is simple: Communist organizations are those to which only Communist states belong, whereas noncommunist organizations are those to which both Communist and noncommunist states belong.

Although the term Eastern Europe is an aggregate category and thus conceals important variations and nuances in the individual international profile of East European states, it is nevertheless true that individual Eastern European states tend to be perceived in terms of stereotypes and hence as "typical" of Eastern Europe as a whole. This is particularly true of those East European states whose associational profiles coincide with the Soviet profile and can thus be defined plausibly as part of a "Soviet bloc." But, correspondingly, this is increasingly less true of Albania, Romania, and Yugoslavia, whose idiosyncratic international behavioral patterns are perceived as those of separate states in Eastern Europe rather than as part of "Eastern Europe." Romania's profile differs less significantly than that of Yugoslavia, whose noncommunist affiliations are more extensive and diverse and whose Communist affiliations are less intensive and less extensive. Albania's deviance is marked by severely limited affiliations in both Communist and noncommunist organizations.

At least five East European states can be defined as being essentially part of a "Soviet bloc," acting as such within both the Communist and general interstate environment. Even in terms of per capita GNP in 1975, the "Soviet bloc" exhibited a general uniformity, which distinguished it sharply from non-European Communist states and even from Albania and Yugoslavia. Of the eight Communist states in Eastern Europe, only Albania, Yugoslavia, and Romania have successfully affiliated or identified themselves with noncommunist interstate groups, most notably the Third World and the nonaligned group, a behavioral trait shared with the non-European Communist states. It is mainly because of the idiosyncratic behavior of Albania, Yugoslavia, and Romania in the international community that Eastern Europe is increasingly perceived even by the Third World as a collection of individual state-personalities rather than simply as a gray mass attached to Moscow. Furthermore, the unsuccessful attempts by Hungary, Poland, and Czechoslovakia to act independently of the Soviet Union can also be more clearly perceived as part of a single behavioral continuum, of which the successful assertion of autonomy in foreign affairs by Yugoslavia, Albania, and Romania is an integral part.

It is apparent that the differential patterns of foreign policy behavior in Eastern Europe reflect in some degree the basic geo-cultural cleavage of Eastern Europe into northern and southern tiers, or more precisely, a north-central group and a southeastern group. Not only in behavioral patterns, but in terms of other indices as well, this distinction persists. There is even a vague and episodic movement in the direction of concerted action by Albania, Romania, and Yugoslavia in their relationship with Moscow, which waxes and wanes in accordance with perceptions of Soviet threats to intervene.

Bulgaria's behavioral pattern, however, interferes with what might otherwise be a tidy and precise demarcation between a subdued northern tier and a defiant southern tier in Eastern Europe. Bulgaria, the prototypical Balkan state, is Moscow's most loyal, faithful, and probably only voluntary client state in Eastern Europe, and apparently has no ambition to behave independently in foreign policy, a trait which distinguishes it from *all* other states in Eastern Europe without exception. Bulgaria is the only country in Eastern Europe where neither a *successful* nor an *unsuccessful* act of defiance has taken place.

Aside from membership and affiliation with interstate groups within the international community, other measurable indices of Eastern Europe's status and visibility in the international community are: (1) development of trade and commerce with different parts of the world; (2) participation in economic and financial assistance programs; (3) participation in military assistance programs; and (4) participation in technical and academic assistance programs.

It should be emphasized that in measuring Eastern Europe's participation in the activities mentioned above, no attempt will be made to disaggregate the data by individual countries. The aggregate data for Eastern Europe conceal wide variations in individual state behavior, and, in some instances, "Eastern Europe" may actually represent the activity of only one or two countries for a particular year or aid given to a particular region. Furthermore, not all East European countries have the same capacity or incentive to become involved in international activity, although it should be noted that all East European states are involved to some degree in all the activities described. The behavioral profile of Eastern Europe will be compared to that of the Soviet

Union and China in order to place it within the behavioral context of
the Communist world as a whole.

In the tables devised to measure East European international activity,
the aggregate data for Eastern Europe include only Poland, Czechoslovakia, East Germany, Hungary, Bulgaria, and Romania, unless otherwise noted.

International Trade and Commerce

Table 4 provides data for the direction of trade, in terms of both
exports and imports for three specific years during the period 1960–75.
The first observation to be made is that the total volume of exports and
imports has increased steadily over the years, as measured in dollars.
Between 1960 and 1975, imports rose over sixfold, while exports increased more than sevenfold. As the volume of trade grew, the direction of East European trade shifted away from the Communist world,
both developed and underdeveloped. In 1960, Eastern Europe's international trade could be described as essentially parochial, but less so than
during the period before 1956. More than 70 percent of its small volume
of trade was with the Soviet Union and within Eastern Europe, and
only 7.6 percent was with the less-developed countries. By 1975, the
Communist share of East European trade had dropped to 66.6 percent
for exports and 59.6 percent for imports, while exports and imports to
the less-developed countries had risen to 10.6 and 6.9 percent, respectively. Trade with the developed countries (United States, Western
Europe, Japan) also increased at the expense of the Communist sector.[6]

Table 4 Direction of East European Trade, 1960–75
(Millions of U.S. Dollars)

	Total Trade	Communist Countries					Noncommunist Countries		
		Total	USSR	Eastern Europe	Far East[a]	Other[b]	Total	Developed Countries	Less Developed Countries
1960									
Exports	7,625	5,525	2,819	2,101	398	208	2,100	1,523	578
Imports	7,761	5,556	2,955	2,084	351	166	2,206	1,712	495
1970									
Exports	18,158	12,545	6,610	4,953	331	647	5,613	4,134	1,478
Imports	18,522	12,500	6,803	4,909	232	556	6,021	4,835	1,186
1975									
Exports	45,213	30,116	15,565	12,211	N.A.	N.A.	15,097	10,312	4,785
Imports	51,229	30,550	16,304	12,269	N.A.	N.A.	20,679	17,132	3,547

[a] Includes data for China, North Korea, and Vietnam.
[b] Includes data for Albania, Cuba, Mongolia, and Yugoslavia.
Source: *Handbook of Economic Statistics, 1977* (Washington, D.C., 1977).

It should be noted that whereas overall trade with Communist countries decreased proportionately, trade with the USSR increased. Expanded East European trade was thus mainly at the expense of intra–East European trade. It should also be noted that variations in dollars are not always congruent with variations in volume, especially with reference to commodities like oil, whose world market price increased substantially. The expanded commerce of Eastern Europe has not been an unmixed blessing, since some countries have developed serious trade imbalances and have accumulated huge hard-currency debts. These imbalances and debts, in turn, have had a deleterious impact on the consumer and agricultural sectors of the domestic economy, most notably in Poland, but also in Romania and Czechoslovakia.[7]

Economic Assistance

For a part of the world that traditionally kept itself uninvolved in affairs beyond those of Europe, Eastern Europe has contributed more than a modest share of total Communist economic assistance to the less-developed countries, particularly when it is noted that both the Soviet Union and China have global pretensions, whereas Eastern Europe does not. What proportion of the East European involvement is simply an adjunct to Soviet policy (whereby the USSR reaps the political benefit and Eastern Europe pays the economic cost) and what share represents a genuine East European involvement designed to lessen its isolation, and hence vulnerability and dependence upon the USSR, is difficult to calculate. Suffice it to say that both processes are involved and, generally speaking, the greater the visibility of Eastern European states in the international community, the greater the potential leverage they may have in their relations with the USSR.

Table 5 provides comparative data regarding the distribution of Communist economic assistance to major regions of the world in the form

Table 5 Communist Economic Assistance to Less-developed Countries, 1954–76
(Millions of U.S. Dollars)

	Total	USSR	Eastern Europe	China
Total	22,197	11,769	6,475	3,953
Africa	5,249	1,249	1,249	2,200
East Asia	809	156	346	307
Latin America	2,044	655	1,236	153
Middle East and South Asia	13,750	8,878	3,644	1,228

Source: *Communist Aid to the Less Developed Countries, 1976* (Washington, D.C., 1976).

of credits and grants during the period 1954–76. Of the total amount extended during this period, Eastern Europe's contribution was 6.475 billion dollars or 29.2 percent of the total, which was more than half of the Soviet share and nearly double that of the Chinese. Although East European assistance went to some sixteen countries in Africa, five in East Asia, ten in Latin America, and fourteen in the Middle East and South Asia, i.e., over forty-five countries, the assistance was highly uneven from one year to the next. To illustrate this unevenness, in 1974, one third of all aid went to Africa, and Romania alone accounted for 54 percent of all East European aid for that year. Romania's stepped up activity in economic assistance is also a good illustration of East European aid that is not a conscious adjunct of Soviet policy but represents individual Romanian initiative in pursuit of its own economic and political interests.

As Table 5 demonstrates, over the entire period, the Middle East and South Asia have received the greatest amount of assistance from Moscow and Eastern Europe, whereas Africa has been the principal recipient of Chinese aid. Again, it must be emphasized that these aggregate figures conceal a highly uneven distribution in numbers of countries receiving assistance and amounts received, as well as in numbers of East European countries granting aid and the amounts granted.

Military Assistance

Military assistance to the less-developed countries can be measured in three dimensions: (a) arms agreements and exports; (b) military assistance personnel stationed abroad; (c) military personnel from abroad being trained. East European military assistance, when compared to economic assistance, is comparatively modest. Table 6 shows that of the nearly 20 billion dollars of Communist arms exports to less-developed countries during the period 1955–76, more than 86 percent was delivered by the USSR, with only 8.3 percent coming from Eastern Europe. China's increment was a bare 3 percent. More than 77 percent of arms assistance went to Middle Eastern countries, while 16 percent was given to Africa. Again, the principal beneficiaries, donors, and amounts varied considerably over the twenty-two-year period.

In 1976, of 21,700 military specialists from Communist countries stationed abroad in less-developed countries, 9,080 were from the Soviet Union *and* Eastern Europe and 11,650 were from Cuba. The East European contingent probably corresponded approximately with East Europe's share of arms exports, i.e., not more than 10 percent. The distribution of military technicians abroad is similar to the distribu-

Table 6 Communist Arms Exports to Less-developed Countries, 1955–76
(Millions of U.S. Dollars)

	1955–69	1970	1973	1976	1955–76
Total	5,975	1,100	3,225	2,760	19,915
USSR	5,025	1,000	3,010	2,190	17,215
E. Europe	775	75	120	200	1,655
China	175	25	25	80	600
Others	—	—	—	290	445

Source: *Handbook of Economic Statistics, 1977.*

tion of arms exports, since (with the exception of Cuban personnel) Soviet and East European military personnel are engaged principally in the training of indigenous personnel in the use, assembly, and maintenance of military equipment. Of the nearly 12,000 Cubans abroad in 1976, 10,000 were concentrated in Angola, and the Cuban contingent accounted for the more than doubling of Communist military personnel abroad from 9,300 in 1975 to 20,730 in 1976.

Military personnel from the less-developed countries are to be found in all East European countries, but again in proportions more modest than East European economic assistance. During the period 1955–76, military personnel came from ten African countries, six Middle East and South Asian countries, and one East Asian country. Of the more than 47,000 military personnel being trained from the less-developed countries over a two-decade period, Eastern Europe was host to little more than 9 percent, while the Soviet Union trained nearly 85 percent of the total (Table 7).

Economic and Academic Personnel

The East European presence in the less-developed countries is most effectively represented by its economic assistance personnel stationed abroad. The East European share of all Communist economic technicians in the less-developed countries is truly extraordinary when com-

Table 7 Military Personnel from Less-developed Countries Trained in
Communist Countries, 1955–76

	Total	USSR	Eastern Europe	China
Total	47,225	39,950	4,375	2,900
Africa	4,075	10,775	775	2,525
East Asia	9,275	7,575	1,700	0
Latin America	550	550	0	0
Middle East and South Asia	23,325	21,050	1,900	375

Source: *Handbook of Economic Statistics, 1977.*

pared to the Soviet and Chinese effort. The larger number of East European states and the fact that some of them are more highly developed and modernized than the Soviet Union enables the East European states to diversify and specialize in their assistance programs. The total of Communist technicians in the less-developed countries during the period 1970–75 was 244,960, of which 47,200 (17.4 percent) were from Eastern Europe, 78,390 (32 percent) were from the Soviet Union, and 118,950 (48.6 percent) were Chinese. The Chinese effort was concentrated in East Africa and includes workers as well as "technicians."

The Chinese presence declined significantly in 1976 to 20,465, whereas the East European contingent nearly doubled to 26,000 and accounted for more than 37 percent of Communist economic technicians for that year, and an even more impressive 57.3 percent of the combined Soviet and East European contingent, stationed in more than forty countries. Table 8 provides comparative data for the distribution of Communist economic assistance personnel for selected years, 1970, 1973, 1975, and 1976, as well as overall totals for the entire period, 1970–1976. This table shows the steady increase of the East European contingent to nearly 40 percent of the total in 1976. Again, it should be

Table 8 Communist Economic-Technical Personnel in Less-developed Countries, 1970–76

	1970	1973	1975	1976	Total 1970–76
Total	24,010	43,960	55,290	70,145	244,960
USSR-Total	10,600	13,095	17,785	19,345	78,390
Africa	4,010	4,590	5,390		
East Asia	100	25	25	—	—
Latin America	35	185	330	—	—
Middle East and South Asia	6,455	8,295	11,500	—	—
East Europe-Total	5,300	7,325	13,915	26,000	47,620
Africa	3,150	5,075	10,290	—	—
East Asia	60	10	30	—	—
Latin America	140	165	225	—	—
Middle East and South Asia	1,950	2,075	3,370	—	—
China-Total	8,110	23,540	23,590	20,415	118,950
Africa	6,960	22,010	21,325	17,915	—
East Asia	150	40	35	40	—
Latin America	—	50	70	105	—
Middle East and South Asia	1,000	1,440	2,090	1,955	—
Cuba-Total	—	—	—	4,385*	—

*3,000 in Angola and 280 in Jamaica.
Source: *Communist Aid to Less Developed Countries, 1975 and 1976.*

emphasized that aggregate data conceal the unevenness of participation and distribution by donor, recipient, and region. For example, in 1976, some 10,000 East European economic technicians were in Libya alone, drawn from no less than five countries (Poland, Hungary, Bulgaria, Czechoslovakia, and East Germany).

It appears from the data that Eastern Europe is much more comfortable and has better capability in providing economic assistance than military assistance, given the dramatic difference in absolute and relative levels of assistance between the two areas. Of course, the data could be interpreted to suggest a rational division of international labor, with the Soviet Union carrying the military assistance burden and Eastern Europe assuming a larger share of the economic assistance effort. A detailed analysis of the East European economic assistance programs, however, would show that many of the projects are of direct economic benefit to the Eastern European countries involved, with the political benefit being a spillover or side-effect, rather than the main incentive. This is true not only of Romanian programs, but of other East European countries' programs as well.

For the past two decades, the Soviet Union and Eastern Europe have conducted an ambitious academic assistance program for Third World countries. During the period 1955–76, nearly 80,000 students from less-developed countries have been reached by these programs. By the end of 1976, some 48,500 students had returned from the Soviet Union and Eastern Europe, about one-third of them from the countries of Eastern Europe. In the same year, over 36,000 students were still studying in the Soviet Union and Eastern Europe, with the East European share double that of the previous three years. Table 9 shows that the number of students departing for the Soviet Union and Eastern Europe has steadily increased from 1970 to 1976.

Of course, the education of foreign students is a chancy business, and the Soviet–East European experience has been very mixed. The results, far from improving the image of the Soviet Union and Eastern Europe, may have actually damaged it. The net consequence depends not only

Table 9 Students Departing for Communist Countries from Less-developed Countries, 1970–76

	1970	1973	1975	1976	Total 1970–76
Total	3,645	5,375	5,060	7,965	34,835
USSR & E. Europe	3,645	5,275	4,995	7,905	34,605
China	0	100	65	60	235

Source: *Handbook of Economic Statistics, 1977.*

upon the treatment of the students by the host society, but also upon the quality of the education, and the reception the students receive at home and abroad when they display their Communist academic credentials.

Aside from the political effects, the extensive interaction between Eastern Europe and the outside world, particularly the Third World, cannot but have enhanced the visibility of countries of Eastern Europe on the world scene, as a region as well as separate personalities. Hundreds of thousands of East Europeans and citizens from remote areas of the world have had contact with one another at various levels and in various parts of the world. Thousands of East European citizens have visited and worked in a wide spectrum of countries, and a corresponding number of citizens from all corners of the globe have visited or have been trained in Eastern Europe. Table 10 provides data for the comparative distribution of trainees from the Third World departing for Communist countries. It shows that more than 77,000 trainees departed for the Soviet Union and Eastern Europe during the period 1970–1976 alone.

CONCLUSIONS

Although the developmental gap between Western Europe and Eastern Europe remains substantial, it has been decreasing rapidly, and Eastern Europe as a whole is generally viewed as part of the developed world and as an integral part of Europe. To be sure, in the traditional trifurcation of the world, Eastern Europe has been consigned to the "Second World," which is an ideological category embracing all Communist states, developed and less developed, but developmental identities increasingly appear to be supplanting ideological identities from the perspective of both developed and underdeveloped states, irrespective of ideology. The traditional tripartite division of the world, based on ideological outlook and alignments, is giving way to new divisions of the world along developmental-continental-civilizational-racial lines. Peking has already declared both the "Communist camp" and the traditional "Second World" as defunct and has restructured the globe into a new tripartite division, with Eastern Europe and Western Europe lumped together as part of a new "Second World," as distinct from a "First World," consisting solely of the United States and the USSR, and a "Third World," consisting of all the developing countries of Asia, Africa, and Latin America:

Table 10 Academic, Technical and Military Trainees Departing from
Less-developed Countries to Communist Countries, 1970–76

	1970	1973	1976	Total 1970–76
Total Trainees	7,845	11,755	16,350	80,475
USSR and				
E. Europe	7,535	11,260	16,135	77,110
China	310	495	25	3,365
Academic	3,645	5,375	7,965	36,060
USSR and				
E. Europe	3,645	5,275	7,905	35,605
China	0	100	65	455
Technical	1,650	3,715	5,320	24,395
USSR and				
E. Europe	1,650	3,715	5,265	24,220
China	0	0	55	175
Military	2,250	2,665	3,065	21,020
USSR and				
E. Europe	2,240	2,270	2,965	18,285
China	310	395	100	2,735

Source: *Handbook of Economic Statistics, 1977.*

In this situation of "great disorder under heaven," all the political forces in the world have undergone drastic division and realignment through prolonged trials of strength and struggle. A large number of Asian, African, and Latin American countries have achieved independence one after another, and they are playing an ever greater role in international affairs. *As a result of the emergence of social-imperialism, the socialist camp which existed for a time after World War II is no longer in existence* [author's emphasis]. Owing to the law of the uneven development of capitalism, the Western imperialist bloc, too, is disintegrating. Judging from the changes in international relations, the world today actually consists of three parts, or three worlds, that are both interconnected and in contradiction to one another. The United States and the Soviet Union make up the First World. The developing countries in Asia, Africa, Latin America, and other regions make up the Third World. The developed countries between the two make up the Second World.[8]

Although the polemical and self-serving character of Peking's recategorization of the world is evident, it is also equally apparent that Peking's image of the world is basically developmental in design. The data in Table 11 show the progressive developmental convergence that has taken place between Eastern Europe and Western Europe and the progressively widening gap between Eastern Europe and the Asian Communist states and the entire underdeveloped world in general.

Table 11 Eastern Europe in Developmental Context, 1963 and 1975

Country or Region	Population (Thousands)		Total GNP (Millions of Constant Dollars)		GNP Per Capita (Constant Dollars)	
	1963	1975	1963	1975	1963	1975
World	3,175,000	4,069,067	1,823,500	5,681,600	821	1,396
Developed	919,327	1,039,355	1,503,099	4,457,200	2,381	4,288
Underdeveloped	2,255,696	3,031,027	319,600	1,224,400	185	404
USSR	225,000	254,300	277,000	870,000	1,678	3,130
USA	189,200	213,631	805,112	1,390,000	4,255	6,490
NATO Europe	287,484	317,724	373,000	1,207,400	2,059	3,800
WTO E. Europe	98,478	106,238	149,459	272,200	1,351	2,562
Bulgaria	8,078	8,741	7,500	16,900	928	1,930
Czechoslovakia	13,900	14,804	27,300	49,900	1,962	3,870
GDR	17,000	16,885	31,359	55,200	1,845	3,270
Hungary	10,100	10,541	13,200	23,300	1,309	2,210
Poland	30,600	34,022	34,500	78,100	1,127	2,300
Romania	18,800	21,245	17,600	48,800	936	2,010
Yugoslavia	19,000	21,346	11,400	32,300	602	1,510
Albania	1,762	2,411	820	1,200	464	497
Total Europe	691,169	767,969	817,700	2,552,700	1,761	3,324
Asian Communist States	751,219	986,119	79,471	288,300	106	292
Mongolia	917	1,444	750	800	818	554
China	716,000	934,600	68,000	274,000	129	293
N. Korea	11,500	16,500	3,100	6,400	273	388
Vietnam	15,300	24,323	2,136	1,250	140	52
Cuba	7,502	9,252	5,485	5,850	731	633

Sources: *World Military Expenditures and Arms Trade 1963–1973* (Washington, D.C.: USACDA, 1974); *World Military Expenditures and Arms Transfers, 1966–1976* (Washington, D.C.: USACDA, 1977).

These developmental trends have generated universal perceptions of a world in which developmental cleavages assume a higher saliency than ideological differences. Thus average per capita GNP for Europe as a whole in 1975 was $3,324, with NATO Europe (excluding Greece and Turkey) standing at $3,800 and WTO Eastern Europe at $2,562, whereas the average per capita GNP for the underdeveloped countries stood at $404 and that for the Asian Communist states averaged out at $292. Even more graphically, Eastern Europe with its 150 million people generated a GNP ($272 billion) nearly as large as that for the four Asian Communist states ($288 billion) with a total population of nearly one billion people. If the data for the Soviet Union are included, the gap between European and Asian communism becomes even more conspicuous.

As a developed part of the world, Eastern Europe, in spite of its already widespread involvement, may be perceived increasingly as not carrying its share of the burden to assist the less-developed countries. The six Warsaw Pact countries accounted for 2.66 percent of the world's population in 1976, but generated 4.5 percent of its gross national product and accounted for 4.8 percent of all exports. On the other hand, Eastern Europe contributed only 1.24 percent of all capital aid to less-developed countries and delivered about 1.82 percent of all arms exports.

Irrespective of the separate identity which the countries of Eastern Europe as a region and as individual personalities have succeeded in developing over the past two decades, the connection with the Soviet Union remains the dominant world image of Eastern Europe. And this is likely to remain so for some time, given the vital stake which Soviet leaders perceive in maintaining their paramountcy in the region. As noted earlier, Eastern Europe is important to the Soviet Union for a number of reasons, the two most important being strategic and ideological. These two purposes of the Soviet presence in Eastern Europe are distinct and independent, yet not easy to disaggregate by both the Soviet leaders and the outside world. The relative priority of these two important purposes, as between one another and other purposes, has changed over time in response to circumstances, events, and perceptions, both Soviet and external.

The purely strategic security purpose of the Soviet presence in Eastern Europe is the most easily understandable and appreciated, but it is not always easy to distinguish from the ideological purpose, which has both defensive and expansionist implications. The crux of the matter is whether Soviet leaders perceive security in traditional territorial, economic, and military terms, or whether they perceive security in ideological terms, i.e., the defense, expansion, validation, and legitimization of a distinctive sociopolitical order inspired by a particular ideology, rather than the simple preservation or promotion of the territorial and economic interests of the Soviet state.

Eastern Europe has historically constituted an invasion channel from the West into Russia, and similarly, it has served as an invasion conduit from Russia into Central and Western Europe. As an important buffer region made up of small, relatively weak states that are divided from one another by ancient historical animosities, it traditionally has been manipulated and exploited by neighboring Great Powers for their own ends. Eastern Europe, by itself, remains incapable of filling the power vacuum that inevitably develops in this region, and it has been the fate of East Central Europe to become the sphere of influence of one of the Great Powers. Since World War II, it has become a part of the Soviet sphere, where it functions as the Soviet Union's single most important geographical defense zone.

Hence, it is not likely that the Soviet leaders will permit Eastern Europe to break away in the foreseeable future. As events in Czechoslovakia demonstrated in 1968, they are prepared to intervene, if necessary, to prevent any significant erosion of their East European empire, although the costs in terms of Soviet international prestige may rise with successive interventions.

The Soviet presence in Eastern Europe thus guarantees, at the minimum, a denial of the region to any other great power; currently, the pertinent great power is West Germany, because Eastern Europe has traditionally been a sphere of influence of either Germany or Russia. Two of the Soviet leaders' great concerns about West Germany's Ostpolitik, initiated by Chancellor Ludwig Erhard in 1965–66 and extended by Chancellors Kurt Kiesinger and Willy Brandt, were that the policy threatened to loosen the bonds between Eastern Europe and the Soviet Union and that it appeared to represent a bid by West Germany to revive its traditional interest in the area.[9] A policy that served to entice the East European states into developing closer relations with West Germany, it encouraged the autonomous defiance of Romania, particularly in the realm of foreign policy. More importantly, it reinforced those internal developments in Czechoslovakia that might have removed the nation from the Soviet orbit.[10]

The strategic aspects of the Soviet presence in Eastern Europe can be viewed separately from the ideological and political aspects, since they are not irrevocably interrelated with any specific ideological purpose or political system; but they cannot be separated when measuring the overall importance of Eastern Europe to the Soviet Union. In a psychological sense, Soviet control of Eastern Europe also serves to validate Moscow's credentials as a regional power, as a leader of a group of states, and as a leader of one of the two principal alliance and political systems in the world. It is important to bear in mind that the United States and the Soviet Union are the only two alliance leaders in the world today, and that a certain amount of prestige is derived from that role. Furthermore, much of the Soviet Union's prestige in international affairs derives from the fact that it is the leader of a group of states.

Thus, the second general purpose of the Soviet presence in Eastern Europe is essentially political and ideological in character, although the ideological aspect has been assuming an increasingly symbolic context. These ideological and symbolic purposes are becoming progressively residual but nevertheless continue to be important for the short run, since the ideological element in Soviet behavior has been eroding for many years and probably will continue to do so. The Soviet Union appears to have no real future as the leader of a universal Communist movement, because China's emergence as a rival has effectively arrested that role. Before the emergence of China as a rival, the policies of the United States had, in many ways, also blocked the expansion of Soviet or Communist power, but in different ways.

In the short run, then, the existence of Eastern Europe as a bloc of Communist states modeled on the Soviet system—and the word "Communist" is emphasized—continues to validate the Soviet Union's credentials as an ideological and revolutionary power, as well as the residual center of a world revolutionary movement.

Eastern Europe thus is not only an imperialistic extension of the Soviet Union, it is also an extension of the Soviet Union's social system; and as the first and most important extension of the Soviet system beyond the borders of the Soviet Union, it represents the residue of Moscow's former ecumenical pretensions. All of the Communist states in Eastern Europe came into being under various forms of Soviet sponsorship. They were all cast from the Soviet mold, and in one way or another represented the first step in universalizing the Soviet system. All have been beneficiaries of Soviet protection, as well as victims of Soviet domination. It might be said that while the Communist regimes have been the beneficiaries of Soviet protection, the populations have been the victims of Soviet domination.

The Communist states of Eastern Europe are, in effect, miniature alter egos of the Soviet Union; and when the Soviet leaders look at

Eastern Europe, they find contentment only if it reflects a reasonable facsimile of themselves. The integrity, viability, and even existence of the Soviet system depend upon the maintenance of the Communist regimes in Eastern Europe; and thus, for psychological reasons alone, the overthrow of any Communist regime in Eastern Europe, even the Albanian, would constitute a threat to the Soviet system. It is important to bear in mind that the Soviet Union does not consider itself to be merely a state; it considers itself as a representative of a particular form of social and economic organization that has universal validity and application. And the East European states are subordinate not simply to Soviet foreign policy; their internal structures are also in some degree subordinate to Soviet will.

On the other hand, East European states (with perhaps the exception of Bulgaria) resent being viewed as extensions of the Soviet system and increasingly perceive themselves as permanent entities, pursuing roads to socialism separate, distinct, and away from Soviet communism and towards the positions of Eurocommunist parties in Western Europe. The advent of Eurocommunism in Western Europe thus may set into motion trends and forces that may convert East European communism, with its separate roads, into a distinctive form of communism which may become a potential bridge between Eurocommunism and Soviet communism, rather than a mere extension of the latter. Of course Soviet power remains decisive in this area and the East European states must pursue their separate roads with prudence and caution.

The defensive function of the Soviet presence in Eastern Europe has been almost universally recognized as valid, certainly by the United States, and has been justified amply by both history and logic. But the second purpose has been a matter of concern to the West, particularly the United States—the function of the Soviet presence in Eastern Europe as a possible first step in the communization of all Europe. As far as Western Europe and the United States were concerned, of course, the ideological-expansionist aspect of the Soviet presence in Eastern Europe dwarfed all other considerations. Since, in Soviet calculations, the defensive and offensive functions of the Soviet presence in Eastern Europe are intricately intertwined, the Soviet leaders seem inherently incapable of disassociating responses that threaten their security from those designed to blunt their ideological offensive. Hence as long as only the United States, Western Europe (especially West Germany), and China remain the principal external champions and supporters of greater freedom for Eastern Europe, the perception of threat will tend to dominate in Moscow.

As an increasingly active participant in the international community of nearly 150 states, and given its recognition as a group of developed, modernized European states of some magnitude, Eastern Europe becomes increasingly incongruous as a group of states still subservient to another state, in a world full of small, exotic, and underdeveloped states subservient to no one.[11] Furthermore, one East European state, Poland, is a substantial state by any objective standard. With an ethnically homogeneous population of about 35 million, it ranks as the fifth largest nation in Europe (excluding the Soviet Union), after Germany, Italy, France, and England. Its aggregate GNP in 1976 was over $90 billion, among the largest in the world, and about as large as that of India with over 600 million people. That a nation of this magnitude can still be subservient to another state in the last quarter of the twentieth century staggers the imagination, and it is only a matter of time until a condition that is merely incongruous in the world community becomes intolerable. Given the national paranoia of the Soviet leadership, Poland and Eastern Europe's hopes for full emancipation can only be furthered by associating themselves with groupings and cultivating constituencies in the world community that can articulate an interest in their freedom without projecting a threat to Moscow. Since the Soviet Union is eager to earn the approbation of countries in the Third World, in the event of future Soviet misbehavior in Eastern Europe, the Soviet leadership may be more sensitive to criticism and condemnation from this direction. Moreover, it can hardly rebut such disapprobation as threatening to its security. Both Yugoslavia and Romania have followed this route, and it appears that North Korea and Vietnam are also enhancing their identification with non-Communist groupings in order to insulate themselves from the threat of Soviet or Chinese domination.

NOTES

1. Quoted from the radio broadcast, as recorded by Columbia Records in "I Can Hear It Now," compiled and narrated by Edward R. Murrow.

2. The total includes Yugoslavia and Albania. The population of the six East European Warsaw Pact states was 107 million in 1976.

3. The West Slavic languages are Polish, Czech, and Slovak; the South Slavic are Slovene, Serbo-Croatian, Bulgarian, and Macedonian. The ten Slavic nations are Poles, Czechs, Slovaks, Slovenes, Croatians, Serbians, Bosnians, Montenegrins, Macedonians and Bulgarians; the four non-Slavic nations are Hungarians, Romanians, Albanians, and Germans.

.4 As reported in "The Train Jan Prochazka Missed," *Literaturnaya gazeta*, May 19, 1972.

5. *The World Socialist System and Anti-Communism* (Moscow, 1972), p. 79.

6. It should be noted that about 70 percent of East European trade is accounted for by Czechoslovakia, East Germany, and Poland.

7. As East European (and Soviet) trade with the outside world has expanded, its hard currency deficit has grown correspondingly. Poland's deficit is particularly serious. The following table charts the increasing deficit.

Hard Currency Deficits in Millions of U.S. Dollars

Country	1970	1973	1975	1976 (est.)
Bulgaria	.7	.8	1.8	2.3
Czechoslovakia	.3	.8	1.5	2.1
GDR	1.0	2.1	3.8	4.9
Hungary	.6	.9	2.1	2.8
Poland	.8	1.9	6.9	10.2
Romania	1.2	2.0	3.0	3.3
TOTAL	4.6	8.5	19.1	25.6
USSR	1.7	3.6	7.5	9.7

Sources: Data for Eastern Europe from Joan Parpart Zoeter, "Eastern Europe: The Growing Hard Currency Debt," in Joint Economic Committee (U.S. Congress), *East European Economies Post-Helsinki* (Washington, D.C.: U.S. Government Printing Office, 1977), p. 1352. Data for USSR, from *Handbook of Economic Statistics, 1977*, p. 52.

The increasing foreign indebtedness of Eastern Europe also increases the interdependence between Eastern Europe and the noncommunist world.

8. From a speech by Vice-Premier Teng Hsiao-ping before the U.N. General Assembly, April 10, 1974, in *Peking Review,* April 19, 1974, p. 6.

9. For an excellent survey, see Andrew Gyorgy, "Ostpolitik and Eastern Europe," in Charles Gati, editor, *The International Politics of Eastern Europe* (New York: Praeger Publishers, 1976), pp. 154–172.

10. For further amplification, see Vernon V. Aspaturian, "Has Eastern Europe Become a Liability to the Soviet Union?" in Gati, *The International Politics of Eastern Europe,* pp. 17–36; V. V. Aspaturian, "The Aftermath of the Czech Invasion," *Current History,* November 1968; V. V. Aspaturian, "Soviet Aims in East Europe," *Current History,* October 1970.

11. For an excellent analysis of international influences on East European behavior, see Andrzej Korbonski, "External Influences on Eastern Europe," Gati, *The International Politics of Eastern Europe,* pp. 253–274.

2   Poland

Andrzej Korbonski

A social scientist asked to analyze political developments in a country over a certain period is faced, first of all, with the task of selecting an approach that is likely to yield some useful and interesting results. This task, complicated to begin with, becomes even more complex when the country in question happens to be Poland, an East European Communist state which for more than thirty years has been undergoing dramatic political and socioeconomic changes; which thus far has defied easy generalizations and classifications; and which continues to be a country of sharp and growing contrasts.

The choice of an approach is obviously largely determined by the questions one seeks to answer. In this case, the major question concerns essentially the performance of the country's political system, or to put it somewhat differently: what makes the Polish system work? In order to answer this question, one must delve into a discussion of such issues as the country's political structure and dynamics, its leadership and elite patterns, socioeconomic and cultural trends, and last but not least, its foreign policy, including its relations with the Soviet Union, the hegemonial power in the region.

The approach that appears most suited for analyzing the political system of contemporary Poland is the "developmental" approach derived from the pioneering work of Gabriel Almond.[1] This approach is based on the assumption that the process of political development is characterized by a number of essential "criteria," "requirements," and "challenges." Thus, all societies passing through the process of political development are bound to deal with at least four developmental requirements—nation-building, state-building, participation, and distribution. Also, all societies undergoing this process have to cope with several crises arising out of the conflicts between the developmental criteria mentioned above. The five crises or challenges most frequently faced are those of identity, legitimacy, penetration, participation, and distribution. For example, a society which has successfully passed through the stages of nation- and state-building must, sooner or later, resolve the problem of popular participation by providing the populace with institutional arrangements for the articulation of their demands and grievances. Similarly, a well-integrated political system must face at some point the problem of distribution by ensuring a decent standard of living for its people, who otherwise can challenge the legitimacy of the system. Almond has suggested that "the way in which political systems encountered these challenges and problems, their order and sequence, and the choices made by elites by confronting them and solving them [go] far toward explaining the peculiar characteristics of [their] structures, cultures and capability profiles."[2]

The greatest virtue of Almond's approach is that, especially in its revised form, it was "precisely designed to deal with the problem of changes and it was also clearly independent of any particular historical context. . . . [It] could be applied to a primitive stateless tribe, a classical Greek city-state, or to a modern nation-state."[3] It follows that it is also suitable for the study of political change in Poland, where the impact of such variables as leadership and international environment, as well as the national political culture, was particularly strong. Moreover, the framework permits one to examine the process of change without pre-judging in advance its ultimate outcome or goal. Hence, in addition to looking at factors causing or inducing "change," "modernization," or "development," we are also able to consider influences affecting the process of "political decay" or deterioration in the level and quality of performance of the political system which seemed to have occurred in Poland with some regularity.

Any political system may also be viewed as being composed of several elements, all of which are undergoing a process of change. Some of these systemic components may be changing at rapid rates, while others may be transformed slowly. Samuel Huntington distinguishes five major components of any political system—culture, structure, groups, leadership, and policies—and suggests that the process of political change is ultimately strongly influenced by the interplay between these components—their type and rate of change and the combination in which they occur.[4] Thus, I propose to analyze the process of political change in Poland since the end of the 1960s by focusing, on the one hand, on the five developmental challenges or crises identified by Almond, and on the other, on the five systemic components analyzed by

Huntington. Since the emphasis is going to be on the most recent developments, the early period in postwar Polish history will receive a rather summary treatment; it has been extensively studied and discussed in Western literature.

THE FIRST TWENTY-FIVE YEARS

The one developmental challenge that postwar Poland, in contrast to several other East European countries, did not have to face was that of national identity. While the process of nation-building in Poland had not been successfully accomplished during the interwar period and the problem of hostile national minorities prevented the achievement of full national integration, the country emerged from World War II as a homogeneous nation-state. The Nazi mass genocide of the Jewish population, the expulsion of the Germans from the newly acquired territories in the west, and the enforced incorporation of Poland's eastern provinces into the Soviet Union resulted in Poland becoming ethnically (and religiously) quite homogeneous, probably for the first time in its long history.

While this phenomenon is usually taken for granted, there is little doubt that it had considerable and lasting impact on postwar developments in Poland. The major beneficiaries appeared to be the country's new Communist rulers, who were spared from having to deal with the kinds of ethnic and national conflicts that influenced political processes in Yugoslavia, Czechoslovakia, and Romania, all of which continued to harbor substantial minorities inherited from the pre-Communist period.

The process of national integration was further reinforced by the mass dislocations and migrations during and immediately after the war. The wartime eastward expulsion of the Polish population inhabiting territories incorporated into the German Reich, followed by the mass postwar settlement of the "Recovered Territories" in the west, did go a long way toward reducing the strong regional antagonisms that had characterized prewar Poland. These antagonisms were the result of striking regional and local differences that had been caused by more than 150 years of Russian, German, and Austrian rule.

While the postwar emergence of an ethnically homogeneous and nationally integrated Poland undoubtedly strengthened the hand of the Communist rulers at least in the initial period, it will be argued below that in the long run it was likely to aggravate some of the other developmental crises, especially those of political penetration and legitimacy. The former crisis implied that the Communist regime has not been able successfully to penetrate Polish society, which meant that large parts of it remained essentially outside the control of the government. The crisis of legitimacy suggested that despite tremendous efforts to generate some voluntary acceptance of, if not obedience to, the new political system, the Communist rulers failed, by and large, to achieve that particular objective. Both crises were due in large measure to the striking persistence of certain features of the country's political culture, among which nationalism continued to play an important role.

The crises or challenges of penetration and legitimacy are usually closely related to the process of state-building. The latter can be identified in the Polish context with the Communist seizure of power which took place in the period 1944–48.[5] The takeover in Poland did not differ significantly from that in some of the other countries in the region: as aptly described by Zbigniew Brzezinski, it represented a synthesis of certain socioeconomic reforms and a fairly substantial degree of Soviet-sponsored terror and violence.[6]

There were two features of the Communist takeover of Poland whose impact still affects political developments in that country today, more than thirty years after the event. One feature was a comprehensive land reform initiated in 1944, which succeeded, on the one hand, in politically neutralizing the peasants, who at that time represented about two-thirds of the country's population, and on the other, in strengthening the peasant class, which subsequently became a major thorn in the Communists' side. The other special feature was the establishment of the Oder-Neisse line and the incorporation and settlement of former German territories with which the new rulers strongly identified themselves. The need to uphold the incorporation of the freshly acquired areas, whose status remained uncertain until 1970, united both friends and foes of the new regime, and also made the process of takeover somewhat easier, as the incoming Communists portrayed themselves as defenders of Poland's national interest. That the new borders made the country even more dependent on the Soviet Union was not generally recognized at that time.

The process of Stalinization (1948–53) that followed the seizure of power might be viewed simply as a continuation of the process of state-building, whereby the Communist polity attempted to penetrate Polish society and to establish total control over it. Here again, the various stages and methods in the gradual establishment of the Soviet political, economic, and societal models followed the traditional path and did not deviate greatly from the policies pursued by the other countries in the region.

However, as in the case of the takeover process, there were some interesting departures from the model, which were to have major repercussions in the future. One of these departures was the relative absence of the high degree of terror and violence that had characterized the Sovietization process in Bulgaria, Czechoslovakia, and Hungary. To be sure, all resistance to the imposition of the Stalinist model was brutally suppressed, yet in the final analysis the various purges of the party and of society at large claimed relatively few victims. An overwhelming majority of those who suffered persecution and imprisonment survived and reappeared after Stalin's death to play a major role in the country's affairs in the late 1950s and beyond.

The same was true with regard to collectivization of agriculture, anti-church policy, and other policies aimed at restructuring Polish society *a la russe*. In each case the pressure from above appeared considerably milder than in the other satellites. The process of Sovietization in Poland turned out to be less bloody and harsh than elsewhere in Eastern Europe.

The first major challenge to the legitimacy of the system took place in 1956. The reasons for the failure of the Communist polity fully to penetrate Polish society—a major contributory factor in the crisis— were convincingly summarized by Brzezinski. According to him, the ability of each East European regime to deal with the consequences of de-Stalinization depended on the intensity of the socioeconomic crisis within the country, the degree of alienation of the working class and the intelligentsia from the rulers, the extent of the given regime's involvement in anti-Titoist policies, and the availability of alternative leadership.[7] Poland and Hungary were much more affected by the above crises than the other countries in the region, and both went through major upheavals in the fall of 1956: a bloody revolt in Hungary and a bloodless changeover in Poland. The latter brought Wladyslaw Gomulka back to power and was accompanied by a series of political and economic changes, among which the collapse of agricultural collectivization was by far the most significant. Gomulka, one of the chief engineers of the postwar Communist takeover, fell victim to Stalinist purges, and his elevation to leadership represented a major break with the past. Although the double crisis of penetration and legitimacy did not last long, it was clear that Poland's politics would never be the same and that the sharp challenge to the supposedly impregnable system would not remain without an echo.

The next decade and a half witnessed an unsuccessful attempt at what may be called "system maintenance" or "consolidation." The regime's efforts to acquire even a modicum of legitimacy failed, most signally in March 1968, when university students and intellectuals rose up in protest against government censorship and increasingly restrictive cultural policy. Thereafter the country entered a period of political stagnation and decay, with the chasm between the rulers and the ruled becoming gradually wider. The explosion of December 1970, when the workers on the Baltic coast rioted in protest against a drastic increase in retail prices and succeeded in bringing down the Gomulka regime, represented the second major double crisis of legitimacy and penetration, the impact of which is still felt today.

The third developmental challenge, that of participation, did not make its appearance until relatively late in the period under discussion. Beginning in 1956, the Polish regime attempted to expand the scope of popular participation at various levels, but until the early 1970s, the progress had not been significant. It may be argued, in fact, that the overthrow of Gomulka in December 1970 represented not only a crisis of legitimacy and penetration but also a crisis of participation, and that in this respect it illustrated rather well the notion of mass politicization leading to social frustration and political instability because of the absence of channels for meaningful participation.[8]

One may generalize, however, that in Poland, throughout most of the period under discussion, the frustration, anomie, and alienation from the system were related more closely to the questions of distribution and welfare than to participation or even legitimacy. In other words, economic demands tended to take precedence over political desiderata, and while both of them probably merged in the first systemic crisis of October 1956, there was no doubt that economic grievances were responsible for the second major challenge to the regime in December 1970. Altogether, despite the impressive progress in industrialization and economic development, the living standard of the Polish population has been growing at a rate slower than in most of the other people's democracies, contributing still further to economic and political discontent.

Thus, on the eve of the seventies Poland was in disarray. Although the political system managed to maintain itself and to withstand the various crises and challenges, its performance was clearly below par and its future uncertain. Except for a very brief period in 1956–57, the Communist regime did not succeed in generating popular acceptance and legitimacy, and by the end of the 1960s it had lost a good deal of support even among its traditional followers. By the same token, the political system was unable to penetrate deeply Polish society, with the result that large segments of the latter, especially the peasantry and the youth, and, as it became abundantly clear in December 1970, also the industrial working class, remained to a considerable degree outside the control of the regime, whose extractive capacity was thereby considerably impaired. This, in turn, had serious repercussions on the performance of the economic system, which failed not only to secure a modest living standard for the majority of the population but also to sustain a moderate rate of economic growth, to guarantee that a better life would be achieved before long.

POLAND IN THE 1970s

The replacement of Gomulka by Edward Gierek in December 1970 seemed to inaugurate a new era in recent Polish history. From the start, Western observers, taking their cue most likely from the personal background and experience of the new leader, who had spent the early part of his adult life in Western Europe—Belgium and France—and had eventually become a successful and popular party leader in Silesia, the most heavily industrialized part of Poland, proclaimed the incoming regime as "dynamic," "pragmatic," and "technocratic," which implied a major contrast to its predecessor and carried a promise of better things to come.

For the first few years these predictions appeared to be largely validated. To begin with, the country's stagnating economy entered a period of rapid growth, stimulated mostly by massive injections of Western credits and technology. Simultaneously, Polish peasants, relieved finally of the heavy burden of compulsory deliveries, responded by sharply expanding their output. The new leadership also belatedly embarked on a drive to overhaul the economic system by appointing a blue-ribbon party-government commission to prepare a blueprint for reforms.

Politically, the new regime also assumed a middle-of-the-road stance by eliminating both the conservative and radical wings in the ruling party oligarchy, and by bringing into leading positions men largely unencumbered by ideological dogmatism or rampant nationalism. The top party leadership included members of the generation who rose to prominence in the postwar period rather than before or during the war. Partly as a result, they tended to be younger and better educated, further reinforcing the view that pragmatism and rationality were to be the chief determinants of policy at the expense of dogmatism and dilettantism.

In line with this approach, the new leadership made an early bid to capture the support of the Polish intelligentsia, focusing on the emerging professional interest and pressure groups, which were promised greater participation in decision making in the name of building a "new Poland." Literary and artistic groups, youth, and even the church were also granted concessions: censorship was reduced in breadth and depth; foreign travel restrictions were largely lifted; and the often crude antireligious propaganda was toned down.

In foreign policy, too, the new team departed significantly from its predecessor. In addition to the continued betterment of relations with West Germany, initiated by the treaty signed in Warsaw on the eve of Gomulka's ouster in December 1970, Gierek made a major effort to improve relations with France, the United States, and other Western countries, by visiting Paris, Washington, and Bonn. His major purpose appeared to be to secure Western credits, which would propel Poland toward rapid industrial modernization.

Closer to home, Poland's relations with the Soviet Union were developing satisfactorily and gave Moscow little cause for concern, as Gierek took great pains to reassure the Kremlin that his overtures to the West represented no threat to Soviet hegemony in the region. The fact that the Soviet Union itself, taking advantage of the spirit of detente, engaged in rapprochement with the West, provided at least some legitimacy to Poland's new endeavors. Insofar as the rest of the East European countries were concerned, Gierek's assumption of power probably made little or no difference, and Poland's relations with them remained essentially unchanged.

Hence, as suggested earlier, it appeared as if a new era had indeed dawned upon Poland, which became permeated with a new spirit of dynamism in sharp contrast to the stagnation and decay of the late 1960s. The honeymoon, however, proved to be short-lived and, for all practical purposes, it was over on the fifth anniversary of Gierek's accession to power. From then on, the political and economic situation deteriorated rapidly, reaching bottom in June 1976, when the regime, making the same mistake as in December 1970, announced a drastic increase in the prices of key foodstuffs. It was then immediately confronted by several major workers' riots and a threat of a general strike, and was forced to retreat and withdraw the increase within twenty-four hours. In the face of multiple challenges by the very same group that had brought it to power only half a decade before—the industrial working class—the image of a pragmatic, dynamic, and relatively popular regime was suddenly replaced by one that bore a striking resemblance to its predecessor, characterized by uncertainty, lack of direction, internal strife, and stagnation.

What had happened and what factors were responsible for this sudden turnabout in the fortunes of a regime that had begun so auspiciously only a few years before? Consideration of the five systemic variables mentioned at the outset of this chapter may prove helpful in explaining what took place.

CULTURE

Culture, as a systemic component, is defined by Huntington as embracing "the values, attitudes, orientations, myths and beliefs relevant to politics and dominant in society."[9] In this context, the concept includes not only mass perceptions and beliefs, many of them with roots established long before the Communist takeover, but also both the official ideology advocated and disseminated by the ruling elite and the antiregime attitudes articulated by political dissenters.

Perhaps the most striking aspect of the cultural variable in Polish politics has been the remarkable persistence of what may be termed "traditional" values, despite the massive socialization and re-socialization campaigns conducted by successive regimes since the end of the war. At the risk of oversimplification, the most relevant of these aspects appear to be basic distrust and disobedience of political or governmental authority; fervent, if not rampant, nationalism; and attachment to certain traditional institutions and social arrangements and structures.

In talking to members of the ruling elite, one often hears the complaint that "building Communism in a country such as Poland is an impossible task." It can be presumed that over the years, the Polish Communist leaders must have become increasingly frustrated with their inability to lay strong foundations for a new political and social system, eyeing with some envy the situation in Bulgaria, Czechoslovakia, East Germany, and Romania, where the obedient population had seemingly accepted and become reconciled to the new order.

There is no doubt that deeply rooted mistrust and dislike of authority has been largely responsible for the failure of the Communist system to penetrate Polish society. It can be argued that although the anti-authoritarian attitudes go back several centuries, they acquired their modern expression during the 150-year period of partitions, further reinforced by six years of German occupation during World War II. The fact remains that in the second half of the 1970s the average Pole, in contrast to his neighbors, most likely considered the present regime essentially illegitimate and imposed from the outside. To be sure, one could expect a similar attitude toward almost any Polish regime, yet the fact that it was a Communist government which, in addition, was imported from the East, made its mass acceptance impossible. Centuries of resistance against foreign domination left marks on the Polish psyche that thirty years of Communist indoctrination did little to eradicate.

Whether one chooses to call it attachment to freedom, rugged individualism, lack of discipline, or simply proclivity to anarchy, the Polish people have steadfastly refused to accept the Communist system as legitimate. This has been as true for the educated classes—traditionally the bastion of independent thought and action—as for the peasants and workers, until recently assumed to be much more malleable and obedient.

There are several interesting corollaries to this phenomenon. First of all, it must be emphasized that the resistance to the system stems only partly from the fact that it happens to be a Communist one. It does not necessarily mean that a democratic system of whatever shape or form would have been universally accepted. On the contrary, traditional Polish political culture tended to be, if not anti-, then at least nondemocratic, embodying to a large degree the values of the old gentry, which were highly elitist, nonegalitarian, and particularistic. These traits seemed to have survived long after the Communist takeover and explain the persistence of deep social cleavages between various segments of Polish society: intelligentsia and workers; workers and peasants; urban and rural dwellers.

A recent striking change in the Polish political and social environment that has greatly impaired the ability of the regime to exercise its authority has been the significant muting of the above conflicts. The process has been slow in coming. German occupation policies did little to reduce the traditional cleavages: directed primarily against the urban intelligentsia, they tended to spare the workers and peasants; indeed, the latter benefited greatly from a sharp rise in food prices. This policy was largely followed by the Communists during the takeover period: land reform benefited the peasants, the industrial working class was elevated to an apparent privileged status, and the intelligentsia continued to suffer. It is not surprising, therefore, that on the eve of Stalinization, the cleavages among the three major classes appeared as wide as ever, and the fact that the Stalinist *Gleichschaltung* policies were directed against *all* classes did little to reduce the existing chasms.

One of the most interesting and significant aspects of the bloodless coup of October 1956 was the emergence of a united front against the

opposition; this concession could have been interpreted as at least a partial victory for the dissenters.

Perhaps encouraged by this success, the intellectual opposition not only took up the cause of the workers against the government in the summer of 1976, but also began to call for greater respect for human rights in general. This was no longer an ad hoc campaign focused on a single, specific issue, but a frontal attack on, and a challenge to, the existing system. The fact that for the first time in modern Polish history the intellectuals were no longer speaking only on their own behalf but also as members of a powerful alliance clearly presented a major problem for the Gierek regime, which thus far had proved unable or unwilling to handle it. There is little doubt that the intellectuals played a major role in the alliance in at least two ways: by giving it national and international exposure and visibility, and by raising its level of politicization by broadening the scope of its demands.

There is considerable evidence that, in comparison with the Soviet Union and the other East European countries, the dissident movement in Poland has been flourishing. In addition to the Workers' Defense Committee, there were two other dissident groups active in the country in early 1978, representing separate political viewpoints. The Workers' Defense Committee—the oldest and best known of the dissident groups —was on the left of the political spectrum. Its programmatic goals appeared to be relatively modest, aimed primarily at achieving a gradual liberalization of the existing system. This was to be accomplished by working within and through the system, rather than by overthrowing it. The Committee's publications have made frequent references to the Polish constitution and various other legal provisions, which, in its eyes, could be utilized to gain and safeguard democratic rights and freedoms. Above all, the Committee's leadership was most anxious to avoid a major political crisis which could result in Soviet intervention *a la* Czechoslovakia. Consequently, the Committee's anti-Soviet pronouncements were relatively rare and muted, and they also tended to play down traditional Polish nationalist sentiments.

The other two dissident groups—the Movement for the Defense of Human and Civil Rights (*Ruch Obrony Praw Czlowieka i Obywatela* or *ROPCiO*) and the Polish Independence Movement (*Polskie Porozumienie Niepodleglosciowe or PPN*)—are much less known. The former was organized by some defectors from the Workers' Defense Committee who were apparently dissatisfied with its relatively moderate program. The latter, a clandestine organization, was even further to the right and, as suggested by its name, it was strongly nationalistic and anti-

Soviet. Between them, openly if illegally, the three groups published from fifteen to twenty separate publications, reflecting the gamut of political opinions.

In light of the above, it is not surprising that the second cultural variable to influence the popular attitude toward the present system has been nationalism, traditionally a powerful force in Polish politics. Although for a variety of reasons Poland never quite succeeded in developing its own brand of national communism, successive party leaders tried, with some measure of success, to utilize nationalist feelings for their own purposes by appearing as defenders of the country's national interest (as in the case of the Oder-Neisse line) or its ethnic purity (as in the case of the virulent anti-Semitic campaign of 1968). On the other hand, the Communist party did not come close to eradicating the traditional anti-Russian feeling that had permeated Polish society for generations and which attached an indelible stigma to anything entering the country from the East. The initial popularity and semi-legitimacy of Gomulka was based on his being identified above all as anti-Soviet rather than anti-Stalinist, and it was this (incorrect) perception that permitted him to enjoy a relatively lengthy honeymoon, certainly a longer one than he otherwise deserved.

The current regime had no such credit to fall back on. With the West German threat to Polish western frontiers gone and the large majority of Polish Jews having left the country, the leadership has been in no position to mobilize nationalist sentiments against real or imaginary enemies, unless it were to be the Soviet Union. This the regime refused to do, at least until now. On the contrary, there is considerable evidence that, if anything, Gierek has been more "pro-Soviet" than his predecessor, judging from his own pronouncements as well as from comments emanating from the Polish media in the past two or three years. As suggested above, the reason for this may have been Gierek's desire to assuage potential Soviet fears regarding Poland's economic and cultural rapprochement with the West. Still, to an average man in the street, the present leadership appeared to be more subservient to Moscow than necessary, and, rightly or wrongly, the Soviet Union continued to be blamed for Poland's recent economic difficulties. This mass perception did little to strengthen the regime's popularity and legitimacy, making it even more difficult for it to make and execute policy.

The final cultural component affecting political processes in the country in recent years was the continued attachment to certain traditional political and social institutions. One of the strongest recent manifestations of this traditionalism was the campaign against constitutional revisions decreed by the government, which mirrored an almost irrational attachment to a constitution passed at the height of Stalinism that was hardly ever respected or observed. To the question of why people protested, the standard response has been that the government had no right to tamper even with a basically undemocratic, quasi-totalitarian constitution, which, after all, represented the most fundamental legal document in the land, one that could not be changed by party fiat. In line with this attitude, the most recent campaign in defense of human rights tends to emphasize constitutional guarantees of individual freedoms.

More relevant for our discussion is the apparently strong attachment to such institutions as the Catholic church and the family farm. Space does not permit a full discussion of church-state relations in Communist Poland. Suffice it to say that after an earlier period of relative calm characterized by a *modus vivendi* between the pragmatic regime of Gierek and the essentially conservative church dominated by Cardinal Wyszynski, the most recent developments suggest that the official policy of the church has swung in favor of the worker-intellectual alliance. The effect of this switch should not be underestimated.

Conventional wisdom has long been that the Poles are strongly religious. This view is based on such evidence as crowded churches, a homogeneous population, and an increase in the numerical strength of the clergy. My own impression is that if indeed the church is still popular today, it is much less because of its religious or spiritual role, and infinitely more because of its function as the only true bastion of independence from Communist control. It could be shown that in the past the church enjoyed its greatest popularity at the height of governmental persecution and that it lost support when church-state relations improved. This relationship was eventually recognized by the Polish leadership, which in the past decade or so has tried to cultivate good relations with the church. For a while, this policy of accommodation seemed successful, as the essentially conservative clergy confined itself to the defense of its own interests, seldom venturing into the purely political arena. However, the deteriorating political and economic situation and the resulting growing reactionary character of the Gierek regime apparently persuaded the church hierarchy to abandon its semi-neutral stance and to add its opposition to that of the workers and the intellectuals, presenting the current regime with still another major challenge.

STRUCTURE

The concept of structure in this context includes "formal organizations through which the society makes authoritative decisions, such as political parties, legislatures, executives, and bureaucracies."[10]

In many respects the Polish Communist party in the mid-1970s did not differ greatly from its counterparts in the other people's democracies. Its membership in mid-1975 stood at 2,359,000, which accounted for roughly seven percent of the population.[11] This percentage had not changed greatly since the mid-1960s, when an intensive recruitment drive was undertaken by the Gomulka regime. In terms of social composition, the Polish party typified a highly bureaucratized structure, with 49.5 percent of its membership accounted for by government officials and white collar workers, 12.2 percent by peasants and farm workers, and only 38.3 percent by industrial workers.[12]

It may be argued that the situation in the middle echelons and in the rank and file of the party in the mid-1970s must have given little cause for joy to its leaders. The growing dissatisfaction with the regime's performance, especially in the economic sphere, meant that the party, the vanguard of Polish society, whose task it was to lead the country to a better future, had not only failed to generate mass support for its policies but it had also allowed a serious challenge to the system's legitimacy to develop almost overnight.

What were the reasons for the malaise within the ruling party? Perhaps the major one was the party's failure to penetrate and become an integral part of Polish society. Throughout most of its existence, quantity rather than quality was the chief determinant of recruitment into the party, with the result that little attention was paid to the caliber of the new entrants, most of whom were joining the party for opportunistic reasons. Periodic purges, in the guise of "verification campaigns" conducted in the name of ideological purity, succeeded only in eliminating the marginal elements of the rank and file, leaving the hard core or the "cadres" largely untouched. The emphasis on sheer numbers resulted in most of the new recruits coming out of the semi-educated classes, who considered party membership a vehicle for rapid career advancement in the government or the economy. This, in turn, was responsible for the rather low intellectual and ideological level of the average party member, who was willing to pay lip service to the regime as long as he derived some tangible benefits from it.

The successive regimes, including the current one, never quite succeeded in defining the proper role for the ruling party. Periodically, especially following radical changes in the top leadership as in 1956 and 1970, there were calls for making the party a rather narrow, elitist organization whose main task was to provide overall guidance and leadership to Polish society, leaving the day-to-day administration and policy implementation to government bureaucrats and specialized groups, regardless of their political affiliation. This policy was usually tied to plans for a major overhaul of the economic system and debates about the importance of "scientific-technical revolution," both of which required major inputs from "experts" rather than from "reds." Usually, this "pragmatic" approach did not last very long, as the firmly entrenched party apparatus resented outside interference and the concurrent loss of power and influence. For all practical purposes, the Gierek regime, just like its predecessors, never managed to make achievement rather than ascription the chief criterion of political recruitment, thus forfeiting its chance of making a real breakthrough on the road toward modernization.

In the mid-1970s party membership continued to be the prerequisite for political and socioeconomic advancement. As a result, the decision-making processes at various levels and in nearly all areas were monopolized by intellectual mediocrities who by and large tended to be ignorant of the real problems confronting the society at large. Periodic calls for the re-establishment of "links with the masses" remained largely unheeded, and the gap between the rulers and the ruled continued to widen. This lack of "contact with the masses" was clearly one of the major reasons for the series of blunders committed by both the Gomulka and the Gierek regimes.

Another reason for these seemingly irrational policies was the apparent inability of the party leadership to establish firm control over the middle-rank bureaucracy and the rank and file. It is well known that in all Communist parties it is relatively easier to purge the top-level leadership than either the middle-echelon apparatus or the membership at large, and the Polish party was no exception. After 1956 it took Gomulka several years to establish full control over the party, and the same was true, albeit to a lesser degree, for the Gierek regime after 1970. The result of this asymmetry between the top and the middle party echelons are frequent difficulties and delays in, and even sabotage of, new policies decreed by the top leadership and implemented by the middle, which, as a rule, tends to be more conservative than the top oligarchy. In Poland, a recent example was the failure of a new agricultural policy favoring efficient individual farmers, which was systematically sabotaged by the local apparatus, supposedly committed ideologically to the socialization of agriculture and opposed to the strengthening of private farming. There was also a sharp disagreement between the party apparatus and the top leadership with regard to the withdrawal of the food-price increase in 1976, which was deplored by the former as a sign of the regime's weakness vis-a-vis the workers.

To sum up, there is considerable evidence to suggest that in the second half of the 1970s the Polish party was divided on a variety of issues; this meant that its ability to govern the country in a rational and efficient fashion was significantly eroded.

Little needs to be said about the remaining Polish political parties—the United Peasant Party (*Zjednoczone Stronnictwo Ludowe*) and the Democratic Party (*Stronnictwo Demokratyczne*). Despite the frequent elaborate show of consultations between the Communist party and its junior partners, for all practical purposes the latter amounted to little more than the traditional "transmission belts" linking the ruling party with the peasants and the intelligentsia. At times they acted as a kind of pressure group, but their influence on decision making has been minimal and they served mostly as a window dressing.

As suggested earlier, both the party and government bureaucracies resembled the traditional Communist stereotypes, characterized by inherent conservatism, fear and distrust of innovations, and determination to defend the status quo. Together with the great majority of the party's rank and file, the party apparatus tended to be opportunistic and careerist, and its level of intellectual and professional sophistication left much to be desired. To be sure, there were sporadic attempts to improve the latter by the cooptation of better-educated individuals, but the overall success was meager. As a result, the standards of bureaucratic performance with respect to decision making and policy implementation were quite low.

Turning to the legislatures, here again, the early promises of greater parliamentary involvement in, and influence on, the political life of the country have not materialized. Both Gomulka and Gierek started off by promising to make the Polish parliament—the *Sejm*—a focal point in the far-ranging discussions of major economic and social issues by making it more visible, and by granting it a greater role in consultations and decision making. Although it seems that in recent years various parliamentary committees have been given more information that enabled them to discuss some specific problems in greater depth and to scrutinize policy implementation, the infrequent and brief plenary sessions of the *Sejm* continued to serve the ritualistic purpose of rubber-stamping governmental decrees and providing a forum for occasional major pronouncements by the party leaders.

To conclude, the political structures in Poland in the mid-1970s tended to conform to the Soviet model emulated by all people's democracies. As such, they frequently acted as a major obstacle on the road to modernization and, thus far at least, periodic attempts to transform them in the direction of greater efficiency have failed in the face of bureaucratic resistance favoring the status quo. Even more importantly, the ruling party appeared to be increasingly divided, with the top oligarchy less and less able to have its policies implemented in a rational fashion.

GROUPS

Groups can be defined as "the social and economic formations, formal and informal, which participate in politics and make demands on the political structures."[13] It may be generalized that in this respect, the Polish record has been much less impressive than that of Czechoslovakia and Hungary, in that the notion of pluralism, however broadly defined, has never been an integral part of Polish political culture. With few exceptions, the performance of formal groups has been rather dismal and there have been only a few examples of particular interest groups acquiring even a semi-legitimate status in the political system.

What were the reasons for this phenomenon? To a large extent, the emergence of functionally specific interest or pressure groups in Poland followed the same path as elsewhere in Eastern Europe, and was the by-product of rapid industrialization and growing complexity and differentiation of the socioeconomic system, which ultimately forced the ruling elite to seek advice from experts in various fields. In Poland, in contrast to some of the other countries in the region, however, only a few of these groups became institutionalized and were brought into the decision-making process. A good deal of the resistance to these groups was due to the character of the Polish Communist party, highly jealous of its prerogatives and resentful of the intrusion of outside specialists. Faced with the strong resistance of the party apparatus, the various groups either meekly surrendered or broke up, with individual members often coopted into the party establishment where they quickly adopted a conservative stance. Some groups never developed a corporatist elan or image of their own, and seemed content with playing the role of traditional "transmission belts."

The most prominent groups of this kind were the trade unions, which even during the relatively liberal periods in recent Polish history never quite abandoned their role of obedient tools of the party. Throughout, their record of defending workers' interests has been most dismal and the fact that they played no part in the two major confrontations between the workers and the regime in December 1970 and June 1976 speaks for itself. Currently, the unions appear to be totally discredited in the eyes of the working class.

The record of most professional groups and associations has not been much better. There is no evidence that such specific groups as journalists, educators, technicians, and managers played a significant role in decision making or, at best, in making their views known. To be sure, individual members of these professions participated, for example, in the work of two recently appointed blue-ribbon commissions entrusted with the task of reforming the economy and the educational system, but they acted as individuals rather than as representatives of interest groups whose right it was to be consulted.

In the absence of empirical evidence, one can hypothesize that the failure of the Polish pressure groups to assert themselves vis-a-vis the government was caused by, among other things, the general dislike of collectivism as a mode of human action. Reference has been made to the deeply rooted mistrust of authority and the attachment to individualism that characterized the traditional Polish political culture. It may be speculated that the idea of interest groups, which in the Communist context would not be truly representative or democratically organized, did not appeal greatly to many individuals who preferred to strike out on their own.

There were, of course, significant exceptions. One of the most articulate and visible groups represented the literary and artistic community, which for the past two decades has been rather deeply engaged in political activities, progressing from the defense of their professional and particularistic interests to demands for greater respect for human rights of all segments of the population. Many writers and artists were heavily involved in the crucial events of October 1956, March 1968, and the most recent period after June 1976. Between these milestones in postwar Polish history, they maintained almost constant pressure on the ruling elite, reminding it of the constitutional guarantees for the freedom of expression. By and large, they proved remarkably effective, possibly because of their high national and international visibility, and there is no doubt that the relatively free Polish cultural and artistic climate owes much to their efforts. The most recent involvement of intellectuals in the human rights campaign in alliance with workers and students obviously represented a watershed in postwar Polish political development. It should be stated, however, that the majority of writers and artists thus far managed by and large to remain neutral, yet

tion was also followed by Gierek who, in addition, granted the peasants important economic and social concessions. It may be argued, however, that especially in the early 1970s, the role of agriculture was greatly overshadowed by the drive for industrial modernization and a rapid rate of economic growth, and the farm sector was almost forgotten. It was only in the aftermath of the food crisis of 1976 that the peasants reappeared as crucial political and economic actors.

Actually, the regime's relationship to individual farmers illustrates well the shortcomings of the Polish system. On the one hand, there is the top party leadership, which appears reconciled to the existence of the private farm sector for many years to come and is openly committed to its support in the name of greater farm output and higher living standards. On the other hand, Polish agriculture has been beset by difficulties such as a continued exodus from the villages, the gradual aging of the farm population, and the fragmentation of individual holdings, making a substantial increase in output highly problematical without additional reforms and governmental aid.

The gap between the regime and the peasants is filled by the bureaucracy—both party and government—which is supposed to implement policy and, at the same time, serve as a channel of communication and information from the peasants to the decision-makers. It is at this juncture that the system clearly breaks down. The local bureaucracy tends not only to either sabotage or delay the governmental "liberal" policies but also to misrepresent the actual conditions in the countryside. As a result, what often appears to be a rational policy never gets fully executed, the peasants become increasingly dissatisfied with the regime, and, in the meantime, the "objective" conditions change, necessitating a new round of decisions, and the vicious cycle continues. This syndrome can be easily applied to almost all branches of political and economic activity, and it serves to illustrate the dilemma faced by the Polish leadership, whose policies are systematically frustrated and whose decision-making powers are being gradually circumscribed by the lack of reliable and correct information.

To sum up, in the second half of the 1970s the Polish regime, for various reasons, still refused to institutionalize a network of pressure groups, thus depriving itself of a potentially valuable ally and partner in decision making. However, it could not prevent the emergence of formal and informal opposition groups which, by articulating increasingly political demands, have been contributing to the already serious problems faced by the system.

LEADERSHIP

It is probably no exaggeration to say that postwar Poland has not been blessed with great political leaders—"the individuals in political institutions and groups who exercise more influence than others on the allocation of values."[14] Throughout its postwar existence, the country has been ruled by four individuals, and although all the evidence is not in, one may generalize that none of them exhibited the kinds of qualities that would have earned them the adjectives "great," "legitimate," or "charismatic."

Despite recent attempts to exonerate and rehabilitate him, Boleslaw Bierut, who ruled Poland during the Stalinist period, must go down in history as essentially a mediocre leader whose major achievement was that he managed to spare the country from the worst excesses of the mass political terror practiced in Bulgaria, Czechoslovakia, and Hungary. While this accomplishment was obviously not unimportant, it was largely offset by his crude policy toward the peasants and the intelligentsia. Bierut's successor, Edward Ochab, was an interim leader whose tenure lasted barely six months. His greatest achievement, in turn, was to pave the way for the return of Gomulka to power.

Wladyslaw Gomulka, who headed the Polish Communist party for roughly twenty years (1943–48 and 1956–70), was not a run-of-the-mill leader.[15] For a brief period (1956–57) he was probably the only genuinely legitimate national leader in postwar Polish history. He was also a man of some principles, as illustrated by his behavior in the early postwar period when his convictions almost cost him his life. Yet, by hindsight, he was also a person of rather limited ability and narrow horizons, whose principles and convictions frequently became transformed into sheer obstinacy and irrational attachment to discredited concepts and ideas whose usefulness was long outlived. He represented a curious blend of pragmatic thinking—as illustrated by his revolutionary decision to dissolve the collective farms—and stubborn refusal to innovate—as reflected by his reluctance to reform and modernize the Polish economy. There is a good chance that he will be remembered chiefly as the leader who took almost fifteen years to squander the great reservoir of credit and confidence granted him by the Polish people in October 1956, and who ended up as a bitter and humiliated man.

By all counts, Gomulka's successor, Edward Gierek, appeared to be a man for all seasons. Unencumbered by ideological baggage from the past, untainted by participation in the factional struggles between the "Muscovites" and the "natives," possessing an impressive wartime resistance record in France, experienced as a party bureaucrat, and famed for his efficient administration of Silesia, economically the most important Polish province, he seemed an ideal choice to lead the country from inertia and stagnation toward a better future. Gierek was immediately hailed as a pragmatist, a technocrat, and a modernizer.

For awhile, all the predictions appeared to have come true. In a relatively short time Gierek succeeded in mollifying the irate working class, granted major concessions to the peasants, improved relations with the church and conciliated the intelligentsia. The often tricky process of political succession proceeded smoothly, with Gierek taking great pains not to antagonize the former leadership by limiting criticism of the past and restricting the purge of the party membership. His rapidly growing popularity was further reinforced by rapprochement with the West, especially in the economic and cultural spheres. Finally, he introduced a new, personalized, and open style into Polish politics, a sharp contrast with the dour and dull style practiced by Gomulka.

Yet, only a few years later, the same leader was forced to call off the drastic increase in food prices, thus rescinding a major policy decision within twenty-four hours in the face of massive resistance by the same workers who had brought him to power less than six years earlier. Although Gierek's role in the decision that triggered off the June 1976 riots is far from clear, he was commonly identified by the masses as being ultimately responsible for it. The laboriously constructed image of the pragmatic modernizer and efficient administrator became tarnished, and the whole system lost credibility overnight. One may hypothesize that the major reason that Gierek was not ousted was the lack of alternatives. No other member of the ruling oligarchy commanded sufficient support—both internal and external—to take over.

Gierek, like Gomulka before him, was clearly a first among equals within the collective leadership. Also, like his predecessor, he was able largely to select his own Politburo, even though initially he had to include in it individuals whom he subsequently purged. Other than that, however, Gierek's oligarchy differed significantly from its predecessor. The Politburo that was ousted in December 1970 included a number of party veterans who had earned their spurs in World War II and who went through the trials and tribulations associated with the construction of the socialist system in Poland, at times paying a rather heavy price for it. Only very few of them remained, albeit briefly, in the new Politburo, which from the start was dominated by "new socialist men" who had made their careers not fighting the Germans or resisting Stalinism, but in bureaucratic infighting.

On the surface the new team appeared better suited to lead Poland into the twenty-first century. The new oligarchs were younger, better educated, essentially nonideological, and technocratically oriented. Following some early purges, they appeared basically to be middle-of-the-roaders, disdaining both the radicalism of the left and the conservatism of the right. As long as the standard success indicators showed rapid progress on all fronts, they enjoyed considerable popularity. This being the case, the notorious decision to raise food prices in June 1976 must have resulted from the ruling oligarchy being largely out of touch with the attitudes and preferences of the citizenry. It must be made clear that the top decision-makers were well aware that the measure would be unpopular. Yet, in the final analysis, they either chose to ignore potential dissatisfaction or remained confident of their ability to ride out the storm. It may be speculated that in either case, the attitude of the leadership reflected lack of contact with, and contempt for, the masses. As one observer of the Polish scene suggested to me in 1976, "As you well know, power corrupts and absolute power corrupts absolutely, and Poland is no exception to this rule."

One may also hypothesize that the growing gap between the rulers and the ruled was at least partly due to the personal backgrounds of individual members of the oligarchy, trained to maintain the leading role of the party at all costs and to treat the general public as the enemy of the system. Members of the previous oligarchy had shared many common traits with large segments of the Polish population: they had fought in the resistance, had been imprisoned in German concentration camps or Stalinist jails, and had tried, at least for awhile, to resist Soviet influence. The leading members of the new oligarchy had no such life experiences; perhaps for that reason they did not enjoy the kind of mass support and legitimacy given initially to Gomulka and his team, although it must be granted that, in the final analysis, such experiences did not prevent the ouster of the latter in 1970.

No leaders anywhere, regardless of their political coloration, can exercise authority or "allocate values" without some degree of popular acceptance—voluntary or coerced. The latter aside, voluntary acceptance, however limited, must involve some belief in the ability of the rulers to make rational decisions at least partially in conformity with the wishes of the majority of the population. This belief has been absent in Poland since the middle of 1976, and the resulting credibility gap has added to the woes of the regime, limiting its freedom of maneuver.

POLICIES

The last systemic component—policies—will be analyzed briefly, since many of them have already been discussed.

On the domestic scene, by far the most important policy decision made by the Gierek regime concerned the new model of Poland's economic development to be based on an extensive modernization of the country's industrial structure with the aid of Western credits and technology. Although the new strategy proved highly successful in stimulating rapid economic growth, it also overheated the economy and added to existing inflationary pressure. While real income and living standards undoubtedly rose in the early years of Gierek's rule, ultimately the output of consumer goods and foodstuffs could not keep up with increased demand fueled by higher wages, and serious shortages began to develop, causing growing dissatisfaction among consumers.

Another major reason for the mounting shortages was that the price of certain key foodstuffs such as meat had been kept frozen since the second half of the 1960s, making Poland probably the only country in the world where food prices remained constant for almost a decade, despite global inflationary pressures. It appeared that Gierek had learned a lesson from the fate of his predecessor and intended to acquire and maintain popular support by keeping food prices frozen. While politically justified in the short run, this decision proved disastrous in the long run, illustrating the vagaries of decision making, even within a supposedly enlightened and pragmatic Communist system.

Other policies initiated after December 1970 also appeared to make considerable sense and testified to Gierek's political acumen. A comprehensive reform of the educational system was clearly needed in light of the rapid socioeconomic transformation of the country. A new approach toward agriculture attempted once again to reassure the peasants about the survival of individual farms while at the same time encouraging them to expand output. Two successive reforms of local government, although politically inspired and aimed at diluting the power of provincial party secretaries vis-a-vis the center, were not devoid of rationality. The conciliatory policy toward the intelligentsia and the church also made good political sense. Thus, on the whole, the initial record appeared most impressive even though, as mentioned above, the implementation of the various measures left much to be desired.

In view of these early successes, it is even more difficult to explain the rationale behind the two highly controversial decisions that ultimately represented a serious defeat for the regime. Clearly, there was little need for Gierek to proclaim the necessity of constitutional revisions at the end of 1975. Since there is no evidence of outside pressure emanating from the Soviet Union or the other people's democracies, it has to be assumed that the initiative originated within the ruling oligarchy, who must have been oblivious to the potential consequences of their decision. While the decision to raise food prices in June 1976 was eminently rational, both the preparation and the timing were faulty, suggesting the leadership's far-reaching ignorance of popular attitudes, rather striking in view of its earlier concern to gain legitimacy and acceptance.

Has the Polish leadership learned any lessons from the crisis of 1976? Although it is too early to pronounce a final verdict, initial evidence seems to suggest that indeed it has. This impression is based on analysis of the regime's behavior since 1976, which may be viewed as relatively restrained, especially when contrasted with the almost hysterical reaction of the other East European governments faced with the human rights campaign in late 1976 and early 1977. While some of the leading Polish dissenters were arrested or persecuted, others were permitted to articulate their opposition not only at home but also abroad. This inconsistent policy may well be the result of sharp disagreements within the ruling oligarchy between those who felt that the last thing the regime needed at this stage was to create martyrs out of a handful of protesters, and those favoring repression as a means of stemming the tide of dissent. At the moment it appears that the pragmatic faction has the upper hand, but its triumph may yet prove illusory.

Insofar as Poland's foreign policy was concerned, Gierek's greatest accomplishment lay in the area of economic policy. By breaking away from Gomulka's fierce and almost irrational adherence to the model of economic self-sufficiency, and by rapidly expanding Poland's economic relations with the West, Gierek quickly succeeded in making Poland one of the fastest growing countries in the world in the first half of the 1970s. To be sure, his timing was admirable and he was also fortunate in that his accession to power coincided with the emergence of the East-West detente. Detente meant that, on the one hand, the West was highly receptive to overtures from Eastern Europe and only too willing to grant it credits and trade concessions, and on the other, the Soviet Union's own growing involvement in East-West trade gave an aura of legitimacy to the Polish initiative. Nevertheless, although the international climate was clearly favorable to the latter, Gierek himself should be given considerable credit for achieving the breakthrough, even though its ultimate cost may prove prohibitive, as Poland's balance of payments deficit at the end of 1976 exceeded $10 billion.[16]

The latter was also due to a combination of factors over which Poland exercised only partial control. The global inflation, caused by the rapidly growing cost of energy and fuel, together with the lasting economic recession in the West, resulted in an increased cost of Polish imports and a reduced value of the country's exports. The poor performance of Poland's agriculture, caused, among others, by an irrational policy of the government, was also responsible for the need to import large quantities of grain and for the decrease in the exports of agricultural commodities, which in the past had accounted for a large share of the country's foreign receipts. The difficult situation in the farm sector was, of course, also related to the scarcity of some of the foodstuffs and the necessity of raising their prices. This, in turn, threatened the stability of the political system, which found itself attacked by irate citizens.

Poland's relations with the Soviet Union and its smaller East European partners also seemed to develop smoothly in the early part of the 1970s. There is considerable evidence suggesting that the December 1970 crisis had serious repercussions throughout the bloc and that the members of the Warsaw alliance welcomed the replacement of Gomulka by Gierek, who was seen as a better guarantor of political stability. The fact that Brezhnev refused to intervene in the Polish succession crisis was a good indication of Moscow's disillusionment with Gomulka, despite the latter's apparent close relationship with the Soviet leadership.

Following his assumption of power, Gierek quickly replaced Gomulka as the Kremlin's favorite East European leader. The Polish attitude toward the Soviet Union, as mirrored in official statements and in the mass media, once again assumed a sycophantic character, almost reminiscent of the Stalinist era. In the international arena, the Soviet lead was followed unswervingly with regard to both the West and the East. Altogether, it may be assumed that Poland's behavior as a junior ally caused little worry to Moscow, at least in the early years of Gierek's rule.

There is little doubt that the June 1976 crisis gave considerable concern to the Soviet leadership, whose memories of the December 1970 Polish workers' riots must still have been quite fresh. It was the mark of growing Soviet sophistication as the leader of a multinational alliance that Moscow refused to intervene. Most likely, in the absence of

credible alternatives, it still viewed Gierek as the leader with the greatest chance to restore stability in the country. A major political crisis in
Poland that would reverberate throughout the region was probably the
last thing the Soviet leaders desired at the time that the specter of
Eurocommunism was beginning to threaten Communist unity. Subsequently, the Kremlin went so far as to bail out the Gierek regime in
November 1976, when the deteriorating economic situation made the
latter's position increasingly untenable. The major Soviet loan made at
that time not only ensured a continuing supply of foodstuffs and essential raw materials for Polish industry, but also signified Soviet confidence in Gierek's ability to weather the crisis. It is too early to make
a judgment as to the full impact of open Soviet support for the faltering
regime, but it may be speculated that the latest show of the Kremlin's
friendship for Gierek did not endear him greatly to the Polish masses,
who continue to blame Soviet exploitation for the country's economic
misfortunes.

CONCLUSION

The picture of Poland in the second half of the 1970s that emerges
from the preceding discussion is of a country in disarray, if not in
decay. Faced with a convergence of several crises, the political system
appeared unable to cope with the various challenges. As a result, the
regime appeared to have lost the purpose and sense of direction that had
made it effective only a few years earlier.

Of the challenges described at the beginning of the chapter, the
questioning of the system's legitimacy seemed most serious in the long
run. The widespread protests against constitutional revisions in the
winter of 1975–76, the workers' riots of June 1976, the growing societal
and political involvement of the church, the establishment of an alliance between the workers and the intellectuals, the increasing restless-
ness of the students, and the human rights campaign, all testified to the
growing alienation of important social groups from the system, which
in a relatively short time succeeded in losing most of its credibility and
appeal.

The simultaneous appearance of the other challenges—those of distribution, participation, and penetration—further aggravated the already difficult situation. The economic crisis characterized by inflation
and escalating shortages of foodstuffs and other consumer goods not
only fueled antigovernment riots but also discredited the regime, bent
upon using "consumerism" as an instrument for acquiring legitimacy.

The arbitrary decisions on all fronts taken without consulting interested segments of the population underscored the continued absence of channels for meaningful participation. Finally, the growing malaise and instability reflected the failure of the political system to penetrate and establish full control over Polish society.

Thus far, at least, the system's response to these multiple challenges and crises indicated confusion as to which course of action to take. The ruling party appeared divided from top to bottom. Although the top oligarchy succeeded in eliminating its most prominent conservative members, this shift has not been followed by any visible change in policy. There is also evidence that the middle-level party bureaucracy continued to maintain its traditional stance, adding fuel to the simmering conflict within the party. The rank and file appeared simply confused. Altogether, the party proved incapable of making and implementing decisions that would remedy the situation, reestablish stability, and restore the system's credibility.

Both the interest groups and the masses remained either aloof or alienated from the system. The groups resented being excluded from participation in decision making and blamed the economic crisis on the government's refusal to consult them. The masses—especially the workers and peasants—accused the regime of indifference, inefficiency, and broken promises of a better life.

It is clear that the second half of the 1970s was a difficult period for Poland. The crisis of confidence in the system, combined with rising but unfulfilled expectations, resulted in a high degree of political instability. But was the country on the verge of a collapse which, ultimately, might force the Soviet Union to intervene in order to safeguard Communist rule? The answer is an emphatic no.

Historically, Communist systems have exhibited an impressive capacity for survival. Since the end of Stalinist rule, they have developed mechanisms for the absorption of internal and external shocks. There is little doubt that the ruling elite not only in Poland but also in the other East European countries has over the years become somewhat more pragmatic and sophisticated, better educated, and politically more sensitive. This meant that although the top oligarchy would not hesitate to apply coercive measures when faced with a critical situation, it was more likely to try to solve the crisis in a pragmatic and nonviolent fashion before resorting to repression. Illustrative is the so far relatively restrained reaction of the Polish regime to the growing political opposition.

Secondly, the frontal challenge to the system might prove to be short-lived, especially if the government does not overreact to the threat. To begin with, the dissident movement, although vocal and visible, has essentially remained confined to a relatively small group of intellectuals and students, and has not succeeded in building multiple bridges to the workers and peasants. In other words, in the late 1970s it remains largely isolated from the bulk of Polish society. It is likely to remain that way, especially if the regime continues its present policy of benign neglect of the opposition, combined with some minor political and major economic reforms.

Insofar as the workers are concerned, it may be argued that the single major source of their discontent has been economic rather than political. If, with luck, the harvests in the next few years prove successful, resulting in a significant improvement in food supply, one may speculate that much of the dissatisfaction will disappear. If, moreover, the government is willing to make some political concessions to the workers—for example, in the area of expanded and more genuine workers' self-government—there is a good chance that this would serve to defuse the current discontent and weaken the opposition.

The same is largely true for the peasants. If the government succeeds in dealing with some of the burning issues confronting Polish agriculture—social security for aging peasants; transfer of privately owned land to the state; and increased availability of inputs into the farm sector—it may be assumed that the peasants' response would be positive, resulting in an expanded farm output. On the political front, maintaining the *modus vivendi* with the church might also help to reduce the distrust of the peasantry.

Finally, the Polish population at large has been well aware of the existence of a certain threshold, the crossing of which would result in Soviet intervention. Consequently it might be less willing to destabilize the system completely. At the same time, in the post-Helsinki atmosphere, the Soviet Union is likely to think twice before intervening to prop up an unpopular regime. Instead, it might well try to help it weather the storm by providing economic aid or making other concessions, as occurred in the Polish case in November 1976.

The immediate question facing the present Polish leadership is what is to be done to restore its credibility and regain popular confidence in the system. In essence, the Gierek regime is faced with three possible courses of action. One choice would be to adopt the "Czechoslovak model," which would imply a suppression of the dissident movement and maintenance of centralized controls over the economy and society at large. In the present configuration of domestic and international forces, the probability of this taking place is not very high. An alternate solution would be the adoption of the "Hungarian model," which would mean far-reaching economic reforms. It can be argued that as long as the economic power centers remain controlled by conservatives —which seemed to be the case in early 1978—the likelihood of broadly gauged changes in the economy is not very great. The final option is the continuation of the present "model," which may be described as muddling through and hoping for the best. In the present circumstances, this solution seems most likely to be adopted, at least in the foreseeable future.

The current difficult political and economic situation precludes the possibility of major reforms. If economic performance improves— which it may do without far-reaching reforms—and if popular dissatisfaction can be contained—which may be possible if the regime does not overreact politically—then it may be speculated that in a few years the regime will regain its confidence and strength, and will be in a position to undertake some meaningful reforms, especially in the economic realm, which is clearly the Achilles heel of the whole system.

NOTES

Research for this article was conducted in Poland in 1976 under the auspices of the International Research and Exchanges Board, whose assistance is gratefully acknowledged.

1. Gabriel A. Almond and G. Bingham Powell, Jr., *Comparative Politics* (Boston: Little, Brown, 1966), pp. 35–37, 306–310.
2. Gabriel A. Almond, "Toward A Comparative Politics of Eastern Europe," *Studies in Comparative Communism,* 4, no. 2 (1971), p. 74.
3. Samuel P. Huntington, "The Change to Change: Modernization, Development and Politics," *Comparative Politics,* 3, no. 3 (1971), p. 320.
4. Ibid., p. 316.
5. For a recent treatment, see Susanne S. Lotarski, "The Communist Takeover in Poland," in Thomas T. Hammond, ed., *The Anatomy of Communist Takeovers* (New Haven and London: Yale University Press, 1975), pp. 339–367.
6. Zbigniew Brzezinski, *The Soviet Bloc,* revised and enlarged edition (Cambridge: Harvard University Press, 1967), pp. 8–9.
7. Ibid, pp. 200 and 205–206.
8. Samuel P. Huntington, *Political Order in Changing Societies* (New Haven and London: Yale University Press, 1968), p. 55.
9. Huntington, "The Change to Change," p. 316.
10. Ibid.
11. *Rocznik Statystyczny 1976* (Warsaw, 1976), pp. 24, 28.
12. Ibid., p. 24.

13. Huntington, "The Change to Change," p. 316.

14. Ibid.

15. For details, see Nicholas Bethell, *Gomulka* (Harmondsworth, England: Pelican, 1972).

16. Richard Portes, "East Europe's Debt to the West: Interdependence Is a Two-way Street," *Foreign Affairs*, 55, no. 4 (1977), p. 757.

BIBLIOGRAPHY

Bethell, Nicholas. *Gomulka*. Harmondsworth, England: Pelican, 1962.

Bromke, Adam. *Poland's Politics: Idealism vs. Realism*. Cambridge, Mass.: Harvard University Press, 1967.

Bromke, Adam, and Strong, John W., eds. *Gierek's Poland*. New York: Praeger Publishers, 1973.

Brzeski, Andrzej. "Poland as a Catalyst of Change in the Communist Economic System." *The Polish Review*, vol. 16, no. 2 (spring 1970), pp. 3–24.

Dziewanowski, M. K. *The Communist Party of Poland*. 2nd ed. Cambridge, Mass.: Harvard University Press, 1976.

Fallenbuchl, Zbigniew M. "The Polish Economy in the 1970s." In *East European Economies Post-Helsinki*, A Compendium of Papers Submitted to the Joint Economic Committee, 95th Congress, 1st Session (Washington, D.C.: U.S. Government Printing Office, 1977), pp. 816–864.

Fiszman, Joseph. *Revolution and Tradition in People's Poland*. Princeton, N.J.: Princeton University Press, 1972.

Kanet, Roger E., and Simon, Maurice D., eds. *Participation and Policy in Gierek's Poland* (forthcoming).

Korbonski, Andrzej. *Politics of Socialist Agriculture in Poland, 1945–1960*. New York: Columbia University Press, 1965.

Lane, David, and Kolankiewicz, George, eds. *Social Groups in Polish Society*. New York: Columbia University Press, 1973.

Lewis, Flora. *A Case History of Hope*. Garden City, N.Y.: Doubleday, 1958.

Milosz, Czeslaw. *The Captive Mind*. New York: Alfred A. Knopf, 1953.

Stehle, Hansjakob. *The Independent Satellite*. New York: Praeger, 1965.

Szczepanski, Jan. *Polish Society*. New York: Random House, 1964.

Zielinski, J. G. *Economic Reform in Polish Industry*. London: Oxford University Press, 1973.

3   Hungary

Bennett Kovrig

TACTICS OF TAKEOVER, 1945–49

The Communist party that entered the Hungarian political stage in late 1944 and proceeded to acquire a monopoly of power over the next five years had the historical distinction of being the first to emulate Lenin's Bolshevik coup in Russia. The military and political collapse of the Austro-Hungarian Empire in the final days of World War I made way in Hungary for a potentially liberal democratic regime under Count Mihaly Karolyi, but Karolyi's regime could not survive the demands of the victorious allies for a drastic dismemberment of Hungary —including the loss of Magyar-inhabited territories—to the benefit of the surrounding successor states. The political vacuum created by the government's resignation was filled on March 21, 1919, by an impromptu socialist-communist dictatorship, a self-styled "republic of councils," in which effective power lay in the hands of Bela Kun and a small band of Communists.[1] Most of its members, like Kun, were former prisoners of war whose socialist sympathies had been converted into fanatical allegiance to Lenin's Bolshevik party, from which they received guidance and financial assistance.

Kun's regime lasted four months. It made ambitious plans for a sweeping social and economic revolution but was hampered by the hostility of the advancing allies and by a state of near-anarchy on its diminishing territory. What popular support Kun attracted was due mainly to his Red Army's initial successes against the Allies. His repressive measures contributed to the rapid alienation of most social classes, notably the peasantry, but the direct cause of his downfall was military defeat. Kun and many of his fellow Communists fled into exile. In Hungary, under the regency of Admiral Miklos Horthy, there followed a succession of governments that paid lip service to multi-party democracy but which were fundamentally authoritarian and conservative. Their appeal rested in large measure on popular revulsion at the Bolshevik experiment and at the territorial truncation administered by the Treaty of Trianon.

The Communist emigres tried to revive the party in exile, in Vienna and Moscow, and to foster some minimal level of activity in Hungary. They also performed a wide range of functions elsewhere as agents of the Comintern. Bitter ideological squabbles and efficient persecution by the Hungarian authorities left the domestic party in disarray throughout the interwar period. Kun and many of his associates fell victim to Stalin's purges in the late 1930s, while the vestigial party at home and abroad wallowed ineffectually behind the tactical shifts from popular front to submergence in the wake of the Nazi-Soviet Pact.

As the inevitability of Allied victory and Soviet occupation of Hungary became evident, the party's Muscovite branch, whose leading figures were Matyas Rakosi, Erno Gero, Jozsef Revai, and Mihaly Farkas, began under Russian tutelage to formulate their postwar strategy. Given their limited power base in Hungary and the uncertainties of future Allied cooperation, they envisaged a gradual "people's democratic revolution," initially in the governing structure and in land tenure, promoted through a multiparty antifascist front.[2] The emigres also dispatched a few partisan groups, whose low number and marginal military significance could not produce the resistance record that was so crucial an element in the Yugoslav Communists' rise to power. Meanwhile, the indigenous Communists, including Laszlo Rajk, Janos Kadar, and Gyula Kallai, existed as a largely ineffectual, dispersed, and beleaguered underground movement, making repeated attempts to join forces with an emerging Independence Front of opposition politicians. These initiatives, as well as the government's desperate efforts to secure a separate peace, were curtailed when in October 1944 the Germans imposed a Nazi-style regime headed by the Hungarian Arrow Cross leader, Ferenc Szalasi.

Upon their return to the liberated territories, the Muscovite Communists proceeded to rebuild the party and to promote the creation of a new government devoted to their initial minimal program. Under the aegis of the Soviet High Command a provisional government came into being in Debrecen in December 1944. Under the premiership of General Bela Miklos, who had crossed lines late in the war, the government included a minority of Communists as well as representatives of the Smallholder, Social Democratic, and National Peasant parties. The government's first major measure, urged by the Communists in the hope of gaining the allegiance of the landless peasant masses, was a sweeping redistribution of land. This and efforts to seize the initiative in economic reconstruction reflected only one aspect of the quest for power by the Hungarian Communist party (*Magyar Kommunista Part* or HCP). The promotion of Communist-influenced national and workers' committees, the prosecution of real and alleged fascists and war criminals by "people's courts," the purge and infiltration of the civil service, the police, and the army, and total control over the political police were other immediate objectives. The Soviet occupiers gave invaluable support in the form of political pressure, advisers, and NKVD agents, and released part of the vast quantities of confiscated foodstuffs for the relief effort engineered by the Communist Zoltan Vas on behalf of the starving population of Budapest. Rapine and pillage by the Red Army, on the other hand, reinforced the Hungarians' historical hatred of Russia and bolshevism.

The HCP's tactics were to wage a battle for power both from above, within the new governing structure, and from below, by mobilizing mass pressures for radical reforms. The party attempted both to seduce the old established Social Democratic party and to weaken its hold over the industrial workers by penetrating the trade unions. Communist sympathizers worked within the SDP, the less important National Peasant party, and even in the Smallholder party. The Smallholder party rapidly became the political umbrella for a broad spectrum of non-Marxist forces.

By the time the HCP held its first national conference in Budapest on May 20–21, 1945, membership had risen from around 2,000 in 1944 to 150,000, and some 1,500 basic party cells were in existence. The Muscovite and indigenous leaderships had merged, with the former predominant under General Secretary Rakosi. The slogan of the day was the "battle for reconstruction." An overoptimistic Rakosi called for municipal elections in the industrial labor stronghold of Budapest, but the outcome on October 7 gave the Smallholders 50.54 percent of the vote, while the United Workers' Front of socialists and Communists gained only 42.76 percent. In the November general elections, with the broadest franchise in Hungarian history, the HCP received 17 percent of the vote; the SDP, now running independently, won 17.4 percent, while the Smallholders received an even clearer majority with 57 percent. All parties espoused the goals of reconstruction and, in varying degrees, of economic and social reform, but the Communists' ill-concealed radicalism and their Soviet connection were clearly repellent to most Hungarians.[3] The Soviet authorities had imposed an agreement to maintain the coalition whatever the election outcome, and such a government came into being under the premiership of the Smallholder Zoltan Tildy. When the republic was proclaimed in January 1946, Tildy became president and was replaced by another Smallholder, Ferenc Nagy.

With its professed ultimate goal an ambiguous "people's democracy" rather than an outright dictatorship of the proletariat, the HCP intensified its battle from above and below. It resorted to manipulated front organizations, street demonstrations, the prohibition of noncommunist youth organizations, the infamous "salami tactics" to weaken other parties by concerted attacks on their "reactionary" elements, attempts to forge a left-wing bloc with the internally divided SDP and NPP, and the acquisition of key administrative offices, beginning with the Interior Ministry. While the Soviet Union imposed huge reparations and joint stock companies and obstructed Western aid, the HCP began to press for greater state control of the economy, starting with the effective nationalization of the coal mines. A Communist-Soviet financial stabilization program was inaugurated on August 1, 1946. Apart from preaching Hungarian-Soviet friendship, the HCP maintained a low profile in foreign policy, aware that Hungary's territorial-ethnic interests in Slovakia and Transylvania (partially satisfied in the Vienna awards of 1938 and 1940) would receive little support in Allied councils, as was confirmed by the Paris Peace Treaty of 1946.[4]

The next step on the road to a "people's democracy," outlined at the HCP's Third Congress in September 1946, was the progressive elimination of the capitalist economy and of its Western-oriented defenders in the government. The discovery by Interior Minister Rajk's operatives of an alleged antistate conspiracy provided the pretext for an offensive against the Smallholder party, and in April 1947 one of the party's leaders, Bela Kovacs, was seized by the Soviet secret police. Prime Minister Ferenc Nagy, who had tried to pursue a policy of compromise in the hope of outlasting Soviet occupation, was thereupon forced to resign, and he chose exile. The United States and Great Britain, junior partners to the Soviet Union in the Allied Control Commission, issued impotent protests at these outrages.

In Hungarian Communist historiography the period from early 1947 to mid-1948 is known as the "year of the turning point." This period encompassed the liquidation of the "conspiracy," the launching of the three-year plan, the national elections of August 31, 1947, the failure of the SDP's right wing to regain control of the party, the progressive nationalization of the banks and other large enterprises, and the unification of the two major left-wing parties in June 1948. The emasculation of the leading anticommunist party, the Smallholders, soon led to the emergence of several extra-coalition parties. Against a splintered opposition, and aided by massive disenfranchisement and balloting fraud, the HCP emerged from the August 31 election as the strongest single party, with an officially reported 22.3 percent of the vote. The coalition as a whole won 60.8 percent, with the more or less Marxist parties within it (HCP, SDP, NPP) getting 45.4 percent.[5]

With Stalin pulling the strings, a conference of Communist parties in Poland in September 1947 adopted as a new revolutionary strategy the creation of "single-party popular fronts" on the Yugoslav model. This meeting, leading to the foundation of the Cominform, marked the beginning of the final phase of consolidation of the Soviet sphere, a process that was both a cause and an effect of the cold war. There ensued in Hungary an accelerated drive to neutralize the new opposition parties, drive their anticommunist leaders into exile, and engineer a power grab in the SDP by its left wing. This drive set the stage for the fusion in June 1948 of the SDP and the HCP into the Hungarian Workers' Party (*Magyar Dolgozok Partja* or HWP), with a combined membership of 1,128,130. During the following year the regime overcame the opposition of the Roman Catholic church by bringing Cardinal Mindszenty to trial on fabricated charges, nationalized the school system, launched the collectivization of agriculture, and eliminated the last remnants of free enterprise. The remaining noncommunist parties were absorbed into a new political umbrella organization, the People's Independence Front, along with the National Council of Trade Unions and other mass organizations. In the May 1949 elections the Front received 95.6 percent of the votes. On August 20, 1949, the constitution of the Hungarian People's Republic was adopted, legitimizing the revolutionary political transformation of Hungary. Aided and abetted by the Soviet Union, and through skillful destruction of the opposition forces, a handful of Communists had succeeded in acquiring dictatorial power.

FROM MOBILIZATION TO MODERNIZATION, 1950–79

The new dictatorship of the proletariat, ostensibly based on Marxism-Leninism, was simply a replica of its Stalinist prototype. The power and collective interests of the "working class" were represented by its vanguard, the party, and implemented through the legislative, administrative, and judicial organs of the state. The latter, together with mass organizations of workers, youth, and women, served as agents of enforcement and mobilization in support of goals formulated by the party leadership. The hierarchical organization of the party followed the Soviet pattern, with the pyramid rising from local through regional committees to the Central Committee and the Politburo. The reality of power was Stalinist, with General Secretary Rakosi enjoying unlimited authority and what subsequently came to be denounced as the "cult of personality." His closest lieutenants were Gero, Revai, and Farkas, in charge, respectively, of the economy, culture and agitprop, and defense. A triennial party congress was formally charged with developing long-term policy and ratifying the Central Committee's decisions. In practice, the principle of democratic centralism meant unquestioning obedience to directives from above.

The estrangement of Tito and Stalin in 1948, together with the growing cold war tensions, led to the imposition by the Soviet Union of even greater orthodoxy and uniformity in the East European satellites. Rakosi participated with exemplary vigor in the ensuing area-wide campaign against alleged Titoists. From 1949 to 1953 more Communists were executed than under the Horthy regime.[6] The major show trial was that of Laszlo Rajk, who was tortured and persuaded to confess to false charges before being executed. Many other Communists, including Kadar (who had participated in Rajk's elimination), were imprisoned. Rakosi's preferred targets in these purges were veterans of the 1919 commune (in which he himself had played a minor role), indige-

Table 1   Membership in Hungarian Communist Party

January 1919	10,000	January 1952	945,606
November 1924	120[a]	January 1956	859,037
December 1929	1,000[a]	December 1, 1956	37,818
February 1945	30,000	January 1957	125,088
July 1945	226,577	December 1957	394,910
January 1946	608,728	December 1961	498,644
January 1947	670,476	December 1967	601,917[b]
July 1948 (HCP)	887,472	November 1970	662,000
July 1948 (HWP)	1,128,130	January 1975	754,353
January 1950	828,695	January 1977	765,566

[a] In Hungary only.
[b] Until 1966 the numbers include candidate members, a category abolished at the Ninth Congress.
Sources: Magyar Szocialista Munkaspart, Legyozhetetlen Ero, 2nd ed. (Budapest: Kossuth, 1974), pp. 22, 63, 82, 162, 169, 175, 179, 185, 193, 204, 224, 236, 250, 257, 285; A Magyar Szocialista Munkaspart X. Kongresszusanak jegyzokonyve (Budapest: Kossuth, 1971), p. 102; A Magyar Szocialista Munkaspart XI. Kongresszusa (Budapest: Kossuth, 1975), p. 6; Partelet, July 1977.

nous (as opposed to Muscovite) Communists, and left-wing socialists. By 1950 party membership had fallen below 830,000 (see Table 1). Over the life of the Hungarian Workers' Party, from 1948 to 1956, more than 350,000 members were expelled from the party.[7] These purges were only one aspect of the police-state terror that affected not only "class enemies" but also the population at large.

The period from 1949 to 1953 was truly totalitarian in the scope of state control over all aspects of life. The official version of Marxism-Leninism, Soviet models, and the glorification of Rakosi pervaded education and culture. In 1949 all enterprises employing more than ten workers and all rental housing were nationalized. State control was imposed on labor mobility and discipline. Coming on top of the ravages of war, Soviet exploitation and the rejection of Western aid by the Communists severely inhibited Hungary's economic reconstruction. The inefficiencies and dogmatic application of the new command economy and the forced reorientation of Hungarian trade toward the Soviet bloc exacerbated the situation. The first five-year plan gave priority to intensive development of heavy industry and to the collectivization of agriculture. In both cases dogmatic insistence on replicating the Soviet model had disastrous consequences. Most of the raw materials necessary to turn Hungary into a "country of iron and steel" had to be imported. Forced industrialization brought a massive influx of new workers to urban areas, where the already critical housing shortage was alleviated by the deportation of "class enemies" to the countryside. Small private farms were arguably not well suited to modern agricultural production, but the brutal collectivization campaign and increasingly heavy levies on farmers only alienated the peasantry, leading to declining productivity and even spontaneous demonstrations in the spring of 1953. Along with an apparently favorable growth rate in the national income and a state of full employment, the government's economic policies brought about a negative balance of trade in 1949 and 1952, an 18 percent drop in the real incomes of workers and employees between 1949 and 1952, and a general neglect of consumer needs.[8] Political participation by the masses was compulsory and ritualistic, and the system's popular legitimacy was abysmally low.

The tensions induced by political oppression and economic hardship were at a peak when in March 1953 Stalin's death ushered in a Soviet interregnum more sensitive to the stresses in the system. Summoned to Moscow, Rakosi was berated for his dogmatism and mismanagement of the economy and ordered to relinquish the premiership (which he had held along with the party's leadership) to Imre Nagy. A veteran

Communist and Muscovite, Nagy had supervised the 1945 land reform but subsequently had become critical of the party's economic policies and had fallen into disgrace.[9] There followed a prolonged tug of war between Rakosi and Nagy, whose "New Course" aimed at abandoning forced collectivization and industrialization, laid greater stress on the satisfaction of personal consumption and welfare needs, and sought to mitigate the more repressive and arbitrary features of the totalitarian system. Collective farm membership fell by nearly 40 percent, investments were redirected to light and consumer industries, the first signs of cultural pluralism appeared, and most Communist political prisoners (including Kadar) were released. An unrepentant Rakosi continued to intrigue against his rival, and as the Moscow political climate evolved, Nagy came to be charged with "right-wing opportunist deviation." In April 1955 he was ousted from the premiership and, seven months later, expelled from the party. Khrushchev reportedly explained the reversal by saying, "I have to keep Rakosi in Hungary, because in Hungary the whole structure will collapse if he goes."[10]

The new Khrushchevian line was a blend of economic neo-Stalinism, modest relaxation of Stalinist terror, "peaceful coexistence" with the West, and reconciliation with Tito. Only the first of these components suited Rakosi. He abhorred detente with Tito, who in turn denounced Rakosi. Rakosi reassigned top priority to heavy industry, but his recapture of absolute power was challenged by an emerging alliance of rehabilitated Communists and of establishment intellectuals who began to relinquish their earlier slavish orthodoxy.[11] Of the liberated party members some, like Kadar, dutifully returned to loyal service; others adopted a more revisionist stance and looked for leadership to Imre Nagy. Khrushchev's anti-Stalin speech at the Twentieth CPSU congress emboldened revisionists and reformers, particularly writers, who began to voice open criticism of Rakosi's totalitarian system.

What began as an intraparty debate rapidly spilled over into the public sphere. One important catalyst was the Petofi circle, a debating forum established under the aegis of the Federation of Working Youth (*Dolgozo Ifjusag Szovetsege*). By July 1956 Gero was describing the Petofi circle as the "second leading center" in the country, a rival to the party.[12] Rakosi made plans for drastic suppression of dissent, but on July 18 he was stripped of office on Moscow's orders. His replacement as first secretary was Erno Gero, an unhappy compromise since the latter was as much a doctrinaire Stalinist as his predecessor. The reformist wave was strengthened by the apparent triumph of the Gomulka revisionists in Poland and by concessions such as the posthumous rehabilitation of Rajk and his ceremonial reinterment on October 6. While Gero traveled to Belgrade in quest of a belated accommodation with Tito, agitation by students and intellectuals took the form of manifestos demanding reinstatement of Nagy to the government, expulsion of Rakosi from the party, public trial for Farkas and others implicated in the Stalinist outrages, publication of foreign trade agreements including Soviet exploitation of Hungarian uranium, freedom of expression in literature, and finally, the evacuation of Soviet troops.

A demonstration before the Budapest radio studios, one of several mass meetings on October 23, was met with gunfire and launched the thirteen-day revolution.[13] There followed the appointment of Nagy as premier and Kadar as first secretary, clashes between the rebels and the party's last line of defense, the secret police, and a limited intervention by Soviet forces. Revolutionary councils sprang up nationwide and pressed Nagy for far-reaching reforms. In summary, the goal of the revolution was pluralistic democratic socialism, encompassing retention of some central planning and nationalization (perhaps with workers' self-management) within a mixed economy; aid to independent farmers and free choice in the formation of agricultural cooperatives; elimination of police terror; economic and political sovereignty and state neutrality; and such basic rights as free unions, the right to strike, and cultural and religious freedom. Unfettered multiparty contests would determine government policy, and the influence of a reformed national Communist party would be proportional to its electoral appeal.

The wave of nationalism and reformism drove Nagy to bring representatives of other former parties into his government and, on November 1, to declare Hungary's neutrality and withdrawal from the Warsaw Pact. An appeal was made for United Nations recognition and support. The Soviet leadership, which had earlier vacillated and issued a conciliatory declaration, now prepared for military repression.[14] Initially, the remnant of the disintegrating HWP had endorsed Nagy's reformist line, but on November 1 Kadar and a few associates were persuaded by the Soviet authorities to leave Hungary secretly.[15] While Soviet forces launched a massive air and land offensive in the early hours of November 4, a broadcast from the Soviet Union announced the formation of a "Revolutionary Worker-Peasant Government" by Kadar and Ferenc Munnich and called upon the Red Army to smash the "sinister forces of reaction."

Entirely dependent on Soviet military might amidst a passionately hostile population, the new regime initially held out the promise of major reforms. Kadar spoke of free elections and voluntary collectivization and held discussions with representatives of other parties and of the revolutionary workers' councils. Committees of economists brought in recommendations for radical change. However, the priority task of rebuilding the party, intraparty factionalism, the revival of Soviet-Yugoslav antagonism and of Moscow's position that revisionism was the principal enemy, all conspired to make the restoration of Communist power a painful and near-totalitarian exercise. Kadar personally eschewed Rakosi's despotic style, but the restoration of order demanded executions, deportations, imprisonment, and other repressive measures. Over two hundred thousand Hungarians sought refuge abroad. Nagy himself was kidnapped by the Russians and later executed. The party's cultural policy, momentarily impelled by Revai's dogmatic intolerance, turned repressive in the face of a writers' strike. Party membership had fallen from a prerevolutionary 860,000 to under 40,000. Thanks to an aggressive recruiting campaign, by the end of 1957 membership in the renamed Hungarian Socialist Workers' Party (*Magyar Szocialista Munkaspart* or HSWP) approached 400,000.

Industrialization remained the primary task of the regime, but Kadar pursued it in the context of his long-term goals of improving the standard of living and legitimizing the party in the eyes of the workers. Another immediate task, required by Soviet orthodoxy and the worker-peasant alliance, was the "socialist transformation of the countryside." After the revolution only 11 percent of arable land remained in the state and collectivized sector. In 1959 a new collectivization campaign was launched, initially with much intimidation and compulsion. The chief culprit in these excesses, agriculture minister Imre Dogei, was dismissed the following year, and other leading dogmatists (i.e., opponents of Kadar's moderate line) were expelled from the leadership in 1962. By that time the collectivization drive had been essentially completed by less severe persuasion, and 92.5 percent of arable land lay in the socialist sector.

The Kadar moderates thus overcame, without entirely eliminating, internal opposition to their pragmatic pursuit of modernization and legitimacy. In December 1961 (following Khrushchev's victory over the "antiparty group" and renewal of de-Stalinization) Kadar forcefully restated his alliance policy. Admitting that the task of modernization could not be fulfilled by the party alone, he called on loyal extra-party Hungarians to assume positions of responsibility and devote their talents to the common goal. To demonstrate his good faith, he gave the green light to literary criticism of the Rakosi regime (as long as there was no implication that the current system bore any resemblance or responsibility). "Those who are not against us are with us"—the converse of the Rakosi axiom—became the conciliatory slogan of the alliance policy. In ideological terms the Kadar line was defined as centrism, or the struggle on two fronts against both the old sectarian-dogmatic mistakes and right-wing revisionist deviations.

The HSWP's Eighth Congress in November 1962 declared that with the completion of collectivization the foundations of socialism had been laid and that Hungary was beginning the construction of a fully socialist society. Socialist democracy would be expanded by a decentralization of authority and a division of labor. Although the party would retain monopoly over ideological questions, definitions of national interest, and major policy decisions, other institutions and groups would be given greater autonomy. The internal class struggle was declared essentially concluded, while the former monolithic view of society was amended to recognize not only collective and individual, but also group interests. One tangible outcome was the abandonment of class discrimination in higher education. There also followed an amnesty for most political prisoners, the end of internment and internal exile, and the attenuation of secret police activity, all in the spirit of "socialist legality." Radio jamming was curtailed, foreign travel restrictions were eased, and cultural and religious activities came under more tolerant control.

Khrushchev's fall in October 1964 and concurrent economic difficulties in Hungary emboldened the more dogmatic elements in the party, but Kadar held fast to his centrist line and succeeded in persuading the Brezhnev leadership of his unimpeachable loyalty to the Soviet Union and of the compatibility of his policies with both Soviet and Hungarian interests. The next major step was to be a reform of the entire economic management structure, a "New Economic Mechanism." Its development, strongly supported by Kadar and promoted by a young former social democrat, Rezso Nyers, was approved at the May 1966 Central Committee meeting by only a narrow margin, over the opposition of advocates of the old command model. Launched in 1968, the NEM introduced some elements of a market economy, with pricing and investment techniques that decentralized planning and placed a premium on managerial expertise, productivity, and competitiveness in the world market.

By implementing his alliance policy, Kadar managed to overshadow the brutal imposition of his regime and reach an accommodation with the Hungarian people. His rule did not enjoy democratic legitimacy in the Western sense, but it gradually earned a degree of pragmatic popular endorsement that was uncommon in Eastern Europe.

CURRENT PARTY STRUCTURE AND DYNAMICS

In May 1972, celebrating his sixtieth birthday, Janos Kadar reflected with some candor upon the Hungarian revolution:

> In 1956, a very serious and critical situation presented itself which is called, scientifically, the counterrevolution. We are aware that this is the scientific definition of what took place in 1956. But there is also another concept which we all might accept: it was a national tragedy. A tragedy for the party, for the working class, for the people, and for the individual. We lost our way, and the result was tragedy. And if we have overcome this now—which we can state with confidence—this is a very big thing.[16]

Three years later, at the conclusion of the HSWP's Eleventh Congress in 1975, Kadar delivered an extemporaneous address in which he tried to dismiss fearful speculation that the party was veering toward a more rigid and dictatorial position. The dictatorship of the proletariat would remain in force, he said, but eighteen years' experience had shown that "it was not such a bad dictatorship after all. One can live under it, create freely, and gain honor."[17] There were no longer any antagonistic classes, only class allies, and the remaining differences were not about the desirability of socialism but about the rate of development of the socialist revolution. The role of the party was to lead and to persuade.

The implementation of the alliance policy and of the NEM had in fact generated persistent opposition among the party's more dogmatic elements. The latter were concerned about an alleged erosion of the preeminence of the party and the industrial proletariat, and at the November 1972 Central Committee meeting Kadar had to forcefully defend his policies, while conceding that liberalization had led to undesirable side effects. Problems in investments, trade, income ratios, and ideology were attributed to the inadequate implementation of earlier party resolutions. Denying the emergence of a "new class," he nevertheless admitted to the existence of arrogance, bureaucratism, and acquisitiveness among party members.[18] A tax on movable property was added to earlier measures to restrict excessive incomes from moonlighting and speculation. A more significant concession was a special "corrective" wage increase for 1.3 million workers in large state and construction industries, followed a year later by another special increase for certain other categories of workers. In an attempt to end debate, Bela Biszku warned that further argument would be incompatible with the Leninist norms of party life and democratic centralism.[19] There followed a campaign to revitalize the party's proletarian image, to curtail ideological and cultural deviations (prompting the investigation and expulsion of some "new left" intellectual critics), and to remedy some shortcomings of the NEM by a reassertion of central planning and control.

At the HSWP's Eleventh Congress in March 1975, Kadar appealed for ideological unity and stressed the need to expand worker participation in decision making.[20] There followed the introduction of a new system of economic regulators, but speculation that continuing economic difficulties would be met by a major recentralization were dispelled by a Central Committee resolution in April 1978; it confirmed the NEM and stressed productivity, managerial efficiency, technological modernization, and the gradual reduction of subsidies and price supports to make the economy more competitive in the world market.

With respect to internal party affairs, Kadar observed at the congress that two-thirds of its members had joined since 1956, and indeed that the membership had become more heterogeneous and subject to intergenerational friction. In the context of the alliance policy, growing numbers of managers, intellectuals, and white-collar workers made the pragmatic choice to adhere to the HSWP. These groups accounted for 46.1 percent of the membership in 1975. The leadership has taken steps to increase the proportion of industrial workers as well as of farmers and women. Although a number of organizational reforms since 1962 have aimed at enhancing intraparty democracy, and while the membership is continually exhorted to exemplary behavior, the diffusion of authority and the stress on secular expertise have induced a measure of alienation and apathy. As one party analyst noted, "The decline in the political content of party life, . . . the ebbing of the critical spirit, the fading away of responsibility, hinder the operation of democratic centralism, the basic rule of party life. Inevitably, this gives rise to liberalism and arbitrary interpretations in the implementation of party decisions."[21] One remedial measure was the 1976 party card exchange.[22] As a result, approximately 3 percent of the members resigned or were expelled, and at the end of 1976 the membership stood at 765,566.[23] By Stalinist standards, the operation was conducted with moderation, and it was construed by the party leadership less as a purge than as a survey of opinion. Ideological deviants are no longer expeditiously liquidated. Rakosi himself died in the Soviet Union, while Gero and other deeply implicated survivors of the Stalinist phase were simply expelled from the party.

Despite the spread of ideological relativism even among the rank and file, the party remains politically supreme. The revised 1972 state constitution proclaims that the "Marxist-Leninist party of the working class is the leading force in society." At the base of the party's pyramidal structure lie 24,450 primary organizations, of which 7,066 are active in industry and construction, 4,215 in agriculture, 1,473 in transportation, and 1,216 in commerce. At the next level there are 97 district party committees and 104 city and Budapest district party committees. County party committees, together with the Budapest Party Committee, number 24. Lower units elect delegates to the next higher level, and conferences of county delegates elect participants in the quinquennial party congress, which is the ultimate legislative body. The 843 delegates to the Eleventh Party Congress elected the 125-member Central Committee. The Central Committee, in turn, elects the Politburo, the Secretaries and Secretariat department heads, and the Agitprop and other key committees. Over the last decade organizational reforms have enhanced the rank-and-file's participation at lower levels with the introduction of secret ballots, procedures for complaints and accountability of leaders, and broader participation in the drafting of congressional guidelines. Elections to the leading organs, however, generally take the form of ratification of Politburo nominations.

The Central Committee meets three or four times a year, normally for two days; it is charged with monitoring the implementation of congressional resolutions and seldom presents a challenge to the policies of the leadership. It routinely hears reports on international affairs and on two or three other current policy issues, and its resolutions are briefly summarized in the media. A preponderant number of current Central Committee members hold key positions of power elsewhere, including 39 in government and in state and local administration, 17 in central party organizations, and 14 in trade union and other mass organizations; the Central Committee also includes a few token full-time workers and intellectuals.

The top party leadership appears more collegial than in Rakosi's day, but its recruitment and deliberations are cloaked in secrecy. The Politburo, the party's executive, has fifteen members. They currently include the prime minister, the head of state, the president of the National Council of Trade Unions, and the first secretary of the Communist Youth League. A partly overlapping circle of power encompasses the eight secretaries of the Central Committee, in charge of the Secretariat's departments. The latter cover all major policy areas and serve in effect as a parallel, but superior, government. Many officers of the Secretariat also hold related government posts, and individuals are frequently shifted from one sphere of authority to the other. All-important interparty relations and liaison with Soviet authorities are conducted by the Secretariat.

The key leader in this political system, Kadar, is both first secretary and a member of the Politburo, but he holds no state office. He has shown consummate skill in preserving his centrist program by trimming the leadership to exclude both reformist and dogmatist critics. Rezso Nyers was dropped from the Secretariat and Politburo in 1974–75 because of his overly enthusiastic promotion of the NEM. Gyorgy Aczel's Western image as a cultural liberalizer probably accounted for his removal from the Secretariat in 1974. More recent personnel changes in the Secretariat include the dismissal in 1976 of the conservative Arpad Pullai and, in April 1978, of Bela Biszku, Kadar's authoritarian deputy, who had controlled the party apparatus as well as the army and security forces. With Biszku's departure, Karoly Nemeth, who had been the secretary in charge of the economy, became Kadar's deputy and putative successor. The periodic reshuffling reflects Kadar's inclination to limit the personal power of his associates and to draw technocrats into the leadership to manage his reforms.

Although party control is less obtrusive than it was in Rakosi's day, it still pervades the Hungarian political system. Senior party members hold all significant positions in government and mass mobilizing organizations, and the party retains full cadre authority (*nomenklatura*) and a generally respected advisory right over many thousands of lesser leadership posts. In the 1971–75 Parliament 71 percent of the deputies were party members. In the police forces, 90 percent of the officers belong to the HSWP, as do 81 percent of the paramilitary Workers' Militia. However, less than half of local and municipal council members belong to the party.

GOVERNMENT AND MASS ORGANIZATIONS

While the party reigns supreme, the promotion of socialist democracy and efficient administration has brought about changes in the nature of governmental authority. The main thrust of these changes has been to give greater scope to elected bodies and to recruit expert talent into administrative service regardless of party membership (though the political education of cadres has received renewed emphasis).

When the 1949 constitution was amended in 1972, the revision was presented less as a political program than as a reflection of achievements. A final version awaits the day when Hungary can be proclaimed a "socialist republic"; the 1972 constitution states that Hungary is a "people's republic." The preamble still pays tribute to the Soviet liberators but now also takes a longer historical perspective, referring to a "millennium" of the people's struggle. The earlier discrimination between "working people" and "citizens" has been abandoned, and all citizens are entitled to participate in public affairs. In addition to the party, the role of mass movements and trade unions in the building of socialism is acknowledged. The equal ranking of state and cooperative ownership is asserted, and private producers are recognized, though they "must not violate collective interests."

The national assembly is described by the constitution as the "supreme representative organ of the people," but it meets only for some ten days each year, and most rules take the form of presidential and ministerial decrees. Since 1966 the electoral law provides for single-member parliamentary constituencies and permits multiple candidacies. In practice, the party, through the Patriotic People's Front (PPF), controls the electoral process. Despite a 1971 law that removed the PPF's exclusive screening power, candidacies opposed to the PPF program are unthinkable, and voters are reminded that they are choosing not between policies but between the personal qualities of candidates. The handful of multiple candidacies that have materialized in the last three general elections (9 in 1967, 49 in 1971, and 34 out of 352 in 1975) hardly represent a pluralistic revolution. In the 1975 election 0.4 percent of valid votes were cast against the PPF, and 299 candidates received over 99 percent of valid votes. The turnover rate between the two parliaments was 38.9 percent. The party and state bureaucracies account for 99 seats, with the rest broadly distributed across the occupational spectrum.[24]

The leadership of party and government was split in 1958, reunited in 1961, and separated again since 1965, with each prime minister being also a member of the Politburo. The initiative for appointment and dismissal of government leaders, formally vested in the Presidential Council, lies with the party. Of the current 23-member Council of Ministers, three are Politburo members, nineteen are on the Central Committee, and only seven are elected members of parliament.

Like other Communist state organs, the judiciary has traditionally been a servant of the ruling party's political goals, and it reached a nadir of subjection and arbitrariness in the purge trials and open class discrimination of the Stalinist period. While it has inevitably remained a defender of the established order, the reformulation of "socialist legality" in the direction of a more consensual, codified, and impartial code of law led in 1972 to a procedural and jurisdictional reorganization of the judicial system.[25] Particularly since 1970 greater administrative constraints have been imposed on the secret police, largely eliminating its old practice of summary justice and reducing its fearsome prominence in the lives of ordinary citizens. All this did not alter its basic political control function, but it is exercised with greater prudence and reliance on quiet persuasion. The very low incidence of reported political crimes can be attributed both to the effectiveness of this deterrence and to the positive socializing impact of Kadar's reforms.

The broadest umbrella for political mobilization is the Patriotic People's Front, whose tasks are defined in the programmatic statement adopted at its Sixth Congress in September 1976:

> The Patriotic People's Front is the most comprehensive framework of the alliance policy of the Hungarian Socialist Workers' Party. . . . It is our task to urge, in the name of this policy, the gathering together of our country's creative forces—party members and nonmembers, materialists and believers, people following different ideologies—and their conscious cooperation in the shaping and execution of this policy.[26]

The PPF works through some 4,000 committees with 112,400 members. Its specific tasks are to organize elections, to stimulate social awareness of public problems (e.g., environmental protection), and to mobilize individuals and groups in support of state and council measures (e.g., the promotion of unpaid "social work"). A related agency is the National Peace Council, with international responsibilities.

Under the alliance policy, the various mass organizations and officially recognized interest groups have emerged as valid interpreters and gatherers of opinion, but only within their narrow technical competence and in accordance with the overall objective of building socialism. The original function of the trade unions as downward transmission belts has been expanded to allow them to serve the "legitimate interests of a smaller community," and the 1967 Labor Code provides for various rights, including that of veto over certain management decisions (but not the right to strike).[27] More recently, the party has instituted new procedures for worker participation in enter-

prise management. Enterprises and agricultural collectives have benefited most directly from the decentralizing impact of the NEM, and
such organizations as the Hungarian Chamber of Commerce and the
National Council of Agricultural Cooperatives serve as advocates of
sectoral interests. While all this does not amount to political pluralism
in the sense of liberty to contest fundamental principles, the mobilization of organized interest groups as active participants in the development of issue-oriented policies is a significant advance over their
erstwhile ritualistic role.

The Communist Youth League has a current membership of over
800,000. A majority of high school and college students, but only a
minority of working youths, belong to the League. At the CYL's Ninth
Congress in May 1976, First Secretary Laszlo Marothy called for better
ideological education while recognizing the impossibility of "inoculat-
ing our youth against petty-bourgeois and bourgeois ideologies and
against an idealist world outlook." Marothy declared that the fundamental task of the CYL is the preparation of members for admission to
the HSWP.[28] The membership profile suggests that being a member of
the CYL facilitates access to higher education and career advancement,
but most young people join for nonpolitical reasons and remain largely
indifferent to indoctrination.[29] Other active mobilizing organizations
include the National Council of Hungarian Women and the Hungarian-
Soviet Friendship Society.

SOCIOECONOMIC AND CULTURAL TRENDS

The key component in Kadar's reform program has been the New
Economic Mechanism, introduced in 1968. The general theory behind
the NEM is that the party sets political targets; government agencies
and local councils translate these targets into concrete economic programs; and enterprises carry out their assigned tasks with a "proper
degree of independence."[30] A three-tier pricing system provides for
fixed, limited-range, and floating prices for different categories of goods.
The state subsidizes essential consumer goods and remains the sole
source of credit and the determinant of major investment priorities.
Nevertheless, the NEM represents a radical departure from the former
command model in its relative decentralization of authority and its
stress on incentives for productivity and on competitiveness.

The early record of the NEM was one of substantial improvement in
national income, consumption, and productivity (see Table 2), but a
number of problem areas soon materialized, prompting continuous
tinkering with the mechanism. A disproportionate growth in incom-

Table 2 Key Economic Indicators in Hungary

	1938	1950	1955	1960	1965	1970	1975
Population (at the beginning of the year), thousands	9,138	9,293	9,767	9,961	10,140	10,322	10,509
Natural increase per 1,000 population	5.7	9.5	11.4	4.5	2.4	3.1	6.0
Index of the national income, 1950 = 100	80	100	132	177	216	300	407
National income by origin, percentage							
Industry	20	26	33	36	42	43	45
Construction	5	9	9	11	11	12	12
Agriculture	58	43	42	29	23	17	15
Other	17	17	16	24	24	28	28
INDUSTRY							
Index of production, 1950 = 100	63	100	186	267	386	523	712
Percentage distribution of persons employed							
state industry	55.4	80.2	82.5	82.6	84.8	83.3	84.0
co-operative industry	—	1.6	9.9	11.5	11.3	13.3	13.4
private craftsmanship	44.6	18.2	7.6	5.9	3.9	3.4	2.6
AGRICULTURE							
Index of gross production, 1950 = 100	113	100	118	120	127	146	185
Percentage distribution of arable land							
state sector	—	5.2	14.4	13.8	14.3	14.2	14.0
co-operative sector	—	4.4	17.9	60.4	80.2	80.1	80.7
private and auxiliary farms	—	90.4	67.7	25.8	5.5	5.7	5.3
EXTERNAL TRADE							
Index of external trade, 1960 = 100	—	35	62	100	164	261	524
INCOME AND CONSUMPTION							
Index of real wages per wage-earner, 1950 = 100	—	100	105	154	168	199	235
Per capita consumption of the population, 1950 = 100	93	100	115	152	176	228	285

Source: Hungary, Central Statistical Office, *Statistical Yearbook 1975* (Budapest, 1977)

pleted investments (accounting for 80 percent of annual investments in 1971) brought stricter guidelines and credit controls in 1972. Growth in private and industrial consumption of imported goods from the West had an unfavorable impact on the balance of trade in the nonsocialist sector. Such shortcomings were blamed on the greater autonomy given to often unskilled enterprise managers. Meanwhile, wage differentiation and the expansion of a relatively affluent middle class provoked an egalitarian backlash on the part of some workers, party dogmatists, and a few new-left intellectuals. The modernization of agriculture has been pursued with some success through mergers of collective farms and the use of Western technology. Peasant incomes have risen more rapidly than industrial wages, and the regime continues to encourage private plot production, which accounts for roughly half of horticultural and livestock output. The initially rapid expansion of agricultural cooperatives into ancillary industrial activities drew manpower away from the state sector, and in 1971 the regime took steps to constrain such diversification.

A dramatic deterioration in the terms of trade for Hungary in the mid-1970s produced an economic crisis, coming on top of the general growing pains of the NEM. The Soviet decision in early 1975 to progressively bring CMEA energy and raw material prices up to world market levels had a severe impact on Hungary. The government introduced a new system of economic regulators designed in part to bring prices more into line with production costs and world market conditions, and moved to withhold a larger share of enterprise profits. The NEM remains a subject of controversy, with criticism focused on the slow transformation of the production structure, low productivity, stockpiling, inadequate investment planning, and a deteriorating trade balance. The government nevertheless denies that the autonomy granted to enterprises by the NEM is being phased out.

The rapid rise in personal income and consumption and the wage differentiation of the late 1960s are being supplanted by a new wave of austerity. In GNP per capita, Hungary (at $2,140 in 1976) ranks fifth among socialist countries and thirty-sixth in the world; the ratio of highest to lowest personal income is 5 to 1. The government's semi-official daily has observed, "We reject what used to be called 'barracks communism,' but the capitalist road of a consumer society is, of course, not our ideal either. So let us seek a future socialist way of life. The question is urgent, as the high income brackets of our society have by now reached, if not surpassed, the relative limits of their requirements."[31] The rapid rise in living standards was accompanied by government efforts to improve other welfare functions, such as pensions and child care, and to eliminate class restrictions in education. Social restratification is evident in educational institutions, where children of the well-educated middle classes are overrepresented. Housing shortages remain a perennial problem in urban areas despite large-scale state construction programs and recent measures to encourage private ownership and construction.[32] Housing problems and other social stresses contribute to Hungary's very high divorce, abortion, and suicide rates.

The low birth rate and a consequently aging population have negative implications for economic growth, and the regime has consequently restricted abortions and improved maternity benefits. The popular identification of upward mobility with white-collar employment has contributed to a shortage of skilled workers, and a December 1975 decree imposed a total or partial freeze on the hiring of white-collar workers. Hungary has a population approaching 10,600,000, of which approximately 3 percent belong to German, South Slav, and Romanian minority groups. A rough profile of the social structure indicates that the ruling elite (party, government, military, security) accounted for 3 percent of the population in 1975 (unchanged from 1965), the middle class (including managers and white-collar workers) for 24 percent (15 percent in 1965), industrial workers for 55 percent (51 percent in 1965), manual agricultural workers for 15 percent (29 percent in 1965), and independent farmers for 3 percent (2 percent in 1965).[33]

Liberalization in the cultural sphere and the social sciences has been a notable feature of the alliance policy, but there are limits that may not be transgressed, and the regime has taken steps to silence intellectuals (such as the sociologist Andras Hegedus) who are allegedly guilty of "pluralizing" Marxism-Leninism. Although most writers and academics dutifully exercise self-censorship, the party periodically issues warnings against abuses of its tolerance. As Politburo member Valeria Benke told the Eleventh Congress, certain intellectuals had "drifted into the troubled waters of revisionism and ultra leftist or other turbid streams," and while open debate was essential, there could be no compromise on certain fundamentals: socialist patriotism (as opposed to "bourgeois" nationalism), proletarian internationalism and Soviet-Hungarian friendship, the leading role of the working class and the HSWP, and the worker-peasant alliance.[34]

Church-state relations have become progressively more normal in the Kadar era. Accord with the Roman Catholic church (which claims at least the nominal membership of 60 percent of Hungarians) was facilitated for both the regime and the Vatican by Cardinal Mindszenty's departure into exile in 1971 from the U.S. Embassy, where he had found haven after the defeat of the 1956 revolution. Mindszenty died in Vienna in 1975, and his successor to the archbishopric of Esztergom, Laszlo Lekai, was installed and named cardinal the following year. The churches receive modest state subsidies (Budapest has the only rabbinical school in the Soviet bloc), but their educational activities are severely restricted. Party policy is to acknowledge the persistence of religious faith and the necessity of tolerating a reduced level of church activity while maintaining the ideological struggle against religion. Said Kadar in 1976: "Without exception the churches are loyal to our system. . . . Is it possible that by doing this the churches may be prolonging their existence? It may be so. . . . It could be said that this is a compromise. . . . But we learn from Lenin that any compromise which advances our revolutionary course is acceptable."[35]

The popular legitimacy of the current system does not bear easy assessment.[36] Older Hungarians remember worse times, while the young suffer from a political apathy that is only infrequently broken by semi-adolescent, semi-patriotic outbursts such as the demonstrations that occurred on the national holiday, March 15, in 1972 and 1973. Overtly deviant behavior, such as intellectual new-leftism and what the regime calls political crimes, is marginal and rare. Instead, one finds a pervasive cynicism or, at best, disinterest regarding the party and its ideology. The pursuit of material wealth and deep-rooted patriotism are the more prevalent popular values, conditioned by a certain acceptance of socialist-collectivist principles.[37]

Lip service to popular participation notwithstanding, the Kadar regime has exploited this depoliticization and has sought to build the system's legitimacy on the satisfaction of material needs. The unspoken but universally understood fact that all change in Hungary is subject to Soviet restraint, and general appreciation that within these limits Kadar has skillfully served Hungarian interests, indicate the nature of the regime's legitimacy. Kadar's pragmatism is rewarded by an ideologically neutral public acceptance that is equally pragmatic. Shortly before his death in 1971, the eminent Marxist philosopher Gyorgy Lukacs expressed deep pessimism regarding the prospects for genuine socialist democracy within the bureaucratic-authoritarian systems of the Soviet bloc.[38] The secrecy of political decision making and leadership selection, pervasive propaganda and limited cultural freedom, an authoritarian and petty bureaucratism inherited from earlier times but aggravated by party norms, a standard of living that, despite improvement, remains well behind that of the affluent West, are all negative features of the system. One can debate the accuracy of a survey by Radio Free Europe in 1976–77 which suggested that in hypothetical free elections barely 5 percent of Hungarians would vote for a Communist party, but there is no doubt that the popular legitimacy of the official ideology, of one-party rule, and above all of Soviet hegemony is far from consensual.[39]

FOREIGN ECONOMIC RELATIONS AND FOREIGN POLICY

The dominant factors in Hungary's foreign economic relations are its membership in CMEA (the Council for Mutual Economic Assistance), its limited resources in raw materials and energy, and its dependence on foreign trade for 40 percent of the national income. Principal domestic raw materials are bauxite, low-grade coal, uranium (exported to the Soviet Union and not reported in trade statistics), and lesser amounts of oil and natural gas. The more important industrial products are pharmaceuticals, electrical and communications equipment, and commercial vehicles. Raw materials and semifinished products account for 28 percent of exports; machinery and other capital goods for 27 percent; industrial consumer goods for 20 percent; and food products for 24 percent. In 1975 the socialist countries accounted for 69 percent of Hungary's trade, and the Soviet Union alone for 36 percent: the largest Western trading partner is the Federal Republic of Germany, with 6 percent.

In recent years the major problems have been a negative balance of trade with the West and the rapid rise in raw material prices. CMEA traditionally served both as an assured supplier of raw materials and as a protected market for Hungary's relatively inefficient industries. With the introduction of the NEM, industrial modernization gained new impetus, but increased purchases of Western technology could not be matched by exports partly because of the European Economic Community's restrictions on food imports and the U.S. government's reluctance until late 1977 to grant Hungary most-favored-nation status. The surpluses accumulated in the socialist sector in the early 1970s could not alleviate the imbalance in Western trade, for the CMEA currencies are not freely convertible. Hungary became a member of GATT in 1973, has pursued joint ventures with Western firms, and has negotiated sizeable hard-currency loans.

The Soviet Union supplies approximately 90 percent of Hungary's requirements for oil (through the Friendship pipeline), iron ore, and

timber, and a high proportion of other raw materials. The renegotiation
of intra-CMEA prices worked to Hungary's detriment, for because of
the commodity structure of Hungarian trade in that sector, the average
increase in import prices was nearly double that of export prices. Along
with the other East Europeans, Hungary has to share in the cost of
developing new Soviet resources, notably the building of the Orenburg
pipeline for Siberian gas. (Hungary also has a share in the new Adria
pipeline, destined to be fed with OPEC oil.) A single Soviet-designed
nuclear power station has been under construction for many years.
Foreseeably, Hungary's ability to buy Western technology will decline
and her economic dependence on CMEA will increase in the years to
come.

Hungary's foreign and interparty policies in the Kadar era have remained firmly aligned with those of the Soviet Union. Apart from the
party, the principal formal links with the Soviet Union and the other
East European states are the Warsaw Treaty, CMEA, and bilateral treaties of friendship, cooperation, and mutual assistance. In the 1968
Czechoslovakian crisis Kadar initially played a mediating role, then
assented to Hungarian participation in the Warwaw Pact intervention.
Kadar has cultivated good relations not only with Khrushchev and
Brezhnev but also with his counterparts in Eastern Europe. The Hungarian economic reforms are regarded with some suspicion by the East
Germans and other more orthodox regimes, but there are no major
disharmonies between Hungary and the rest of the Soviet bloc. One
exception is Romania, which harbors close to two million ethnic Hungarians in Transylvania and has employed brutal measures of dispersal,
discrimination, and cultural assimilation.[40] The fate of the Hungarian
minority in Romania is of passionate concern to most Hungarians, and
as a result relations between the two regimes have been noticeably
cool. There are smaller Hungarian minorities in Slovakia and in the
Voivodina region of Yugoslavia, but more tolerant treatment, particularly in Yugoslavia, has attenuated historical animosities. Relations
with Yugoslavia have signally improved since the tense period following the invasion of Czechoslovakia.

One foreign policy defeat for Kadar has been Hungary's relegation to
observer status at the mutual force reduction talks in Vienna in 1973.
At Soviet insistence, Italy's nonparticipation was matched by that of
Hungary, excluding from the negotiations Hungary's armed forces
(103,000 troops plus 27,000 paramilitary forces) as well as the 48,000
Soviet troops stationed on Hungarian territory. In endorsing the 1975
Helsinki Final Act, Kadar noted that it did not mean mutual ideological

acceptance and intimated that Hungary's policies were already consistent with the act's prescriptions.

In Communist party relations, Kadar normally gives a muted echo to the Soviet line. Communist China is regularly denounced for its anti-Sovietism and rapprochement with the West. In the schismatic debate over Eurocommunism, Kadar has tried to profess moderation, rejecting Western criticism of the East European model, while suggesting that other paths to socialism are conceivable as long as the experience of the Soviet party is kept in view.[41] The Hungarian party has adopted the Soviet model of detente in its pursuit of trade expansion and domestic ideological retrenchment. Full diplomatic relations with West Germany were restored in 1973, and diplomatic and commercial contacts with the West have multiplied. It was a measure of Kadar's success that in 1977 he not only was awarded the Lenin Peace Prize but also secured the return of the ancient crown of St. Stephen from the United States, where it had been held in safekeeping since the end of World War II. Third World contacts are nurtured both to show solidarity against colonialism and imperialism and to pursue commercial objectives. In sum, Kadar's foreign policy has been to normalize relations with all states subject to the limitations of Soviet interests. Meanwhile, through tourism and unjammed radio broadcasts (and Austrian television in western Hungary), Hungarians are uncommonly exposed to external influences which reinforce a historical Western cultural orientation whose ideological content the regime has great difficulty in counteracting.

PROBLEMS AND PROSPECTS

The Hungarian regime's pursuit of economic modernization and socialist democracy leads inevitably to a dilemma: as one Western analyst put it, "How to achieve democratic legitimacy (a Western concept) without destroying the leading role or supremacy of the Party (a Communist concept) in Hungarian society."[42] The regime needs the cooperation of a large, well-educated middle class that is no longer inhibited by past affiliations and which lays claim to material rewards, cultural freedom, and a role in decision making. The regime must also placate the demands of the industrial working class, not only for the sake of higher productivity but also to authenticate the ideologically preordained leading role of that class. In the absence of a free contest of political interests, the party alone must choose among priorities, persuade the public of the wisdom and inevitability of that choice, and forestall any independent challenge to its decision. As memories of the 1956 revolution's tragic repression fade, the task of mobilizing a politically apathetic younger generation to actively support a monolithic system that tolerates no pluralism becomes pressing but is also fraught with risks.

While the current Hungarian version of proletarian dictatorship bears no resemblance to the pluralistic political system that was anticipated in the 1956 revolution, it is also far removed in its day-to-day operation from Rakosi's totalitarianism. With the obvious exception of agricultural collectivization, which in the long run has had a largely positive economic outcome, the Kadar system owes much to the original orientation of the New Course. Thus the Hungarian system is differentiated in some respects from the rest of the Soviet bloc. Compared to the Soviet and other East European versions, it manifests a more rational and flexible economic mechanism, fewer cultural constraints, and an unusual official sensitivity to popular opinion.

In the latter half of the 1970s, however, there is little likelihood of further democratization of the system and of sustenance of the economic growth rates of the preceding period. The ideological consolidation of the Soviet bloc in the face of detente and of President Carter's advocacy of human rights imposes a ceiling on Hungarian experimentation with socialist democracy and economic decentralization. World economic changes and their repercussions within CMEA will have a severe negative impact on the rate of development of the Hungarian economy. Meanwhile, the absence of credible constitutional guarantees, the ever-present shadow of the Kremlin, and the imminent necessity of finding a successor to the aging Kadar inspire popular apprehension even about the permanence of the current alliance policy. "I believe," said Bela Biszku in 1969, "that the supreme guarantee has already been given—namely the Party itself, which has never forgotten the lessons of 1956 and which, in its inner life, incessantly fosters democracy. We are doing everything to prevent any group from ever again monopolizing the party and the socialist system and abusing power."[43] The circumstantial legitimacy of the Kadar regime rests on such promises, on the tangible benefits of the alliance policy, and on the fear of worse dictatorships.

NOTES

1. See Rudolf L. Tokes, *Bela Kun and the Hungarian Soviet Republic* (New York: Praeger, 1967). For a brief historical overview, see Bennett Kovrig, *The*

Hungarian People's Republic (Baltimore: Johns Hopkins Press, 1970). A more comprehensive history of the Hungarian party can be found in Kovrig, *Communism in Hungary from Kun to Kadar* (Stanford: Hoover Institution Press, 1979).

2. Balint Szabo, *Nepi demokracia es forradalomelmelet* (Budapest: Kossuth, 1970), pp. 77–106.

3. Cf., Charles Gati, "Hungary: The Dynamics of Revolutionary Transformation," in Charles Gati, ed., *The Politics of Modernization in Eastern Europe* (New York: Praeger, 1974), pp. 51–84.

4. On Allied policy regarding Hungary, see Bennett Kovrig, *The Myth of Liberation* (Baltimore: Johns Hopkins Press, 1973), pp. 30, 52, 64–71.

5. Sandor Balogh, *Parlamenti es partharcok Magyarorszagon, 1945–1947* (Budapest: Kossuth, 1975), p. 525.

6. Paul Ignotus, "The First Two Communist Takeovers of Hungary: 1919 and 1948," in Thomas T. Hammond, ed., *The Anatomy of Communist Takeovers* (New Haven: Yale University Press, 1975), p. 398.

7. Magyar Szocialista Munkaspart, *Legyozhetetlen ero,* 2nd ed. (Budapest: Kossuth, 1974), p. 224.

8. See Bela A. Balassa, *The Hungarian Experience in Economic Planning* (New Haven: Yale University Press, 1959), pp. 31–35, 216ff; cf., Ivan T. Berend, *A szocialista gazdasag fejlodese Magyarorszagon, 1945–1968* (Budapest: Kossuth, 1974), pp. 86–93.

9. Wrote Nagy: "The 'left-wing' deviationists, primarily Rakosi and Gero, in the years 1949 to 1953 brought the socialist reorganization of agriculture to a dead end, bankrupted agricultural production, destroyed the worker-peasant alliance, undermined the power of the People's Democracy, trampled upon the rule of law, debased the people's living standards, established a rift between the masses and the Party and government—in other words swept the country towards catastrophe" (Imre Nagy, *On Communism: In Defence of the New Course* [New York: Praeger, 1957], p. 194).

10. Quoted in George Mikes, *The Hungarian Revolution* (London: Deutsch, 1957), p. 61.

11. See Tamas Aczel and Tibor Meray, *The Revolt of the Mind* (New York: Praeger, 1960).

12. Paul E. Zinner, *Revolution in Hungary* (New York: Columbia University Press, 1962), p. 195.

13. Among the numerous accounts of the Hungarian revolution, two of the best are Zinner, *Revolution in Hungary,* and Ferenc A. Vali, *Rift and Revolt in Hungary* (Cambridge: Harvard University Press, 1961).

14. See "Principles of Development and Further Strengthening of Friendship and Cooperation Between the Soviet Union and Other Socialist States," in Paul E. Zinner, ed., *National Communism and Popular Revolt in Eastern Europe* (New York: Columbia University Press, 1956), pp. 487–89. For the Western response to the revolution see Kovrig, *The Myth of Liberation,* ch. 5.

15. See William Shawcross, *Crime and Compromise* (New York: Dutton, 1974), pp. 82–85.

16. *Tarsadalmi Szemle,* June 1972, p. 9.

17. Radio Free Europe Research, Situation Report, March 22, 1975.

18. *Partelet,* December 1972.

19. *Nepszabadsag,* December 24, 1972.

20. *A Magyar Szocialista Munkaspart XI. kongresszusa* (Budapest: Kossuth, 1975), pp. 70–124.

21. Laszlo Rozsa, "Aktivitas, kiallas, demokracia," *Tarsadalmi Szemle,* May 1976, p. 29.

22. *Nepszabadsag,* October 24, 1975.

23. *Partelet,* July 1977.

24. For further analysis of the composition of the national assembly, see Peter A. Toma and Ivan Volgyes, *Politics in Hungary* (San Francisco: Freeman, 1977), pp. 57–62.

25. See Toma and Volgyes, pp. 74–82.

26. *Nepszabadsag,* September 20, 1976.

27. *Nepszabadsag,* January 16, 1971.

28. *Nepszabadsag,* May 11, 1976.

29. Toma and Volgyes, pp. 96–98.

30. *Partelet,* September 1973. An excellent analysis of the development and implementation of the NEM can be found in William F. Robinson, *The Pattern of Reform in Hungary* (New York: Praeger, 1973), chs. 2–6.

31. *Magyar Hirlap,* August 8, 1976.

32. Social welfare programs are outlined in Toma and Volgyes, ch. 10.

33. Ibid., pp. 45–46.

34. Radio Free Europe Research, Situation Report, March 20, 1975. Earlier cultural policies and problems are examined in Robinson, ch. 9.

35. *Tarsadalmi Szemle,* March 1976, p. 18.

36. On socialization, the media, and the political culture, see Toma and Volgyes, chs. 8, 9, and 11.

37. Observed the president of the Patriotic People's Front, Gyula Kallai: "We must take into account that a significant part of the masses . . . is still not unified in its world outlook. This is linked to the fact that there remain traces of the old system's ideology, and indeed in certain political and economic circumstances this harmful inheritance may and does reemerge. We must confront calmly but determinedly the fact that the philosophy of individualism and egotism is, under the ostensible veneer of socialism, spreading through not negligible strata of our society" (Nepszabadsag, June 27, 1976).

38. Interview with Yvon Bourdet in *L'Homme et la societe,* April–June 1971, pp. 3–12.

39. Radio Free Europe, Audience and Public Opinion Research Department, "Political Orientation and Listening to Western Radio in East Europe," July 1977.

40. See Robert R. King, *Minorities under Communism* (Cambridge: Harvard University Press, 1973), chs. 8 and 9.

41. *Beke es Szocializmus,* January 1977.

42. Toma and Volgyes, p. 63.

43. Quoted in Robinson, pp. 263–64.

BIBLIOGRAPHY

Aczel, Tamas, ed. *Ten Years After.* New York: Holt, Rinehart & Winston, 1967.

Aczel, Tamas, and Meray, Tibor. *The Revolt of the Mind.* New York: Praeger, 1960.

Hungarian Socialist Workers Party, Party History Institute. *History of the Revolutionary Workers Movement in Hungary, 1944-1962.* Budapest: Corvina, 1973.

Ignotus, Pal. *Hungary.* New York: Praeger, 1972.

Kecskemeti, Paul. *The Unexpected Revolution.* Stanford: Stanford University Press, 1961.

King, Robert R. *Minorities Under Communism.* Cambridge, Mass.: Harvard University Press, 1973.

Kovrig, Bennett. *The Hungarian People's Republic.* Baltimore: Johns Hopkins Press, 1973.

————. *Communism in Hungary from Kun to Kadar.* Stanford: Hoover Institution Press, 1979.

Laszlo, Ervin. *The Communist Ideology in Hungary.* Dordrecht: Reidel, 1966.

Nagy, Imre. *On Communism: In Defense of the New Course.* London: Thames & Hudson, 1957.

Radvanyi, Janos. *Hungary and the Superpowers.* Stanford: Hoover Institution, 1972.

Robinson, William F. *The Pattern of Reform in Hungary.* New York: Praeger, 1973.

Shawcross, William. *Crime and Compromise: Janos Kadar and the Politics of Hungary Since Revolution.* New York: Dutton, 1974.

Sinor, Denis, ed. *Modern Hungary: Readings from* The New Hungarian Quarterly. Bloomington: Indiana University Press, 1977.

Toma, Peter A., and Ivan Volgyes. *Politics in Hungary.* San Francisco: Freeman, 1977.

Vali, Ferenc A. *Rift and Revolt in Hungary.* Cambridge, Mass.: Harvard University Press, 1961.

Volgyes, Ivan, ed. *Political Socialization in Eastern Europe.* New York: Praeger, 1975.

Zinner, Paul E. *Revolution in Hungary.* New York: Columbia University Press, 1962.

4   Czechoslovakia

Otto Ulc

TACTICS OF TAKEOVER

With a mere 50,000 square miles (the approximate size of North Carolina) and a population of 15 million, Czechoslovakia is not a large country, but it is strategically located in the geographic center of the European continent. When the Czechoslovak Republic was founded in 1918, it inherited the largest part of the industry of the dismantled Austro-Hungarian monarchy. The advanced level of economic development and the numerical strength of the working class thus provided an auspicious setting for testing Marxist visions of social transformation.

In 1945 when World War II ended, of all the European lands east of the Elbe, Czechoslovakia was in the most fortunate position. It had not suffered substantial war destruction (as had occurred especially in Poland and Yugoslavia) and it was not treated as a defeated enemy (as were Hungary, Romania, and Bulgaria) or burdened by reparations and foreign occupation. Czechoslovakia was regarded as an ally by the victorious powers. In a rare exception to the pattern in the other countries it occupied, the Red Army left Czechoslovakia before the end of 1945. The government-in-exile of President Eduard Benes in London was allowed to return to the Soviet-bound part of Europe, at least as a symbol of statehood and preservation of its continuity. However, symptomatic of things to come was the return route taken by the Benes government: it traveled to Prague via Moscow, where Benes, who had little faith in the West and few options left to him, signed a pact of friendship with Stalin.

There is enough evidence available to argue that Communist rule was *not* imposed upon Czechoslovakia from the outside. This particular

Communist takeover was not a foregone conclusion, and the main credit for the outcome belongs not to the Kremlin in general or to Stalin in particular but to domestic forces—especially to the effort of the Communist Party of Czechoslovakia (hereafter CPCS). In contrast to neighboring Poland and Hungary, Czechoslovakia did not harbor anti-Russian sentiment. The CPCS had been a fairly strong legal party in the prewar years, with its leaders sitting in parliament and not in jail. The total prewar CPCS membership was 80,000. The Munich Pact had left a legacy of betrayal. Bitterness toward the West was enhanced by gratitude to the Soviet Union for its main share in crushing Hitler. The war polarized and radicalized the country, and by 1945 the CPCS membership exceeded one million. Membership included not only prewar Bolsheviks but also nostalgic Slavophiles, ardent anti-German patriots, ex-collaborators, and opportunists of all shapes.

Under Nazi rule some suffered and others collaborated. As in other East European lands, Communist party membership was an effective protection for the collaborationists. Political involvement also provided an opportunity to settle accounts with personal enemies. Three million Sudeten Germans—i.e., one-fifth of Czechoslovakia's total population—were expelled from the country, leaving behind considerable property: houses, villas, shops, factories, fields, and farms. A CPCS official was invariably in charge of distributing ex-German property. Not surprisingly, the electoral success of the CPCS was greatest in these Sudeten counties.

The first governmental program was signed in April 1945 in the East Slovak town of Kosice. It called for a National Front government, state control of large industries, land reform, punishment of wartime collaborators, and the expulsion of Germans and Hungarians from the country. "National Front" denoted a coalition government without, however, any provision for an eventual parliamentary opposition. All conservative and rightist parties were banned. The most notable casualty was the Republican (Agrarian) party, powerful in the prewar years.

In the Czech lands, i.e., in Bohemia and Moravia, four political parties —the Communists, the Social Democrats, the Czech Socialists, and the Catholics—and in Slovakia two parties—the Communists and the Democrats—shared power. In accordance with the pattern of sovietization in other countries, the first prime minister, the left-wing Social Democrat Zdenek Fierlinger, was not an overt Communist but a fellow traveler. The chairman of the Communist party, Klement Gottwald, was one of his four deputies. In the coalition government the Communists obtained the key ministries: interior, information, agriculture, education, and social welfare. Thus they were put in control of land distribution, propaganda, the police, and the administration of social welfare benefits.

The Communists followed the usual blueprint of takeover: infiltrating and gaining control of mass organizations (notably the trade unions and the youth movement), splitting the noncommunist parties by encouraging the formation of left wings, and attacking anticommunists with charges of a fascist past or fascist intentions.

Under Gottwald's leadership the Communist party espoused the allegedly Czechoslovak road to socialism. In May 1946 parliamentary elections were held, and in a free contest with other parties the CPCS was a winner, receiving 38 percent of the votes (43 percent in the Czech lands) and 114 of 300 parliamentary seats. Gottwald became the prime minister.

A two-year plan of postwar reconstruction was introduced. At the same time the political mood in the country, affected by the fading postwar euphoria, started to hurt the CPCS—which was engaged in a drive to obtain a 51 percent majority of public support. The CPCS conducted a public opinion survey only to find that not more than 28 percent of the Czechoslovak electorate was expected to vote the Communist ticket in the elections scheduled for May 1948. With this gloomy prospect of an electoral loss, the CPCS leadership resolved to seize power. In February 1948 a governmental crisis was staged and skillfully exploited. The Communist minister of interior, Vaclav Nosek, refused to comply with a cabinet decision to reinstitute the dismissed noncommunist police commissioners. Twelve noncommunist ministers resigned as a result, causing the fall of the government. Their alleged plan was that President Benes would call for an immediate election, the Communists would be defeated, and the country would become a pluralistic democracy.

Though loyal to his agreement with the Soviet Union, President Benes did not want to sever ties to the West. He conceived of Czechoslovakia as a bridge between East and West. However, after six critical days, a visit from the Soviet ambassador Valerian Zorin, and Communist threats of violence, Benes succumbed and instead of calling for free elections that might have neutralized the CPCS, he issued a virtual mandate for one-party rule. Events followed swiftly: several noncommunist leaders fled to the West; others were arrested; the popular Jan Masaryk, minister of foreign affairs and son of T. G. Masaryk, the founder of the Republic, was found dead (officially a suicide, unofficially the victim of a political murder). President Benes refused to sign the new constitution in May 1948, resigned his office in June, and died in September of the same year. Within less than six months Czechoslovakia and its leadership had completely changed.

Gottwald, as head of the Communist party, became president, while Rudolf Slansky remained secretary general of the CPCS. (Slansky was hanged as an "enemy of the people" in 1952.) Antonin Zapotocky became prime minister in 1948 and succeeded Gottwald in the presidency after the latter's death in March 1953.

The National Front now became a vehicle for one-party rule. Noncommunist members of the National Front included only a few puppet parties and mass organizations. In May 1948, a single slate of candidates allegedly received 86.6 percent of the votes cast. A new constitution was promulgated in the same month. Although its form was democratic, its contents were not.

THE MAIN LINES OF POLITICAL DEVELOPMENT

The postwar course followed by the Warsaw Pact countries may generally be characterized as Stalinism, superseded by de-Stalinization, inaugurated by Khrushchev in 1956. The Czechoslovak version of Stalinism was particularly durable and virulent. In the post-Stalin period Antonin Novotny, who was first secretary of the CPCS from 1953 to 1968 and president of Czechoslovakia from 1957 to 1968, maneuvered to extricate his regime and himself personally from responsibility for the Stalinist terror.

Novotny's strategy of whitewash retarded de-Stalinization for several years. This delay deepened the social crisis, until it erupted in the Prague Spring of 1968. At that time the scope of liberalization dwarfed all other reformist efforts in Eastern Europe, those of Yugoslavia included. Significantly, the impetus toward change was not directed against Communist party rule (as was the short-lived revolt in Hungary in 1956) but was led by Communist reformers themselves.

In August 1968, however, the Soviet Union, enforcing the Brezhnev doctrine of limited sovereignty, suppressed with arms the Czechoslovak challenge to the status quo. The few months of euphoric emancipation, with civil liberties restored and censorship abolished, were followed by a period officially termed "normalization." With the possible exception of Albania, Prague became the foremost European center of neo-Stalinism.

It has been argued that the probable success of the Stalinist model of socialist construction is in inverse proportion to the general advancement of the country in which the model is to be tested. The Stalinist variant, designed for backward, rural, autocratic Russia, was more likely to be successful when applied to backward, rural, and autocratic Bulgaria than to industrially advanced Czechoslovakia, with a tradition of pluralistic democracy. The imposition of a crash program of heavy industrialization and the building of steel mills in industrialized but iron-ore poor Czechoslovakia was designed to satisfy an alien doctrine and not domestic needs. Not surprisingly, in comparing the economic advancement of the East European countries, Czechoslovakia's record has been the least distinguished.

Economic activities down to the street-corner ice-cream vendor were nationalized, all agricultural land was collectivized, and the first five-year plan went into force in 1949. These changes were accompanied by a thorough personnel turnover. Political loyalty was declared the supreme recruitment criterion for any job. A special category of "proletarian executives" emerged. Persecution of "class enemies," e.g., cuts in social security benefits for orphans from bourgeois families, became the rule. The damage to the economic structure and to personnel has been felt ever since.

For reasons that have never been satisfactorily explained, Gottwald's leadership departed from the Leninist principle of elitist recruitment into the party ranks. Instead of strict admission requirements for the select few, the CPCS gates were open to mass enrollment. The Communist party, 1.59 million strong, in March 1946, swelled to 2.5 million by March 1948. One in every three adults became a Communist. A subsequent purge reduced the CPCS ranks to some 1.5 million, which has been a fairly constant figure to the present.

Another difficult issue of the Stalinist period was the nationality question and the sharing of power. In Czechoslovakia there are twice as many Czechs (inhabiting Bohemia and Moravia) as Slovaks (in Slovakia). The two nations have similar languages and a very dissimilar past, socioeconomic development, and political culture. In the postwar years the Slovak demands for federation were not met; instead, an unsatisfactory compromise, called "asymmetry," was introduced. This arrangement provided the Slovaks with a restricted type of autonomy, later to be diminished even further. Slovak grievances were to contribute significantly to the collapse of Novotny's regime in 1968.

Czechoslovak Stalinism was characterized also by political trials and executions of the innocent. Among the victims was Milada Horakova, a member of the parliament and a survivor of a Nazi concentration

camp, one of the few women in postwar Europe to be tried and executed
for a political crime. The main wave of political arrests took place in
1951 and affected one of the most prominent terror-makers, the secretary general of the CPCS Rudolf Slansky. He, along with thirteen code-
fendants, most of them Jewish, were found guilty; eleven were
executed, and their ashes were scattered on a road south of Prague. In
1954 Gustav Husak, the leading Slovak Communist, was sentenced to
life imprisonment for being a bourgeois nationalist. He was later released and in 1969 he became the first secretary of the CPCS, a post that
he still holds. In the early 1950s a new generation of political prisoners,
estimated at well over 100,000, languished in 422 jails and concentration
camps.

Even after the deaths of Stalin and of Gottwald in March 1953 the
Czechoslovak phase of Stalinism was not yet over. Antonin Novotny,
the colorless new leader, continued Stalinist policies. More political
trials were staged, and on May 1, 1955, an eighteen-thousand-ton statue
of Stalin, allegedly the largest in the world, was unveiled in Prague.

In February 1956 Khrushchev denounced Stalin in his secret speech
at the Twentieth Party Congress; Poland rebelled in the summer of 1956
and Hungary erupted in a revolution in the autumn. The dramatic
challenge to Communist rule in Budapest generated in Prague an atmosphere of nervous vindictiveness and intensified intolerance. It was in
this period of renewed call for class struggle and Bolshevik vigilance
that the forced collectivization drive reached its peak.

A new constitution was adopted in 1960, officially terminating the
transitional period of "people's democracy" which had lasted twelve
years, and heralding the arrival of socialism. This bold self-assessment
put Czechoslovakia next only to the Soviet Union: no other country had
attained the distinction of having achieved "scientific socialism." Accordingly, the Czechoslovak Republic (*Ceskoslovenska republika*—
CSR) was renamed the Czechoslovak Socialist Republic (*Ceskoslovenska socialisticka republika*—CSSR). The new Czechoslovak constitution
even surpassed its Soviet model by declaring Marxism-Leninism the
state ideology, and anchoring the leading role of the Communist party
in this basic law of the land. To cover up the political past, Novotny
chose a complex road of procrastination, whitewash, and salami tactics
of rehabilitation, which lasted a decade. As a gesture toward de-Stalinization several commissions of inquiry were established after 1956, each
reporting a different version of the Czechoslovak emulation of the Stalinist terror. One commission found nothing irregular or inappropriate
with regard to the trials; a second commission held that minor techni-

calities were in error; a third detected major deficiencies. Finally, in 1963, under the impact of Khrushchev's renewed attack on Stalin at the Twenty-second Party Congress in 1961, the last commission pointed to some of the guilty parties and their crimes, although not to Novotny. The greatest cadre change since the purges of the fifties ensued: the old guard, including the premier, Viliam Siroky, was retired. Siroky's place was taken by a Slovak party bureaucrat, Jozef Lenart. Some of the executed party members who had been rehabilitated were posthumously readmitted into the party.

Novotny's last five years in power were crisis-ridden and culminated in the fall of his increasingly ineffectual regime in January 1968. The troubled state of the economy, the Slovak question, and general social malaise characterized the eclipse of Novotny's rule.

After 1961 the rate of production growth slowed significantly, and in 1963 Czechoslovakia experienced a decline in its gross national product. The five-year plan for 1959–63 had to be abandoned. Economists began to attack openly the "cult of planning," as an awkward, ineffective system. The economy was in urgent need of rational criteria for recruitment, management, decentralization, and production. Yet, the CPCS apparatus feared that giving more autonomy to economic units would threaten its own monopoly of power, and would lead to gradual loss of control over the state and over society. The need for a New Economic Model (NEM) was recognized, but political considerations prevented its genuine implementation. The realization had been growing within the top CPCS leadership that a successful economic reform could not be carried out without a change in the political system, that the economy would not prosper as long as the CPCS retained its monopoly of power. After three years of preparation, a compromise policy was adopted, but it satisfied neither the reformers nor the conservatives.

Criticism of the economic system, along with the rehabilitation of the victims of Stalinism, were signs of a more relaxed political climate. Franz Kafka was rehabilitated in 1963; censors became more tolerant; good literature was published; and Czechoslovak artistic creativity, especially in the film industry, became well known abroad. Czechoslovak citizens were issued passports and were allowed to travel abroad in increasing numbers. Class discrimination subsided, academic degrees were restored, and even some objectivity prevailed in the official assessment of Czechoslovakia's precommunist past.

The protracted crisis of Novotny's rule had many causes, of which the Slovak issue was perhaps the most formidable. The marriage of the Slovaks with the twice-as-numerous Czechs had been, at best, a marriage of convenience, with the inconvenient aspects of the liaison increasingly visible. Except for linguistic and geographical proximity, these two nations had little in common. During World War II the Czechoslovak state was destroyed, the Czech lands were occupied by the Germans, and the Slovaks became semi-independent in a pro-German alliance. After the war the Czechs voted for the Communists, while the Slovaks sided with the anticommunists. Again, the Slovak aspirations for a federal solution were not met. Prague, the Czech center, ran the affairs of the entire state. The 1960 constitution further curtailed the powers of the authorities in the Slovak capital of Bratislava, thus adding to the credibility and vigor of the Slovak complaints.

The Stalinist purges of the fifties had affected the Slovak elites with particular harshness and, indeed, the very concept of Slovak nationhood was condemned as bourgeois nationalism. Thus, the rehabilitation of the victims of Stalinism in the 1960s was seen also as a rehabilitation of Slovak national identity. It was in Bratislava, and not in Prague, that the first attacks on Novotny's regime were launched.

In 1967, the year preceding the Prague Spring, the Czechoslovak leadership came under increasing criticism. Two political events of importance to Czechoslovaks occurred in June: the Six Day War in the Middle East and the Fourth Congress of Czech Writers in Prague. Israel, very popular in small Czechoslovakia, demolished its Arab adversaries, the friends and allies of the Soviet Union. Soviet weapons were defeated. At the writers' congress in Prague thoughtful and eloquent indictments of the Communist establishment and its rule were articulated: the narrowmindedness of the bureaucracy, the vulgarity of the censorship, and the subversion of socialist principles in general. The congress was highlighted by a masterful speech by the novelist and CPCS member Ludvik Vaculik, who accused the regime of having failed in its twenty years of unlimited rule to solve a single one of the problems facing Czechoslovak society.

The leadership, under attack, reacted with repressions: expulsions from the party, prohibition of publications, and the like. But Novotny's regime was losing ground. In December 1967 the Central Committee of the CPCS convened. The intraparty struggle came to an end in January 1968, when Slovak bureaucrat and compromise candidate Alexander Dubcek was chosen to replace Novotny as the new leader of the ruling Communist party.

The appointment of Dubcek marked the beginning of the eight months known as the Prague Spring. The events of 1968 catapulted Prague into the role of a challenger of the Soviet monopoly over applied

Marxism. The aim of Czechoslovak reformers was to combine socialism with democracy and economic security with civil liberties—and
to eliminate Leninism as a crippling distortion of Marxism. In this
ambitious quest sacrosanct and hitherto unchallenged articles of faith
were attacked and eventually rejected.

Hundreds of books have been written about the Prague Spring.[1]
Here, we can mention only the most fundamental observations relating
to this experiment in "socialism with a human face." For one, it was
an interrupted process. Soviet intervention prevented full implementation of the experiment. From the Soviet viewpoint Dubcek's cardinal
error was weakening the leading role of the Communist party. Such
heresies were enunciated in the Action Program of April 1968. This
document, drawn up by the CPCS, in some respects resembles Western
Eurocommunist pronouncements of the 1970s, but in other respects it
was a compromise, eclectic and quite general. Bold promises were
muted by qualifying clauses. In this "first step toward a new democratic
model of socialist society" little was said about the leading role of the
Communist party, but the CPCS had nonetheless issued the Action
Program without consulting the minor parties, other components of
the National Front, or the nation at large.

The abolition of censorship significantly enhanced the political role
of the mass media. The press, radio, and television became "schools of
democracy." They discussed quite openly the darker aspects of the
previous twenty years of socialist construction: the purges, tortures,
show trials, concentration camps and the like. The airing of these previously taboo subjects served as an effective socialization program, and
after a few months the Soviet type of one-party rule was thoroughly
discredited. Public opinion surveys confirmed the overwhelming popularity of the new course: Dubcek's team received some 90 percent of
popular support.

In June 1968 a Rehabilitation Law was passed. The law submitted to
review the punitive record of the state over the preceding two decades.
Any person convicted of a political crime in the state period was entitled to a retrial. Retrials could be initiated by a relative or heir. An
overwhelming majority of those who chose this venue of belated redress were rehabilitated.

The Soviet leadership may have misunderstood and misinterpreted
the Czechoslovak developments in 1968, but only in part. Whereas
Prague did not plan to secede from the socialist camp and join the
capitalist West, this loyalty in foreign affairs was not matched by similar loyalty in domestic matters. Dubcek's plans for domestic transfor-

mation were substantially alien to the Soviet autocratic understanding of socialism. Prague did indeed weaken the leading role of the Communist party. It was Moscow's fear that the success of such a course in Czechoslovakia would endanger the Soviet regime and would even touch off a collapse in Poland and East Germany. In the eyes of the Kremlin the Czechoslovak heretics had to be stopped. Soviet efforts at persuasion escalated: first consultations and warnings; then reprimands, intrigues, and military maneuvers; and finally military intervention, after all the previous measures had failed.

The Soviet invasion of August 21, 1968, was a textbook example of military efficiency and political ineptitude. The armies of the more dogmatic members of the Warsaw Pact moved into Czechoslovakia in response to an invitation that never arrived. The Czechoslovak populace did not greet with sympathy those rendering "fraternal assistance in defense of socialism." Indeed, the Soviet invasion caused the most profound shift in the Czechoslovak political outlook since World War II: people who were divided in 1948 became united in 1968. The rift between the Communists and the anticommunists, between the supporters and the opponents of the regime, disappeared; wounds were healed by acute patriotism and anti-Sovietism.

The imposed process of "normalization" led to the annulment of the innovations introduced in 1968—except for the federalization of the country, which was retained albeit in a modified form. However, the restoration of the status quo ante proved to be beyond reach. The Czechoslovak experiment with humanized socialism and its military suppression destroyed whatever base of mass support the ruling Communist party had enjoyed in the past. There has not been such a gap between the ruler and the ruled since the Nazi occupation. The alienated populace is compliant but committed to the pursuit of private interests. The leaders are insecure, and in their insecurity they tend to overreact, which further widens the gap.

CURRENT POLITICAL STRUCTURE AND DYNAMICS

Czechoslovak political institutions and processes, as they have evolved since 1948, have closely emulated the Soviet model. Accordingly, inherited precommunist structures were either abolished entirely (e.g., the administrative courts—a citizen's avenue of redress against bureaucratic decisions) or retained in form, though not in content (e.g., the independent judiciary was converted into an instrument of "class justice"). Other institutions of purely Soviet inspiration were introduced (e.g., the *Prokuratura,* an institution that is part public prosecutor, part watchdog, and part ombudsman).

For reasons of geography alone, the Czechoslovak copy could not be an exact replica of the Soviet master design. The imitation of all things Soviet which the Prague leadership obstinately pursued was often counterproductive. For example, an attempt to convert Czech fields to corn, in imitation of Khrushchev's infatuation with planting corn, resulted in considerable economic loss.

In the 1970s Husak has adhered very closely to the Soviet model in substance and even in form. A Czechoslovak party congress has been invariably scheduled just after each Soviet party congress. In 1976 Husak dismissed three cabinet ministers to conform with a similar reshuffle in Moscow. The CPCS structure and functions are similar to the Soviet model: the Politburo initiates policies and supervises their implementation, which is left in the hands of the executive branch of the government, including the cabinet, various ministries, and other offices of a ministerial rank. The Secretariat of the Central Committee of the CPCS is the nerve center of the party bureaucracy, and the first secretary is the most powerful person in the country. The country is divided into provinces and the provinces into districts. Each unit is headed by a party bureaucrat of appropriate rank.

The presidency and the federation are the two constitutional features that deviate from the Soviet model. Czechoslovakia has retained the precommunist system of the singular presidency in preference to the Soviet collective presidency, represented by the Presidium of the Supreme Soviet. Gottwald, the head of the CPCS, became in 1948 also the head of the state. This combination of his CPCS office and his government seat led to the post mortem accusation that he had pursued the cult of personality. Irrespective of this stigma, Novotny acquired both the offices in 1957, and in 1968 this lust for dual power was cited among the reasons for Novotny's political fall. Prominent among the accusers at the time was Husak, but in 1975, First Secretary Husak also acquired the presidency. This weakened rather than strengthened Husak because it made him vulnerable to the kinds of attacks that had been launched against his predecessors.

The second and more significant departure from the Soviet blueprint concerns the federalization of the country. Moscow shares power with the Soviet union-republics only in form, whereas in Czechoslovakia the sharing of power by Prague and Bratislava is meaningful in content. It should be recalled that Slovak national aspirations were instrumental in the fall of the Novotny regime. On October 28, 1968, the day of the fiftieth anniversary of the foundation of the Czechoslovak Republic by T. G. Masaryk, a Constitutional Law on Federation was promulgated. In response to demands for maximum autonomy, separate institutions, such as the Slovak Ministry of Justice, were set up, and even dual citizenship was established: one could become a citizen of the Czechoslovak Socialist Republic (CSSR), on the one hand, and of either the Czech Socialist Republic (CSR) or the Slovak Socialist Republic (SSR) on the other.

The nationalistic euphoria was bound to subside. Dual citizenship, about as practical as dual citizenship in the United States and, say, North Dakota, was found too cumbersome and was abolished, as were some other innovations of decentralization. An element of the original 1948 asymmetry has remained, calling into question the achievement of genuine federalization. The state was federalized, but the Communist party was not. No *Czech* Communist party, as opposed to the Slovak Communist party, has ever been brought to existence.

Since 1948 the Czechoslovak electoral system has followed the Soviet system of a single slate of candidates. Since the Soviet invasion in 1968 two general elections have been held. In 1976, Czechoslovak voters allegedly broke records of electoral loyalty by casting 99.97 percent of their votes for the candidates of the regime.

LEADERSHIP AND CHANGING ELITE PATTERNS

In the first period of one-party rule, when Communist power was achieved and consolidated after 1945, the leadership consisted mainly of veteran Czechoslovak Bolsheviks of the prewar era—Gottwald, Slansky, Kopecky, Dolansky, and Siroky. By the 1970s, all of these leaders were dead. However, the current first secretary, Husak, can be counted as a survivor of this early group.

The old Bolshevik elite was augmented by postwar CPCS recruits, by former left-wing Social Democrats, and by opportunists of various types. Since 1968, the leadership has been dominated by the beneficiaries rather than by the co-architects of Communist rule. Changes in personnel after the 1968 invasion, culminating in a massive party purge in 1970, provided numerous vacancies which were filled with individuals with often manifestly inferior qualifications, with careerists, and with a disproportionate number of persons of Slovak nationality.

At the top of the hierarchy is Gustav Husak, the first postwar ruler of Slovakia, who was subsequently sentenced to life imprisonment. Rehabilitated during the 1960s, he returned to the political arena in 1968, an outspoken liberal, yet an autocrat; a supporter of Dubcek, yet after the invasion his denouncer. Like the Hungarian leader Janos Kadar, Husak experienced torture and incarceration by his own comrades, but in other respects Husak's background and record are quite different from those of the leaders of the other Warsaw Pact countries —Honecker of East Germany, Gierek of Poland, Kadar of Hungary, Ceausescu of Romania, and Zhivkov of Bulgaria. Husak is a university-educated intellectual of nonproletarian background, not a member of the dominant Czech nationality. His reputation is burdened by a dubious wartime record as a resistance fighter tainted by collaboration with the Slovak pro-Nazi regime. For twenty years, Husak, now first secretary of the CPCS, was prevented from holding any post in the CPCS apparatus. This profile makes Husak atypical not only in comparison to his East European counterparts but also in comparison to other members of the Czechoslovak Politburo.

Husak was expected to emulate the policies followed by Kadar after 1956. However, whereas Kadar followed a centrist course opposing both the left and the right wing of the party, Husak steered a dogmatic course, attacking only the progressive reformers. As a result, he isolated himself from his potential centrist allies and increasingly has become identified with the policies of the CPCS conservatives.

The "progressive" versus "conservative" dichotomy is inappropriate for the Czechoslovak political leadership of the 1970s. Rather the distinction is between the conservative and hard-line factions. Husak is the main representative of the conservative wing, practicing what is sometimes referred to as "reluctant terror," i.e., no great excesses in policies of repression. To the man-in-the-street, Husak represents the lesser evil.

The leader of the hard-liners is Vasil Bilak, an ethnic Ruthenian, a tailor by training, an outspoken and consistent Stalinist, and the Politburo member in charge of ideology and relations with foreign Communist parties. In the 1960s he was among those opposing rehabilitation of Husak. Bilak's group functions as a watchdog over the Husak group. Moscow plays the two factions against each other without permitting a victory to either party. At the moment no politician in good standing with the Soviets is a credible successor to Husak.

Personal compatibility between the Soviet and individual East European rulers is certainly an advantage, but it is insufficient guarantee of a lasting career. All East European leaders are judged first of all on their capacity to govern. If this capacity is lost, so is Soviet support.

Conservatives and hard-liners differ only in degree with regard to harshness and intolerance toward supposed enemies, such as religious believers, nationalists, nonsocialists, non-Marxists, and above all, former members of the Communist party.

Politically, Czechoslovak society consists of three layers:

1. CPCS members and their families. Party membership is the key to promotion, better jobs, better housing, college admission, and privileges such as travel to Western countries.

2. Those who have never been members of the CPCS. As a rule, persons in this category cannot reach the top of their professions, but at the same time they are not particularly victimized and are allowed to lead an undisturbed life within the range of modest expectations.

3. Former Communists who either quit the CPCS (as occurred frequently after the Soviet invasion in 1968) or were expelled. People in this category are the current pariahs of Czechoslovak society, replacing the classic enemies of 1948 vintage: capitalists and big landowners.

As a rule, party membership means lifetime involvement. Except for serious illness or advanced age, there is no other way for a Communist to retire but in disgrace. In Czechoslovakia, a country of 15 million, there are half a million former party members, who have been demoted, harassed, and frequently persecuted along with their families. In the post-invasion purge of 1970, a full one-third, around 500,000 of the total 1,500,000 membership, was removed from the ranks. While in the post-1948 purge, opportunists and bourgeois elements were weeded out, in 1970 committed Communists, among them prewar party veterans, were purged. The 1970 purge affected the Czechs (constituting 90 percent of all casualties) more than the Slovaks, and singled out individuals with higher education, party seniority, and positions of responsibility. Of the total purged, some 75 percent were assigned to manual labor. Entire scholarly disciplines were decimated.

The existence of this large body of dismissed party members frightens the current leadership more than would the spectre of a handful of executed innocent comrades. Former party members who are bound by their common past experiences and their present outcast status represent, in the words of former Central Committee member Alfred Cerny, a shadow "party of the future," and constitute a threat to the present neo-Stalinist establishment. A situation unique among the Soviet-type countries has developed: the creation of an alternative, shadow Communist party, consisting of Communists who were purged but not killed.

The current ruling elite in Czechoslovakia is marked by its insecurity. In contrast to the genuinely popular leaders of 1968, their successors, placed in power by the invading Soviet forces, evoked neither affection nor respect. Leading roles in political and economic institutions, in culture, and in academia, have often been filled by individuals of insufficient talent and ability.

The tenure of these elites depends solely upon the continued sponsorship of the Kremlin. Awareness of this precarious status and of the absence of public support serves to unite these insecure power holders. Developments at the Fifteenth CPCS Congress, held in Prague in April 1976, illustrate the cohesion between the conservatives and the hardliners. At issue was a proposed amnesty, blanket or partial, for the purged Communists, who, if readmitted to the party, undoubtedly would challenge numerous incumbents for their jobs. Only Husak spoke in favor of a reconciliation, and only a token amnesty was adopted. The danger to present officeholders was thus thwarted, and the policy of wasting talents, injurious to the state and economy, was reconfirmed.

Given its limited sovereignty, Czechoslovakia's politics closely reflect Soviet politics. After the uneventful Twenty-fifth Congress of the Soviet Communists in 1976, the Fifteenth Congress in Prague did not produce any major changes in elite composition or in policy. The Politburo remained unchanged (except that the ailing Ludvik Svoboda was dropped), and the 30 percent turnover in the Central Committee remained within the range of a normal exchange. The equilibrium between the conservatives and the hard-liners was preserved, and the precarious balance precludes any fundamental policy changes in the short run. It appears that Husak will remain in power for the foreseeable future. At least he was not among the signatories of the letter urging the Soviet Union to invade and liberate Czechoslovakia from Dubcek's socialism with a human face in 1968. (Politburo members Vasil Bilak, Karel Hoffman, Alois Indra, and Antonin Kapek are known to be among the forty signatories.)

Husak's policy of normalization has not been without its successes. Standards of living have risen and there is no prospect of riots of the Polish type. The political activism exhibited by Czechoslovaks in the late 1960s has turned into political apathy. However, this apathy has had repercussions in the economic realm, impairing efficiency and production in general. By 1975 the economy had begun to exhibit serious strains.

FOREIGN POLICY AND FOREIGN ECONOMIC RELATIONS

The reforms of the Prague Spring of 1968 aimed at domestic democratization and not at foreign policy reorientation. Whether because of prudence or genuine preference, the reformers did not fall into the Hungarian trap of 1956 in demanding neutrality and abandonment of the Warsaw Pact. The restraints shown in Prague notwithstanding, the Soviet Union intervened militarily in August 1968.

The Moscow Protocol that finalized the act of invasion, signed by the kidnapped Czechoslovak leaders, was to be the cornerstone of the normalization process. Under its terms Soviet military units would be stationed in Czechoslovakia until normalization was achieved. Ostensibly, this goal has not yet been attained, despite the 99 percent electoral victories of the normalizers.

In 1970 Czechoslovakia and the USSR signed a new friendship treaty which incorporated the principle of limited sovereignty and retroactively legalized the 1968 invasion. Under the terms of this treaty, should war erupt between the USSR and China, for example, Czechoslovakia would automatically become a party to the conflict.

If Czechoslovak foreign policy is a reflection of Soviet policy, in the sphere of the foreign trade, however, such uniform conformist measures cannot be easily duplicated. Obviously, two trading partners cannot both be creditors at the same time on the basis of their mutual trade. During the 1960s Czechoslovakia was the banker for the less-developed socialist allies. For example, in 1966 Czechoslovakia granted a $500 million loan to the USSR to modernize and expand its oil fields in Western Siberia. However, since 1974, Czechoslovakia has for the first time experienced a trading deficit in dealing with its socialist partners.

After the 1968 invasion an economic decline in Czechoslovakia was widely predicted. Yet, the standard of living did not deteriorate. To the contrary, the rate of consumption rose, keeping Czechoslovakia in second place in the socialist bloc (after East Germany) with respect to this aspect of economic performance.

The price for "consumer pacification" was the exhaustion of credits and foreign currency reserves. The 1973 oil boycott, the quadrupling of crude oil prices, and the energy crisis, along with the economic crisis in the West, were applauded in Eastern Europe. This elation proved to be premature. The Soviets, as suppliers of crude oil, gradually raised the prices of their exports to East European countries aiming to match the OPEC price level. Secondly, socialist importers now had to pay inflationary prices for capitalist exports. In this way inflation has affected socialist economies. Compared to that of the USSR and Poland, the indebtedness of Czechoslovakia to the West is relatively minor (an estimated 2 billion dollars in 1976). Czechoslovakia's foreign trade problem stems largely from its growing trade deficits, its dependence on imports, and the difficulty it has reaching hard currency markets with its own industrial products.

PROBLEMS AND TRENDS

The post-invasion regime under the leadership of Gustav Husak deserves credit for some improvement in the supplies of consumer goods, for its attempts to suppress corruption, for the preferential allocation of resources in Slovakia so as to catch up with the more developed Czech lands, and also for the application of some restraint in applying repression in both the judicial and the extra-judicial spheres.

These positive marks are overshadowed, however, by the negative aspects of the regime's performance, notably, its perpetuation of the Communist party monopoly, its intolerance, persecution of presumed political adversaries, enforcement of strict censorship, and mutilation of the arts and sciences. In addition to the post-invasion diaspora of some 130,000 refugees (almost 1 percent of the total population), there is a domestic diaspora which includes practitioners of entire scholarly disciplines.

In addition to the regime's political liabilities, there are the frequently mentioned symptoms of the Czechoslovak economic malaise: unnecessary and unfinished investment projects; underutilization of industrial capacity by one-half; exhaustion of labor reserves; a high percentage of manpower and resources channeled to war-related research and production. Like Great Britain, Czechoslovakia is handicapped by the obsolescence of its industrial equipment, which to a large degree escaped destruction in World War II. The political passivity of the population is reflected in poor economic performance, as energies are channeled into private and often illicit materialistic pursuits to the detriment of the public good.

A further liability is that political loyalty is the prime and frequently the only determinant of employment and educational opportunities. The Labor Code was amended to allow the immediate firing of anyone accused of a political impropriety (e.g., signing a petition, supposedly a constitutionally guaranteed freedom). Wage and salary scales are based not only on qualifications and performance but also on the extent of one's political activism. All college admissions applicants are subjected to what is termed "complex evaluation," in which the parents' social class and political standing are rated in a discriminatory point system. As a rule, children of former CPCS members are denied access to higher education. Fortunately the impact of these repressive measures is blunted by widespread corruption. This relatively new phenomenon penetrates all spheres of life and reaches into high political offices, the Secretariat of the Central Committee included.

If corruption is one of the symptoms of post-totalitarian socialism, the most profound post-totalitarian phenomenon in contemporary Czechoslovakia is the existence of an implicit social contract: the rulers rule and the citizens, left alone to attend to their private affairs, do not meddle in public affairs. Largely absolved from ritual political involvement, the population has become preoccupied instead with the material rewards of a consumer society. Overt "consolidation" has been achieved at the cost of a spiritual and moral crisis pervading Czechoslovak society.

While this social contract does not produce socialists, neither does it produce challengers of the system. Still, one may question how long the consumerist pacification program can last in view of Czechoslovakia's growing economic difficulties.

Despite the prevailing public apathy, the leadership is prone to breaking its commitment to the unwritten social contract. In the post-Dubcek period, for example, the Party leadership initially preferred political noninvolvement among youth to wrongheaded political involvement. Something akin to an armistice developed. The party gave up its fight against long hair and beat music, and even persuaded young people to fill vacancies created by the thorough post-invasion purges. Yet, for reasons so far not fully explained, in 1976 the party terminated this spirit of detente with a crackdown on rock music.

Dissent is an increasingly vexatious problem for the Czechoslovak establishment. Since 1973 persons prominent in the reformist movement in 1968—politicians such as Alexander Dubcek, Josef Smrkovsky, Zdenek Mlynar, and Jiri Hajek; scientists such as Ivan Malek, Karel Kaplan, Vilem Precan, and Karel Kosik; writers such as Vaclav Havel, Pavel Kohout, Ludvik Vaculik—have been sending open letters to various party and governmental officials and institutions.[2] To assure that these messages received attention abroad, copies were delivered to Western journalists stationed in Prague. The response of the leadership to these letters has often been vitriolic.

The 1975 spirit of Helsinki bore its best fruit in "Charter 77," characterized by the Yugoslav dissenter Milovan Djilas as "the most mature and accomplished program produced by Eastern Europe from the war up to today."[3] "Charter 77," issued in January 1977 in Prague and signed by several hundred Czechoslovaks from all walks of life, is an appeal to the government to obey its own laws. It cites the provisions of valid Czechoslovak statutes and ratified international conventions and stresses the necessity of living up to these commitments. The signatories of the Charter emphasize that they do not challenge the government nor do they form an opposition.

Beginning with the main party daily, *Rude pravo,* on January 12, 1977, all the Czechoslovak mass media have vilified the signatories of the charter, declaring it a hostile, antistate pamphlet, a product of CIA-inspired anti-Communist hysteria. While not a single sentence of it has appeared in any Czechoslovak publication, thousands of citizens have been forced to append their signatures to the condemnation of the charter, which they have not been permitted to read. Refusal to sign poses the threat of employment termination for the individual and implies ruin for the entire family. Actually, this campaign, by publicizing the charter, has helped rather than harmed it.

The events of 1968 united the nation against the occupying outside force and against the local rulers imposed by this force. In the following years political commitment gave way to political inertia, without narrowing the gap between the rulers and the ruled. Intense anti-Soviet, or, more specifically, anti-Russian attitudes, triggered by the invasion, still prevail among the Czechoslovak populace.

Another byproduct of the invasion is the growing rift between the Czechs and the Slovaks, which in the opinion of some observers represents the most serious nationality conflict in the history of the country. Though the responsibility for this destructive development lies largely with Husak's leadership, the origins of the present rift may be traced back to the Prague Spring. When the armies of several Warsaw Pact countries invaded Czechoslovakia, the tanks were aimed at the Czech rather than the Slovak heretics. It was a punitive expedition against the Czech nation, evidenced, *inter alia,* by the results of the 1970 purge of the Communist party: of the half million members purged, 90 percent were Czechs. Nine out of ten subsequent political trials were Czech affairs. Whereas in Slovakia the assignment of an intellectual expelled from the CPCS to manual labor is an exception, in the Czech lands such an assignment is the general rule. Many vacancies in prominent positions are filled by outsiders from Slovakia and the Slovak representation in the federal offices in Prague is (in Czech public opinion) disproportionately high. The Czechs, twice as numerous as the Slovaks, also resent the preferential treatment of Slovakia with respect to the allocation of investment resources. This type of affirmative action to redress the imbalances of Slovak history is not at all appreciated by the Czechs. Even if some of the grievances may be more imaginary than real, this policy is potentially destructive to the cohesiveness of the Czechoslovak Socialist Republic.

ADAPTATION TO AND DEVIATION FROM THE SOVIET MODEL

The transformation of the pluralistic political system of prewar Czechoslovakia into a Stalinist, and subsequently a neo-Stalinist, system may be viewed as a "great leap backward." After some fifteen years of socialist construction, this country's economic performance was the most disappointing in the bloc, and the political system under Novotny's leadership was reaching the point of immobility.

Nothing of substance materialized out of Gottwald's postwar pledge to embark upon a Czechoslovak road to socialism. Instead, the Soviet version of Stalinism was adopted. The aim of the reformers in 1968 was to undo the main damage caused by the exaggerated emulation of all things Soviet. Implementation of the reformers' program precipitated the formulation and application of Brezhnev's doctrine of limited sovereignty. After the Soviet invasion of Czechoslovakia, the status quo ante was restored, and all the reforms were rescinded except one: the federalization of Czechoslovakia. The creation of parallel Czech and Slovak state structures, though weakened somewhat since 1968, does remain in existence.

Self-interest commands the Czechoslovak political elite to preserve the state of limited sovereignty. Awareness and fear of public hostility promotes a unity of convenience and indeed of necessity within the leadership. Under these circumstances Communist party rule is bound to be noninnovative. The Politburo fears that any innovation may contribute to the destabilization of the political system. In time, however, a timid, static system is apt to exhibit signs of aging and decrepitude.

At present, whereas the average Soviet citizen seems to accept the legitimacy of Communist party rule and is essentially loyal to the system, the average Czechoslovak citizen is not. Such a seemingly irreparable division points to a paradox and a certain irony: in 1948 the imposition of the Soviet model put Czechoslovakia on an unenlightened and in many respects a backward course.

It is not unlikely that under both internal and external pressure some change toward moderation and modernization of the present dysfunctional Czechoslovak regime will be achieved in the remaining years of this century.

NOTES

1. Among the most recent works is H. Gordon Skilling, *Czechoslovakia's Interrupted Revolution,* (Princeton: Princeton University Press, 1976).
2. See Jan F. Triska, "Messages from Czechoslovakia," *Problems of Communism,* November–December 1975, pp. 26–42.
3. *The New York Times,* April 14, 1977.

BIBLIOGRAPHY

Dubcek, Alexander. *Czechoslovakia's Blueprint for Freedom.* Edited by Paul Ello. Washington, D.C.: Acropolis, 1968.

Golan, Galia. *The Czechoslovak Reform Movement.* Cambridge: Cambridge University Press, 1971.

———. *Reform Rule in Czechoslovakia: The Dubcek Era, 1968–1969.* Cambridge: Cambridge University Press, 1973.

Jancar, Barbara W. *Czechoslovakia and the Absolute Monopoly of Power.* New York: Praeger, 1971.

Korbel, Josef. *Twentieth Century Czechoslovakia: The Meaning of Its History.* New York: Columbia University Press, 1977.

Kusin, Vladimir V. *The Czechoslovak Reform Movement.* Santa Barbara: ABC-Clio, 1973.

———. *The Intellectual Origins of the Prague Spring: The Development of Reformist Ideas in Czechoslovakia, 1958–1967.* Cambridge: Cambridge University Press, 1971.

Krejci, J. *Social Change and Stratification in Postwar Czechoslovakia.* London, 1972.

Oxley, A. et al. *Czechoslovakia: The Party and the People.* London: St. Martin, 1973.

Remington, Robin A., ed. *Winter in Prague: Documents on Czechoslovak Communism in Crisis.* Cambridge, Mass.: MIT Press, 1969.

Selucky, R. *Czechoslovakia: The Plan That Failed.* London, 1970.

Skilling, H. Gordon, *Czechoslovakia's Interrupted Revolution.* Princeton: Princeton University Press, 1976.

Suda, Zdenek. *The Czechoslovak Socialist Republic.* Baltimore: Johns Hopkins Press, 1969.

Svitak, Ivan. *The Czechoslovak Experiment, 1968–1969.* New York: Columbia University Press, 1971.

Taborsky, Edward. *Communism in Czechoslovakia, 1948–1960.* Princeton: Princeton University Press, 1961.

Ulc, Otto. *Politics in Czechoslovakia.* San Francisco: W. H. Freeman, 1974.

Zinner, Paul E. *Communist Strategy and Tactics in Czechoslovakia, 1918–1948.* London: Pall Mall, 1963.

5   German Democratic Republic

Arthur M. Hanhardt, Jr.

THE GDR TODAY

In recent years, the German Democratic Republic (GDR) has been steering a hazardous course between the integrative demands made by the Soviet Union and the pressures of the world economy. The ability of Erich Honecker, general secretary of the ruling Socialist Unity party (SED), to deal with these problems is hindered by the fact that his options are limited by the Soviet leadership and by the domestic situation in the GDR. Thus, the GDR's leaders have limited room for effective maneuver in dealing with rising domestic expectations that conflict with the demands of the international economy. Why does the GDR find itself in this predicament?

The Soviet Union is the principal trading partner of the GDR. Ever since the East German "economic miracle" of the early 1960s, which in some ways rivaled the rapid development of the West Germany economy in the early 1950s, the GDR and the Soviet Union have become increasingly intertwined economically. The interrelationship between the economies is especially important since it has approached the level of integration. That is, the GDR supplies the USSR with finished goods, while, in return, the Soviets send raw materials, including over 90 percent of the GDR's oil requirements. This trade structure has bound the GDR very closely to the Soviet Union, and the Soviet leadership has exploited its advantage systematically, although in the late 1960s the terms of trade showed a trend favoring the GDR.

In the 1970s, and particularly since the 1973–74 OPEC boycott, the economic position of the GDR has deteriorated. The economic decline has had two aspects. First, within the framework of greater integration within the Council for Mutual Economic Assistance (CMEA), the GDR and other East European states have had to help finance the development of Soviet natural resources. This has added a substantial, but unknown, amount to the GDR's financial burden. Second, and more important, the Soviets have gradually raised the prices of delivered raw materials while insisting that the prices it pays the GDR for finished goods remain unchanged. Higher costs and stable prices have put the GDR into an uncomfortable squeeze.

The economic discomfort of the GDR has several sources. The relationship with the USSR is one; another is the GDR leaders' commitment to keep domestic prices stable. According to official pronouncements the inflation affecting the capitalist world will not affect socialist economies. The SED leadership is painfully aware of the social unrest that would ensue, should prices for staples, fuel, and housing rise. The Polish experience of 1970 has not been ignored or forgotten. The SED leadership has responded by exhorting the work force to achieve greater productivity in order to hold off price increases.

Another source of GDR economic problems is its relationship to the world economy. If productivity is to rise to pay for more expensive raw materials and to subsidize domestic prices, then relief must be sought in Western markets. The GDR had great expectations in this respect in the mid-1970s, when increased international recognition ended GDR political isolation from the West. In 1974 the United States finally recognized the GDR, and East Germany became a full member of the United Nations.

Access to international markets was seen as a means by which the GDR could modernize and expand its economy. The industrial skill of the GDR, particularly in specialized areas of manufacture such as precision instruments, would gain the recognition and rewards that had previously been denied to a country that before its partition had shown up on nearly every list of the world's "top ten" industrial nations. Expanded Western trade had an unspoken political aspect as well. Trade flexibility might give the GDR some leverage vis-a-vis the Soviet Union: benefits denied by the Soviets might be obtained elsewhere.[1]

Diplomatic recognition and participation in international commerce came hard on the heels of the oil boycott and consequent economic problems in the West. Trade figures rose but so did prices; the GDR was becoming increasingly indebted as a result of its expanded Western trade. The best estimate for 1976 indicates that about 24 percent of GDR foreign trade went to the West. Still, exports were insufficient to cover the cost of Western imports. In 1976 the U.S. dollar indebtedness of the

GDR rose to 5.1 billion, up from 4.2 billion in 1975.[2] Exact figures are difficult to obtain, but it is clear from the trends that the GDR has not escaped the effects of world trade conditions.

Despite these problems, the SED has remained ostentatiously loyal to the Soviet Union. This loyalty was clearly demonstrated in the 1975 GDR-USSR Friendship Treaty, at the Ninth Congress of the SED in 1976, and at the Conference of European Communist Parties also in 1976. Most recently, during the sixtieth anniversary of the Russian Revolution in 1977, the SED went all out to demonstrate its unity with the Communist Party of the Soviet Union. Erich Honecker declared at the Moscow celebration of the October Revolution: "We know that the alliance with the Communist Party of the Soviet Union and with the Union of Soviet Socialist Republics is an alliance with the future."[3] This theme was repeated so often in the GDR that it became too much for some East Germans to bear.[4] Indeed one researcher found that in the October 1977 issues of the official SED newspaper, *Neues Deutschland,* coverage of "the sixtieth anniversary of the Bolshevik Revolution ... was accorded roughly six times as much space as was devoted to the observation of the founding of the GDR (October 7)."[5]

In the GDR today popular lack of enthusiasm for the bond with the USSR is a significant source of tension. Indeed, some segments of public opinion think that the industrially advanced GDR, with its high standard of living (by Soviet bloc measures), should not slavishly follow the Soviet lead on the road to socialism, and that German conditions, German experience, and German leadership should modify Soviet models.

Manifestations of tension take a variety of forms, ranging from rowdyism to support for the kind of reform communism espoused by Rudolf Bahro.[6] While anomic manifestations are easily dealt with by the state security apparatus, the ideas generated by Bahro and other intellectuals—mostly writers—who have challenged SED orthodoxy are more difficult for the state and the party to handle. There have been several occasions when oppositional groupings have challenged the dominant authority, first of Walter Ulbricht, who led the SED from 1949 to 1971, and then of his successor, Erich Honecker, who has had to cope with critical voices since mid-1976.

In comparing the political system of the GDR with that of the East European states, it must be remembered that the GDR has had a unique pattern of emergence and growth. In a generation, East Germany has been transformed from a vanquished and hated foe to a firm and integral member of the Soviet bloc.

THE SOVIET ZONE OF GERMANY:
AN HISTORICAL FRAMEWORK

The Communist system in the GDR owes its origins to the complex
and interrelated events that accompanied the end of World War II in
Europe and led to the division of what remained of the German Reich
into three—later four—Allied zones of occupation. Although the Allied
Control Council was meant to be an administrative agency for all of the
zones, its formal capacities as a central administration were few. This
meant that as time passed and as the wartime alliance all too quickly
degenerated into competition and conflict, the commitment at Potsdam
to treat Germany as a whole faded. Compounding this growing fragmentation was the addition of France as the fourth occupying power.
France had not been present at Yalta and Potsdam and refused to be
bound by any notion of a unified approach to a future Germany.

The "Ulbricht group," German communists sent to Soviet-occupied
Germany from Moscow in April 1945, carried instructions reflecting
Soviet intentions of treating postwar Germany as a single unit.[7] Ulbricht and his colleagues from the Communist Party of Germany (KPD),
all of whom had spent much of their time during the 1930s and the war
years in the Soviet Union, were under orders to go slowly in the recon-
stitution of the KPD, concentrating instead on placing "their" people in
important administrative posts in close cooperation with the Soviet
Military Administration in Germany (SMAD).

The Soviet Union's initially cautious approach was motivated by the
idea that Soviet influence could be maximized throughout postwar
Germany by a low-profile presence, emphasizing cooperation among
democratic, antifascist forces. This strategy met with some success.
There was considerable feeling among German survivors on both the
left and the right that only broadly based cooperation among political
forces could lead to policies that would prevent a recurrence of Nazism
in Germany.

It soon became apparent that the all-German approach had limitations from the Soviet point of view. Inter-Allied cooperation had revealed severe problems, and the SMAD was aware that its influence
was going to be insignificant beyond the Soviet Zone. Consequently the
SMAD issued Order No. 2 on June 10, 1945, authorizing creation of
antifascist democratic parties and labor unions.

The day after Order No. 2 was issued, the KPD was formally organized. Three other parties were also founded in the Soviet Zone: the
Social Democratic Party of Germany (SPD), the Christian Democratic

Union (CDU), and the Liberal Democratic Party of Germany (LDPD). All four parties were joined in August 1945 in an Antifascist Democratic Bloc. With the establishment of this bloc the first period in the history of the Soviet zone/GDR, known as the Antifascist Democratic Order, began.

The Antifascist Democratic Order is the name given to developments in Soviet Zone politics from 1945 to the foundation of the GDR in October 1949. These four years brought massive changes in the political system, economy, and social structure in the area under Soviet control.

Changes in political life in the Soviet Zone came swiftly, once political parties had been organized. From the beginning the SPD moved toward a unification of the socialist forces. However, the idea was coolly received by the KPD, which preferred to build on its special relationship with the Soviet Military Administration and to consolidate its own position vis-a-vis the public. Early elections held in Berlin in the fall of 1945 indicated considerable support for an independent SPD in the Western sectors of that divided city. These election results plus strong opposition to unification from the Western zones led to a changing of the fronts. Now the Communists were pressing for unity with the support of the SMAD. In April 1946 the Socialist Otto Grotewohl and the Communist Wilhelm Pieck clasped hands, symbolically uniting the two socialist movements in the Socialist Unity Party (SED). Initial parity between Social Democrats and Communists in the SED leadership yielded to dominance by the latter. Increasingly the SED became the mixed cadre and mass party which it has remained ever since.

The Christian Democratic Union represented unification of another kind. Conflict between Catholics and Protestants had been seen as a factor contributing to the rise of Nazism in prewar Germany. A union of Protestants and Catholics would tie them together in a political force that would forward the cause of democratic politics and Christian values. Although its first programs took liberal social positions, including public ownership of major industries, the CDU came increasingly into conflict with the occupation authorities and the SED over religious and political issues. One leader after another was forced out of the party and subsequently left for the West. By 1949 the Christian Democrats had accepted SED leadership.

German liberalism, represented by the Liberal Democrats, was the fourth political tradition to be represented in the new party structure. This organization articulated the needs of the bourgeoisie and private business. The importance of the Liberal Democrats has diminished as the private sector has declined, but it remains as a symbolic base of support for the Socialist Unity Party. The presence of several political parties in the GDR indicates the need to bind the groups which those parties "represent" (e.g., the middle class, the religious believers) to the leadership of the SED. While similar parties were banned elsewhere in Eastern Europe, the GDR remains in a state of transition to one-party rule, which may yet take years to achieve.

The CDU and LDPD were joined by other parties and mass organizations to complement the work of the SED. The Democratic Farmers' Party of Germany and the National Democratic Party of Germany were established in 1948. The Farmers' Party was designated to aid the SED in organizing the agricultural sector. The National Democrats were founded following an amnesty of former Nazis and military officers. Many of its members had become associated with the "National Committee 'Free Germany'" while in Soviet captivity. They represented a source of support for the newly emerging system and were organized toward that end.

In addition to the parties, several mass organizations helped to transform the political scene in the 1945–49 period as part of what became the "National Front of Democratic Germany." The Free German Trade Union Federation was founded shortly after the Soviet Military Administration's Order No. 2. Originally the Trade Union Federation was the vehicle used by the Socialists in an effort to build their strength in competition with the Communists. As the Trade Union Federation came under the increasing influence of the Socialist Unity Party, it was integrated into the economic changes sweeping the Soviet Zone.

Three further mass organizations were gathered into the National Front. The Free German Youth was based on earlier German models and the Soviet Komsomol. Especially important in the formation of new cadres as the SED consolidated its position, the youth organization has produced many of the current GDR leaders, including SED General Secretary Erich Honecker.[8]

The Democratic Women's Association of Germany and the Cultural Association were the other mass organizations of the National Front. These organizations and parties have provided a symbolic pluralism in the political system of the GDR. During the early years they frequently articulated vital interests, some of which clashed with the program of the SED. The SED prevailed. In the 1945–49 period, many activists, particularly those associated with the Social Democrats, the Christian Democrats, and the Liberals, left the Soviet Zone.

Changes in the economy of the Soviet Zone were manifold. Among them was the Soviet reparations program. Originally Soviet reparations were to come from its own zone plus a percentage of the production of the other zones. In exchange the Soviets were to supply food to the West. This arrangement broke down and the Soviets stepped up their reparations program, dismantling and carrying off over 1,000 factories and converting over 200 industrial operations into Soviet stock corporations. Production from these corporations was taken by the Soviets. Other changes resulted from Soviet policies aimed at nationalizing banks, large industrial enterprises, Nazi holdings, and the property of people who had fled from the Soviet Zone. Nationalization and socialization further hindered the productivity of an already truncated economy.

The social and economic policies of the Soviet Military Administration and the SED also had far-ranging effects in agriculture. The large landed estates were converted into state farms. All holdings of over 100 hectares were expropriated. The land seized was distributed to landless farmers, agricultural laborers, and German expellees from Eastern Europe. Thus the conditions for later collectivization were established. The Farmers' Party played a significant role in this "revolution on the land" by helping the SED bridge the ideological gap between the urban and rural elements of the working class. Thus the countryside was transformed, while those who could not accept the change left for the West.

The large-scale migration to the West had an impact on the social structure of the Soviet Zone that was as profound as changes in the political system and economy of the early postwar years. There was a considerable leveling of the "heights" of German society in the Soviet Zone. Dispossessed landholders were joined in the West by many leaders of political organizations and economic enterprises who saw the policies of the Soviets and the SED severely restricting their freedoms. This out-migration had two implications. First it meant that the social structure was adapting to the Soviet model of a workers' and peasants' state. Secondly, potential opponents of political and social change were leaving the field to those who either accepted the new order or had made their peace with the emerging socialist system. Although this did not mean an end to opposition from within, it did simplify matters.

By 1949, when the two German states were officially established, the antifascist era was drawing to a close, and the SED felt secure enough to make significant changes, which were announced at two key SED meetings: the Third Party Congress (1950) and the Second Party Conference (1952). The Third Party Congress transformed the SED into a Leninist party fully recognizing the disciplines of democratic centralism and Soviet leadership. The Second Party Conference called for the coordination of GDR development with the Soviet Union in a process which continues to this day. In addition the SED called for increasingly intense class conflict to assure the triumph of the workers and peasants. Together, these pronouncements launched the GDR on a road which led from Soviet occupation in 1945–49, to its status as the always reliable "junior partner" of the Soviet Union in the 1970s.

POLITICAL DEVELOPMENTS, 1949–1971

The following discussion of the main lines of political development in the GDR from 1949 through 1971 will follow the chronological periods the SED has itself defined. These periods are the construction of socialism, from 1949 through 1958; the completion of socialist production relations, from 1958 through 1963; and the comprehensive construction of socialism, from 1963 to the Eighth SED Party Congress (1971), which ended the "Ulbricht era."

The period of the construction of socialism in the GDR was characterized by several significant developments. Politically, the dominance of the SED was established. In the economy the expansion of the socialist sector was accelerated. And the social system moved toward an idealized socialist model.

The predominance of the SED had been apparent in the 1945–49 period. In fact the National Front, which fielded a single list of candidates in the first election to the People's Chamber (Parliament) in 1949, clearly showed the superiority of the SED which has continued ever since. The SED held 100 seats, while the Christian Democrats and Liberals had 60 each. The National Democrats and the Farmers' Party each had 30 seats, the Trade Union Federation had 40, and the other mass organizations, a total of 80 parliamentary seats. Since many of the members of the Trade Union Federation and mass organizations were also SED members, SED preeminence was assured.

SED influence quickly spread through the state apparatus as well. At the national level the ministries were dominated by the SED and the decisions of the SED Politburo were made binding on the government apparatus. Central control over state governments was assured in 1952 with the transformation of the traditional *Laender* into 14 administrative districts.

While the SED was establishing its dominance over the framework of government, its leadership had to overcome challenges from within its own ranks and from the people. A major challenge from within the party came in the wake of the revolt of June 1953, the first of the massive uprisings in the Soviet bloc. Insecurity following the death of Stalin in March 1953, combined with a distressed economy, led the SED to announce a "New Course" which aimed unsuccessfully at reducing popular dissatisfaction. The intraparty debate on what path to follow in the light of uncertain developments in the Soviet Union resulted in the formation of a group opposed to Ulbricht, led by the minister of state security, Wilhelm Zaisser, and the editor of the party newspaper, *Neues Deutschland,* Rudolf Herrnstadt.

Following the revolt, the Soviet leadership felt compelled to support Ulbricht, opting to preserve continuity while attending to its own problems. Since Ulbricht's opposition had connections with the defeated Beria faction in Moscow, it was possible for him to strike back and reassert his leadership in a purge of Zaisser, Herrnstadt, and their sympathizers.

The next challenge from within the SED came after the Twentieth Party Congress of the CPSU in 1956. De-Stalinization and the discussion of a "third (socialist) path" between the Soviet model and capitalism led to a lively debate among party philosophers and economists in 1956–57. The debate clashed sharply with Ulbricht's orthodoxy. Again the course of events, this time in Poland and Hungary, turned a rising oppositional tide in Ulbricht's favor. Not willing to risk another 1953 in the GDR, the Soviet leadership backed Ulbricht in a purge of Wolfgang Harich and others associated with ideological and economic revisionism. This was to be the last major intraparty threat to Ulbricht's leadership until his ouster.[9]

A severe challenge to the SED came in June 1953, when German workers rioted in East Berlin and elsewhere in the GDR, as a result of economic pressures generated by the expansion of the socialist sector of the economy. While the socialist sector grew rapidly during the first five-year plan (1951–55)—first as a result of nationalization and later with the return of the Soviet stock corporations—the infrastructure, in terms of plant, equipment, and investment, was inadequate. High work norms, unrealistic plan goals, lack of trained personnel, and agricultural collectivization together created unbearable pressures. The New Course sought to relieve rising dissatisfaction by slowing the tempo of socialization, but the attempt failed. Driven to higher productivity without higher wages, workers went on a rampage in East Berlin and at 271 other locations in the GDR on June 17. Soviet troops and tanks were used to quell the worst riots.[10]

The revolt made clear that socialist consciousness had not penetrated the GDR citizenry sufficiently to sustain the pace of the first five-year plan. Consequently the plan was revised downward several times, while allowing for progress toward building the energy and industrial base for future development. The revised plan was also coordinated with the newly established CMEA, in which the GDR was to play an increasingly important role.

The second five-year plan encountered so many problems that it was discarded in 1958 in favor of a seven-year plan designed to harmonize with the rhythm and demands of Soviet plans. The seven-year plan assured the increasing dependence of the GDR on the economy of the Soviet Union. All of the plans favored the development of heavy industry and required increased imports of raw materials, since the GDR has few resources beside lignite ("brown coal"), salts (for chemicals), and uranium (exported to the Soviet Union).

While the events of 1953 had shown that socialist goals and socialist reality were still far apart, it was clear that the construction of a socialist society was progressing. During this period efforts were undertaken to collectivize the land parcelled out in the postwar land reform. Although the pace was slow, the SED delegated party workers to assume leadership roles in rural areas and to run collectives. In the cities, the middle class and private businesses were systematically undercut. Middle-class children had difficulty obtaining access to higher education. Private businesses faced problems with finance and supplies. At the same time thousands of workers were enrolled in the Workers' and Peasants' Faculties, where they could attain university matriculation standards and gain career advantages upon graduation. These policies had long-range effects on the social structure of the GDR and cultivated its image as a workers' and peasants' state progressing toward socialism.

The second period proclaimed the completion of socialist relations in production. Beginning with the Fifth SED Party Congress in 1958 and ending with the Sixth Party Congress in 1963, the period was characterized by mobilization and consolidation. Mobilization took several forms, ranging from the proclamation of "ten commandments of socialist morality," through educational reforms and the propagandistic goal of surpassing the Federal Republic of Germany in important areas of consumption, to the comprehensive collectivization of agriculture. These acts of mobilization caused a flood of emigration. In turn, this massive movement to the West led to an act of consolidation: construction of the Berlin Wall in 1961.

By 1958 Walter Ulbricht, strengthened by his survival of the challenges of 1953 and 1956–57, issued a socialist ten commandments (e.g., "Thou shalt protect and multiply the people's property"). Ulbricht's proclamation was part of a concerted action to expand socialist consciousness and to propagate the socialist personality through secular parallels to religious institutions such as socialist marriage and socialist communion, the latter a ritual for Youth initiation.

More effective than socialist rites in mobilizing youth was the transformation of the educational system. A mandatory ten-year polytechnical curriculum was introduced in 1958–59. The aim of educational reforms was to give students strong preparation in the sciences and technical fields along with thorough training in the disciplines of labor (a weekly "day of practical work") and of Marxism-Leninism. Advanced education was made available on a broad basis through evening and correspondence curricula as well as at expanded universities and technological institutes. Massive efforts were undertaken to encourage working-class people to advance through education. The educational system has become a source of considerable and justified pride in the GDR. And there is evidence that the political socialization that is taking place throughout the educational system is having a positive impact in inculcating the values and beliefs of socialism. Students who have passed through the system owe their place and status in good measure to training provided by the state.[11]

The GDR economy was relatively strong in 1958–59, and perhaps as a consequence Walter Ulbricht promised that the GDR would surpass the Federal Republic of Germany (FRG) in per capita consumption of important foodstuffs and consumer products. This goal was unrealistic. Other planned goals also proved to be unrealistic, in part because they relied on unachievably high rates or productivity. The need to produce more without increasing investments, costs, and labor has been a constant theme in GDR economic development. Failure to improve productivity led to the scrapping of the seven-year plan begun in 1958.

The seven-year plan was supposed to bring the GDR economy in line with that of the Soviet Union, but a combination of impossible goals (e.g., an 84 percent increase in productivity, 110 percent increase in machine construction and 85 percent increase in consumer goods), the agrarian collectivization drive, and the construction of the Berlin Wall led to a cancellation of the plan in 1962. The gap between promise and performance was too wide to bridge, even with the good start of 1958–59.

The full collectivization of agriculture, that is, the transformation of all farms into agricultural cooperatives by 1960 was a goal ratified by the Fifth SED Party Congress. This goal was achieved, albeit at considerable cost. While collectivization had been pursued since 1952, the pace had been slow. By 1956 there were roughly 6,300 agricultural cooperatives. By mid-1960 this figure had jumped to over 19,000 with half of the increase coming after 1958. Collectivization met with considerable resistance, which in turn was met by massive SED intervention in the rural areas. Factory workers were assigned to the countryside. Endless debates and discussions were undertaken to convince farmers to give up their independence and join a cooperative. Eighty-four percent of the arable land of the GDR was put under the control of the cooperatives by 1961. For all practical purposes the goal of full socialization of agriculture had been achieved. The costs came in lowered productivity (at least in the short run) and the massive emigration of farmers to the FRG.

Farmers were not the only ones leaving the GDR in 1960 and 1961. The intensity of the collectivization campaign led Germans employed in other sectors of the economy to question their future prospects in the GDR. Also contributing to massive emigration was the positive attraction of the "good life" in the FRG, with its availability of consumer goods and other rewards. While the greatest number of emigrants had been registered in the turbulent year 1953 (over 300,000), nearly 200,000 arrived in the FRG in 1960, and in the first eight months of 1961 over 150,000 people had left the GDR.

This population drain, a total of over 2.5 million in the twelve years between 1949 and 1961, could not be tolerated by the GDR leadership, especially since the great majority of those leaving were in their productive years and represented skilled crafts and professions. The SED response was the construction of the Berlin Wall on August 13, 1961.

Although widely interpreted as an act of desperation, which it was, the sealing of the Berlin sector boundary and the enhanced fortification of the East-West demarcation line also meant that, for the first time since its establishment, the GDR leadership could begin to consolidate its regime within its own borders. The population of the GDR now had to either oppose or accept the system without the alternative of leaving. The lack of large-scale overt opposition since August 1961 would indicate that most GDR citizens—either actively or passively—have accommodated themselves to the post-1961 realities.

In the last phase of the Ulbricht era—that of the comprehensive construction of socialism (1963–71)—dynamic elements emanating from economic reforms guided the lines of political development. At the Sixth SED Party Congress (1963) a "New Economic System" was proclaimed, modifying important aspects of the central planning system, which had deteriorated into chaos in the early 1960s. The New Economic System was accompanied by changes in party organization, the emergence of a "state consciousness" among the East German population, and strained relations with the Soviet Union leading to Ulbricht's ouster in May 1971.

The planned economy of the GDR was having considerable difficulty fulfilling the demands of an expanding socialist industrial sector while attempting to provide more and better consumer goods. Clearly the way out lay in the direction of decentralized management and a system of economic incentives. Both paths were taken in the New Economic System. Associations of nationally owned enterprises created rationalized industrial complexes. Although managers were given responsibilities within a planned framework, they and their work were judged by standards of profitability, turnover, and cost effectiveness. This was in accord with the theories of the Soviet economist Yevsei Liberman, who also suggested material incentives for both managers and workers. Ideology was toned down while the "economic levers" of profitability and personal rewards were emphasized.

In tandem with the New Economic System was a shift to party organization according to the production principle, then favored by Khrushchev for the Soviet party. By organizing the SED along the lines of activities in construction, agriculture, industry, and ideology, party organization could parallel the economic organization. This reorganization led to an infusion of young and technically competent party members at the middle level of responsibility. Their intrusion threatened older party cadres to the extent that the production principle was abandoned in 1966 in favor of a return to the territorial principle of state and local party organization, which had never been completely abandoned. Again this shift was in line with changes in the Soviet Union, where the territorial principle was restored shortly after Khrushchev's ouster in 1964. In spite of the failure of the production principle, the dynamic influence of the new cadres was felt in the SED as well as the economy.[12]

An emphasis on youth and education during this period, along with continuing improvement in the standard of living, led to the emergence of what West German analysts have called a "state consciousness" in the GDR. Cut off from the West, citizens of the GDR began to take pride in what was becoming their own "economic miracle." Western observers noted increasing identification of citizens with a state that was providing comprehensive social security and an increasingly better life.[13]

In the second half of the 1960s there was considerable stress on the role of technology in the comprehensive construction of socialism. The success of the economy and of the SED was seen in the expansion of the economy through technological sophistication, in what was termed a "scientific-technical revolution." Industries such as instrumentation, electronics, and chemicals received special attention and investment funds. Training in these fields was also emphasized and led to rapid growth on a relatively weak infrastructure. This weakness led to economic difficulties in 1970, when the economy could no longer keep the pace. The New Economic System, which had undergone modification, was finally abandoned in 1970.[14]

To Walter Ulbricht, the scientific-technical revolution was an important means by which the GDR could assert itself within CMEA and also show the West what socialism was capable of producing. Because of his seniority among Communist leaders, Ulbricht began formulating the theory that a technologically based and developed socialist society was a special stage on the way to full communism with its own laws. The transition to a communist society, according to this interpretation, would be a long process. Increasingly—and irritatingly—Ulbricht began to lecture other Communist leaders, including the Soviets, and to pose as the "father" of the GDR.

Tensions grew between Ulbricht and the Soviet leadership under Brezhnev. Not only did there seem to be a clash of personalities based on Ulbricht's "more Communist than thou" attitude, there were also substantive differences between East Berlin and Moscow over detente and policy toward the FRG. Ulbricht was very uncomfortable with Brezhnev's approach to the West. After all his political career had been saved by the East-West conflict in 1953 and 1956–57, and a "front-line" mentality was good propaganda. The Soviet Union was also promoting the normalization of relations between the two Germanys and cultivating Soviet-FRG trade. Both policies were anathema to Ulbricht. Improved relations with FRG threatened an intolerable influx of Western influence. Ulbricht viewed Soviet trade with the FRG as a diminution of GDR influence.

By the spring of 1971 it was time to replace the uppity and footdragging Ulbricht. Ulbricht was ousted between his appearance at the Twenty-fourth Congress of the CPSU in the spring of 1971 (where he spoke of his personal acquaintance with Lenin) and the Eighth SED Party Congress in June 1971. In contrast to the experience of other East

European countries and the USSR, the transition was smooth, as Erich Honecker, former leader of the Free German Youth, took over the party reins. Ulbricht went into honorable retirement as titular SED chairman and died in 1973 at the age of 80. He left behind a stabilized social and political system, which was on the verge of receiving the international recognition that Ulbricht had so urgently desired. The economy had been stabilized as well, although a weak infrastructure and dependence on imported raw materials hampered access to the heights of achievement and world markets.

THE HONECKER LEADERSHIP

The SED claims that the GDR is presently a "developed socialist system" in the process of making the transition to communism under the leadership of Erich Honecker. Honecker made significant changes in the SED's political line at its Eighth Party Congress. While not easing up on the need for scientific-technical development in the GDR, he emphasized that the party must return to the basic principles of Marxism-Leninism. That is to say, the welfare of the workers and peasants must have first priority in a socialist state.

A return to ideological basics was swiftly reflected in the economy with the conversion of the remaining private sector into nationally owned enterprises. Also nationalized were enterprises with mixed private and state ownership (borrowed from Chinese practice of the 1950s). Over 100,000 enterprises were affected by this move, which effectively eliminated any significant private production.

A new line was also evident in Honecker's emphasis on the GDR's ties to other socialist countries and to the Soviet Union. Gone was the notion that the GDR was somehow different from the other socialist countries. This shift was reflected in the constitutional changes adopted in 1974. The revised constitution no longer spoke of a German nation divided into two states. The GDR was now defined as a "socialist workers' and peasants' state . . . forever and irrevocably allied with the Soviet Union."

In fact the course set by Erich Honecker in 1971 has been steadfastly followed, bringing the GDR into closer alignment with the Soviet Union both in economic and in political affairs. This course was confirmed by the GDR-Soviet Friendship Treaty of October 1975 and at the Ninth SED Party Congress in 1976, which adopted a new party program and statute.

The new statute made Honecker general secretary of the party in line with the current Soviet usage. The party now numbers about two million members and candidates, or about 11 percent of the GDR population of nearly eighteen million. This percentage is almost twice the ratio (6 percent) of CPSU members and candidates to the Soviet population. Rather than an exclusively elite party, the SED functions as a mass and cadre (elite) party. Indeed the SED is an instrument of mobilization and leadership. That there is concern over the relative size of the SED was articulated by Honecker in his report of the Central Committee to the Ninth Congress, wherein he urged that Leninist principles be used in the selection of new members and announced that there would be no increase in total membership.

The National Front of the GDR (formerly the National Front of Democratic Germany) continues to serve as an umbrella for the parties and mass organizations. Overall the importance of the minor parties has decreased. In spite of the fact that the Christian Democratic Union has experienced a slight growth in membership, its relative position has declined. Traditionally first among the fraternal National Front parties, it has recently yielded its place to the Democratic Farmers' Party, signaling the relative importance of the agricultural sector. Although the multiparty system is a "deviant" and perhaps declining feature of the GDR political system, it shows no immediate signs of being phased out.

The mass organizations represented in the National Front continue to serve the SED. The trade union, youth, and women's organizations are of particular importance in this respect. The women's association deserves special mention because of the key role that women play in the GDR economy, which suffers chronically from an acute labor shortage. Just under 50 percent of the labor force is female and over 85 percent of the women of working age are either employed or under apprenticeship. A World Congress of Women was held in East Berlin in 1975, and much is made of the legal equality of women in the GDR, which was firmly established by the Family Law Code of 1965. The economic importance of women is not reflected in the political leadership of the SED or the other mass organizations. Only about 13 percent of the SED Central Committee are women and less than one-third of the trade union association presidium are female. There is no evidence that this situation is the source of any active protest by East German women.

The varying composition and character of the top political leadership reveals much about change in the GDR. The Ulbricht group, charged with restoring political life in the Soviet occupation zone in cooperation with the Soviet Military Administration, formed the nucleus of the elite that guided the fortunes of the GDR in its early years. These top functionaries, who had been in exile in the Soviet Union, asserted themselves in the crises of 1953 and 1956–57. Not only did members of the Ulbricht group have strong Soviet backing, they were also extremely effective at political infighting and were able gradually to coopt loyal new members into the SED inner circle.

The post-1961 consolidation along with the emphasis on economic and technological development required the recruitment and advancement of a new type of elite member, one who was technically trained and competent as well as politically loyal to the SED.[15] Many of the potentially dissatisfied had left the GDR before 1961. Those who remained owed their advancement and education to the system. It is symbolic that Ulbricht's successor had been the first chairman of the Free German Youth in 1946. Indeed since Honecker replaced Ulbricht, more and more form youth organization leaders have been coopted into the top ranks of the SED apparatus, replacing the Ulbricht group as its members grew old, retired, and died.

Honecker himself has consolidated his leading position. In addition to being SED general secretary and chairman of the National Defense Council, he was made chairman of the Council of State in October 1976, thus combining all major roles in the GDR leadership, much as Brezhnev does in the Soviet Union. Earlier in 1976 Konrad Nauman and Werner Felfe had joined the SED Politburo. Both men were colleagues of Honecker in the Free German Youth. It is interesting to note as well that the SED inner circle, again following current Soviet practice, includes the ministers of state security and national defense.

Honecker's promise to improve the lot of the workers and peasants was implemented by a series of measures aimed at raising wages at the low end of the income scale and providing better housing and increased benefits in terms of vacations, pensions, and working conditions. Honecker also promised stable prices. Since then, the worldwide inflationary trend has placed enormous pressure on the GDR's economy, which is dependent on imported raw materials. Economic pressures are compounded by the SED's commitment to a comprehensive system of welfare and public services.

The SED has responded to these problems with a program of "socialist intensification," aimed at raising labor productivity. At the same time, prices for imports from East and West continue to rise, while export prices are not keeping pace. With the Polish specter constantly in mind, the SED leadership has responded by bringing back to power the technocrats who had been successful in the mid-1960s. The urgency of the situation is reflected in virtually every edition of the party newspaper, *Neues Deutschland.* The goal of the intensification campaign is a 30 percent increase in labor productivity by 1980 through more efficient utilization of materials and increased automation.

Socioeconomic difficulties have been accompanied by problems related to cultural policy. While a feeling of state consciousness has broadened the SED's base of support, intellectuals—particularly writers —have been a source of grave concern to the SED. This concern has been heightened because much of the literature and art to which the SED objects has been "socialist"-inspired. The East German cultural community took seriously Honecker's statement at the Eighth SED Party Congress that if one proceeded from a firm socialist basis, there could be no taboos in art and literature. The expectations of cultural liberalism which this statement aroused were not fulfilled by subsequent policies.

Two incidents in 1976 demonstrated the limits of what the cultural policy of the GDR would tolerate. Wolf Biermann, a popular poet and balladeer, had emigrated to the GDR from West Germany in 1953 for ideological reasons, attracted by the communist promise in the East. His songs, while condemning Western capitalism, also criticized socialist bureaucracy in the GDR. His uncompromising communism brought him into conflict with the SED, which banned his public appearances in 1964. Following a semipublic concert in an East Berlin church in the fall of 1976, Biermann was given permission to undertake a concert tour in the FRG. Once Biermann was out of the country, his GDR citizenship was revoked. Biermann's exile caused a wave of protest among East German artists and writers. The protesters were, in turn, subjected to reprisals, forcing some to withdraw their public support for Biermann.

In a related case, Rainer Kunze, who published his novel *The Wonderful Years* in West Germany, was expelled from the GDR Writers' Association in November 1976. Kunze's stories were apparently not sufficiently "positive" in character and the Writers' Association accused him of "revisionism."

The Biermann and Kunze cases underline the difficulty the SED has had bringing cultural life into line with the demands of socialist realism. During the earlier years of the GDR, efforts to encourage worker-writers and to create proletarian art forms failed. East German writers have produced some outstanding literary works—the writings of Volker Braun, Anna Seghers, Christa Wolf, and others—but the relationship between the requirements of artistic excellence and the demands of the cultural bureaucracy has often been unsatisfactory.

INTERNATIONAL RELATIONS

The political development of the GDR must be seen against the background of international politics.[16] This background is essentially a triptych of three overlapping panels: GDR interactions with the Soviet Union and Eastern Europe; GDR-West German relations; and detente between the Soviet Union and the United States.

Beginning with the occupation, ties between the Soviet Zone/GDR and the Soviet Union have had ranking importance. Once prospects for reunification did not materialize, the interests of the SED leadership lay in the closest possible relationship with CMEA and the Soviet Union. Indeed, the economic development of the GDR has been closely related to its evolving status as a "junior partner" of the Soviets. This relationship has enhanced the GDR's prestige in Eastern Europe, where since 1963 it has enjoyed the highest standard of living of the East European countries. On the cost side, the GDR has had to pay dearly in terms of unfavorable trade relations with the Soviet Union. The Soviets supply the GDR with all of its natural gas, 90 percent of its oil and 60–70 percent of its nonferrous metals. The prices for these raw materials have gone up, while those of GDR exports have only been able to recoup about two-thirds of the increase.

Relations with the Soviet Union were somewhat strained in the latter part of the Ulbricht era. Since then they have been restored to the inseparability confirmed by the Friendship Treaty and the GDR constitution. The GDR and the Soviet Union rely on each other for support. For example, during the 1976 Conference of European Communist Parties in East Berlin, *Neues Deutschland,* while remaining true to its commitment to publish all speeches, including those of the Eurocommunists, mounted a vigorous campaign before the meeting to make clear that the Soviet experience with the dictatorship of the proletariat was a necessary phase in any transition from capitalism to communism.

Such loyalty has had a mixed reaction in Eastern Europe. Wartime memories linger. The wealth of the GDR promotes jealousies. Nonetheless the key military importance of the superbly equipped National People's Army within the Warsaw Treaty Organization has been accepted. The cultural orthodoxy and conservatism of the GDR, however, has not enhanced its popularity among its eastern neighbors.

GDR policy toward the Federal Republic of Germany is aimed at *Abgrenzung,* or the barring of West German influence. Throughout its history, the GDR has had to deal with influences from West Germany and West Berlin, which exert a strong attraction on the East German population. Western TV is available in most of the GDR and, since the normalization of relations between East and West Germany in 1972, there has been a huge influx of visitors from the Federal Republic and West Berlin. The SED feared this influx and has waged a continuous campaign against West German influence, in spite of its commitment to peaceful coexistence. Border incidents, visa charges, financial arrangements, the status of West Berlin and particularly emigration, all remain points of friction between the two Germanys. Applications for emigration from the GDR to West Germany have numbered well over two hundred thousand and have been turned into an expression of protest by those dissatisfied with their lot. The drive toward greater integration with the Soviet Union and CMEA is closely related to *Abgrenzung* in German-German relations.

Much the same holds for GDR foreign policy within the framework of detente between the United States and the Soviet Union. As the GDR moves toward socialist integration, it narrows its capacity to trade with the West. Economic resources cannot be stretched far enough to reap maximum benefit from East-West trade, which is becoming increasingly expensive to the GDR.

On the political front, relations with the West are tempered by the fact that the Four Powers still have responsibility for Berlin, as determined by the Quadripartite Agreement on Berlin of 1971. This arrangement sets limits to what can be done in Berlin without endangering relations between the Soviet Union and the United States. Berlin remains a touchstone for detente, and the GDR must keep this in mind as it pursues *Abgrenzung.*

Across all threee aspects of the international picture is the common theme of the GDR-Soviet connection. This relationship is crucial for the future of the GDR. There is a residue of anti-Soviet feeling in the GDR that more than thirty years has not expunged. No matter how far socialist integration progresses in theory, it remains to be seen to what extent and for how long it will be accepted by the East Germans. At this point they have no alternatives. Not even the dissidents provide a viable competing perspective. Meanwhile, economic troubles in the West are prompting many to count their blessings in the security that the GDR system provides.

CONCLUSIONS AND PROSPECTS

The GDR is highly integrated into the Soviet bloc. The course of its development as a socialist system has led East Germany into a period of relative prosperity and high economic achievement. Indeed a reading of the official report on the GDR economic plan for 1977 would lead one to the conclusion that the plan went well: all goals were achieved or surpassed.[17]

Yet the same document contains as undertone of uncertainty that has been present in the GDR since 1976. Although all may have been well in 1977, the balance sheet concludes, more will have to be done in 1978 and subsequently to consolidate earlier "historic" achievements. The fact that exhortations to the workers to "give their all" in the name of the thirtieth anniversary of the GDR were circulated two years in advance of the event is evidence of a painful awareness that the worker, through ever-increasing productivity, will be the source of economic salvation. Even though the GDR has done well in improving the workers' standard of living, there is uncertainty about how much more can be accomplished without increased investment in plant and equipment. Expanded investment would have a negative impact on the availability of consumer amenities. Such a development would conflict with popular expectations and might lead to unrest that transcends the currently small circle of dissident intellectuals and writers.

Popular discontent, encouraged by a constant flow of people, values, and hard currency from the Federal Republic, may overcome the passivity evident now among the broader population. The publication in January 1977 of a "dissident manifesto" in the West German magazine *Der Spiegel* may well have been an inter-German cause celebre about a faked document.[18] Authenticity aside, the fact remains that the accusations of SED corruption and mismanagement made in the manifesto had people "talking politics" as seldom before in the GDR. The Soviet Union may have been expressing its concern about what might have happened when, in *Neues Deutschland,* it reminded all involved—including the West—that over twenty Soviet divisions are stationed in the GDR.[19]

The military situation in Central Europe is of great concern to the GDR leadership. Relaxation of tensions between East and West tend to undermine the domestic position of the SED, which thrives on its "front-line" position in the confrontation and demarcation between socialism and capitalism.

Similarly, the SED carefully monitors relations between the Soviet Union and the Federal Republic. The Soviets need good relations with West Germany to encourage trade and the importation of technology. Good relations between Bonn and Moscow are viewed with suspicion in East Berlin, for the SED is jealous of its preferred position vis-a-vis the USSR.

Prospects for the future of the GDR are controlled as much from Washington and Moscow as they are from East Berlin. Through its ups and downs, the detente relationship between the United States and the USSR helps to regulate the balance in Central Europe. As long as neither side is willing to accept or impose a change at the point where East and West meet, ways will be found to keep the GDR economy from faltering.

The twin traumas of inflation and unemployment are still keenly felt in both Germanys. If the worst effects of both can be contained and controlled in the GDR, then the general line of development will continue. Ten years ago I concluded a survey of the GDR with the following speculation about its future:

> The prospects, then, are for a continuation on course, even if Ulbricht is no longer at the helm. This is even more the case when Ulbricht's possible successors are taken into account. There is no one among the hopefuls who has the qualities of leadership and authority to move the German Democratic Republic from its present place in the formation of the communist party state system.[20]

If Honecker were substituted for Ulbricht, the same could be said today. Firmly at the side of the USSR, the GDR leadership has little room to maneuver, no matter who may be at the helm.

NOTES

1. The GDR already had access to the European Economic Community through its special relationship with the Federal Republic of Germany. Trade between the two Germanys is considered intra-German trade under the terms of the Treaty of Rome.

2. Hans-Dieter Schulz, " 'Alles andere als ein Spaziergang' Die Wirtschaftslage der DDR Ende 1977," *Deutschland Archiv,* vol. 10, no. 12 (December 1977), p. 1240.

3. *Deutschland Archiv,* vol. 10, no. 12 (December 1977), p. 1247.

4. At a celebration of the founding of the GDR on October 7, 1977, in East Berlin the audience got out of hand when a rock band was replaced by a Russian balalaika ensemble. The ensuing scuffle had strong anti-Soviet overtones.

5. C. Bradley Scharf, "East German Accommodation to Soviet Foreign Policy Requirements," unpublished paper presented at the Western Slavic Association meeting, Reno, Nevada, February 1978, p. 18.

6. Rudolf Bahro, *Die Alternative* (Frankfurt a/M: Europaeische Verlagsanstalt, 1977).

7. Wolfgang Leonhard, *Child of the Revolution* (Chicago: Regnery, 1958). This remains one of the best "inside" accounts of the Moscow sojourn and postwar return of KPD leaders.

8. See Heinz Lippmann, *Honecker* (New York: Macmillan, 1972).

9. Intra-SED struggles are covered in Carola Stern, *Ulbricht: A Political Biography* (New York: Praeger, 1965).

10. For a treatment of the 1953 revolt see Stefan Brant, *The East German Rising of 17th June 1953* (London: Thames and Hudson, 1955).

11. For a discussion of political socialization see A. M. Hanhardt, Jr., "East Germany: From Goals to Realities," in Ivan Volgyes, ed., *Political Socialization in Eastern Europe* (New York: Praeger, 1975), pp. 66–91.

12. Thomas A. Baylis, *The Technical Intelligentsia and the East German Elite* (Berkeley: University of California Press, 1974).

13. Gebhard Schweigler, *National Consciousness in Divided Germany* (Beverly Hills: Sage, 1975).

14. Michael Keren, "The Rise and Fall of the New Economic System," in Lyman H. Legters, ed., *The German Democratic Republic: A Developed Socialist Society* (Boulder: Westview Press, 1978), pp. 61–84.

15. Peter C. Ludz, *The Changing Elite in East Germany* (Cambridge: MIT Press, 1972).

16. For a more detailed discussion see Melvin Croan, *East Germany: The Soviet Connection* (Beverly Hills: Sage, 1976).

17. Staatliche Zentralverwaltung fuer Statistik der DDR, "Gute Bilanz der Arbeit zum Wohle des ganzen Volkes," *Dokumente zur Politik der Deutschen Demokratischen Republik,* no. 1 (1978), pp. 3–6.

18. For an extract from the manifesto in English see "Eurocommunism Reaches East Germany," *Atlas,* vol. 25, no. 3 (March 1978), pp. 19–21.

19. Ellen Lentz, "Soviet Acts Worried About East Germany," *New York Times,* January 29, 1978, p. 15.

20. Arthur M. Hanhardt, Jr., *The German Democratic Republic* (Baltimore: Johns Hopkins Press, 1968), p. 113.

BIBLIOGRAPHY

Baylis, Thomas. *The Technical Intelligentsia and the East German Elite.* Berkeley: University of California Press, 1974.

Brant, Stefan. *The East German Rising 17th June 1953.* London: Thames and Hudson, 1955.

Croan, Melvin. *East Germany: The Soviet Connection.* Beverly Hills: Sage, 1976.

Hangen, Welles. *The Muted Revolution.* New York: Alfred A. Knopf, 1966.

Hanhardt, Arthur M., Jr. *The German Democratic Republic.* Baltimore: Johns Hopkins Press, 1968.

Herspring, Dale. *East German Civil-Military Relations.* New York: Praeger, 1973.

Legters, Lyman H., ed. *The German Democratic Republic.* Boulder, Colorado: Westview Press, 1978.

Leonhard, Wolfgang. *Child of the Revolution.* Chicago: Regnery, 1958.

Lippmann, Heinz. *Honecker.* New York: Macmillan, 1974.

Ludz, Peter C. *The Changing Elite in East Germany.* Cambridge: MIT Press, 1972.

Schweigler, Gebhard. *National Consciousness in Divided Germany.* Beverly Hills: Sage, 1975.

Smith, Jean Edward. *Germany Beyond the Wall.* Boston: Little, Brown, 1969.

Starrels, John, and Anita Malinckrodt. *Politics in the German Democratic Republic.* New York: Praeger, 1975.

Stern, Carola. *Ulbricht: A Political Biography.* New York: Praeger, 1965.

6   Romania

Robert R. King

Contemporary Romania has distinguished itself principally through its foreign policy. Although it has maintained institutional links with the Soviet Union, Romania has followed a foreign policy that is autonomous from—and in some cases defiant of—the Soviet Union. Romania remains a full member of the Warsaw Pact, although it has not participated in joint military maneuvers since the mid-1960s. It is a member of CMEA, but Bucharest has frequently expressed reservations about that organization's economic integration schemes. Romania signed a new Treaty of Friendship and Alliance with the Soviet Union in 1970, but the provisions of that agreement were quite different from similar documents signed by the Soviet Union and the other Warsaw Pact member states earlier, and the Soviet-Romanian treaty acknowledged Romania's unique place.

This policy has been skillfully carried out by Romania's leaders since the early 1960s. They have utilized and exploited every opportunity to widen the scope for their autonomous action. While the Soviet Union has not been provoked into using force, at times this possibility has been threatened and the Romanians have wisely adjusted their course.

Domestic policy, however, has not been as unique. It is an oversimplification to state that while Romania follows an independent and innovative foreign policy, it pursues an orthodox or even Stalinist internal policy. But generally it has followed the Soviet pattern of internal development, although occasionally its policies have shown some unique features and adjustments peculiar to Romanian circumstances. Basically, its course in foreign relations has had little effect upon its internal policies. It can be argued, in fact, that this is not contradictory but necessary under the circumstances. The Romanians toe the mark internally in order to avoid Soviet anxiety and ultimately intervention, thus securing greater leeway in external affairs. The Hungarians have taken the opposite course—their loyalty to the Soviet Union in foreign affairs has given them the flexibility to introduce certain far-reaching domestic economic and political reforms.

There is little in the country's past that explains its activities in foreign relations. Its history is not markedly different from that of the other East European states. Its experience under Communist party rule until the autonomous foreign policy was initiated in the early 1960s likewise offered few clues or causes for the interesting foreign policy developments that have taken place.

As did most other countries of Eastern Europe, modern Romania emerged as an independent state in the nineteenth century, as the empires that dominated the region gradually began to lose their grip. The Romanian principalities came under Turkish domination in the early sixteenth century, and although they maintained a degree of *de jure* sovereignty, they were a Turkish vassal state. As Ottoman power began its long decline, local Romanian nobles gradually increased their influence. Two dates were important in this struggle. The first was 1859, the year the provinces of Walachia and Moldavia were united under a single prince, and the second was 1877, when the Romanian state declared its complete independence from Turkey during the course of the Russo-Turkish war.

Although Walachia and Moldavia united and became the Kingdom of Romania, the new state did not include all Romanians. Two important provinces remained under foreign control—Transylvania, which had an ethnic Romanian plurality but substantial Hungarian, German, and Serbian minorities, was a part of the Austro-Hungarian Empire, and Bessarabia, with a Romanian majority but substantial Ukrainian, Russian, Jewish, and German minorities, had been part of the Russian Empire since the tsars won it from the Turks in 1812. National unity became a major preoccupation of the Romanian state during the first half-century after it gained its independence. Both territories were added to the kingdom in 1918 in the aftermath of the collapse of the Habsburg and Tsarist Empires during World War I.

Although national unity had been formally achieved, the new "Greater Romania" was hardly a united country. Only 70 percent of the population was ethnically Romanian, and Hungary and the Soviet Union refused to recognize their loss of the territories of Transylvania and Bessarabia. In addition, social and cultural cleavages in the country were significant. A democratic form of government never really took root, and during the political and economic upheavals of the interwar

period Romania was ruled by a succession of authoritarian governments dominated by the wealthy aristocracy, later by the king, and
finally by Marshal Ion Antonescu.

During the period before 1944 the Communist party played a very
limited role in the country's political life. The Romanian Communist
party (RCP) was founded in 1921 with the splitting of the Socialist party.
Three years later, however, the government declared it illegal, and it
remained outlawed until 1944. Although the party continued to operate
underground, it never achieved a large following and its front organizations had a minimal impact on interwar Romanian politics. There
are a number of reasons for its limited success before 1944. First, the
working class, the traditional communist recruiting ground, was small,
and the trade union movement had minimal influence. Second, the
party never developed a successful program to appeal to the sizeable
and impoverished peasantry. Third, the party, at least for the first
twelve years of its existence, was rent with serious factional strife.
Fourth, Soviet and Comintern interference in the party's internal affairs
and policies prevented the development of programs that would meet
the peculiar needs of Romania. Finally, and perhaps most significant,
the party was identified as being an anti-Romanian institution. At the
direction of the Comintern it advocated the return of Bessarabia to the
Soviet Union and the right of self-determination, including secession,
to the national minorities. Thus, on the eve of its rise to power the RCP
had little following in Romania and the reputation of being a foreign
institution.

THE TACTICS OF TAKEOVER, 1944–48

The advent of the RCP to power was clearly a function of the presence
and power of the Soviet Union. Without the assistance of the Soviet
Army it is certain that it would never have succeeded in achieving its
dominant role. In this regard, the takeover in Romania does not differ
from those that took place in the rest of Eastern Europe, with the
exception of Yugoslavia and Albania. The unusual feature of the
Romanian takeover was the coup d'etat of August 23, 1944. On that day
King Michael, with the cooperation of the leaders of four leading political parties, including the RCP, arrested Marshal Antonescu and his
government, broke Romania's adherence to the Axis alliance, terminated hostilities against the Allied powers, and declared war on Hungary. This Romanian *volte face* was largely a recognition of the flow
of events—German and other Axis troops (including Romanian) were

being driven back from Soviet territory. The Soviet Army had retaken Bessarabia in the spring of 1944, and by August a major Soviet offensive was developing against German and Romanian positions in Romania itself. Three weeks later, on September 12, an armistice between Romania and the three principal allies was signed in Moscow. In view of the obviously important role the USSR would play in postwar Romania, inclusion of the RCP (with its close links with the Soviet Union) in the group of parties to participate in the new government was merely an example of good politics.

Once the Antonescu government was replaced, the RCP, with Soviet assistance, lost little time in asserting itself. Between August 1944 and March 1945 there were three rearrangements of the government, and in each reshuffle the Communist party came out in a stronger position. In February 1945 a government crisis was provoked by the Communists and their allies; on this occasion Soviet Deputy Foreign Minister Andrei Vishinsky ordered King Michael to appoint as prime minister Petru Groza, the head of the Plowman's Front, a peasant party which had allied itself with the RCP. The king had little choice but to comply, and Soviet approval of the new government was immediately forthcoming.

The Groza government was formally a government of the People's Democratic Front, a group of leftist parties and organizations including among others Groza's Plowman's Front, the Social Democratic Party, and the RCP. In fact the key ministries (Interior, Justice, Armed Forces) were firmly in Communist hands and the RCP quickly undertook to consolidate its position. The new government immediately took steps to move against those who had collaborated with the Antonescu regime and the Nazis. A liberal definition of collaboration was adopted, and opposition political leaders were eliminated along with the fascists. The Groza government also announced an extensive agrarian reform designed to win the support of the peasantry and to weaken the former landowners. At the same time a number of Soviet-Romanian joint companies were established, giving considerable influence over basic sectors of the Romanian economy to the Soviet Union, and the government began to exercise greater control over the economy in general.

The first postwar elections were held in November 1946. The law under which they were conducted was drawn up by the Groza government and administered by the Interior Ministry. Thus it was no surprise that when the results were tabulated, the Communist-led People's Democratic Front was found to have secured 347 seats in the parliament and the other political parties 36.

The year 1947 saw further consolidation of the Communist position. In February the peace treaties with the former minor Axis states (Italy, Finland, Bulgaria, and Hungary, as well as Romania) were concluded. This formally put an end to the very limited influence Great Britain and the United States had been able to exercise over Romanian affairs under terms of the armistice agreement. Once the legal situation was clarified and Romania again became nominally independent, the party was able to consolidate its position still further. The security organs began to take more overt action against opponents of the regime, and in October Iuliu Maniu and a number of other leaders of the National Peasant Party were brought to trial and found guilty of treason. The next step was the removal of King Michael in December; he was forced to sign a statement of abdication, and Romania was proclaimed a people's republic.

Having removed all sources of organized and institutionalized opposition to the Communist regime, the party proceeded to tidy up loose ends. Among their more important acts was abandoning the pretense that the government was composed of a group of allied parties. In February 1948 what was left of the Social Democratic party was merged with the RCP to form the Romanian Workers' party (RWP), in keeping with the pattern that had been established for all of Eastern Europe. The Plowman's Front was also eventually absorbed into the RWP, as were all other political groups: although the front continued to exist, its importance declined and it gradually became an umbrella for the various mass organizations (trade unions, youth and women's groups, etc.).

The remainder of the Soviet framework was quickly added. A new constitution was adopted in April 1948, and though it differed in certain details it was nevertheless in the Soviet mold. In June 1948 the Grand National Assembly adopted a law nationalizing all industrial, banking, insurance, mining, and transportation enterprises, and the following month a central planning organization was established to provide integrated direction for the economy. The decision to proceed with the collectivization of agriculture, another key element in the Soviet model being applied in Romania, was adopted in March 1949. To further ensure party dominance in the country, new legislation on local government organization was introduced and educational reforms were carried out, mainly to restructure the curriculum to ensure proper socialization of the new generation in the official ideology and to produce the specialists required by the industrialization program.

Between 1944 and 1950 the party moved from a position of very limited political influence to domination of Romanian life, thanks mainly to the presence of overwhelming Soviet might. The party, owing little allegiance to the population, was dependent upon Soviet favor to remain in power, and thus the party leadership had little hesitation in transplanting the Soviet model onto Romanian soil, regardless of local needs and peculiarities.

THE MAIN LINES OF POLITICAL DEVELOPMENT, 1950–75

After the imposition of the Stalinist *Gleichschaltung* throughout Eastern Europe, the system and pattern of events in Romania diverged little from those in evidence elsewhere in the Soviet sphere. Collectivization and industrialization were pursued ruthlessly, and a second major currency reform was carried out in 1952 which substantially reduced private savings and also reduced the purchasing power of most economic groups. Also in 1952 another new constitution was introduced, which followed the Soviet model even more closely than had the one adopted four years previously.

This was a period of purge both in the party at large and among the top leadership. At about the time the Social Democratic party merged with the RCP in early 1948 the admission of new members was completely halted and a "verification" of all previous party members was carried out. In the less than four years between the RCP's legalization in 1944 and the founding of the RWP in 1948, the membership swelled from about one thousand to over one million. This turbulent growth resulted in the admission of many opportunists, careerists, and questionable elements, and the party felt it necessary to consolidate its position and weed out the undesirables. Over the years this process, similar to that being carried out elsewhere in Eastern Europe, resulted in a drop in membership of over 40 percent, from 1,060,000 in 1948 to 595,400 in 1955.

During this period a purge was also carried out in the top ranks of the party leadership. Secretary-General Gheorghe Gheorghiu-Dej, who had held the post since April 1944, shared power with Ana Pauker and Vasile Luca, and as he began to increase his dominance over the party organization through the verification campaign he came into conflict with them on the issue of their independent authority. In May 1952 Pauker, Luca, and Teohari Georgescu, one of their collaborators and the minister of the interior, were all purged from their party positions.

Gheorghiu-Dej was successful, thanks to his strong position in the party and because he had won the confidence of the Soviets. In a significant reversal of the general pattern elsewhere in Eastern Europe, the native Communist (Gheorghiu-Dej, who had spent the years 1933 to 1944 in Romanian prisons) won the factional struggle against the Muscovites (Pauker and Luca, who had spent the war years in the Soviet Union handling Romanian Communist affairs there). Gheorghiu-Dej had won over the Soviets by his handling of party affairs during the eight years of his tenure as party chief. The anti-Semitic campaign (which was initiated in Eastern Europe with the Slansky trial in Czechoslovakia and the Rajk trial in Hungary, and which Stalin was following up in 1952 with his own "Doctors' Plot" in the USSR) was beneficial to Gheorghiu-Dej, since Pauker was Jewish.

Having purged his most powerful rivals, Gheorghiu-Dej followed the Stalinist pattern and in June 1952 assumed the post of chairman of the Council of Ministers (premier) in addition to that of leader of the party. The death of the Soviet dictator in March 1953 resulted in a lessening of Stalinist excesses throughout Eastern Europe, however, and in Romania Gheorghiu-Dej headed the list of those indulging in self-criticism for the revolutionary enthusiasm that had resulted in the extremes of the previous period. In conformity with the Soviet emphasis on collective leadership, but following the Malenkov model, Gheorghiu-Dej gave up his post as first secretary of the party from April 1954 until October 1955. After Malenkov's demise, however, he returned to the leading party position and gave up the premiership. Although significant progress in the sphere of heavy industry was achieved, results in light industry, agriculture, and other areas of the economy were less positive. The relaxation that followed Stalin's death was also felt in these areas, and collectivization was pursued less harshly than previously.

The Twentieth CPSU Congress and Khrushchev's secret speech on that occasion had a profound impact in Romania, as they did elsewhere in Eastern Europe. Gheorghiu-Dej, in a report on his return from the Twentieth Congress, was critical of Stalin but argued that the Stalinists in the Romanian party had been purged in 1952 (i.e., Pauker, Luca, and Georgescu). Despite this attempt to shift the blame, however, the party leader was apparently accused of being responsible for the adoption of Stalinist principles and the use of Stalinist methods by Miron Constantinescu and Iosif Chisinevschi, two Politburo members who had accompanied Gheorghiu-Dej to the Twentieth CPSU Congress in Moscow. Among those most influenced by the new anti-Stalinism were the writers, who were chafing under the party's literary dogmatism and control.

The events in Hungary and Poland in October 1956, however, resulted in a general effort to quell the ferment. The intellectuals among the Hungarian minority in Romania were strongly affected by the upheaval in Hungary. There was no language barrier to their understanding, and they had traditionally been greatly influenced by events in Budapest. Romanian students were also impressed by the events in Hungary and the general ferment of the times, and some workers in Romanian industrial centers used the occasion to express dissatisfaction. As developments in Hungary raced along out of control, Gheorghiu-Dej cut short a visit to Yugoslavia to return to Bucharest. Through a combination of concessions (higher living standards for workers, restoration of rights and benefits to ethnic Germans, etc.) and the threat of reprisals, the Romanian leadership succeeded in maintaining control. But the experience had nevertheless shaken their confidence. The Romanians were among the first to praise Soviet intervention in Hungary, and provided assistance in restoring party and secret police authority in that country.

The concessions made under extreme circumstances in 1956 were continued for a time as the party sought to reestablish its authority and control. Once this was done, however, more stringent measures were taken. Among the first to suffer were the members of the Hungarian minority. The intellectuals, among the most affected by the Budapest events of 1956, engaged in party-directed self-criticism and some of the autonomous rights the group had been granted earlier were gradually reduced. Two of the more dramatic and symbolic steps in this process were the merging of the Hungarian-language university in Cluj with the Romanian-language institution in the same city and the alteration of the boundaries of the Hungarian Autonomous Region in Transylvania in order to increase the proportion of ethnic Romanians and reduce the percentage of Hungarians.

Although the pace of the collectivization of agriculture slackened in 1956, it was taken up again with greater insistence after 1959, and in 1962 the party proudly announced the full collectivization of agriculture. The slowdown in the pace of industrialization in January 1957 ended in late 1958 with the decision to pursue economic development more vigorously. The writers and intellectuals, too, found themselves subject to increasing pressure to conform to more restrictive literary and cultural policies.

An important event which took place in 1958 and had a significant impact upon the evolution of Romanian policies was the decision to withdraw the Soviet troops stationed in Romania. These military forces had been in the country since 1944 and had played a major role in the rise of the Communist party and in maintaining Soviet influence there. Their withdrawal was a reflection of the geographically safe location of Romania and of Soviet confidence in the leadership of Gheorghiu-Dej.

Although the troops were withdrawn, Romania remained under the influence of the USSR. When Khrushchev denounced the excesses of Stalin and his cult at the Twenty-second CPSU Congress in 1961, Gheorghiu-Dej was again required to deal with Stalinism. At a Central Committee plenum in December 1961 Pauker, Luca, Georgescu, Constantinescu, and Chisinevschi were again singled out as Romania's Stalinists and linked with the antiparty group purged by Khrushchev in the USSR. Again Gheorghiu-Dej's arguments were hardly convincing, but he did succeed in maintaining his position.

In the early 1960s Romania began to follow a course independent of that pursued by the Soviet Union. Although this was most evident in the sphere of foreign relations, it also had an impact upon domestic policies. The process of establishing a degree of autonomy was a gradual and contradictory one. One of the main factors behind the evolution of differences with the USSR was the fact that the Soviets favored industrial specialization while the Romanian leadership was committed to comprehensive industrialization. (This was not a matter of the Soviets demanding that Romania remain a supplier of raw materials and agricultural products, as some have suggested, but a question of the scope of specialization.) At any rate, by early 1963 the differences between Romania and the other CMEA countries (and the Soviet Union in particular) had come into the open. Romanian insistence ultimately forced the Soviet Union to yield ground on the key CMEA issues that divided them. The Romanians widened their autonomy by adopting a position of cautious neutrality regarding the Soviet-Chinese differences that played such an important role in the world Communist movement in the early 1960s and by developing closer economic and political relations with the Western countries. (These aspects of Romania's foreign relations are discussed in more detail below.)

The new autonomy from the Soviet Union had a more limited impact on internal developments. The innovative foreign policy was accompanied by a rather orthodox domestic policy, although nationalism was gradually permitted to resume a more prominent role in the country's life and many aspects of Sovietization were gradually eliminated.

Among those party leaders who came increasingly to the fore under Gheorghiu-Dej was Nicolae Ceausescu, who became the Central Committee secretary responsible for party organization and cadres. When Gheorghiu-Dej died in March 1965, it was not surprising that Ceausescu assumed the position of party chief. He began the task of consolidating his position in the hierarchy, a process that required some four years, during which time he purged several members of the old guard who had been confidants of the previous party leader, as well as a rival from his own generation. One important achievement was his assumption of the title of president of the State Council (titular head of state) in addition to his leadership of the party.

Ceausescu, always an energetic individual, lost little time in putting his own stamp on the party's policies. At the Ninth Party Congress in July 1965—just a few months after he had assumed control of the party—he had his title upgraded from first secretary to secretary-general, the name of the party was changed from Romanian Workers' party to Romanian Communist party, the leading organs of the party were restructured with the creation of the Executive Committee, and conditions for party membership were changed. Shortly after the congress a new constitution was adopted and Romania was elevated from a "People's Democracy" to a "Socialist Republic." In March 1974 the constitution was changed and Romania acquired a president, to which position Ceausescu was duly elected.

In domestic policies he has been identified with the vigorous campaign to lift Romania into the ranks of the industrialized countries, and he has repeatedly called for greater sacrifice and effort in order to hasten economic development. He has also been responsible for emphasizing the importance and role of ideology in the nation's life, in an effort to create a "new man with advanced socialist awareness." He is also known for his fostering of efforts to identify the RCP with Romanian national tradition and to play up the "progressive" aspects of the national heritage. His style of leadership is clearly paternalistic, and it has been evident on a number of occasions (most dramatically in August 1968, when he vehemently criticized the Soviet invasion of Czechoslovakia) that he has struck a responsive chord among his countrymen.

THE CURRENT POLITICAL STRUCTURE

According to the Romanian constitution the RCP is "the leading political force in the entire society" and plays "the leading role in all fields of socialist construction and guides the activity of the mass and public organizations and of the state organs."[1] And indeed the party is the leading force in society, owing to its power to determine who will fill the leading positions in government, cultural life, and social organizations in general. It has also drawn into its membership most of the leading figures in Romanian society, and is thus able to influence many aspects of the country's life.

The supreme organ of the party is its congress, to which delegates are selected at regional conferences. It meets every five years to hear and approve reports on party activity, to establish basic policy, and to elect the Central Committee, a Central Auditing Commission (which controls party finances), and the Central Collegium (formerly the Control Commission, which deals with questions regarding party membership).

Between congresses the Central Committee is the seat of power, but this is a large body (205 full and 156 candidate members were elected to it in November 1974) and it meets infrequently. Real power thus devolves upon the Political Executive Committee (PEC), the Bureau of the PEC, and the Central Committee Secretariat.

The RCP at present has no Presidium or Politburo, as do most other East European parties, although such a body existed until March 1974. A unique feature of its organizational structure, however, is the Political Executive Committee (formerly known as the Executive Committee). This body was created in 1965 at the Ninth Party Congress, shortly after Ceausescu became party chief, as a place to which the new party leader's supporters could be promoted while the old retained their seats in the Permanent Presidium. The PEC has gradually assumed a status somewhat between the level of the Politburo and that of the Central Committee. It is a bit too large for real deliberation and decision making (in mid-1977 it had 23 full and 15 alternate members), but it serves as an agency that can legitimize statements and party directives that do not require Central Committee endorsement.

From its advent to power in 1944 until March 1974 the party also had a Politburo, which after July 1965 was called the Permanent Presidium. Its membership varied but averaged about nine, and it included the most influential figures in the party. In March 1974 the Permanent Presidium was abolished, but a new body, called the Permanent Bureau of the Executive Committee, was created. Membership in it, however, was to be ex officio, a departure from past practice with regard to the Presidium, in which membership was accorded to individuals. Thus the secretary-general of the party (Ceausescu) and all Central Committee secretaries were automatically members of the Permanent Bureau, as were the president of the republic (also Ceausescu), a vice-president of the State Council, the premier, the first deputy premier, one or two deputy premiers, the chairman of the Central Council of Workers' Control of Economic and Social Activities, the chairman of the State Planning Committee, and the chairman of the trade union organization. The amendments to the party statute adopted at the March plenum specified that other persons could be designated members of the bureau by the Executive Committee.

At the Eleventh Congress, in November 1974, further changes were made in the composition and structure of the Permanent Bureau. The party statute was again amended to specify that bureau members are to be chosen by the Executive Committee from among its members, and that it is to be led by the party secretary-general; ex officio designation of members was dropped. After the congress the new Executive Committee named only five persons to the bureau—Ceausescu, the party leader; Manea Manescu, the premier; Gheorghe Oprea, a deputy premier; Ion Patan, another deputy premier and minister of foreign trade and international economic cooperation; and Stefan Andrei, a Central Committee secretary responsible for foreign relations of the party.

A unique feature of the new organizational structure is the fact that the Permanent Bureau is responsible to the party's Executive Committee rather than to the Central Committee. Members of the Permanent Presidium, which was abolished when these changes were made, had been chosen by, and were responsible to, the Central Committee, as is still the practice with regard to the other East European parties. No official explanation was given for this two-stage elimination of the Permanent Presidium, but it seems probable that, since it comprised the most powerful individuals in the party, it had become more influential than Ceausescu desired, and it may also have become a forum in which opposition to his programs could be expressed. The first step, replacing it by a bureau composed of ex officio members, was a graceful way of dropping those whose views differed from Ceausescu's. The other change that came about during the party congress may have been prompted by the unwieldiness of the larger bureau and a desire to increase its efficiency; it is also possible that the smaller body was what Ceausescu originally had in mind, and that he found a two-step elimination of the old Presidium to be politically the most expedient way of achieving his end.

In January 1977, however, further changes were made in the composition of the Permanent Bureau, and its membership was increased from five to nine. The addition of four individuals (including Elena

Ceausescu, wife of the party leader) with responsibility for areas other than international economic relations suggests that this body may again be assuming the role of a Politburo.

The Central Committee Secretariat plays much the same role in Romania as it does in other East European Communist parties. In mid-1977 there were ten Central Committee secretaries in addition to the party secretary-general.

As of December 31, 1976, party membership was officially reported at 2,655,000, including some 106,000 members who joined during that year. About 50 percent were classed as workers (up from 43 percent in 1969), 20 percent as peasants (down from 28 percent in 1969), and 22 percent as intellectuals and white-collar personnel. The party's ethnic composition remained approximately the same as that of the country as a whole—87.7 percent Romanian, 7.7 percent Hungarian, 1.9 percent German, and 2.7 percent other nationalities.[2]

The RCP is organized into basic units or cells in factories, on farms, and in the smaller political subdivisions; in 1974 there were about 70,000 such units. The next higher step is represented by the party organizations in communes (rural territorial subdivisions) and municipalities, in which there were 2,706 and 235 organizations, respectively. Finally, there are party organizations for each of the 39 counties and the municipality of Bucharest; these supervise the lower-level party organizations within their territories.[3]

In addition to the party organization there are a number of mass organizations which function under party leadership. The Union of Communist Youth, for young people in their teens, operates in essentially the same fashion as does the party. Children between eight and fourteen are members of the Pioneer organization, and for those from four to seven there is a new organization called Falcons of the Fatherland, set up in 1976. The General Confederation of Romanian Trade Unions is another important mass organization that functions under party guidance. As with the other East European trade unions (except in Yugoslavia), the Romanian unions serve essentially as transmission belts for purveying party policy to the workers. Women also have their own organization, the National Council of Women.

In 1968, after opposing the Soviet-led invasion of Czechoslovakia, the party sought to mobilize mass support and created the Front of Socialist Unity (FSU) to replace the largely inactive People's Democratic Front. (The latter was an outgrowth of the National Democratic Front, created in October 1944 to link the RCP, the Social Democrats, and other left-leaning political groups in order to seize power.) The FSU includes trade union, youth, and women's front organizations, as well as associations representing the various national minorities living in Romania. The RCP is the only political party, but the FSU provides the permanent organizational framework for mass participation in politics at all levels. It plays a primary role in coordinating the activities of other front organizations and in the election process. Its leadership includes the leaders of the party, and Ceausescu is its chairman.

Romania's governmental structure varies little from that of other East European countries. The representative legislative body, the Grand National Assembly, is theoretically the supreme government organ, but it meets infrequently (two or three times a year) and only for a few days at a time, leaving the real work of governing to the Council of Ministers, the president, and the State Council. The State Council is elected by the assembly, and in 1976 it was composed of a president, three vice-presidents, a secretary, and twelve members. It acts on behalf of the legislature between sessions. Until 1974 the president of the State Council was titular head of state, but in March of that year the constitution was amended to provide for a president of the Socialist Republic of Romania who is ex officio president of the State Council. He has the authority to issue decrees and take certain other actions by virtue of his office without State Council approval.

The actual management of the government is in the hands of the Council of Ministers, elected by the Grand National Assembly. The council is presided over by a chairman (prime minister or premier). In mid-1977, in addition to the premier, 12 deputy premiers, 22 ministers, and 15 other heads of organizations were members of the Council of Ministers.

CHANGING PATTERNS IN THE ELITE

The RCP has played the leading role on the Romanian political scene for over thirty years, and during this period there have been substantial changes in the composition of its elite, not only in terms of individuals but—more importantly—in terms of the groups involved.

Owing to its attraction for minorities between the two world wars, the party leadership during the period of its illegal existence and also during its early years in power included an unusually large proportion of ethnically non-Romanians. Among the leading figures were a number of Jews (e.g., Ana Pauker, Chivu Stoica), Hungarians (e.g., Vasile Luca, Alexandru Moghioros), and others (e.g., Emil Bodnaras, who had a Ukrainian father and a german mother).[4] Gradually this situation has been altered. In part this represents a deliberate effort at Romanianization, which some regard as having begun with the purge of Pauker and Luca in 1952. The party's efforts to draw leading individuals into its ranks, and particularly its attempt (since the mid-1960s) to link the RCP with Romanian nationalism, have perhaps been more important, however. In general one can say that the party elite has become increasingly Romanian in ethnic composition, although a careful effort is made to include representatives of the minorities (particularly the Hungarians) in the higher echelons.

Over time the average age and length of service in the party have increased so far as its elite is concerned. The average age of Politburo (1945–60) and Political Executive Committee (1965–74) members rose from 41 in 1945 to 54 in 1974; the average length of party membership increased from 17 years in 1945 to 36 years in 1974. In addition to increasing age and greater party experience, there has also been a tendency for a higher proportion of full members of the Central Committee to be reelected (about 57 percent in Central Committees elected at congresses since 1960) and for new full Central Committee members to come from the ranks of the alternate members (an increase from 10.0 percent of full Central Committee members in 1955 to 21.5 percent in 1974).[5] Thus members of the party elite are increasingly subject to longer periods of socialization in the party before reaching leading posts, and as a consequence there is a greater tendency toward conservatism and maintenance of the status quo in the organization.

Another change is that the educational level has risen over the years. Initially a large proportion of party leaders had little higher education and a great many of them were workers. Some were members of the intelligentsia, but for the most part these were trained as lawyers or in the humanities. The number of leading party officials with technical or economic backgrounds has now increased significantly, however. In part this represents the concern that party bureaucrats acquire skills that will enable them to deal with an increasingly complex economy and society, and in part it represents an effort by the party to coopt members of the technical and managerial elite into the political leadership.

Although it would be imprudent to conclude that the party elite has undergone or is undergoing critical changes in composition that will alter the nature of the party or the regime, the elite has become more national in its outlook, more conservative in approach, and better qualified by education and experience to deal with the complexities of modern society. The elite still retains a distinctive institutional focus, however; the career party bureaucrats continue to dominate the system, and there is little reason to expect any change in this situation in the immediate future.

SOCIOECONOMIC AND CULTURAL TRENDS

Romania was a predominantly agricultural country in 1945, despite the economic development that took place during the interwar period. (In 1930 some 78.6 percent of the population lived in rural areas.) Under the program of industrial development that has been carried out under RCP direction, the economic and social structure of the country has altered considerably. By 1975, for example, it was estimated that the rural portion of the population had declined from 76.6 percent in 1948 to 56.8 percent.[6]

In 1975 industrial production was some 21 times the figure for 1950, which represents an annual average growth rate of 12.9 percent. There were, however, significant differences between the growth of heavy industry and producer goods, which increased at an average annual rate of 14.4 percent, and that of light industry and consumer goods, which increased at an annual average of 10.6 percent. These changes were also accompanied by a shift in the proportion of the work force employed in industry, from 12.0 percent in 1950 to 30.6 percent in 1975, and a corresponding decline in the number of persons employed in agriculture, from 74.1 to 37.8 percent.

This impressive growth in industry was achieved at the expense of agriculture and consumption. Between 1950 and 1975 agricultural production rose at an average annual rate of 4.3 percent, in large part because it suffered from a persistent shortage of investment funds coupled with organizational difficulties. This sector remains a weak spot in the Romanian economy, despite the fact that agricultural products are still important in the country's exports. Between 1950 and 1975 real personal income rose only by an average of 4.8 percent per year, and there has been a consistent policy of keeping down the production of consumer goods for domestic use. Resources have been devoted to heavy industry rather than to those areas calculated to raise the standard of living (food production and processing, consumer products, housing, etc.). During the 1970s there have been increasing indications —including reports of strikes in some areas—that the population would prefer increased availability of consumer goods. Thus far, however, Ceausescu has successfully resisted such pressures. Romanian workers, with the notable exception of the Jiu Valley miners, seem to be much more acquiescent than their Polish counterparts.

The RCP has also been concerned with education, for two principal reasons. First, trained specialists and technicians must be provided for the country's rapid industrialization and economic development. Thus the number of students and the length of time they spend in school have increased substantially since the RCP came to power. (In 1975–76 the number of students in primary schools was double the figure for 1938–39, and in secondary schools there were some 26 times as many.) The second reason for party interest in education and in the cultural field generally is the need to ensure the political indoctrination of the population, and the younger generation in particular. Although ideology was an important area of party interest in the early years of the regime, it was given less emphasis during the 1960s, but since Ceausescu launched his ideological campaign in July 1971 (which was reaffirmed in 1976) it has been given greater prominence.

Though the population is principally of Romanian ethnic origin, minorities represent over 12 percent of the total. The largest of these are the Hungarians (which in 1977 numbered 1,700,000, or 7.9 percent of the population) and the Germans (with 348,000, or 1.6 percent).[7] The Germans have declined in number since 1945, primarily owing to emigration to West Germany and Austria, although the Romanian government has officially expressed its opposition to this and measures have been taken to stem the flow. The Hungarians were a favored minority immediately after the Communists came to power, while the Germans (some of whom had supported Nazi Germany) were discriminated against. In the wake of the unrest in the Hungarian community in 1956, their privileges were gradually reduced, and measures directed against the German minority were removed. Under Ceausescu a more conciliatory policy toward the minorities has been followed than was the case in the last years of Gheorghiu-Dej's rule, but minority activity is still restricted and links with Romania are emphasized.

FOREIGN POLICY AND FOREIGN ECONOMIC RELATIONS

Contemporary Romania's claim to uniqueness is based on its foreign policy. Through skillful diplomacy and exploitation of opportunities presented by the international situation, Romania has cautiously expanded its autonomy from the Soviet Union, but at the same time has maintained its membership in the Warsaw Pact and avoided Soviet military intervention. Although there are differences of view over the timing of and reasons for Romania's policy of autonomy, the initial overt disagreement with the Soviet Union (and the first step in establishing Romanian autonomy) was the dispute over economic integration within the Council for Mutual Economic Assistance (CMEA). Romania's attempts during this period to diversify its foreign trade and —particularly—to expand its trade with Western states increased the country's freedom of maneuver. With Romania's attempts to mediate between the Soviet and Chinese parties in 1963 and the issuing of the Romanian party's April 1964 declaration,[8] autonomy was codified and expanded to include political as well as economic relations.

The death of Gheorghe Gheorghiu-Dej and Nicolae Ceausescu's assumption of the party leadership in March 1965 led to certain changes. Although Ceausescu's foreign policy continued to follow much the same lines as that of Gheorghiu-Dej, he has been more directly identified personally with the expansion of Romanian autonomy, and he has been more explicit and systematic in enunciating this policy and relating it to Marxist-Leninist ideology and Romanian nationalism. Although the first few months of his tenure as party leader (which coincided with the initial period of the Brezhnev-Kosygin leadership in the Soviet Union) were marked by caution and even by a certain improvement in Romania's relations with the USSR, under Ceausescu autonomy has been further expanded and legitimized. Soviet attempts to strengthen the Warsaw Pact organization in late 1965 and early 1966 were finally abandoned in the face of energetic opposition from the Romanians. In a speech on the forty-fifth anniversary of the founding of the Romanian party Ceausescu responded to Soviet initiatives by reiterating Romania's view that military pacts were obsolete, criticizing Soviet interference in the affairs of other parties under the Comintern, initiating thinly veiled claims to Soviet territory, and reasserting the sovereignty and independence of Romania.[9] In 1967 he further strengthened Romania's claim to autonomy and provoked a crisis within the Warsaw Pact by establishing diplomatic relations with West Germany and refusing to support the Soviet Middle East policy following the Arab-Israeli conflict.

The high point of Romania's defiance of the Soviet Union was its refusal to participate in, and its explicit condemnation of, the Soviet-led invasion of Czechoslovakia in 1968. Although, under Soviet pressure, Romania's position on the Czechoslovak events was moderated within a short time, relations with the Soviet Union continued to be strained. The terms of a new twenty-year Treaty of Friendship, Alliance, and Mutual Assistance with the Soviet Union, signed in July 1970 despite the limited normalization of relations which it implied, confirmed

Romania's unique position in the Warsaw Pact. Ceausescu's daring visit to Peking in the summer of 1971 and the Soviet pressure which followed it further confirmed Romania's autonomy.

Perhaps the most graphic illustration of Romania's foreign policy is the shift in trade partners that has taken place since 1960. (See Table 1.) The decline in the percentage of trade with the USSR is dramatic, although that country remains Romania's number one partner in terms of trade volume. Two other shifts are also noteworthy—the increase in trade with the developed industrial countries, which seems to have leveled off in the 1970s, and the sharp increase in trade with the developing countries, mainly since 1970.

Although one must not underemphasize the internal factors that were involved in the Romanian leaders' pursuit of autonomy from the Soviet Union, the international factors that permitted them to follow this policy were skillfully exploited to that end. Romania's innovative foreign policy began during a time when the cold war confrontation between the Soviet Union and the United States was still the predominant feature of the international landscape. The East-West division was still clearly marked in Europe, and both major powers were seeking to seduce wavering members of the opposing alliance. Also, though serious differences developed between the Soviet Union and China, their conflict was fought within the Communist movement, and Peking was largely isolated from the rest of the world. This gave Romania an opportunity to expand its autonomy within the international Communist movement by bargaining Romanian support for Soviet concessions, and at the same time the Chinese were interested in supporting the Romanians in their search for autonomy from Moscow. Another factor that influenced this policy was the example and support of Yugoslavia.

Changing conditions in the early 1970s, however, have also led to subtle alterations in Romania's policy. As the Soviet-American con-

Table 1 Percentage of Total Romanian Trade by Political Group of States

Trade with	1960	1965	1970	1975
USSR	40.1	38.8	27.0	18.6
CMEA (without USSR)[a]	26.5	21.5	21.9	19.4
Other Communist states	6.4	4.6	7.0	6.8
Developed industrial states	21.6	27.6	34.8	37.3
Developing countries	5.4	7.5	9.3	17.9

[a]Including Cuba after 1972. Prior to this Cuba is included in the "other Communist states" group.

Source: *Anuarul Statistic al R.S.R. 1976*, pp. 377–383.

frontation has given way to detente and as the bipolar world has
evolved into a multipolar one, the interest of the Soviet Union and the
East European states in expanding political and economic relations
with Western states has increased, and for the latter such ties have also
assumed greater importance. When Romania was almost the only East
European state anxious to further economic and political ties with the
West, there was considerable interest in and support for its independent foreign policy. Now that improved East-West relations have expanded to include the Soviet Union and most of the rest of Eastern
Europe, Romania's position is no longer unique. Although its autonomous foreign policy is still considered praiseworthy, other considerations have come to play a more important role.

The Romanians had expected great things from the Conference on
Security and Cooperation in Europe when the preparations for it began
in the early 1970s. They hoped the gathering would result in legal and
moral support for their foreign policy position and in further economic
and political advantages through improved relations with Western
states. While the conference in Helsinki did create a better atmosphere
in East-West relations, it has not proved to be as directly beneficial to
Romania as was apparently hoped initially. Furthermore, Western interest in humanitarian questions (the so-called Basket Three issues) has
given rise to certain strains, and this has had the effect of emphasizing
Romania's common interests with the Soviet Union and the other Warsaw Pact states. In short, the Helsinki conference contributed to the
gradual erosion of Western interest in Romania and has done little to
perpetuate the uniqueness that characterized its position vis-a-vis the
West in the past.

The policy of the Chinese People's Republic was another factor that
helped to establish Romania's autonomy from the Soviet Union in the
1960s, and in fact, in 1970–71, when Romania was searching for an
alternative to the West as a political and economic counterweight to the
USSR, China became a serious candidate for that role, but for a short
time only. During the period of Soviet pressure against Romania in the
summer of 1971, following a visit by Ceausescu to Peking, both
Romanian and Chinese leaders apparently came to the conclusion that
China had only a limited ability to defend Romania against the USSR.
In addition, the Chinese seem to have concluded, after President Nixon
visited Peking in 1972, that they could influence international affairs
and deal with the potential Soviet threat more effectively by establishing good relations with the United States, Japan, and other major nations than by promoting the autonomy of a miscellaneous assortment

of small Balkan states. Thus China's growing acceptability and status in the world make Romania of less importance to Peking. And China's succession problem, which had been apparent at least since the Lin Piao affair in the early 1970s, raised further questions about its ability to support Romania. This is not to suggest that Romania and China are no longer interested in maintaining good relations—in fact, Ceausescu was in Peking and Chairman Hua visited Bucharest in 1978—but the aura of importance evident in the past has disappeared.

Yugoslavia's support also began to appear less certain, mainly for domestic political reasons. That country's unstable internal situation, primarily a consequence of its ethnic and to some extent its ideological fragmentation, is exacerbated by Tito's advanced age. Whatever takes place in the post-Tito succession struggle (and this struggle is already under way), the probability is that Yugoslavia will be less secure domestically and less important internationally, at least for a period of time.

Thus the elements of the international scene that permitted and encouraged Romania to develop autonomy in the early 1960s have been altered, but having achieved a degree of autonomy from the Soviet Union, the current Romanian leadership is committed to continue that policy. As a result there has been a serious search for alternative sources of support, for new ways to maintain and perhaps expand the sphere of independent action. Although this search continues, there has also been an effort to cover exposed flanks by reducing differences with the Soviet Union in nonessential areas. But despite a general trend toward "normalization" with Moscow since the invasion of Czechoslovakia in 1968, there have been periods of renewed stress, as when the Soviet Union exerted pressure on Romania in the summer of 1971, after Ceausescu's visit to China. Generally, however, there have been fewer overt differences between the two. The relaxation reached its high point thus far during 1976, when Ceausescu visited Brezhnev in the Crimea in August and the Soviet leader paid a return visit to Bucharest just before a Warsaw Pact summit was convened there in November.

While the Soviets' motivation for achieving more normal relations with Romania has been primarily political and diplomatic, Bucharest's interest appears to be primarily economic. Its need to balance trade with the West and the growing demand for raw materials and capital equipment for industrialization are important factors here. The Soviets have increasingly demanded better-quality goods from the East European states, but the latter's technological level and the quality of their output are probably still below that required for successful competition in the industrialized West. Another deterrent is the difficulty of marketing products on the unfamiliar and fragmented Western markets. Still more important, perhaps, is the fact that the CMEA states have similar state trading monopolies, and this simplifies the negotiation of unified export and import contracts. While these economic ties are more important to Romania than to the USSR, both states benefit and there is a common interest in developing relations. This does not mean that Romania has abandoned its interest in autonomy, but rather that present conditions favor the development of economic relations with the CMEA states.

Perhaps the most significant shift in Romanian policy to result from these changes in the international setting in the early 1970s was the decision to pursue closer relations with the developing countries. Initially the motivating factors were principally economic, the consequence of Romania's ambitious industrialization program. As its productive capacity and its need for raw materials expanded, Romania found increasing difficulty in marketing its products in the West, and its dependence upon Soviet raw materials increased. Thus the developing countries appeared to be ideal trade partners. The demand for quality and the problems of marketing were less serious than in the West, and raw materials were among the principal exports these states could provide. Also, no political complications would result from such exchanges, as might be the case with the Soviet Union. Over time, however, as Romania has succeeded in improving its trade balance with the West and shown a greater willingness to expand economic ties with the CMEA states, the political and diplomatic aspects of relations with the Third World have assumed greater importance. The economic dimension remains a significant factor, however, as is evident from Romania's expanding trade with these countries.

NOTES

1. Text of the Constitution of the Socialist Republic of Romania as amended, *Buletinul Oficial*, December 27, 1974.

2. *Scinteia*, August 8, 1969, and April 7, 1977.

3. Ibid., July 25, 1975; *World Marxist Review*, no. 5, 1973.

4. On this aspect of the Romanian elite, see D. A. Tomasic, "The Romanian Communist Leadership," *Slavic Review*, 20:3 (October 1961), pp. 477–494.

5. See Robert R. King, *A History of the Romanian Communist Party* (Stanford, Calif.: The Hoover Institution, forthcoming), chapter 4.

6. Figures are all from *Anuarul Statistic al R.S.R. 1976* (Bucharest: Directia Centrala de Statistica, 1976).

7. *Scinteia*, June 15, 1977.

8. Ibid., April 23, 1964. English text is in William E. Griffith, *Sino-Soviet Relations, 1964–1965* (Cambridge, Mass.: MIT Press, 1967), pp. 269–296.

9. See *Scinteia*, May 8, 1966. On the Warsaw Pact dispute, see Robin A. Remington, *The Warsaw Pact: Case Studies in Communist Conflict Resolution* (Cambridge, Mass.: MIT Press, 1971), pp. 80–99; and Fritz Ermarth, *Internationalism, Security, and Legitimacy,* Rand Memorandum Rm-5909-PR (March 1969), pp. 33–40.

BIBLIOGRAPHY

Cretzianu, Alexandre, ed. *Captive Rumania: A Decade of Soviet Rule.* New York: Praeger, 1956.

Fischer-Galati, Stephen. *The New Rumania: From People's Democracy to Socialist Republic.* Cambridge, Mass.: MIT Press, 1967.

———. *Romania.* New York: Praeger, 1957.

Gilberg, Trond. *Modernization in Romania Since World War II.* New York: Praeger, 1975.

Ionescu, Ghita. *Communism in Rumania 1944–1962.* London: Oxford University Press, 1964.

Jowitt, Kenneth. *Revolutionary Breakthroughs and National Development: The Case of Romania, 1944–1965.* Berkeley and Los Angeles: University of California Press, 1971.

Montias, John Michael. *Economic Development in Communist Rumania.* Cambridge, Mass.: MIT Press, 1967.

Roberts, Henry L. *Rumania: Political Problems of an Agrarian State.* New Haven: Yale University Press, 1951. [Reprinted, Hamden, Conn.: Archon Books, 1969.]

Seton-Watson, Robert William. *A History of the Roumanians: From Roman Times to the Completion of Unity.* Cambridge: Cambridge University Press, 1934. [Reprinted, Hamden, Conn.: Archon Books, 1963.]

7   Bulgaria

Robert R. King

Of the East European states, Bulgaria has attracted the least attention and interest. There are three principal reasons for this neglect. First, with the exception of Albania, Bulgaria is the smallest and economically least developed of the East European countries. Second, since 1945 it has suffered none of the spectacular upheavals that have focused world attention on most of the other East European states, at least for a time. Third, Bulgaria has been the most loyal follower of the Soviet Union. Although the Bulgarian regime has shown a degree of innovation and divergence from the Soviet pattern in agricultural policy and in a few other areas, Bulgaria's adherence to the Soviet model has been even "more Catholic than the Pope."

Bulgaria, however, is more important than its lack of attention would suggest. It is a key state in the Balkans, and the principal country through which Soviet influence is projected into this important region. In the Balkans the interests of the major powers converge and all have allies there—Bulgaria, as mentioned, has close ties with the USSR; Turkey and Greece are linked with the United States through the North Atlantic Alliance; Romania, though a member of the Warsaw Pact, has sought to assert its autonomy from Moscow; Yugoslavia has been a leader of the nonaligned countries and has jealously maintained its independence; and Albania has had close links with China, although these have recently deteriorated. If these external connections are not enough, there are also local quarrels (Cyprus and Macedonia) which have the potential to become wider conflicts. Geopolitically, Bulgaria has a greater importance than its placid postwar history would suggest.

That Bulgaria has managed to avoid "those profound lacerations" which put other countries of Eastern Europe on the front pages of the world's newspapers may "serve as an excuse for lack of attention."

Italian Communist journalist Giuseppe Boffa, however, argues that "this very characteristic is one of the most interesting and original features of socialist construction in Bulgaria."[1]

It can be argued that Bulgaria deserves the obscurity it has received. Unsensational continuity has been the hallmark of its postwar history. It has been a most faithful follower of Soviet foreign policy initiatives; its domestic political and economic policies have been in some respects competent, but they have never exceeded the bounds of ideological orthodoxy. Nevertheless, Bulgaria's recent history has been interesting, and its experiences under communism have been relevant.

A Bulgarian kingdom existed as an independent state in the early Middle Ages, but it gradually came under Byzantine dominance. When the Turks swept up the Balkan Peninsula in the fourteenth century, Bulgaria was among the first territories to be taken, and it remained a part of the Ottoman Empire for over five hundred years. As the empire of the Sublime Porte began to disintegrate, Bulgarian national awareness began to awaken. These two factors, coupled with Russian military assistance during the Russo-Turkish War of 1877–78, led to the creation of the modern Bulgarian state. Originally it consisted only of the northern part of what is contemporary Bulgaria, but additional territory was annexed to it in 1885 and in 1912. Since it was one of the last of the Balkan states to achieve independence, it came late to the struggle for territory, and was therefore frequently at odds with its neighbors—Serbia (later Yugoslavia), Greece, Romania, and Turkey— over territorial issues. Mainly in order to gain areas it claimed on ethnic and historical grounds, Bulgaria entered World War I on the side of the Central Powers and World War II on the side of the Axis countries. Although during these wars Bulgaria achieved some of its territorial aims, these gains were taken from it in the peace negotiations that followed defeat. The drive to obtain what was considered rightfully Bulgarian, coupled with a low level of political and social development, led to authoritarian governments between 1923 and World War II.

The Bulgarian Communist party (BCP) established strong roots and played an important role in Bulgarian politics during the interwar period, although its fortunes varied considerably during that time. It developed from the Social Democratic party and assumed the name Communist in 1919; it was one of the earliest parties to affiliate with the Soviet party. A negligible organization in 1912, the BCP had become Bulgaria's second largest party by 1920, owing to the debacles the country had suffered in the Balkan wars and World War I under the regime of the largest party, the Bulgarian Agrarian People's Union. The BCP took the position that the Union represented the "rural bourgeoisie," and fought it as implacably as it did the urban parties. In the rightist coup d'etat against the peasant government of June 1923, the BCP decided on a course of "neutrality," but this decision was quickly reversed by the Comintern, and the party was ordered to stage an uprising in cooperation with the Agrarian Union's left wing. The abortive insurrection of September 1923 resulted in the decimation of BCP cadres throughout the country and the flight of its leading officials (e.g., Vasil Kolarov, Georgi Dimitrov) to the Soviet Union; during the underground period (1923–44), however, it recovered some strength.

THE TACTICS OF TAKEOVER, 1944–49

Although Bulgaria was allied with Nazi Germany during World War II, its position was a peculiar one: Bulgaria declared war on Great Britain and the United States, but not on the Soviet Union. This was in part due to the unpopularity of a conflict with the Russians, but it was also a calculated effort on the part of Tsar Boris to gain the greatest advantage from the war with the least amount of direct involvement. When the Soviet Army swept across Romania in the summer of 1944, the USSR refused to acknowledge Bulgaria's nonbelligerency, and declared war on September 5; the Soviet Army entered Bulgarian territory shortly thereafter.

The BCP was active in Bulgaria during the war, although its efforts at armed resistance were minimal until shortly before the arrival of Soviet troops. The main political effort during the conflict was directed toward creation of a broad antifascist coalition of all factions opposed to the regime. Under the guidance of Dimitrov in Moscow the BCP joined the left wing of the Agrarian Union, the "Broad" Socialists, and other groups to form the Fatherland Front in September 1943. The Front government took power on September 9, 1944, aided not only by the arrival of the Soviet Army but also by the gradual disintegration of the fascist regime following the death of Tsar Boris in August 1943.

Initially the Communist presence in the Fatherland Front government was not conspicuous. There were only two Communists among the sixteen members of the Council of Ministers, but they held key positions—the Ministries of the Interior and of Justice. Holding these two important posts, they began to root out the leaders of the previous government. This they did with vigor, thus earning for the BCP the distinction of having the bloodiest beginning of any of the new regimes in Eastern Europe. Meanwhile local government was being reorganized under the auspices of the Fatherland Front by a Communist leader, and local government committees were responsible to the Front rather than to the central government in Sofia.

As the BCP consolidated its power, it began bringing the Front fully under its control. It used splitting tactics to eliminate first one and then another of its erstwhile allies. The process was well under way when Dimitrov returned from Moscow to take over personal direction of the BCP in late 1945. He became prime minister shortly afterward, and following a plebiscite in September 1946, the monarchy was abolished and Bulgaria was declared a people's republic.

In October elections were held to select a national assembly, which was to produce a new constitution. An opposition Agrarian Union group that had formerly been in the Fatherland Front and was led by Nikola Petkov was permitted to participate in the elections, and despite the Communist-inspired atmosphere of terror they won some 30 percent of the vote. The Fatherland Front, nevertheless, won handily, and this "tolerated opposition" was not tolerated for long. The peace treaty with Bulgaria (and the other small Axis allies) was signed in February 1947; it recognized Bulgarian sovereignty, and the day after it was ratified by the U.S. Senate Petkov was arrested and subsequently executed.

The remainder of the Communist-imposed superstructure was quickly installed. The new "Dimitrov" constitution was approved in December 1947, a virtual copy of the 1936 Stalin Constitution adopted in the Soviet Union. Also during 1947 nationalization was extended to all important branches of industry, banks and insurance companies, and all foreign and some domestic trade firms. Even before nationalization was complete, central planning was initiated.

The one interesting Bulgarian deviation from the pattern that prevailed in the remainder of Eastern Europe was the solicitude shown by the authorities for the Bulgarian Orthodox church, of which most Bulgarians were members. Following Orthodox tradition, the church was closely linked with the state, and thus did not become an alternative center of power as was the case with the Roman Catholic church in Poland, Hungary, and Czechoslovakia. Some church leaders were sent into exile or banned from exercising their functions, but cooperative clerics were found and the government even supported the elevation of the exarchate to the status of a patriarchate in 1951. In part this was because the church was a symbol of Bulgarian national unity which the BCP wished to exploit, but it also served to further Soviet foreign policy aims by supporting the Russian patriarchate against the ecumenical patriarch in Constantinople.

The last step in the process of consolidating BCP power was the purge of the "nativist" faction of the party leadership by the "Muscovite" wing. Essentially, the pattern set elsewhere throughout Eastern Europe was followed in Bulgaria. The leading native Communist was Traicho Kostov, who had remained in Bulgaria and supervised party affairs on the spot, while Dimitrov and others had lived in the Soviet Union for some twenty-five years. In 1949 Kostov was accused of harboring nationalist and anti-Soviet sentiments and was dismissed from the Politburo and as deputy premier. He was tried and executed in December of that year. Other prominent home Communists were also purged at this time, including Interior Minister Anton Yugov. Although Stalin clearly wanted a Muscovite loyalist in charge of the BCP, the candidates were limited. Dimitrov, already sixty-three when he returned to Bulgaria in 1945, died in July 1949. The other prominent Muscovite, Vasil Kolarov, was five years older than Dimitrov, in poor health, and died just six months later. There were several prominent and experienced native Communists who could have taken over the party leadership, but the Soviets promoted Vulko Chervenkov. He had spent over twenty years in the Soviet Union before returning to Bulgaria in 1946, and he was not particularly well known even in Communist circles. His first post on returning was that of chairman of the Committee on Science, Art, and Culture, hardly a key position. Nevertheless, four years later he was secretary-general of the BCP and prime minister of Bulgaria.

MAIN LINES OF POLITICAL DEVELOPMENT, 1950–75

In the three years between his assumption of power in 1950 and the death of Stalin in 1953, Chervenkov succeeded in achieving a greater degree of control in Bulgaria than did any of his counterparts elsewhere in the Soviet sphere of Eastern Europe. The death of the Soviet dictator, however, marked the beginning of a new era. Unrest in Bulgaria (a tobacco workers' strike in Plovdiv in 1953 being the most obvious evidence), coupled with the relaxation decreed by the new Soviet leaders, led the regime to take measures to restrict police terror, reduce prices on important food items, cut back compulsory deliveries for collective farms, and improve conditions for workers in industry. In January 1954 new directives for the 1953–57 plan called for increased investment in agriculture, light industry, and housing. This was useful from the point of view of appeasing the population, which had suffered much under the rigorous earlier five-year plan, but it was also good from the economic point of view to permit the economy a breathing spell after five years of strenuous efforts to promote industrialization.

In keeping with the Kremlin's new pattern of collective leadership, Chervenkov gave up his post in the party but retained the premiership. One reason for this was that Stalin's heir, Georgi Malenkov, held the top government post in the USSR. Another reason was that in Todor Zhivkov, he thought he had a safe manipulatable first secretary to handle party affairs. This decision proved Chervenkov's undoing, because he lost direct control of the party apparatus; also, he had chosen the wrong Soviet patron. Until 1956, however, Zhivkov played a minor role—he was not even a member of the BCP delegation to the Twentieth CPSU Congress. At the Sixth BCP congress in February 1954 a number of Chervenkov's Communist rivals, including Yugov, were promoted to high party and government positions, a clear indication of his slipping status. Furthermore, native Communists who had been linked with Kostov were being quietly released from prison and rehabilitated. After Khrushchev's visit to Yugoslavia to mend fences with Tito, the CPSU first secretary's disapproval of the Stalinist leaders in Eastern Europe became increasingly apparent. Thus the coming demise of Chervenkov became ever more obvious after 1955.

The Soviet party's Twentieth Congress in February 1956, at which Khrushchev delivered his secret speech attacking Stalin, hastened Chervenkov's decline. The BCP Central Committee held a plenum April 2–6, 1956 (thenceforth known as the April plenum), at which Zhivkov delivered a report on the implications of the CPSU congress—although, as noted above, he had not been present at it. The plenum issued a "unanimous" resolution on the importance of Leninist norms, collective leadership, and struggle against the personality cult. Chervenkov was criticized openly for having permitted the development of a personality cult of his own.[2] Ten days later the National Assembly accepted his resignation as premier, but he was designated a deputy premier. The new head of government was Anton Yugov. Although Chervenkov's power had been considerably curtailed, he was by no means out of the picture, and for some time he remained a force to be reckoned with in the BCP.

Contemporary BCP writings inspired by Zhivkov hail the April plenum as a major turning point for the party, but that assessment is symbolically rather than factually valid. There was indeed a new, more open atmosphere after April 1956, but after the events in Poland and Hungary the following autumn the timid Bulgarian leadership moved to restrict the implications of the April plenum. The Central Committee session was a logical continuation of events since 1953, but hardly marked a turning point.

One rather curious episode at the end of the 1950s was Bulgaria's "great leap forward." The 1958–62 plan approved in June 1958 was rather moderate compared with previous ones, emphasizing that industrial branches should be developed only when favorable natural conditions and resources existed or when they were essential to the economy as a whole. This plan led to greater emphasis on the light and food industries, although heavy industry was still given preference. Less than six months later, however, a national movement was initiated to fulfill the plan in three to four years, and the new drive was spelled out by Zhivkov in a series of theses adopted by the Central Committee in January 1959.[3] Several reasons have been advanced for the great leap. Economically, despite considerable progress the Bulgarian economy was still not functioning at full capacity, it was not properly balanced, and there were problems in its foreign trade picture. Politically, the influence of China was a significant factor. The fact that the campaign was launched shortly after Chervenkov returned from a visit to Peking and that it was called in the Bulgarian press "the great leap forward" suggests Chinese influence. At the end of 1960 the government claimed that the 1958–62 plan had been fulfilled two years ahead of schedule, but a closer look showed that the targets had been lowered to coincide with what had been accomplished. The fact that the 1961 plan abandoned such an approach to the economy is perhaps the best testimony to its failure.

The strains introduced in the BCP by the "great leap" exacerbated the factionalization that already marked the party. Between 1958 and 1962 at least four factions emerged: the Chervenkov-Muscovite group, still influential though out of favor in the Kremlin; the Zhivkov–younger domestic Communist group; the Yugov–older domestic Communist group; and another older domestic Communist faction grouped around Dimitur Ganev. The existence of such factions was something of an anomaly in Eastern Europe, since after 1957 Khrushchev had established his clear ascendancy in the CPSU and his example was followed throughout the rest of the area, except in Bulgaria. Although there were purges of important BCP leaders in 1957 and early 1961, the most important step followed the Twenty-second CPSU Congress in October 1961, when Khrushchev revived his anti-Stalin campaign with renewed vigor. At the Central Committee plenum called to hear Zhivkov's report on the Soviet congress, Chervenkov was dismissed from the Politburo, the Central Committee, and his deputy premiership for being guilty of making "serious mistakes and employing vicious methods" both before and after the April plenum. This action was followed by the expulsion of "not a few" members from the party.

The final demise of Chervenkov after an eight-year decline left Zhivkov and Yugov as the two principal contenders for power. Khrushchev clearly favored Zhivkov, and made this quite apparent in a special visit to Bulgaria in May 1962. Despite the obvious support of the Soviets, however, Zhivkov had considerable difficulty forcing Yugov out. A Central Committee plenum that opened on the eve of the Eighth BCP Congress in late 1962 did not vote to drop Yugov until Zhivkov made a sudden trip to Moscow between sittings of the committee. Finally, in his opening address to the party congress, Zhivkov announced the expulsion of Yugov from the Politburo and the premiership, the expulsion of Georgi Tsankov from the Politburo and a deputy premiership, and the expulsion of Chervenkov from the party. Yugov and Tsankov were accused of various Stalinist crimes. At the congress and immediately afterward a number of Zhivkov loyalists were promoted to party and government positions, while Zhivkov himself acquired the premiership in addition to remaining first secretary of the party.

Although Zhivkov succeeded in establishing his authority over the party and essentially eliminating the factionalism that rent the party prior to the Eighth Congress, one extraordinary incident raises questions about the extent of his control and support. In April 1965 a conspiracy to unseat him was uncovered, involving several important party and military officials, most of whom had been involved in partisan activities in Western Bulgaria during World War II. The fact that the conspiracy was discovered just a few months after Khrushchev had been removed from office by his Kremlin colleagues suggests that the Soviet coup prepared the ground for the attempted Bulgarian one. Subsequent reports indicated that in Western Bulgaria and in the military there was a significant amount of sympathy with those who plotted the coup.[4]

At the time of the Ninth BCP Congress in 1966 there was some hope that it would speed up certain reforms that had been initiated after the April conspiracy, but it became only too evident after the congress that the process of reform was being slowed rather than accelerated. This was particularly evident in the economy, where the party was attempting to come to grips with the consequences of modernization. The cautious economic reforms launched in December 1965 were modest by any standard, but in July 1968, after almost three years of half-hearted attempts to implement them, the party leadership opted for a return to centralization. This retrenchment in the economy was paralleled by a tightening of ideological control in other areas of society, most notably the cultural field.

The one area in which Bulgaria has shown a degree of innovation is the organization of agriculture. In 1969 agro-industrial complexes (AICs) were established on an experimental basis, and by the end of 1970 they encompassed over 90 percent of the country's arable land. AICs are large enterprises intended to achieve horizontal integration of agricultural production units, to encourage specialization over larger areas, thus raising production, and to permit mechanization at lower cost. The Bulgarians have taken a flexible approach to the AICs, experimenting on a small scale and then implementing those measures found to be the most successful. While the AICs have not radically improved agricultural output, there is evidence that the organizational changes have been beneficial to production. The approach to agricultural organization, however, represents an exception to the general picture of political, economic, and ideological conservatism that has marked Bulgaria under Zhivkov.

THE CURRENT POLITICAL STRUCTURE

The BCP plays the dominant role in Bulgarian politics, both in fact and according to the country's current constitution, which specifies that the party "is the leading force in Bulgarian society." This basic document also specifies that the country is a member of "the world socialist community," and thus is committed to "developing and strengthening friendship, cooperation, and mutual assistance with the USSR and the other socialist countries."[5] Although the BCP is cited as the leading force, how it exercises that role is not spelled out.

The party itself is organized along standard Soviet lines. Its highest authority is the party congress, which meets every five years and delegates to which are selected from lower-level party organizations. This gathering approves policy statements and "elects" the Central Committee, which wields power between congresses. The Central Committee meets two to six times a year and is largely a platform from which to legitimize and publicize party policies. It "elects" a Secretariat and Politburo, where the actual power resides. In mid-1977 the Politburo was composed of eight full and six alternate members; the Secretariat consisted of First Secretary Todor Zhivkov, four secretaries, and five members.

At the Eleventh Party Congress in March 1976 the BCP had 789,796 members, an increase of over 90,000 in the five years since the previous congress in 1971. One out of every eight Bulgarians over the age of eighteen is a member of the party. The BCP's social composition has remained relatively constant for some time: 41.4 percent blue-collar workers; 30.2 percent white-collar workers; and 23.0 percent collective farmers. At the end of 1975 women made up 27.6 percent of its members.[6]

The usual gamut of mass organizations operates under party control: the *Chavdarche,* an organization for children between the ages of seven and nine; the *Septemvriiche* (Septembrists), the equivalent of the Pioneers in the USSR, for slightly older young people; the Dimitrov Communist Youth Union or Komsomol, for teenagers; the trade union organization; the Committee of Bulgarian Women. All function in much the same manner as their Soviet models.

The Fatherland Front continues to exist, though it plays a less prominent role now than it did in 1944, when it was the instrument for seizing power. The Front is completely under BCP influence. It is the largest mass sociopolitical organization in Bulgaria, and in mid-1977 its membership was over four million. It acts as an umbrella for all other public and mass organizations and provides the principal vehicle for mass participation in politics. All candidates for public office at national and local levels are elected on the Fatherland Front ticket, and it is the main institution for organizing government elections.

The only unique organization is the Bulgarian Agrarian Union (BAU), which is referred to as the second political party in the country. It is the remains of the once influential organization of the same name which played such an important political role in the interwar period. Although it continues to maintain an independent organizational existence as a party, it is controlled by the BCP and in fact is merely another means of carrying out BCP policy. At its last congress (in December 1976) the BAU reported a membership of 120,000, unchanged since 1957. Primarily because of its past services the BAU has been allocated an unexpectedly large number of seats in the National Assembly. Since 1966 this number has remained constant at 100, or about one fourth of the assembly members. The BAU is mainly concerned with agricultural questions, but its role in agricultural management is small and appears to be declining with the introduction of AICs. It does play something of an international role, however, maintaining contacts with other agrarian parties. Since the Soviet Union has no agrarian party of its own, the BAU has occasionally taken the lead in multilateral functions sponsored by the USSR. This international role is perhaps the main reason for the BAU's continued separate existence; it certainly does not diverge in any respect from the policies of the BCP.

The government structure is specified in the 1971 constitution. The State Council is the highest body of state administration. It has certain representative functions and exercises the functions of the National Assembly when the latter is not in session. The head of the State Council (Todor Zhivkov was elected to the post when it was created in 1971) is the head of state. The National Assembly is described as "the supreme organ of state power" and is composed of some 400 deputies. Since it meets only a few times each year and for only a few days each time, it is principally a body that announces, publicizes, and legitimizes decisions taken elsewhere. The government is headed by the prime minister, who presides over the Council of Ministers; in mid-1977 this council had thirty-five members—the prime minister, a first deputy and six deputy prime ministers, twenty-two ministers, and five agency heads with ministerial rank.

THE LEADERSHIP AND CHANGING ELITE PATTERNS

On the whole the members of the Bulgarian elite are well into middle age (in 1977 the average age was fifty-eight); not altogether homogeneous (i.e., not all are of proletarian background); and not highly educated (less than half have university degrees). They have on the average served more than thirty-five years in the party. Within the top elite, certain important distinctions should be noted. The full members of the Politburo are somewhat older (average age sixty-three) than the candidate members (average age fifty-five) and the members of the Secretariat (average age fifty-six); they are also less well educated, and have longer service in the party.

An analysis of the career patterns of the Bulgarian elite indicates that there are three chief avenues to power: advancement within the party hierarchy; advancement within the state apparatus; advancement first in the party and then in the state apparatus. The most common road to the top is, as might be expected, through the party hierarchy; three-fifths of the top elite have followed this road.

The most typical example of this career pattern is the present first secretary, Todor Zhivkov, whose whole career has been in the party apparatus. Zhivkov was born of peasant stock in a rural area and had less than a secondary education. He joined the Young Communist League in 1930 and spent the next twelve years as a secretary in various districts. He was active as a partisan during the war, and after September 9, 1944, became second secretary of the district party committee in Sofia. In 1945 he was elected a candidate member of the Central Committee, and in 1948 became a full member as well as a member of the Organizational Bureau. In January 1950 he was elected a Central Committee secretary, and in November of that year he became a candidate member of the Politburo. The next year he was elected to full membership in that body. At the Sixth Party Congress (February–March 1954) he became first secretary of the Central Committee, a post he still holds. Zhivkov typifies the bureaucrat who has risen through the ranks—a colorless, disciplined official who has spent his career dealing with organizational-ideological problems rather than with specialized problems of the economy.

The second most common way to the top is to alternate work in the party and the state apparatus. The prototype of this route is Tano Tsolov. He joined the Communist youth organization in 1934 and became a party member six years later. He was active in underground party activities and in a partisan detachment before 1944. He was a regional party official from 1944 to 1950, when he became head of the Central Committee Industry and Transportation Department. His switch to government took place in 1952 when he was appointed head of the Ministry of Heavy Industry. From 1959 to 1962 he returned briefly to party work as a Central Committee secretary, but in 1962 he became a deputy premier and a candidate member of the Politburo. In 1966 Tsolov became a full Politburo member. He has remained a deputy premier since 1962 but his responsibilities have changed during this period; he has served as Bulgaria's permanent representative in CMEA (1966–68) and as head of the State Planning Committee (1968–71). In 1971 he became first deputy premier. Thus Tsolov has spent time in both party work and the state apparatus. His long experience in economic matters differentiates him from members of the elite like Todor Zhivkov, whose careers have been solely within the party apparatus.

Stanko Todorov, the present prime minister, took the third route to power. While he spent his first several years in party work, his career since 1952, when he was appointed minister of agriculture, has been predominantly in the state apparatus. He subsequently served as deputy chairman of the Council of Ministers and chairman of the State

Planning Commission, deputy prime minister, chairman of the Commission on Economic and Scientific-Technical Collaboration, and permanent representative to CMEA. His rise has been little less than meteoric, and in July 1971 he replaced Zhivkov as prime minister. While he is not highly educated, his administrative experience has given him an overall familiarity with technical and economic questions, which distinguishes him from men whose careers have been solely in the party apparatus.

The Bulgarian elite is essentially composed of "ideological generalists"—that is, men who have spent most of their careers in party and organizational work—rather than "pragmatic" technocrats. Technological know-how is *not* an avenue to power. On the other hand, there is a minority in the elite—represented in particular by Todorov, Tsolov, and Pencho Kubadinski in the Politburo—whose career patterns differentiate them from less-well-educated "ideological generalists" like Todor Zhivkov, and who, owing to their past experience and organizational associations, may be presumed to have a different, somewhat more flexible outlook. One should avoid labeling such men "liberal," however; they are "pragmatic neoconservatives" whose primary interest is to increase the efficiency of the system.[7]

ECONOMIC DEVELOPMENT AND SOCIAL CHANGE

Traditionally, Bulgaria has had a primarily rural economy, and at the end of World War II it was still a predominantly agricultural country. Although modest efforts were made to encourage the development of industry before 1939, progress in this area was limited, and in 1948 some 81.9 percent of the working population was still engaged in agriculture, and only 9.9 percent in industry and construction. At first, under the two-year reconstruction plan (1947–48), and with greater emphasis when the first five-year plan (1949–53) was launched, investment was focused on the industrial sector. In 1949, 33.6 percent of total investment was in industry and construction, and only 11.7 percent was allocated for agriculture. This imbalance has continued, although investment in both areas has increased. Between 1965 and 1971 investment in industry and construction averaged 48–52 percent of total annual investment, while agriculture received 15–17 percent a year.

The results of the industrial priority have been evident in the development of the Bulgarian economy since the late 1940s. The percentage of the work force employed in agriculture declined from 81.9 in 1948 to 33.4 in 1971, and during this period employment in industry and construction climbed from 9.9 to 39.8 percent. The contribution of agriculture to the gross national product likewise declined, from 31 percent in 1952 to 14 percent in 1971, while that of industry and construction increased from 54 percent to 74 percent over the same period. The proportion of industrial production stemming from agriculturally related areas (food processing, forestry, leather processing, textile and clothing manufacture) was 83.4 percent in 1939; by 1952 it had declined to 69.3 percent, and by 1971 the figure was 43.8 percent. Although it is obvious that the Bulgarian economy is still heavily dependent upon agriculture, the change is dramatic. Industrial production not related to the processing of agricultural goods (heavy engineering, machine building, chemicals, ferrous and nonferrous metallurgy, and the production of electricity and fuel) accounted for only 11.7 percent of total industrial output in 1939, but by 1971 it was responsible for 56.2 percent.[8] A good measure of the progress achieved is the fact that in 1950 Bulgaria's per capita national income was 66 percent of the Soviet per capita national income for that year, but by 1969 the Bulgarian figure had reached 85 percent of the Soviet figure.[9]

Despite this significant shift toward industry, however, agriculture continues to play an important role in the Bulgarian economy. In 1971 over 33 percent of the population was still employed in it. (The only two East European states with a higher proportion of the work force engaged in this area were Romania, with 46.6 percent, and Poland, with 35.2 percent; in East Germany—the most heavily industrialized country in Eastern Europe—the figure was only 12.6 percent.)[10] Economic progress has been significant, but Bulgaria has not yet reached the level of an advanced industrial country.

A number of social changes have accompanied the shift from agriculture to industry. The peasantry was the largest social class in prewar Bulgaria, but today industrial workers can make this claim. Although most members of the new working class are no more than a generation away from the farm, and as a result are still influenced to some extent by peasant traditions, they have concerns and problems quite different from those of their agrarian countrymen.

From being predominantly rural, the population has become predominantly urban. During the decades before World War II the urban population remained roughly constant at about 20 percent of the total. By 1956 it had reached 33.6 percent, in 1965 it was 46.5 percent, and in 1973 it was estimated at 57 percent.[11]

Another social change that has accompanied the economic changes is a rise in the level of education. When the country achieved its independence, the Bulgarian population was largely illiterate, but by the end of World War II this condition had been almost eliminated among the younger generation. In pursuing its ambitious industrialization program the Communist government has needed a population with a higher level of education, particularly in scientific and technical fields, and has therefore concentrated on expanding educational facilities. In particular, opportunities for advanced study have increased. An indication of this is the fact that at the end of 1944 the ratio of students in advanced training to the total population in the 15- to 25-year-old group was 5.4 percent; at the end of 1971 the figure was 29.1 percent. The number of university-level students per 10,000 inhabitants was 16.0 in 1939–40, but had reached 97.8 in 1967–68, placing Bulgaria fifth among the countries of the world in terms of ratio of students to total population.[12]

ORTHODOXY IN FOREIGN POLICY

Bulgaria is the East European state that is probably most loyal to the Soviet Union. Various explanations have been offered for this. Some observers have suggested that the existence of factions within the BCP has prevented the development of a strong, united party, and hence Moscow has been able to play one faction against another to the benefit of Soviet interests. While this explanation may have had a certain validity during the 1950s, after the Eighth party congress in 1962 factionalism within the party was largely eliminated. Others have attributed the BCP's loyalty to the strong historical and cultural bond between Russians and Bulgarians. These ties do of course influence Sofia's foreign policy, but this explanation seems inadequate by itself to justify the extraordinarily close adherence of Bulgaria to Soviet foreign policy, particularly since popular opinion has generally had only limited impact on postwar government policy. Still another explanation is that Bulgaria's geographical location is of such importance that the Soviet Union has insisted upon maintaining a very firm foothold in the country, but the fact that Soviet troops are not stationed in Bulgaria suggests that it is not an unwilling follower of the Soviet line.

Although the above considerations undoubtedly account in part for Bulgaria's superloyalty to the Soviet Union, other elements are obviously involved. Just as the conservatism of the Bulgarian party seems to govern its orthodox domestic policies, the fear of risk-taking and change appears to be a key element in its foreign policies. Rather than take chances, Bulgaria has preferred to follow a foreign policy that at times could be described as being more Soviet than that of the Soviet Union.

This conservatism is reinforced by the advantages Bulgaria has gained from its close relationship with the USSR. The economic assistance provided by that country is so important that the potential cost of an autonomous foreign policy makes Bulgarian leaders unwilling to take the risk. The rewards for adhering to the Soviet policy line have indeed been significant. Of all the East European states, Bulgaria ranks first in trade with the Soviet Union and the CMEA states, and last in trade with the "developed capitalist countries." In 1974 its trade with the USSR amounted to 46.9 percent of the total, and 70.2 percent of the total was with CMEA states (including the USSR).[13] How closely the Bulgarian economy is linked with that of the Soviet Union is indicated by the fact that two-thirds of Bulgaria's imports of fuel, mineral raw materials, and metals come from there, and 60 percent of the output of the Bulgarian machine-building industry is exported to Russia. On the other hand, 13–14 percent of all Soviet machine and equipment exports go to Bulgaria. The USSR has assisted in the construction of 180 enterprises and units which constitute the foundation of Bulgaria's heavy industry, and some 150 additional units are to be built during the course of the 1976–80 plan.[14]

The increasing coordination between the two countries is not just an economic phenomenon; it is being extended to all spheres. In discussing this growing closeness during Brezhnev's visit to Sofia in 1973, Todor Zhivkov asserted that the USSR and Bulgaria would increasingly have the same rhythm of development, and that coordination and integration would take place not only in the economic field but in the political, ideological, scientific, cultural, and military fields as well. "In other words," he went on, "Bulgaria and the Soviet Union will act as a single body which breathes through the same lungs and is nourished by the same blood stream."[15]

An organizational reflection of the closeness of the two countries is that the Bulgarian ambassador in Moscow is now ex officio, a minister in the Bulgarian government, and his deputy is a deputy minister.

The area of Bulgaria's greatest foreign policy interest is its relations with its Balkan neighbors. Although it has generally followed the Soviet lead even in this region, there have been indications that divergencies between Soviet and Bulgarian interests do indeed exist. In recent years Bulgaria has followed the Soviet-inspired line of opposing multilateral Balkan cooperation and working only to improve bilateral relations with its neighbors, but its policy was not always so oriented. Sofia responded favorably to the Khrushchev-inspired Stoica proposals in the 1950s, and the first half of the 1960s was marked by repeated and persistent expressions of Bulgarian support for a nuclear-free zone in the Balkans. This support was essentially a matter of principle, however, and was not accompanied by concrete suggestions about how to reach agreement on the subject.

Nonetheless there are certain indications that despite the lack of concrete action during this period Bulgaria had not abandoned the idea that many of the Balkan countries' problems could be solved on a multilateral basis. A statement advocating "steps of a regional Balkan character—e.g., multilateral Balkan parliamentary and government meetings," was made by Foreign Minister Ivan Bashev in 1970.[16] A year later an incident in connection with the Tenth BCP congress provided an indication that Zhivkov was still (or again) in favor of a high-level Balkan conference but was prevented from making a suggestion to this effect, presumably because of Soviet disapproval. A passage in his report to the congress was obviously deleted at the last moment, but through an error became known to Western newsmen. The passage in question called for a common declaration by the Balkan countries on respect for territorial integrity, noninterference in internal affairs, and renunciation of the use or threat of force. It went on to say that the preparation of such a declaration "could provide a favorable occasion to discuss these questions on a bilateral basis and to hold a multilateral meeting of government representatives or heads of governments of the Balkan states." Although Zhivkov renounced his original advocacy of a multilateral meeting of Balkan leaders, his report as read and printed still contained outspoken support of multilateral undertakings.

The positive attitude to multilateral undertakings expressed at the Tenth BCP congress was soon reversed, however. Premier Stanko Todorov said in an interview that despite the favorable atmosphere prevailing in the Balkans, "one must be satisfied with strengthening bilateral neighborly relations." He later repeated this view, stating still more explicitly that "the situation is not yet ripe for establishing multilateral relations in the Balkans."[17] Thereafter Bulgaria consistently advocated bilateral relations as the only possibility for the Balkan countries. This Bulgarian policy was reemphasized at the Athens conference on Balkan cooperation in January 1976, where the Bulgarians showed less willingness than any other participating state to accept the idea of Balkan cooperation.

Because of Sofia's ultra-Soviet foreign policy, there is a possibility of

conflict between that policy and Bulgarian nationalism. Despite strong
historical, cultural, and emotional ties with Russia, a desire for international recognition and an independent role in world affairs, which are
elements of nationalism, conflicts with Bulgaria's pro-Soviet policy.
Strong national sentiment on the part of the population could easily
lead to anti-Sovietism, and this has posed a difficult problem for the
BCP, which has sought to foster both patriotism and love of the Soviet
Union.

With the Bulgarian leadership so firmly united with the Soviet
Union, the country's foreign policy offers few opportunities for actions
satisfying to Bulgarian nationalism. This fact, however, provides a
useful clue to Bulgaria's position on the troublesome Macedonian question, which continues to disrupt relations with Yugoslavia. At issue is
the nationality of the inhabitants of the Yugoslav republic of Macedonia and the Bulgarian district of Blagoevgrad. The Yugoslavs have
vociferously maintained that the Slavic inhabitants of both areas are of
Macedonian nationality. The Bulgarians have quietly maintained that
they are ethnic Bulgarians, but they appear to be more willing to accept
a separate nationality for Macedonians in Yugoslavia. Although the
positions taken by the two parties could provide a basis for territorial
claims, both have renounced such demands, and at present the dispute
centers around interpretations of the history of this area and Bulgaria's
refusal to admit the existence of a Macedonian minority in Bulgaria.
Questions relating to the Macedonian language also do not appear to be
completely resolved. Representatives of both Bulgaria and Yugoslavia
have expressed serious interest in good relations, and efforts have been
made to expand political and economic ties. In all cases, however, the
unresolved Macedonian issue continues to be the principal obstacle to
further improvement. From the Yugoslav point of view the Bulgarians
must first admit the existence of a Macedonian nationality, both contemporary and historical, and second, recognize the existence of a
Macedonian minority in Bulgaria which is entitled to full nationality
rights.

For the Yugoslavs, securing Bulgarian recognition of the Macedonian nationality is a significant issue. The Yugoslav claim to the
southern part of its territory (the socialist republic of Macedonia) is
based on the presumption that the Macedonians are one of the peoples
of the Yugoslav federation. Until 1912 the Slavic inhabitants of the
Blagoevgrad district were part of the same Turkish region and were
considered part of the same ethnic group; hence, securing Bulgarian
recognition of a Macedonian minority becomes a necessary concomi-

tant to securing recognition of the existence of a Macedonian nationality in Yugoslavia. With the potentially unstable internal situation in
Yugoslavia this problem has assumed greater significance and urgency.
The Yugoslavs have been quite aggressive in asserting their "historical" claims about Macedonian nationality. Public polemics and scholarly disputes over the question of whether Samuil's Tenth-century
kingdom was "Bulgarian" or "Macedonian" are hardly relevant, since
our present concepts of national identity are inaccurate measures by
which to assess events of that time. The dispute over the nationality of
the inhabitants of Macedonia, particularly the revolutionary leaders of
the Macedonian independence movement during the nineteenth century, is somewhat more relevant, but again, hardly of decisive importance. Yet these historical issues are a primary reason for the repeated
outbursts on the Macedonian question.

Although Bulgaria has apparently accepted the fact that people of
Macedonian nationality live in Yugoslavia, treatment of historical issues in some Bulgarian periodicals still provokes Yugoslav wrath. Comments offensive to Belgrade could be eliminated by a directive from the
party leadership, whose power is sufficient to enforce compliance; in
fact, offending statements appear to vary according to the state of
Soviet-Yugoslav relations. For the Bulgarians to grant minority rights
to the Macedonians in the Blagoevgrad district would be more difficult.
In the first place, it is doubtful whether many of the local population
would choose to be identified as Macedonians rather than Bulgarians;
they would probably consider themselves somewhat different from
other Bulgarians, but regional peculiarities do not necessarily imply
consciousness of a separate nationality. It would seem, however, that
some mutually acceptable compromise could be worked out.

The fact that Yugoslav-Bulgarian differences have not been resolved,
despite the sincere desire to improve relations and despite occasional
Soviet pressure on Sofia to do so, indicates the strength of Bulgarian
feeling. In this case the Macedonian question—which is closely linked
with Bulgarian nationalism—may serve as a safety valve for national
feelings, since the Bulgarian leaders have chosen to subordinate Bulgaria's interests to those of the Soviet Union. As a highly emotional
issue directed against a country that is not fully within the "socialist
camp," it provides a useful release for national feelings that might
otherwise develop anti-Soviet overtones. The Macedonian question,
however, remains unresolved and thus is likely to be an important
issue for post-Tito Yugoslavia and a factor in Soviet-Yugoslav as well
as in Bulgarian-Yugoslav relations.

NOTES

1. Giuseppe Boffa, "Bulgaria's Road," *L'Unita* (Milan), February 14, 1974.
2. *Rabotnichesko Delo,* April 8, 1956.
3. Ibid., January 20, 1959.
4. The best account of this incident is found in J. F. Brown, *Bulgaria Under Communist Rule* (New York: Praeger, 1970), pp. 173–189.
5. *Rabotnichesko Delo,* May 9, 1971.
6. Ibid., March 30, 1976.
7. On the Bulgarian elite see "The Bulgarian Party Leadership," Bulgarian Background Report/10, Radio Free Europe Research, September 8, 1972.
8. Figures from *Statisticheski Godishnik na N.R.B., 1972* (Sofia: Tsentralno Statistichesko Upravlenie, 1972), pp. 66, 87, 93, and 110.
9. G. E. Zhelov, *Problemy vosproizvodstva i mezhdunarodnogo razdelenia truda v stranam chlenam SEV* [Problems of Production and the International Division of Labor in the Member Countries of CMEA], (Moscow: Ekonomika, 1971), p. 145.
10. Constantin Grigorescu and Marcu Horovitz, "Economic Development of Romania and Other Comecon Countries Compared," *Probleme Economice* (Bucharest) no. 7 (July), 1973.
11. *Statisticheski Godishnik,* 1974.
12. *Statisticheski Godishnik,* 1966 and 1972, and *Narodna Mladezh,* May 1 and 24, 1968.
13. See *Statisticheski Godishnik,* 1974, and *Statisticheskii ezhegodnik stran chlenov soveta ekonomicheskoi vziamopomoshchi* (Moscow: 1972), p. 325.
14. Tsvyatko Bozhkov, "Economic Integration with the USSR Is a Decisive Factor in Building a Developed Socialist Society," *Planovo Stopanstvo,* no. 6/1973.
15. *Rabotnichesko Delo,* September 20, 1973.
16. Ibid., February 18, 1970.
17. *Helsingin Sanomat* (Helsinki), April 1, 1973.

BIBLIOGRAPHY

Brown, J. F. *Bulgaria Under Communist Rule.* New York: Praeger, 1970.
Dellin, L. A. D. *Bulgaria.* New York: Praeger, 1957.
King, Robert R. *Minorities Under Communism: Nationalities as Source of Tension Among Balkan Communist States.* Cambridge, Mass.: Harvard University Press, 1973.
Kofos, Evangelos. *Nationalism and Communism in Macedonia.* Salonica: Institute for Balkan Studies, 1964.
Miller, Marshall Lee. *Bulgaria During the Second World War.* Stanford, California: Stanford University Press, 1975.
Oren, Nissan. *Bulgarian Communism: The Road to Power, 1934–1944.* New York: Columbia University Press, 1971.

————. *Revolution Administered: Agrarianism and Communism in Bulgaria.* Baltimore: Johns Hopkins Press, 1973.

Palmer, Stephen E., and Robert R. King. *Yugoslav Communism and the Macedonian Question.* Hamden, Conn.: Archon, 1971.

Rothschild, Joseph. *The Communist Party of Bulgaria: Origins and Development, 1893–1936.* New York: Columbia University Press, 1959.

8   Albania

Nicholas C. Pano

Although it is the smallest and least developed of the East European Communist states, the People's Socialist Republic of Albania has at various times since 1945 enjoyed a prominence far out of proportion to its size and power. To a considerable degree Albania's notoriety has stemmed from the fact that its rulers have steadfastly pursued the goals they established for themselves upon their advent to power in November 1944. These were to maintain and strengthen their hold on Albania, to preserve the country's independence and territorial integrity, to modernize its economy and society, and to build socialism in accordance with the Leninist-Stalinist Soviet model. Since the early 1970s the Albanians have attracted further notice as a consequence of the efforts of their leaders to establish themselves as arbiters of "Marxist-Leninist purity."

Albania's efforts to realize these objectives have brought it into conflict first with Yugoslavia in 1948, then with the Soviet Union and the greater part of the Communist world during the 1960s, and with its most recent patron and ally, China, in the 1970s. By the late 1970s, the People's Socialist Republic of Albania enjoyed the dubious distinction of being the most isolated and dogmatic of the East European party states.

The Albanians are considered to be the descendants of the Illyrians, among the earliest inhabitants of the Balkan Peninsula. In 167 B.C. the Romans conquered the Illyrians. Subsequently, the Albanians were overrun by the Goths, Bulgars, Slavs, Serbs, Normans, Byzantines, and Ottoman Turks. Except for the years 1443–68 when the Albanians temporarily freed themselves from Turkish control under the leadership of their national hero Skanderbeg, Albania remained under Ottoman rule until 1912.

The Albanians, however, were disappointed that some 500,000 of their compatriots residing in what is today the Yugoslav autonomous province of Kosovo-Metohija were not included in the boundaries of the new Albanian state. After winning its independence, Albania experienced a period of political instability which lasted until 1925, when Ahmed Zogu, a northern tribal chief, seized power. In 1928 he proclaimed Albania a monarchy and ruled until 1939, when Italy invaded and occupied Albania.

Following the Italian invasion, Zog fled the country. Zog's departure and the failure of the World War II Allies to recognize his regime in exile set the stage for the power struggle between the wartime Communist and noncommunist resistance forces.

THE COMMUNIST TAKEOVER: 1941–46

Prior to 1941 communism had been only an inconsequential factor in Albanian political life. During the 1920s a handful of Albanian students, intellectuals, and young workers developed an interest in Marxism and sympathy for the new Soviet regime; about twenty-five of them went to the Soviet Union for ideological and political training after the fall from power in December 1924 of the short-lived Fan Noli government, which they had backed. The first Communist cell in Albania was formed in 1927, but the movement attracted little support during the 1930s. When Italy invaded and occupied Albania in April 1939, the Communists were few in number (about 200), lacked leadership and discipline, had little contact with the masses, and were divided into four contending factions.

Differences among these factions being apparently irreconcilable, a number of prominent Communists, among them Enver Hoxha, a thirty-three-year-old schoolteacher turned revolutionary, began to agitate for the dissolution of the existing Communist groups and the formation of a united Albanian Communist party. This plan was given impetus by the Nazi invasion of the USSR in June 1941 and assisted by the Yugoslav Communist party, which had maintained a loose liaison with the Albanian Communists since 1939. In November 1941, at a secret meeting in Tirana, representatives of three of the Albanian groups along with two Yugoslav advisers agreed to establish an Albanian Communist party and elected an eleven-member Central Committee with Hoxha as secretary. The entire party leadership and most of the 130 persons subsequently admitted to the party were relatively young Communists who had not been trained in the Soviet Union and who had no ties with the Comintern. Approximately two-thirds of the original party members were students or young intellectuals of upper- or middle-class backgrounds, and the rest were mostly laborers and artisans.

The most pressing problems confronting the newly formed party were to establish an organizational structure, expand its membership, improve its ties with the people, and gain control of the resistance movement. The realization of these tasks was facilitated by the disorganization of the prewar power elite. King Zog had gone into exile in the early hours of the Italian invasion, taking with him many political leaders; most of those who remained in Albania were collaborating with the Italians, and those who weren't were not yet ready to act. Taking advantage of this leadership vacuum and the organizational and military advice of their Yugoslav advisers, the Communists had made substantial progress, by the end of 1942, toward the realization of their objectives.

By January 1942 they had formed eight district party committees, which in turn established local party organizations to supervise the operations of the cells and other basic party units. As the district and local party organizations began to function, they recruited, on a highly selective basis, individuals who were actively opposing the Italians. The Communist Youth Organization, created in November 1942, also served to swell the ranks of Communist sympathizers among younger Albanians. Throughout the summer of 1942 Communist guerrilla units conducted military actions which they extensively publicized and which seem to have been well received by the people. Communist propaganda efforts were further enhanced when the party newspaper *Zeri i Popullit* commenced publication in August.

With their numbers growing and their prestige rising, the Communists convened a meeting of representatives of all the Albanian resistance organizations at Peza in September 1942. The Peza Conference established the National Liberation Movement (NLM), a coalition of the majority of the active Albanian antifascist groups, and authorized the creation of popularly elected national liberation councils throughout Albania to conduct the war effort on the local level and to exercise political control when the occupation forces had been expelled. Better organized and more politically astute than the other groups comprising the NLM, the Communists easily dominated the organization. Thus, by the stratagem of an antifascist popular front, the Communists had assumed by the end of 1942 a leading, though not exclusive, role in the struggle to liberate Albania.

In November 1942 a number of prominent liberal and moderate politicians established a staunchly anticommunist organization, the National Front (NF), which advocated the formation of a republican regime in Albania after the war, and the preservation of the ethnic Albanian state created in 1941 by the Axis powers with the incorporation of the Yugoslav provinces of Kosovo and Metohija into Albania. During the first half of 1943 both the NLM and NF conducted military operations against the Italians and waged war with each other; the NF forces were larger, but the NLM appears to have been more active in fighting the enemy and more effective in publicizing its successes.

As a result of peacemaking efforts by patriotic noncollaborationist Albanian politicians and members of the British military mission, which had entered Albania in April, the NLM and the NF sought to resolve their differences on August 2, 1943, with the Mukaj Agreement. This pact provided for equal representation of both groups on a "Committee for the Salvation of Albania," designed to direct the war effort; the reorganization of the national liberation councils to ensure proportional representation for the NF; and the holding of a plebiscite in Kosovo after the war to determine the future of the region.

The Albanian Communist leadership refused to approve the agreement, however, fearing loss of NLM control to a coalition of NF and noncommunist elements, and their Yugoslav advisers objected to the proposed plebiscite on the grounds that Kosovo-Metohija was an integral part of Yugoslavia. The Communists then called for an all-out struggle against both the NF and the Germans, who had occupied Albania in September following the Italian surrender. Repudiation of the Mukaj Agreement and the resumption of warfare with the NF led to the resignation from the NLM of Abas Kupi, its last important noncommunist leader. Kupi, an ardent monarchist, now formed the Legality Organization, which favored the restoration of King Zog. As 1943 drew to a close, the NLM found itself opposed by the combined forces of the German Army, the pro-German Albanian puppet government, the NF, and the Legality Organization.

The winter of 1943–44 marks the turning point of the Albanian power struggle. Despite the best efforts of the formidable military forces of the opposition and the ravages of one of the bitterest winters in Albanian history, the NLM managed to survive and in turn launched a massive offensive against its enemies in the spring of 1944. Aware of the consequences of an NLM victory, the British military mission made repeated efforts to arrange a truce among the contending Albanian factions and to bring the noncommunist forces into the war against the Germans.

But their efforts were unsuccessful, and as a result, during the final stages of the "national liberation war," the Communists had little difficulty in convincing most of the people that their opponents were "collaborationists," "traitors," and "war criminals."

When most of southern Albania had been freed from Nazi control, the NLM convened a congress on May 24 at Permet. At this meeting the NLM became the National Liberation Front (NLF), Hoxha was appointed supreme commander of the National Liberation Army, King Zog was forbidden to return to Albania, and all treaties concluded by the Albanian government prior to 1939 were declared null and void. In late October, when about three-fourths of Albania had been liberated, the NLF convoked a congress at Berat. The congress established a provisional government headed by Hoxha and dominated by Communists. The NLF pledged to hold free elections for a constituent assembly, and expressed its desire to maintain good relations "with the great allies, Great Britain, the Soviet Union, and the United States."

By late November 1944 the Germans evacuated their last position in Albania and the Communist-dominated provisional government was installed in Tirana, with the apparent support of the majority of the people and with the sympathy (because of the NLF contribution to the war effort) of the U.S. and British governments. Thus, even before the end of World War II in Europe, communism had triumphed in Albania, the only country in Eastern Europe where Communists had seized power without any Soviet assistance. The young, ambitious, nationalistic, indigenous Communist leadership that had emerged during the war now confronted the immediate task of consolidating and legitimatizing its authority.

During 1945–46 the Communists moved swiftly to strengthen their hold on the Albanian political system. After eliminating virtually all their active opponents by purges and "war crimes" trials, they renamed the NLF the Democratic Front (DF) and in its name ran a slate of Communists and their sympathizers for the constituent assembly convoked by the provisional government. On December 2, 1945, the DF slate polled 93 percent of the ballots cast, and on January 11, 1946, the newly elected constituent assembly formally abolished the monarchy and proclaimed Albania a "people's republic." On March 14 the new constitution of the People's Republic of Albania was promulgated. Thus, by the spring of 1946, the Communists had legitimized their position in Albania. Enver Hoxha, secretary general of the Albanian Communist party, was now also prime minister, foreign minister, defense minister, and commander-in-chief of the armed forces in the new government.

POLITICAL TRENDS, 1946–76

Between 1946 and 1956 Hoxha successfully withstood three major challenges to his leadership. The first came from Koci Xoxe, Hoxha's powerful deputy, who, representing the older, less well-educated proletarian faction of the party, favored an accelerated socialist revolution and exclusive ties with Yugoslavia and the Soviet Union. With the United States and Britain becoming increasingly hostile, Hoxha temporarily accepted the Xoxe program in 1946, but the Yugoslavs, unplacated, backed Xoxe in the spring of 1948 in an effort to overthrow Hoxha. Hoxha, however, exploited the Soviet-Yugoslav split, which occurred at this time, and succeeded in purging Xoxe and his followers at the First Congress of the Albanian Party of Labor (APL) in November 1948. After a public trial, Xoxe was executed in June 1949.

The next major challenge to Hoxha's leadership came in the early 1950s, when a segment of the Albanian leadership headed by Politburo members Bedri Spahiu and Tuk Jakova began to urge, among other things, a slowdown in the industrialization program, a delay in the collectivization of agriculture, a softer line toward religion, a "democratization" of the party, and, after 1953, the initiation of a program of de-Stalinization. Hoxha, who had during the late 1940s enthusiastically embraced the Stalinist line, strenuously opposed these positions as hindrances to the successful construction of socialism, and by June 1955 he had purged most of his principal antagonists, including Jakova and Spahiu.

The final challenge to Hoxha's leadership during the 1950s came on essentially the same issues at the Tirana city party conference in April 1956. His opposition this time came mainly from middle-ranking bureaucrats and military officers, but Hoxha again prevailed and definitively established his control over the APL at the Third Party Congress in May, when he filled the Politburo and Central Committee with his loyal followers. There were no further significant challenges to his leadership until the 1970s.

Hoxha's success was due not only to his superior political skills and personal popularity but also to the support of the Soviet Union. At the Albanian Third Party Congress, however, after perfunctorily endorsing the line proclaimed at the Soviet Twentieth Party Congress and promising to improve relations with Yugoslavia, Hoxha proceeded to defy the USSR by refusing to rehabilitate Xoxe and announcing his intention to rapidly collectivize agriculture and to accelerate the pace of industrialization.

In retrospect, it is clear that Hoxha's decisive victory over his domestic opposition in 1956 and his public defiance of the Soviet Union at the Third Party Congress represented a major turning point in Albania's postwar history. Developments both within and outside Albania during 1956 enhanced Hoxha's position and further unified the Albanian ruling elite. The experiences of Poland and Hungary convinced them that any serious deviation from the Stalinist model would lead to internal unrest and perhaps rebellion, which would, in turn, provide the Soviets and Yugoslavs with an excuse to intervene in Albania and impose a regime more to their liking. This world view united the Albanian leadership and profoundly influenced its policy decisions during the late 1950s and early 1960s.

Tirana's persistence in Stalinism along with its unwillingness to align its foreign and economic policies with those of the USSR culminated in the Soviet-Albanian ideological and diplomatic break in December 1961. Albania's successful defiance of the USSR on this occasion was made possible by support from China as well as by the solidarity of her own leaders, the only member of Hoxha's inner circle to question the party's stand toward the Soviet Union having been purged over a year before the split. Between 1961 and 1964, the most pressing concern of the Albanian regime was to prevent an economic collapse following the termination of all Soviet aid programs. By 1964, when the Chinese had filled this gap and the economic situation had been stabilized, Hoxha moved to implement his ideological and cultural revolution, whose main features he had outlined in 1961.

As conceived by Hoxha, the ideological and cultural revolution would, first, destroy those attitudes, traditions, and institutions that had up to this point impeded the regime's efforts to build a modern nation-state. Specifically, he aimed to eliminate the influence of religion, excessive family and sectional loyalties, prejudices toward women, "bourgeois" economic and social outlooks, poor labor discipline, and a general indifference toward political authority. Second, the movement sought to ensure that Albania, unlike the Soviet Union and the East European party states, would not fall into the revisionist heresy and would make the transition to communism in accordance with the principles of Marxism-Leninism, as interpreted by Tirana. Hoxha appears to have been influenced and encouraged by China's unfolding cultural revolution during the 1960s, and this common development served to strengthen the bonds between Tirana and Peking at this time. But the Albanian cultural revolution, unlike the Chinese, did not mask a power struggle between rival factions in the leadership and was consequently better planned and controlled.

At its height, 1966–69, the Albanian cultural revolution took the form of a massive party attack on the military and state bureaucracies in an attempt to forestall the rise of an Albanian "new class" and to strengthen party supremacy in all areas of the nation's life. One of the most spectacular aspects of this movement, not yet duplicated in any of the East European socialist countries, was the destruction of the institutional church and the proclamation of Albania in 1967 as the world's first atheist state. Other noteworthy results of the cultural revolution were the achievement of the total collectivization of agriculture, the reduction in size of collective farmers' private plots, a women's emancipation campaign, and the reform of the educational system.

As China phased out its cultural revolution during 1969, there was apparently agitation by some party leaders as well as by intellectuals and young people for Albania to follow Peking's example. Although the objectives of the ideological and cultural revolution had not been fully realized, Hoxha recognized that the Albanians were ready for a respite from the constant demands that had been made on them since 1966. Between 1970 and 1973 Albania thus enjoyed a period of somewhat relaxed party controls and, like China, opened its door a crack to tourists and other foreign influences.

Between 1973 and 1975, however, Hoxha reversed his course. In response to what he perceived to be dangerous developments and threats to his leadership, he cracked down, successively, on the youth and cultural sectors, the military, and the technocrats.

In March 1973 Hoxha became alarmed by reports of mounting school dropouts and academic failures at all levels of instruction; high rates of unauthorized absences from work by young people; a substantial increase in crimes committed by juveniles; the growing popularity of "western" dress, hair styles, and music among the country's younger generation; and the open repudiation of "socialist realism" by some writers and artists, who exhorted their colleagues to turn to the "West" for inspiration. Consequently, the Albanian party leader began to reinstitute strict party controls over youths and intellectuals, and major leadership changes took place in the League of Albanian Writers and Artists and the Union of Albanian Labor Youth. Todi Lubonja, Fadil Pacrami, and Agim Mero, the three Central Committee members who had apparently argued convincingly for the more moderate line toward youth and culture, were purged.

By 1974, aware of the military establishment's desire to decrease party influence in such areas as military training and discipline, to downgrade the importance of mass popular mobilization (Hoxha's concept of "people's war") in defense strategy, and to lessen Albanian dependence on China, Hoxha seems to have feared a military putsch. Accordingly, between July and December 1974, he deposed the entire top level of the military establishment, including Defense Minister and Politburo member Beqir Balluku, reputedly the fourth-ranking member of Albania's ruling hierarchy.

During 1975, when the differences between the technocrats and party leadership over planning priorities for the 1976–80 five-year plan and the desirability of Albania's seeking new sources of economic aid became acute, Hoxha launched a massive purge of the nation's economic and managerial elites. This move also provided him with scapegoats for the failure of the 1971–75 five-year plan to realize its goals.

Thus, by the mid 1970s the internal stability and cohesive leadership that had characterized Albanian politics since 1956 had broken down. At the Seventh APL Congress in November 1976, three of the thirteen Politburo members and three of the four Politburo candidates elected at the 1971 congress were not renamed to their posts, and nearly 50 percent of the 1971 Central Committee members were dropped from that body. There were, in addition, seventeen cabinet changes between October 1974 and December 1977. These extensive leadership changes appear to be attributable to two major factors. First, differences had obviously developed within the Albanian leadership over such matters as the Sino-Albanian relationship, the regime's hard-line cultural policies, and, above all, the definition of the respective roles of the party and state bureaucracy in the military and economic sectors. Second, Hoxha found it necessary to remove from top positions individuals loyal to him, when their failure to carry out their responsibilities posed a threat to his regime. It appeared that Hoxha hoped to undercut his domestic opposition and to make his policies binding on his eventual successors by incorporating his views on key ideological and political issues into the new Albanian constitution promulgated in December 1976.

POLITICAL STRUCTURE

According to the 1976 constitution, the Albanian Party of Labor is "the vanguard of the working class and the sole leading political force of the state and society" (Article 3). As emphasized throughout this document, the party is dominant in all aspects of the nation's life.

In organization and structure the APL resembles its East European and Soviet counterparts. Theoretically, the party congress which meets every five years is the APL's highest organ, but in actuality it merely approves the leadership's policies and its nominees to the Central Committee. The APL Central Committee elected in 1976 consists of 115 members and generally meets twice a year. In reality the Politburo and Secretariat are the most important party organs. The Politburo is the locus of power in the APL and the nation's leading policy-making body. In 1977, it consisted of seventeen members (twelve voting members and five nonvoting candidates). The APL Secretariat, which supervises the work of the party bureaucracy, is headed by First Secretary Enver Hoxha and four other secretaries.

Below the national level there are party organizations at district, city, village, and ward levels. There were also in 1976 approximately 3,000 basic party organizations on farms and in factories, offices, and military units. Although about 66 percent of the Albanian population live in rural areas, a majority of the basic party organizations are in the cities. This discrepancy reflects the fact that the party, except during the late 1940s, has recruited its members mainly from among office workers and laborers. As Table 1 shows, white-collar workers comprised the largest social group in the party during the 1950s and 1960s. Since the onset of the ideological and cultural Revolution, the leadership has sought to increase the representation of laborers to give the party a more strongly proletarian flavor. After holding steadily at about 10 percent between 1948 and 1961, the proportion of women party members rose to about 23 percent in 1971 and 27 percent in 1976 as a consequence of the women's emancipation campaign.

Since 1948 APL membership has averaged between 3 and 4 percent of the total population, the smallest ratio of party members to population in Eastern Europe. As Table 2 indicates, there was only a modest

Table 1 Composition of the Albanian Party of Labor, 1948–76
(In Percentage of Total Membership)

Year	Laborers	Peasants	White-Collar Workers	Others
1948	23	67	10	0
1952	12	31	55	2
1956	20	31	45	4
1961	29	27	42	2
1966	33	26	37	4
1971	36	30	34	0
1976	38	29	33	0

Source: *Zeri i popullit*, November 11, 1948; April 1, 1952; May 26, 1956; February 14, 1961; November 2, 1966; November 2, 1971; November 2, 1976.

Table 2   Growth of the Albanian Party of Labor, 1941–71

Year	Membership
1941	130
1944	2,800
1948	45,382
1952	44,418
1956	48,644
1961	53,659
1966	66,327
1971	86,985
1976	101,500

Sources: *Rruga e Partise*, 6 (November 1959), p. 88; *History of the Party of Labor of Albania* (Tirana, 1971), pp. 327, 369, 411, 474, 572; *Zeri i popullit*, November 2, 1971; November 2, 1976.

growth in APL membership between 1948 and 1961. This reflects the frequent purging of the party ranks that accompanied the leadership struggles between 1948 and 1956.

Since only a small percentage of the population belongs to the party, various mass organizations serve as its auxiliaries. The most important of these is the Democratic Front (DF), the mass political organization open to all citizens of voting age (eighteen years and over). In theory the principal function of the DF is to nominate and campaign for candidates for local and national elective posts. In practice it is the chief agency for the transmission of the party line to the masses and for the mobilization of popular support for the policies of the regime.

The Union of Albanian Labor Youth, comprised of young adults between fourteen and twenty-six, in addition to inculcating loyalty to the regime, serves as a recruiting agency for the party. The United Trade Union of Albania is charged with maintaining high worker morale and a high level of productivity among the nation's laborers. It also seeks to ensure that party and state economic directives are carried out. A major responsibility of the Union of Albanian Women is to raise the economic and social consciousness of the nation's females by encouraging women to enter the labor force and to become more actively involved in social and cultural activities. Since APL members hold key leadership and staff positions in the mass organizations, their activities are thus closely controlled by the party.

The structure of the Albanian government is similar to that of other Communist states. According to the 1976 constitution, the 250-member People's Assembly, which is elected for a four-year term and meets twice a year in two- or three-day sessions, is the "supreme organ of state power." The constitution further stipulates that all actions taken by the Assembly must conform to "the general line and orientations of the Albanian Party of Labor" (Article 67). In practice the Assembly does little more than approve the legislative proposals submitted to it and ratify the actions taken by the government and the Assembly Presidium between legislative sessions. Although the Assembly elects its Presidium and the cabinet, the composition of both these bodies is determined by the party.

The fifteen-member Assembly Presidium, which is dominated by top-ranking party members, serves as the nation's legislature when the Assembly is not in session. In addition it awards decorations, ratifies treaties and international agreements, appoints and discharges diplomatic officials, and supervises the work of the district peoples' councils. The Presidium chairman is the Albanian head of state, an exclusively ceremonial position in the Hoxha regime.

Headed by the prime minister, the Council of Ministers is the government's leading executive and administrative authority. It serves as the instrument whereby APL policies and directives are transmitted to the state bureaucracy. With few exceptions, cabinet ministers have been members of either the Politburo or the Central Committee. The 1976 constitution created a Presidium of the Council of Ministers, chaired by the prime minister and comprised of all deputy prime ministers. This body's main function is to check on the implementation of cabinet decisions and directives.

Local government organs consist of people's councils at the district, city, and village levels. The authority of these bodies is exercised primarily through their executive boards. They have jurisdiction over administrative, economic, and sociocultural matters within their respective geographic areas. Their decisions, however, may be set aside by action of a higher-ranking people's council or the Assembly Presidium.

The Supreme Court, elected by the People's Assembly for a four-year term, is the highest judicial organ. A reform of the judiciary in 1968 abolished the district appeals courts. On the local level justice is dispensed by the people's courts, whose judges are elected by their constituents for four-year terms. Appeals—which have become rare in recent years—from decisions of the people's courts are heard directly by the Supreme Court. Rounding out the legal establishment is the Attorney General's Office, which represents the government in legal proceedings and verifies the constitutionality of legislation and ministerial decrees. With the explanation that the process of establishing the socialist legal system had been completed, the Ministry of Justice was abolished in September 1966.

Three constitutions have been promulgated in Albania under the Communist regime. According to party spokesmen, each of these reflects a specific stage of Albania's "uninterrupted revolution."

Since Albania was only in the initial stage of its socialist revolution, the March 1946 constitution made no mention of such matters as the special role of the Communist party, the collectivization of agriculture, the nationalization of trade, or other aspects of the socialist order. It was therefore necessary to frame a new constitution correcting these shortcomings in July 1950, as Albania embarked upon her program of intensive socialist development. This document was essentially similar to those adopted by the East European "people's democracies" in the late 1940s and early 1950s.

At the Sixth APL Congress in November 1971, Enver Hoxha announced that Albania had entered "the stage of the complete construction of socialist society." In the light of this development and the experience of the ideological and cultural revolution, he claimed that the 1950 constitution had become obsolete. It was, however, only after he had squelched his domestic opposition that Hoxha gave a high priority to the drafting of a new constitution in October 1975. The tone and content of this document, which was drafted by a committee dominated by Hoxha and his associates, seem to have been influenced by the developments of the early 1970s in Albania. Although the 1976 constitution did not significantly alter the structure of the Albanian political system, it did change the name of the country to the People's Socialist Republic of Albania (Article 1). This latter gesture was intended to underscore Tirana's contention that Albania, alone among the European Communist states, was building socialism according to the tenets of Marxism-Leninism.

The constitution emphasizes the supremacy of the party in every sphere. In commenting on this underlying theme of the constitution, Albanian leaders have repeatedly stressed that they have no intention of limiting the party's role to that of a guide or teacher, as has allegedly occurred in some "revisionist" and "ex-socialist" countries. Rather, in Albania the party will continue to be deeply involved in the direction and control of every activity and institution. The constitution thus is intended to ensure there will be no retreat from the hard-line Stalinist domestic, military, and foreign policies that Albania has steadfastly pursued since the late 1940s, and which have come to distinguish it from the remainder of the East European socialist community.

Specifically, the constitution proclaims Marxism-Leninism as the nation's official ideology (Article 3); commits Albania to support "revolutionary" national and social liberation struggles (Article 15); abolishes private property except for wages, personal residences, and articles for personal or family use (Articles 16, 23); prohibits the granting of concessions to "bourgeois and revisionist capitalist monopolies and states," or obtaining credits from them (Article 28); forbids the practice of any religion and obliges the government to maintain a program of "atheistic propaganda" to develop a "scientific materialistic outlook in people" (Article 37); requires universal military service "for the defense of the socialist homeland" (Article 62); stipulates that the armed forces are led by the party and designates the first secretary of the Albanian Party of Labor as commander-in-chief of the armed forces (Articles 88, 89); declares it an act of treason for anyone "to sign or approve ... the surrender or occupation of the country" (Article 90); and bans the establishment of foreign military bases and the stationing of foreign troops on Albanian soil (Article 94).

LEADERSHIP AND CHANGING ELITE PATTERNS

Between 1956 and 1971, the Albanian leadership was among the most stable in Eastern Europe. During this time only one Politburo member, Liri Belishova, and five Central Committee members were removed from their posts for ideological or political errors. Enver Hoxha (born 1908) was the most important member of the ruling elite. His inner circle included Politburo members such as Prime Minister Mehmet Shehu (born 1913), Central Committee Secretary Hysni Kapo (born 1915), Defense Minister Beqir Balluku (born 1917), cultural specialist Manush Myftiu (born 1919), ideologist Ramiz Aliq (born 1925), and economic trouble-shooter Spiro Koleka (born 1908).

Party leadership posts up to the mid-1970s were held almost exclusively by early converts to communism who had fought in the national liberation war. About half of the fifty-three members elected to the Central Committee at the Fourth APL Congress in 1961 were also related by blood or marriage. With few exceptions, those elected to the Central Committee and other important party posts between 1956 and 1971 were recruited from the ranks of the party and state bureaucracies headquartered in Tirana. The leadership was also relatively young. The average age of the Albanian Politburo up to the mid-1960s was less than fifty.

The unity of the Albanian leaders appears to have been strongest during the 1960s when there seems to have been a consensus on key domestic and international issues. Hoxha's associates also seem to have appreciated that they owed their positions to the powerful APL first secretary and that their fates were tied to his.

By the early 1970s, in the aftermath of the intensive phase of the ideological and cultural revolution, the solidarity of the APL leadership began to crumble as the cultural, military, and economic elites sought to assert a greater voice in decision making in their respective domains. At this point Hoxha responded to what he perceived as a threat to his regime by purging or disciplining the bulk of the first generation Albanian specialists in these areas. By this action the APL first secretary underscored his determination to prevent the emergence of powerful and potentially disruptive interest groups within the leadership and demonstrated that he would not hesitate to take harsh actions even against long-time colleagues and former friends. Of the thirty-five Central Committee members dropped from that body or demoted to candidate status between 1973 and 1976, three had been elected in 1948, two in 1952, eleven in 1956, seven in 1961, five in 1966 and seven in 1971.

As Hoxha began to rebuild the party and state leaderships in the mid-1970s, he turned, in a marked departure from past practice, to the district party organizations as well as to successful managers of farms and factories for the new blood that this task required. All the new Politburo members and candidates elected at the 1976 party congress as well as the recent cabinet appointees are relatively young, in their late thirties or early forties, with fairly extensive experience at the district and local levels. It remains to be seen whether they have the requisite talents to deal with the problems they have inherited and whether they will find it any easier than their predecessors to conform to Hoxha's demands.

In November 1976, Lenka Cuko, first secretary of the Lushnje district party organization, was among those elevated to the Politburo. This marked the first time since 1960 that there was female representation on this body. Approximately 20 percent of the newly elected members of the Central Committee were also women. At the local level the percentage of women holding party offices has increased, along with that of officials of proletarian background. The latter now comprise 86 percent of local party officeholders. Although former laborers and individuals from working class backgrounds reportedly hold 40 percent of the administrative positions in the state bureaucracy, there are no data available concerning the representation of this group in the party central bureaucracy.

Despite the recent turmoil in the APL leadership, Enver Hoxha appeared to be firmly entrenched in power in mid-1978. He and Tito were the senior Communist rulers in Eastern Europe. Hoxha continued to rely heavily on his Politburo intimates such as Shehu and Kapo. As a consequence of the purge of the economic establishment, First Deputy Prime Minister Adil Carcani (born 1922) has been delegated the major responsibility for the management of the economy. Shehu, Kapo, and Carcani would most likely assume significant roles, at least for the short run, in a post-Hoxha regime.

SOCIOECONOMIC AND CULTURAL TRENDS

In 1945 Albania was a war-devastated, underdeveloped agricultural nation. After devoting its initial efforts to repairing the damage Albania had suffered during World War II, the regime moved swiftly to nationalize industry and to set the stage for agricultural collectivization. The long-range economic objective of the Albanian leaders since the late 1940s has been to transform their homeland from a backward agrarian nation into a modern industrial-agricultural state. Although this ambition had not been fully realized by 1978, Albania had, as Table 3 demonstrates, made considerable progress toward this goal.

In the development of the economy, Albania's rulers have also, owing to the nation's pre- and post-World War II experiences, given a high priority to making their homeland virtually self-sufficient and thus largely immune from external economic coercion. Albania's persistence in this policy since the late 1940s contributed to the development of tensions in its relations with Belgrade and subsequently with Moscow. Both Yugoslavia and the Soviet Union regarded Albania's development strategy as unrealistic, uneconomic, and above all, inimical to their own interests.

Table 3 Sources of Albanian National Income by Sectors (In Percentages)

Sector	1938	1950	1960	1970	1975[a]
Industry and construction	4.4	15.6	43.6	52.6	51.7
Agriculture	92.4	76.3	44.4	34.5	35.8
Transportation, trade, etc.	3.2	8.1	12.0	12.9	12.5

[a]Planned

Sources: Harilla Papajorgji, *The Development of Socialist Industry and Its Prospects in the People's Republic of Albania* (Tirana, 1964), p. 137; *Ekonomia Popullore*, 19 (Jan.–Feb. 1972), p. 25.

Albania embarked on its program of long-range economic planning in 1951. From the outset the leadership has given a high priority to the rapid development of industry as well as to the exploitation of the country's natural resources such as oil, chrome, copper, iron, and hydropower. As is evident from Table 4, the industrial sector registered relatively high growth rates during the first and second five-year plans because of Albania's minuscule industrial base. The dramatic falloff in industrial growth during 1961–65 reflects the halt in Soviet aid programs in 1961. Albania experienced a high level of growth between 1966 and 1970, owing to the assistance she received from China and the strict discipline imposed on the labor force during the ideological and cultural revolution. The decline in industrial growth since 1970 stems from the breakdown of labor discipline in the early 1970s and the apparent inability of the Albanians to absorb the aid provided by China because of shortages of skilled labor and management deficiencies. These as yet unresolved problems as well as a reduction in the volume of Chinese aid for the 1976–80 period appear to have resulted in a cut of about 33 percent in the original industrial growth rate estimates for this period. Albanian planners project that by 1980 domestic production will be sufficient to meet 90 percent of the nation's requirements for consumer goods and spare parts. Albania's first steel mill is also expected to be in full operation by that date.

As in other Communist-ruled nations, Albanian economic planners have been deeply concerned by the chronic problems plaguing the agricultural sector of the economy. After abandoning his initial collectivization drive in 1954 in response to a Soviet request, Hoxha launched a massive collectivization campaign in 1956. By 1960 approximately 86 percent of the nation's farm land was incorporated into the socialist sector. The collectivization drive, however, caused much resentment in the countryside and resulted in a temporary decline in farm output.

Table 4   Average Annual Growth Rate of Albanian National Income by Sector (In Percentages)

	1st FYP 1951–55	2nd FYP 1956–60	3rd FYP 1961–65	4th FYP 1966–70	5th FYP 1971–75	6th FYP 1976–80 (Planned)
National Income	11.2	7.0	5.8	9.1	6.7	7.0
Industry	21.5	18.9	8.0	13.4	8.7	7.5
Agriculture	4.8	0.6	6.2	4.1	5.9	7.1
Construction	16.7	18.6	5.0	9.4	n.a.	n.a.
Transportation, trade, etc.	24.2	7.6	1.8	8.0	n.a.	n.a.

Source: *30 Vjet Shqiperi Socialiste* (Tirana, 1974), p. 187. *Zeri i popullit*, November 5, 1976.

Full collectivization was achieved in 1967, and since that time the size of farmers' private plots has been reduced to about a quarter to three-quarters of an acre. During the 1960s and early 1970s Albanian agriculture regularly achieved only about 50 percent of its assigned production targets. In 1976 the regime claimed the nation had achieved self-sufficiency in the production of bread grains and would meet virtually all its food needs from domestic production in 1980. To improve agricultural output, the government has expanded the output of chemical fertilizers and sought to increase the number of agricultural specialists.

Up to the late 1970s Albania has been able to develop and survive largely as a result of the outside economic and technical assistance it has received. In July 1978, as a consequence of the growing ideological rift between Peking and Tirana, China, which had been Albania's chief foreign aid donor since the 1960s, abruptly terminated its economic and military assistance programs in Albania. It will be interesting to note the extent to which this action will affect Albania's goal to achieve near economic self-sufficiency by 1980 as well as the impact it will have on the nation's future development.

Between 1944 and 1977 the Albanian population increased from 1,-100,000 to 2,500,000. Approximately 60 percent of Albanians alive in 1977 have grown up in the period of Communist rule; because of Albania's policy of isolation, few have had any direct contacts with foreigners or the outside world. According to 1975 census data, peasants comprised about 50 percent of the population, laborers 36 percent, and white-collar workers 14 percent. Approximately 66 percent of the population still lived in rural areas.

Since 1945 Albania has had the highest birthrate of any European country and in the early 1970s the population was still growing at an average of 2.6 percent annually. At the beginning of the 1970s Albania's population was predominantly young, with about 42 percent under age 15.

The ultimate social objective of the APL leadership has been to create the "new socialist person." In order to achieve this goal the regime has emphasized the need to wage unrelenting class war. Consequently there have been campaigns to eradicate "bourgeois" attitudes and outlooks, emancipate women, destroy religion, break down the distinction between physical and mental labor, and bridge the gulf between the urban and rural areas.

Although some progress has been registered in all these areas, it seems unlikely the Albanians will be any more successful in efforts to create their "new socialist person" than have their comrades in Eastern Europe and the Soviet Union. Despite the intensive regimentation of the ideological and cultural revolution and the post-1973 cultural crackdown, the Albanian press in 1978 still devoted much space to exposing the "social evils" that persisted in the country. The alacrity with which Albanian youth and intellectuals embraced "alien influences" during the relaxation of the early 1970s suggests that the regime's social doctrines command only a superficial allegiance. Furthermore, the government concedes it can do little to halt the transmission of "bourgeois ideas and values" into Albania by means of foreign radio and television broadcasts.

Although subjected to what are probably the most rigid ideological strictures among the European Communist states, Albanian culture, measured in terms of its output and breadth, has flourished under the Communist regime. The rapid expansion of the educational system and the virtual elimination of illiteracy in the country have played major roles in this development.

In the mid-1970s there were over 700,000 students enrolled in the school system. Nearly one in three Albanians was attending an educational institution. The schools are one of the most important agencies of political socialization in Albania. A 1969 educational reform was designed to upgrade the ideological aspects of the instructional program. Under the reformed curriculum students spend six and a half months in academic study, two and a half months at physical labor, and one month in military training each year. To be eligible to attend an institution of higher education, a student must work for one year on a factory or farm.

With the growth of an educated and literate population, there has been a marked increase in literary and artistic output. Most works of fiction center around the themes of the war of national liberation and the building of socialism. By the early 1970s there were over 800 books published annually in Albania. Music, drama, art, and the cinema have also developed in recent years. These, too, are closely bound by the canons of "socialist realism."

With the complete electrification of the country in 1970, radio and television have become increasingly important. Most significantly for the regime, they have brought the Albanian masses into contact with foreign cultures and ideologies. As of the mid-1970s it did not appear as if Albania was jamming foreign broadcasts.

FOREIGN POLICY AND FOREIGN ECONOMIC RELATIONS

There have been four distinct phases in Albania's international relations since the end of World War II. Between 1944 and 1948 Albania was a Yugoslav dependency and its foreign policy was strongly influenced by Belgrade. During 1949–60 Albania was a Soviet satellite and its external policies were closely aligned with those of the other members of the Communist camp. From 1961 to 1969 Albania enjoyed a special relationship with China. Since 1970, however, Chinese-Albanian relations have steadily deteriorated as Peking and Tirana have differed over both domestic and foreign policy issues.

Immediately following the Communist seizure of power, Yugoslavia, with the apparent approval of Stalin, assumed a dominant role in Albania. Tito discouraged Albania from establishing diplomatic and economic ties with Western Europe and the United States and sought to bring Tirana's foreign policy into line with that of Yugoslavia. As a consequence of a series of agreements concluded in 1946, the Albanian and Yugoslav economies were closely integrated. At the same time, Belgrade, with the help of Koci Xoxe and the other pro-Yugoslav elements in the Albanian leadership, was paving the way for the transformation of Albania into one of the constituent republics of the Yugoslav Federation.

An indication of Albania's unique position in the Communist camp at this time was that the Albanian Communist party was the only ruling party not invited to participate in the Cominform. The Soviet-Yugoslav rupture in mid-1948 enabled the Albanians to end the special relationship with Yugoslavia that Belgrade had imposed on them.

Following the break with Yugoslavia, Albania drifted into the Soviet camp. Although there was still sentiment within the Albanian leadership for normalizing relations with the United States and Great Britain, Hoxha was angered by their refusal to recognize his regime, by their opposition to Albania's admission to the United Nations, and by their perceived support for Greek claims to parts of southern Albania. What finally confirmed Hoxha in his decision to align Albania totally with the Soviet Union and in his resolve to develop a Stalinist-type regime were the joint Anglo-American-sponsored clandestine operations to overthrow his government between 1949 and 1953. These ventures were betrayed and thwarted as a result of information supplied to the Soviets and the Albanians by the Russian agent H. A. R. (Kim) Philby.

As a full-fledged member of the socialist camp, Albania was admitted to CMEA in 1949 and was one of the signatories to the Warsaw Pact in 1955. During the 1950s approximately 90 percent of Albania's foreign trade was with the CMEA countries, and the USSR was Albania's major trading partner and source of foreign aid. The Albanians have acknowledged that the assistance they received from the Communist camp was crucial to the economic gains registered during the periods of the first and second five-year plans.

By the last half of the 1950s, however, serious differences had arisen between the USSR and Albania. Hoxha was unnerved by the Soviet-Yugoslav rapprochement of the mid-1950s. This, he feared, might be a prelude to a new Yugoslav move to annex Albania. The Albanian leaders also opposed wholesale de-Stalinization in their homeland on the grounds that it could lead to internal unrest, possible Soviet intervention, and their eventual removal from power. Tirana was further concerned about Soviet proposals to establish an "international socialist division of labor" among the CMEA countries. Under this arrangement Albania would have been restricted to supplying the CMEA community with foodstuffs and raw materials. This situation, it was believed, would keep Albania in a state of perpetual dependency and make its leaders more vulnerable to Soviet coercion.

These were the major considerations that led to the 1961 Soviet-Albanian break. Albania, however, could not have taken this drastic action without the assurance of Chinese support. As in 1948, it was a development within the Soviet camp—this time the Sino-Soviet rift—that made it possible for the Albanian leadership to remain in power and to continue to pursue its own line. Although Soviet-Albanian diplomatic and economic relations were severed in 1961, Tirana did maintain its ties in both these areas with the East European Communist states. Albania, however, ceased to participate in the Warsaw Pact and in CMEA, and in September 1968, in the aftermath of the Soviet invasion of Czechoslovakia, officially renounced its membership in the Warsaw Pact.

China's economic and military aid contributed significantly to Albania's survival following the Moscow-Tirana split. During the 1960s China and Albania developed a special relationship which became particularly close between 1966 and 1969 when both countries were in the throes of their respective cultural revolutions and when China was virtually isolated from the rest of the world.

The Sino-Albanian relationship underwent a transformation in 1969, as China phased out its cultural revolution and sought to strengthen its ties with the West, including the United States. Tirana was especially distressed that the developments in China were reinforcing the domestic agitation that brought about the brief period of relaxation in Albania during the early 1970s. The Albanian leaders also appear to have been disappointed with the nature of the support they received or were promised from Peking following the Soviet invasion of Czechoslovakia, and by China's apparent decision to scale down the level of its economic aid to Albania following the conclusion of the fifth five-year plan.

Since the early 1970s Albania has responded to these developments by attempting to lessen its economic dependence on China. To this end it has sought to improve diplomatic and economic relations with Yugoslavia and Greece. By the mid-1970s, Yugoslavia had become, next to China, Albania's most important trading partner. Tirana has expressed interest in expanding its commercial and cultural ties with Third World countries and other nations, with the notable exceptions of the United States, the Soviet Union, Israel, West Germany, and Great Britain.

Sino-Albanian relations rapidly deteriorated following the death of Mao Tse-tung in September 1976 when China's new leaders opted for a moderate domestic course and continued to court the United States, the countries of Western Europe, and many Third World nations. Tirana viewed these developments as a "betrayal" of both Marxism-Leninism and its own national interests. By early 1978, Albania had begun to take the Chinese to task for alleged delays in the delivery of promised economic assistance. The Albanians were also distressed by China's rapprochement with Yugoslavia as well as by what they termed Peking's "imperialistic" policy toward Vietnam.

In July 1978, obviously angered by the continuous and escalating Albanian attacks on their policies and leaders, the Chinese responded by halting their economic and military assistance programs. This action marked the formal end of the Sino-Albanian alliance.

PROSPECTS AND PROBLEMS

As the 1970s draw to a close, Albania finds itself at another crucial historical juncture. As Albania's post-World War II experiences have demonstrated, the country's fate has been profoundly influenced by developments within the Communist world. Within less than a year after Mao's death, new and more serious strains had arisen in the Sino-Albanian relationship. Albania's future will also be affected by developments in Yugoslavia after the passing of Tito. Tirana's relations with Belgrade will be further complicated by the growing nationalism of the Albanian minority in Yugoslavia. What makes Albania's present situation even more perplexing is that, unlike in 1948 and 1960, it seems to be entering a new period of trial without the backing of a major Communist or noncommunist power.

The Albanian economy will continue to be a major source of concern to the leadership. Should Albania fail to achieve the relatively modest goals of the current five-year plan, there could well be a new challenge to Hoxha from the technocrats. There are also indications that if the increasing economic expectations of the Albanian masses are not soon satisfied, this situation could result in some serious difficulties for the regime.

As the educational level of the Albanian people continues to rise and as radio and television ownership becomes more widespread, the leadership will find it increasingly difficult to insulate the population from outside influences. Should China remain committed to a moderate course, this development will likely intensify the pressures on the leadership to modify its austere revolutionary regime.

Finally, there could be significant changes in the Albanian leadership itself by the early 1980s. The two most prominent members of the ruling elite, Enver Hoxha and Mehmet Shehu, have not enjoyed the best of health in recent years. Their passing could further undermine the cohesiveness of the leadership and, given the domestic and external problems Albania faces, could cause their successors to modify or abandon the hard-line policies that have been the hallmark of the Hoxha regime.

BIBLIOGRAPHY

Amery, Julian. *Sons of the Eagle: A Study in Guerilla War.* London: Macmillan, 1948.

Bardhoshi, Besim, and Kareco, Theodhor. *The Economic and Social Development of the People's Republic of Albania During Thirty Years of People's Power.* Tirana: "8 Nentori," 1974.

Fontana, Dorothy Grouse. "Recent Sino-Albanian Relations," *Survey,* 21 (autumn 1975), pp. 121–44.

Frasheri, Kristo. *The History of Albania: A Brief Survey.* Tirana: "Naim Frasheri," 1964.

Griffith, William E. *Albania and the Sino-Soviet Rift.* Cambridge: MIT Press, 1963.

Hamm, Harry. *Albania: China's Beachhead in Europe.* New York: Praeger, 1963.

History of the Party of Labor of Albania. Tirana: "Naim Frasheri," 1971.

Keefe, Eugene K. *Area Handbook for Albania.* Washington, D.C.: U.S. Government Printing Office. 1971.

Logoreci, Anton. *The Albanians: Europe's Forgotten Survivors.* London: Victor Gollancz Ltd., 1977.

Marmullaku, Ramadan. *Albania and the Albanians.* Hamden, Connecticut: Archon Books, 1975.

Pano, Nicholas C. "Albania in the Era of Kosygin and Brezhnev." In *Nationalism in the USSR and Eastern Europe,* edited by George W. Simmonds. Detroit, Michigan: The University of Detroit Press, 1977, pp. 474–494.

———. "Albania in the Sixties." in *The Changing Face of Communism in Eastern Europe,* edited by Peter A. Toma. Tucson: University of Arizona Press, 1970, pp. 244–280.

———. "Albania in the 1970s," *Problems of Communism,* 26 (November–December 1977), pp. 33–43.

———. "The Albanian Cultural Revolution," *Problems of Communism,* 23 (July–August 1974), pp. 44–57.

———. *The People's Republic of Albania.* Baltimore: The Johns Hopkins Press, 1968.

Peters, Stephen. "Ingredients of the Communist Takeover in Albania," *Studies on the Soviet Union,* 11 (no. 4, 1971), pp. 244–263.

Prifti, Peter R. "Albania." In *The Communist States in Disarray, 1965–1971,* edited by Adam Bromke and Teresa Rakowska-Harmstone. Minneapolis, Minn.: University of Minnesota Press, 1972, pp. 198–220.

———. "Albania and the Sino-Soviet Conflict," *Studies in Comparative Communism,* 6 (autumn 1973), pp. 241–279.

———. *Socialist Albania Since 1944.* Cambridge: MIT Press, 1978.

Skendi, Stavro (ed.). *Albania.* New York: Praeger, 1956.

Thomas, John I. *Education for Communism: School and State in the People's Republic of Albania.* Stanford, California: Hoover Institution Press, 1969.

Tretiak, Daniel. "The Founding of the Sino-Albanian Entente," *China Quarterly,* no. 10 (April–June 1962), pp. 123–143.

9   Yugoslavia

Robin Alison Remington

The Yugoslav state rose from the ashes of World War I in 1918 only to be dismembered with the approach of World War II. Out of the chaos and devastation of the Second World War, Yugoslavia was reunited under the leadership of the Communist Party of Yugoslavia (CPY). Unlike most of their East European comrades who rode to power on the coattails of the Soviet army, Yugoslav Communists fought an indigenous battle of national liberation. Led, sometimes driven, by the Croatian peasant turned locksmith, turned revolutionary, Josip Broz—who under the name of Tito was to become one of the most important statesmen of postwar Europe as well as its most controversial Communist leader—the party followed Chinese methods that had yet to succeed in China. There is evidence that the Yugoslavs were keenly aware of their model. Take the following statement by Mosa Pijade, veteran ideologue and Tito's instructor in Marxism during his prison days: " 'The people are water, a partisan is a fish; fish cannot live without water.' That principle of the Chinese partisans holds here too."[1]

Such a pattern of revolutionary takeover had the advantage of building a large, genuine constituency that looked to the party for leadership. The integrating myth of partisan solidarity became the foundation of a "revitalized belief system" in support of the second try at uniting the South Slavs into a common Yugoslav state.[2] As in the interwar years, and with considerably more success, the CPY attempted to become an effective, cross-ethnic, nationwide party. It is a continuing attempt, and one that must be understood in the context of Yugoslav political cultures and historic legacies. Otherwise present-day Yugoslavia makes no sense.

THE REMNANTS OF HISTORY

To grasp the impact of historic ethnic considerations on Yugoslav communism, Americans must shed a good deal of culture-bound intellectual baggage. Yugoslavia is the heart of the Balkans. In that part of the world a state is an internationally recognized entity with the formal attributes of territorial integrity, sovereignty, and control of its domestic affairs that conducts foreign policy on the basis of legal (if sometimes fictitious) equality with other such internationally recognized entities. A country is the piece of real estate occupied by the state. Neither a country nor a state is a "nation." Rather, a "nation" is a group of individuals united by common bonds of historical development, language, religion, and their self-perceived collective identity. A "nation" may or may not be recognized as such by the international system. It may be coterminous with a state, but in the Balkans it usually is not. Bluntly, there is no Yugoslav nation.

Yugoslavia is a state—a state perhaps in the process of becoming a nation. The official ideology of the League of Communists of Yugoslavia (LCY) is committed to nation-building and national (ethnic) integration. To what extent the commitment has been translated into reality is hotly debated. At a minimum one can identify the goal. A conservative estimate is that substantial work has been done on the foundations.

According to the 1971 census, the Yugoslav population is 20.5 million including five official "nations" and a variety of nationalities. The nations are the Serbs, 8.4 million; Croats, 4.8 million; Slovenes, 1.7 million; Macedonians, 1.2 million; and Montenegrins, 608 thousand. The national minorities include Albanians, Hungarians, Turks, Slovaks, Bulgars, Romanians, Czechs, Italians, Germans, and Gypsies. The criteria for distinguishing between "nations" and "national minorities" is in part whether or not the group in question has another potential homeland. In short "nationalities" are members of nations whose "native countries border on Yugoslavia."[3]

The nations of Yugoslavia share a common, visceral knowledge of foreign domination. Trying to survive on a pivotal intersection between Europe and the Ottoman Empire, they knew only too well the running battles of international crossroads. The Slovenes were ruled by Charlemagne, then by the Germans (Austrians) until the end of World War I. The Croats, existing in a state of token autonomy under the Hungarians dating from 1102, lived on memories of an independent Croatia. From 1018 the Macedonians were ruled alternately by the Turks, Bulgarians, and Serbs. The Serbian empire that under the Nemanja dynasty in the fourteenth century included the territory of present-day Albania, Bulgaria, Macedonia, and much of Greece submitted to Turkish occupation after the battle of Kosovo in 1389. The Montenegrins, Serbs who retreated to the black mountains from which they took their name, held out for another hundred years before they too yielded to the Turkish yoke at the end of the fifteenth century.

For our purposes the salient consequences of this star-crossed South Slav history are the following:

1. The two largest nations of Yugoslavia, the Serbs and the Croats, survived hundreds of years of domination by feeding on heroic legends of past empires. This historic consciousness solidified their sense of "nationhood," i.e., separateness from each other. Such an attitude was instrumental for national survival, but it became extremely dysfunctional when the Serbs and Croats attempted to unite in the Kingdom of Serbs, Croats, and Slovenes in 1918.

2. The nations of Yugoslavia suffered under radically different imperialisms. Consequently they brought with them into the twentieth century diverse legacies in terms of political culture, economic development, and religion; there were even two alphabets for Serbo-Croatian. Under Austrian influence, the Slovenes and Croats were ardent Catholics, western, European. For the Serbs, Macedonians, and Montenegrins, the Turkish heritage meant much more than economic backwardness. Orthodox or Muslim, these nations were influenced by oriental politics and culture in ways that can be seen even today.

These varied political experiences helped shape the future political tactics of the South Slavs in dealing with one another. The Serbs, whose nineteenth-century history reads like a serialized epic of repression and revolt led by simultaneously feuding families, tend toward centralism and authoritarian military solutions. As Bogdan Denitch has perceptively pointed out, the historic relationship of violence to social structure in those areas previously within or on the borders of the Turkish Empire created a political elite unavoidably linked to the tradition of war.[4] Conversely, in their attempt to carve out substantial home rule under the Hungarians, the Croats became well versed in passive resistance and political obstructionism, with which the Serbs have had scant patience.

Mutual wartime atrocities sharply worsened interwar antagonisms. Yugoslavs fought each other in a savage civil war that did nothing to create the ethnic trust so essential for postwar national integration. That conflict, reinforced by Serb/Montenegrin military traditions, meant that the partisan army was heavily Serbian and disproportionately Montenegrin.[5] Given the exigencies of wartime recruitment, the party itself reflected a similar ethnic composition. Vows of brotherhood and equality notwithstanding, the resultant credibility gap has done much to determine the politics of Communist Yugoslavia.[6]

MAIN LINES OF POLITICAL DEVELOPMENT, 1948–1970

By the end of World War II, the Yugoslav party had grown from an estimated 12,000 members to 140,000. Most of these new members were drawn from the ranks of the partisan army. They were young, predominantly peasants, and dedicated more to Tito personally than to the dimly understood principles that he supported. In the euphoria of victory, party and army were almost dizzy with success. Not only had the country been liberated from the German invaders largely by its own efforts, but also a social revolution was underway. Everything seemed possible, and individuals were swept forward on a wave of political optimism that tended to hide harsh economic realities. Even before the occupation and civil war, Yugoslavia had struggled with the unenviable economic legacy of the Turks. At the end of the war, it was still a small, economically backward Balkan country with the added burden of having suffered almost unbelievable devastation. Some 1.7 million people, roughly one of every nine inhabitants, had died in battles, concentration camps, or as a result of ethnic-inspired atrocities. Another 3.5 million had been left homeless. Much of the manufacturing industry had been destroyed or seriously damaged. In these circumstances the first job of the new Communist government was to repair the damage, with the ideological imperative that the economy should be reorganized according to what were considered proper socialist principles.[7]

Yugoslav economists looked to the Soviet model. The efforts of the CPY to rebuild the economy were Stalinist in both goals and methods. Emphasis was on extensive, rapid industrialization starting with the most basic industrial infrastructure. Financing was at the expense of depressed agricultural prices, facilitated by unskilled labor moving from the countryside into the factories. Planning was centrally organized and based on an administered credit system with marked disregard for costs. This course lasted from 1945 to 1949, when the split with Moscow intervened.

The Soviet-Yugoslav differences that climaxed with Yugoslav expulsion from the Cominform in 1948 have been well documented elsewhere.[8] For our purposes, it is important to avoid the commonplace that Tito was expelled from interparty circles because he was a "national communist." True, the Yugoslav party was proud and not overly fond of accepting Soviet military advisers, advice, or the political-economic penetration that had become the norm in Soviet relations with the other East European regimes. Nonetheless, the difficulty from Moscow's perspective was not Yugoslav nationalism so much as Tito's revolutionary ambitions in the Balkans.

The Yugoslav leader aided the Greek guerrillas after Moscow had abandoned them for fear that the civil war in Greece would sabotage what was left of the wartime alliance. He demanded public Soviet support for a Yugoslav Trieste and pressed towards a Balkan federation despite Stalin's lack of enthusiasm for the project. In short, Yugoslav expansionism clashed with Soviet foreign policy priorities. At the same time, domestically, the Yugoslav party was more, not less, ideologically dogmatic than the other East European regimes, still cautiously attempting to establish the nature of "peoples democracies" as distinct from the Soviet model. While Stalin was mistaken to think he could shake his little finger and Tito would fall, he was correct that at bottom his problem with the Yugoslavs was "conceptions that are different from our own."

From 1948 until 1956 the Soviet-Yugoslav split became the fundamental fact of Yugoslav domestic and foreign policy. The Yugoslav leadership's number one problem was the nature of the party rank and file. How to explain the break to the young, for the most part ideologically immature and enthusiastic cadres that had been weaned politically on myths of Soviet infallibility and love of Stalin? How to cushion the personal pain and disillusionment of the core of seasoned Communists who had survived the purges of the 1930s and the war? The ideological self-image of the Yugoslav leadership plus the practical fear of demoralizing the party rank and file ruled out simply denouncing the Soviets and switching sides in the East-West struggle over the fate of Eastern Europe. To do so would have risked party disintegration as well as Soviet invasion. Moreover, even had these restraints not existed, there was no immediate political welcome waiting in the West. Rather, the first reaction to the split was disbelief. Indeed, many Western observers openly speculated that Yugoslavia was Moscow's Trojan horse in the emerging cold war. The Yugoslav policy of minimizing their expulsion from the Cominform as "a mistake" and continued expressions of loyalty to the Soviet Union and to Stalin personally, combined with an attempt to shore up Belgrade's socialist credentials by an intensified collectivization drive, did nothing to still such Western suspicions.

Until the Tripartite Agreement of 1951 began to repair some of the damage caused by the Cominform economic blockade, Yugoslavia was crushingly isolated in Europe. Distrusted by the West, Tito was denounced as a "tyrant, murderer, spy" by his former Cominform comrades. East European show trials of "Titoist" heretics increasingly ruled out all hope of reconciliation, while maneuvers on Yugoslavia's borders underlined the Balkan socialist maverick's precarious military position.

Both politically and economically, the Stalinist model had become patently inappropriate. The search for alternatives began. In 1952 the historic Sixth Congress announced that the "leading role" of the Communist party was to be confined to political and ideological education. The resolution called for open party meetings, decentralization of party organization, autonomy for local party organs, elimination of bureaucratism, and socialist democracy. The name of the CPY was changed to the League of Communists of Yugoslavia (LCY) to symbolize the new decentralized organizational structure; the Politburo became the Executive Committee to eliminate Stalinist terminology. In short, the Soviet model was publicly dumped on the rubbish heap of Yugoslav party history. The political consequence of this act was immense: it signaled the end of the official party monopoly of political life.

Worker's Self-Management

Having rejected the Soviet example, the Yugoslav leadership worked desperately to fill the political-economic vacuum with an ideologically acceptable alternative. Party theorists turned to such classics as Marx's analysis of the Paris Commune and Lenin's *State and Revolution* and to the thinking of British socialists such as G. D. H. Cole. The new system emphasized worker democracy—the truly radical assumption that factories belong to the workers. In principle, workers in each factory or enterprise became the trustees of socially owned property. As such they elected workers' councils, which in combination with management boards decided what and how much to produce, at what prices, and for what wages. These decisions were expected to take into account demand (market), production costs, and general rules laid down by the government in the form of annual and medium-range social plans. The key changes in economic management are shown schematically below.[9]

	Stalinist model	*Self-management*
Goals:	1. Socialism by means of state power	1. Withering away of the state
	2. Equalization of the positions of the workers in relation to state-owned means of production	2. Worker management of social property
	3. A new social order for its own sake	3. personal happiness of individuals
Agents:	Hierarchically organized state apparatus	Autonomous enterprise
Means:	1. State ownership	1. Social ownership
	2. Central planning	2. Social planning
	3. Administrative allocation of goods	3. Market mechanism
	4. Administrative rules	4. Financial instruments
	5. Administrative wage	5. Worker decided wages
	6. All-embracing state budget	6. Decentralized state budget for economic operations
	7. Consumption as residual	7. Consumption as an independent priority or factor in development
	8. Collectivization of agriculture	8. Business cooperation of peasants

The difficulty was not so much in principle as in implementation.
Centralized economies cannot be dismantled overnight. The first actual
steps toward a self-managing socialist economy were cautious. The idea
was not well understood, and in the beginning, workers controlled very
little. Medium-range goals of the system remained much the same—
extensive and rapid industrialization emphasizing infrastructure—as
did the problems of capital accumulation and distribution. Some feared
that instead of the best of both worlds, Yugoslavia had taken the worst.

Consequently, there began a see-saw centralization/decentraliza-
tion/centralization pattern that has characterized the Yugoslav economy ever since. This pattern reflects a basic conflict between the pro-
ponents of more emphasis on the "market" aspects of self-managing
socialism, economic rationalizers rather inaccurately often considered

"liberals," and their opponents. At stake are fundamental conflicts over the nature of regional development, social priorities, and at bottom, the question of who must pay the cost of change.[10]

Thus from the moment the LCY rejected Stalinism for self-managing socialism, the party has been faced with conflicting political-economic demands in circumstances where the LCY had abdicated the right to decide by fiat. In the long run this shift proved more important for Yugoslav politics than did the fluctuating international environment, marked by the collapse of Khrushchev's 1955–56 reconciliation attempts, the Polish and Hungarian crises of 1956, caused in part by the Soviet leader's campaign to bring Yugoslavia back within the fold, and the 1958 Soviet-Yugoslav dispute over the nature of Yugoslavia's road to socialism and its legitimacy within the post-Stalin international Communist movement. For by the 1960s it was clear that a serious political struggle was underway in the guise of economic debates. Moreover, the party itself was divided on these issues. Hence they were not resolved, and continued to fester into the 1970s.

The Economic Issues and Actors[11]

Economic rationalizers within and outside the LCY assumed not only that economic Stalinism was distasteful for political reasons but also that Yugoslavia had reached a "take-off" stage in terms of the economy. At this stage artificially depressed standards of living in order to finance basic industrial infrastructure were considered harmful rather than helpful. Basically, the complaint of the economic rationalizers in the early 1960s was that Yugoslavia suffered from enormous waste, unnecessarily low personal consumption, and unutilized industrial capacity; all of these factors provided workers with no incentive to work. The economic rationalizers' solution was to make reality out of the fiction of market socialism. According to their scheme, individual enterprises, in conjunction with banks, were to be given greater control over earnings, pushed to make profitable investments, and allowed to go out of business if they could not earn a profit. Personal consumption would be gradually allowed to increase. The credit system would be reorganized. Prices would be moved in the direction of reflecting supply and demand. Monopolies would be allowed in those sectors where they were necessary to an economic scale of production.

By 1964 the Yugoslav leadership appeared to have accepted this platform for rationalization almost intact. Tito personally spoke of the need to raise standards of living. The trade unions came out in favor of the plan. The program was forcefully reiterated at the Sixth Central Committee Plenum. Yet implementation still appeared bogged down. The problem was not so much the resistance of economic "conservatives" but that a genuine "socialist market economy" had drastic implications for the well-being of several sectors of Yugoslav society. For our purposes these groups will simply be called the opposition.

The opposition reflected national-regional differences in the most graphic, painful way. First, as might have been expected, people in unprofitable enterprises and those in underdeveloped regions of the country were flatly against the reform. Although the two categories were not always synonymous, there was considerable overlap because of earlier policies favoring "political" factories in underdeveloped areas of Serbia, Montenegro, Macedonia, and Bosnia-Hercegovina. These were factories established as rewards (sometimes for wartime performance), as incentives for development in poorer regions, or as personal/political favors. Since these factories had never been assumed to have an economic base, the likelihood of their survival under the proposed reforms was small. However, whether or not a factory had been established for political reasons, potentially all factories in the less industrialized, formerly disadvantaged areas of the country would be in trouble.

Whereas economic rationalizers operated on the assumption that the Yugoslav economy had reached the point of economic take-off, the opposition disagreed. Those opposed to the reforms emphasized that even if one could make such an assumption with respect to Croatia, Slovenia, and the Vojvodina, the same could not be said for the less industrialized south. They insisted that in Kosovo, Macedonia, Montenegro, and Bosnia-Hercegovina, forced investment be maintained for the sake of equalization.

Opposition arguments were based on social priorities rather than economic rationalism. Oppositionists argued that the reforms were antisocialist. A state with welfare commitments could not accept the consequences of unemployment, restricted social services, and a widening of the gap between developed and underdeveloped regions of the country. In individual rather than regional terms, the consequences implied increasing wage differentials at a time when food prices were rising. It stressed capitalist norms of competition rather than socialist egalitarianism. Equally important, the opposition pointed to some economic realities. The economy could not survive the simultaneous collapse of many enterprises in terms of either the economic or the social consequences that would surely occur if the subsidized factories were forced to do without their subsidies and show a profit.

Those who would feel the weight of the economic cost of reforms found allies among those who would have to face a political cost. The ranks of middle- and lower-level party and government functionaries stood to lose significant power with any depoliticizing of the economy. These bureaucracies stubbornly resisted implementation of the reforms despite approval at the top of the party. Thus the opposition found its strength in national, regional, and bureaucratic bastions. At the highest level, vice president and head of the security service (UDBA) Aleksandar Rankovic served as the protector of these forces, and only after his fall in 1966* did the program of the rationalizers push ahead.

The result was much as had been predicted. The party responded to increased unemployment by allowing large numbers of Yugoslavs to work abroad. This massive labor migration eased the pressure of unemployment and brought much needed foreign currency into the economy. Yet it had a variety of undesirable side effects. The foreign workers, particularly those working in more industrialized European nations such as West Germany, Austria, and Sweden, raised the standard of expectations within Yugoslavia. The workers came home to marry, to bring a cousin out with them, or to show off a new car. Such rising expectations only intensified frustration with Yugoslav economic reality. As one economist rather bitterly expressed it, "We can't have a West German standard of living on the basis of a small, backward Balkan economy. And everyone now wants one."

As the consequences of the economic reforms began to surface in severe social-political dislocation in 1968, international events intervened. In August the Soviet Union and its more orthodox East European allies invaded Czechoslovakia to put an end to the Dubcek regime's experiment with "socialism with a human face." By September that action had been expanded into the Brezhnev doctrine, by which Moscow reserved to itself the right to intervene militarily or otherwise if developments in any other socialist country threatened either (1) socialism within that country or (2) the basic interests of other socialist countries.[12] Again Yugoslav security was directly threatened.

Not since 1948 had the country appeared so united. The LCY attacked the invasion of Czechoslovakia as a violation of socialist norms and reminded all parties involved that in case of need the Yugoslav army was ready to defend Yugoslavia's borders. Domestically, party member-

---

*Formerly considered Tito's successor, Rankovic was ostensibly removed for letting his UDBA agents go too far in bugging Tito's bedroom. However, the commission investigating the charges against him was headed by the subsequent head of the Croat CP, Miko Tripalo, and there is reason to think that Rankovic's economic policies played not a little role in his political retirement.

ship went up, with more young people joining than at any time in recent years. Militarily, the Yugoslav People's Army (JNA) adopted a mixed partisan strategy called "all people's defense," and accepted Territorial Defense Units (TDU's) as partners of the regular armed forces. The National Assembly passed a law declaring it treason for any citizen to fail to resist foreign occupation. In 1969 Tito, euphorically and, as it turned out, prematurely, pronounced the "national question" solved.[13]

In sum, the fundamental economic/political conflicts that had intensified with the economic reforms of 1966 remained unsolved. Pushed aside by international crisis, these tensions returned in full force in the 1970s, complicated by an organizational power struggle, this time between the federal center and the republic party/bureaucratic elites. To understand these developments, they must be seen in the present political context.

CURRENT POLITICAL STRUCTURE AND DYNAMICS

Yugoslavia is a federation composed of six republics and two autonomous provinces. Five of the republics are the territorial base of the Yugoslav nations identified in the first part of this chapter—Serbia, Croatia, Slovenia, Montenegro, and Macedonia. The sixth, Bosnia-Hercegovina, is divided roughly equally between Serbs, Croats, and Moslems with no single ethnic group having a majority. Nor are the "national" republics ethnically homogeneous. Croatia has a Serbian minority of 17 percent. Serbia includes the autonomous provinces of Kosovo, with its majority of ethnic Albanians, and of the Vojvodina, where there are large Hungarian, Croat, and Slovak minorities. Albanian enclaves exist in both Montenegro and Macedonia. These overlaping ethnic and territorial boundaries create complex political problems.

The League of Communists of Yugoslavia is the only official political party. Each republic has its own party organization, however, creating regional party elites who, given the ethnic dimension of their political base, have interests that frequently conflict with one another and with the central party organization. Paralleling the party organization, there is a federal governmental structure involving a collective presidency, a federal assembly or parliament consisting of two chambers (the Federal chamber and the Chamber of Republics and Provinces) with a federal executive council acting as the executive body of the parliament, federal agencies and courts. Each republic has its president, as-

sembly, and governmental bureaucracy as well, with the assembly
structure reaching down to the local government level in the form of
commune assemblies.

The Eleventh LCY Congress in June 1978 reorganized top party bodies in a manner that appears to move away from the centralism imposed
by the Tenth Congress in 1974. Thus until the next congress, the Yugoslav party will be run by a 165-member Central Committee, and a
twenty-four-member Presidium with its own Secretary and a number
of executive secretaries. This is roughly parallel to the Central Committee, Politburo, and Secretariat in the Soviet and more orthodox East
European party structures. Due to the manner of selection and the
relationship of the individual republics to that process, however, the
end result in terms of where power actually resides is very different
from the Soviet situation.

The Central Committee is composed of twenty representatives from
each republic, including the president of the republic; fifteen representatives from each autonomous province, including the president of the
provincial committee; and fifteen representatives from the army party
organization. The Presidium has three members from each republic,
two from each autonomous province and one from the army. The nine
executive secretaries also represent the respective republic, autonomous province, and army party organizations. Tito is a member of both
the Central Committee and the Presidium. Yet for the future it may be
more important that all the republic presidents and presidents of the
provincial committees are members of both bodies. In short, the top
hierarchy of the LCY has been firmly tied to proportional representation for the regional party organizations, while the role of the army has
been formalized at the highest party levels.[14]

The twelve-member Executive Committee of the 1974 Presidium has
been eliminated. That only three of its members were included in the
new, expanded body may be considered an index of the Executive
Committee's general impotence. Conversely, seven of the eight-mem-
ber collective state presidency are members of the new Presidium, once
again blurring the distinctions between the top party and state leadership which can be seen as a form of interlocking directorate. With the
exception of LCY secretary Stane Dolanc, the other executive secretaries
are not members of the Presidium, but rather work under Dolanc to
provide "liaison" between the LCY and republic and provincial parties.

Next to the party-state apparatus, the armed forces is the most significant all-Yugoslav institution. Indeed, the JNA has its own League of
Communists, which in terms of numbers is larger than the party orga-

nizations of two of the republics. Given the historic image of the Yugoslav army as an instrument of Serbian hegemony, considerable effort has been made to assure multi-ethnic representation among the officer corps. These efforts appear successful at the top of the command structure, although it is impossible to tell to what degree they have penetrated the middle and lower levels, which in the early 1970s conservative estimates considered 70 percent Serbian. The political influence of the army is reinforced by that of the Veterans' organization, SUBNOR, also statewide and because of the nature of the partisan struggle, most likely largely Serbian and Montenegrin, except perhaps in Slovenia.

The trade unions also provide an institutional framework that spans the republics and provinces, although it is difficult to estimate their importance as compared to the daily influence of administrative and economic institutions that exist on regional, local, and enterprise levels.

Lastly, the Socialist Alliance (SAWPY) is an umbrella organization that functions much like a primary system in single-party electoral systems. It includes officially sanctioned interest groups such as women's organizations, professional groupings, and students, and legitimate social-political organizations that may have issue-oriented impact but little systematic input into national policy.

The nature of these institutions and their interaction tends to be obscured by formal functional descriptions. Charts are misleading. Present-day political reality involves institutional jockeying for position in the struggle to determine not only who but what will control the future of Yugoslavia after Tito. Rooted in history, this confrontation is being fought out through conflicting interpretations of the experiment with self-management. It is a political drama motivated by the power of an idea that has swept the actors far beyond their intended goals, changed some parts, and willy-nilly introduced others. Self-managing socialism, as an alternative to Stalinism, has inadvertently legitimized ethnic politics within Yugoslavia.

Nation Versus Class: The Organizational Dilemma

When Yugoslavia split with Moscow in 1948, the Yugoslav leadership was demanding *national* emancipation from Soviet hegemony and *socialist* emancipation from CPSU ideological domination. The Yugoslav road to socialism was to be a modernized version of the society Marx sketchily described in his analysis of the Paris Commune of 1871. Politically, self-management was to extend beyond the factory to the commune and the republic. It was a truly radical approach which gave legitimacy to wide-scale political participation at all levels and, despite sporadic attempts at back-tracking such as the determined recentralization efforts since 1972, irrevocably undermined democratic centralism as an organizing principle. It is a hard fact that it is impossible to have issues decided at both the top and the bottom simultaneously.

The logical political implication of self-management was increased autonomy of decision making at the republic and commune levels with inevitably increased importance of the republican party organizations. Given the coincidence of key republics with certain "national" (ethnic) groups already discussed, this autonomy soon led to demands for national self-determination, which was the last thing that the League of Communists of Yugoslavia had in mind. Soon, the contradiction of preaching the right of "national communism" at the international level and prohibiting it within Yugoslavia became increasingly hard for the party to live with.

For years the answer to this problem had been Tito himself. Unfortunately, Tito's personality cult guaranteed the appearance of state and party unity at the expense of negotiated settlement of basic conflicts. By 1970 the Yugoslav leader himself had become uncomfortable with a system that considered his person indispensable. Hence the mammoth constitutional amendments of 1971.

On the most basic level the amendments amounted to Tito's attempt to manage his own succession. Drafted by a mixed commission of political leaders and legal advisers, rather than by a commission of legal experts as with earlier constitutional amendments, their writing took two months. Tito himself presided over the final meeting. Yet the result surely was not what he had intended. Swept forward by demands once again for a genuine participatory federalism, the amendments reflected both national (ethnic) ambitions and bureaucratic power struggles, first, between federal (LCY) and republic party elites; second, between the state and party bureaucracies.

At first it almost seemed that the federation had disappeared in the process. Although the central government retained responsibility for defense, foreign policy, and a "united market" (no one seemed quite sure just what such a market meant), one might almost have said that the Yugoslav state had "withered away" into a confederation of coequal republics. Interrepublican committees were set up to negotiate political and economic conflicts of interest. The rule was by consensus, so in effect each republic had a veto. A collective presidency consisting of members from each republic and each of the autonomous provinces was to replace Tito, who was allowed by amendment 36 to retain the position of president for life.[15]

The interrepublican committees soon reached a stalemate over the unresolved issue of economic rationalization versus social priorities. Croatian nationalism became identified with the leadership of the League of Croatian Communists. Thirty thousand Zagreb students struck demanding revisions in the foreign currency regulations that, from their perspective, unfairly drained off foreign exchange that came into the country via the Croatian coast into Belgrade banks. Tito attacked the strike as "counterrevolutionary" activity. The nationalist (and, incidentally, economic reform-minded) Croat leaders Miko Tripalo and Dr. Savka Dabcevic-Kucar resigned. Heads rolled at all levels of the Croat party apparatus; high-ranking Croats in the army appear to have been purged as well.

At the time and for the most part in retrospect, these events have been considered a Croatian crisis, i.e., a nationalist-separatist move that failed.[16] From an organizational-political perspective, there was another crucial consideration. The unintended consequence of the constitutional amendments of 1971 had been to generate demands that self-management be taken to its logical conclusion in terms of the Yugoslav party organization itself. As the former head of the Croat Central Committee ideological commission put it:

> He who is ready to accept the concept of Yugoslavia as a federative state composed of equal nations and national minorities, and not ready to discuss the LCY as a federation of national parties, shows his true attitude concerning the former concept. There cannot be a federation of equal, self-managing communities, if there are no possibilities for formation of the League of Communists both on the class and national basis.[17]

Bluntly, one may say (as was often said to me by Yugoslavs) that Yugoslavia had not one political party in 1971 but eight, representing each republic and the two autonomous provinces.

Tito's determination to end that situation was at the heart of the Croatian crisis of 1971. He struck in favor of a reformed, strengthened, and most importantly, *united* Communist party that had the power "to interfere" when necessary, and to which the republican Communist parties were to be strictly accountable. The emphasis on Croatia being only one of the offenders and the seemingly senseless expanding of the purge to other republics were a part of Tito's plan to recentralize the League of Communists of Yugoslavia, streamlining it until he felt secure that the party as an organization could survive him.

The Tenth Party Congress in 1974 ratified the party centralization. It is difficult to evaluate the long-run impact of that reorganization despite the apparent rehabilitation of the regional party organizations at the June 1978 Congress. Tripalo is gone, and by 1972 so are the chairman of the Serbian party, Marko Nikezic; the Macedonian leader Krste Crvenkovski; the Slovene, Stane Kavcic. A whole generation of republican party leaders who had political experience and credibility with their constituencies, and who, despite strong differences, could work together, is a resource that was sacrificed for party recentralization. Their departure from the political scene is a logical place at which to consider the changing nature of the Yugoslav political elite.

POLITICAL LEADERSHIP AND CHANGING ELITE PATTERNS

Despite the formal renunciation of the party's monopoly on political life, political leadership in Yugoslavia remains the function of the League of Communists. The nature of that leadership is undoubtedly influenced by the other institutional interest groups already discussed. Nonetheless the decisions that determine high-level Yugoslav domestic and foreign policy take place within the League of Communists or such governmental organs as the collective presidency, which can best be understood as an interlocking directorate with top party bodies. It would be naive to assume that numbers equate with influence on policy in the Yugoslav party, yet they do provide information on access to the policy-making process. We know for sure that those outside the party do not make key decisions. Therefore the composition of the LCY can serve as a rough index of who decides the allocation of power and resources in Yugoslav society.

According to Yugoslav sources, party membership in absolute numbers grew as follows:[18]

1946	253,000	1958	829,000
1948	482,000	1968	1,146,000
1952	772,000	1971	1,025,000
1954	654,000	1977	1,400,000

If one assumes that the 1948 figure essentially reflects membership before the Soviet-Yugoslav split, by 1958 more than half the membership had joined the party after the break with Moscow. Notwithstanding a drop following decentralization and deemphasis of party power,

1958 membership had surpassed the 1952 mark. If one makes allowances for those who dropped out of the party or who were pushed out because they could not adjust to their new role, it is a fair assumption that the majority of the 1.1 million members in 1968 had been politically socialized into the values of self-managing socialism by a party organizationally and ideologically unique within the international Communist movement. At the top, where those most familiar with the Soviet model remained, personal political survival and the need to assure the party's domestic legitimacy continually necessitated public affirmation of the Yugoslav way.

In short, numbers tell us that with the exception of brief periods of disorientation—1952–54, during radical organizational change, and 1970–71, presumably due to political chaos and ambivalence of direction—the Yugoslav party has grown steadily. Spurts of membership followed perceived external threats in both 1948 and 1968. The majority of these members entered the party at periods that would strongly suggest continuing commitment to an independent, i.e., nonaligned, Yugoslavia. Self-management is accepted as an axiom of Yugoslav political life with the day-to-day substance of that symbolic commitment to expanding participation decided by political struggle.

The steady shift in social composition of party membership is even more striking than its growth. Figures are subject to dispute, but trends are clear. The sharpest is the drop in peasant members, who declined from more than 50 percent in 1952 to 6.7 percent in 1971. Manual workers fell slightly in the same period from 32.2 percent to 28.8 percent. Conversely, the most dramatic jump was in the catch-all category of white collar workers, which moved from 18.9 percent in 1952 to 45.5 percent in 1971. In a rough fashion, this confirms Branko Horvat's claim that as of the mid-1960s "employees" (white-collar workers such as administrative officials, academics, managers, and security personnel) have above average membership in all categories, whereas workers, whether skilled, semiskilled, or unskilled, are below average.[19] Moreover, not only has the rate of joining been three times higher among employees than among workers, but employees with only primary education outnumber skilled workers in the party.

Denitch's breakdown gives a concise picture of the current Yugoslav party.[20] Group I (heavily overrepresented in terms of percentage of the population) includes managers, technical and general intelligentsia, and students; as Denitch succinctly put it, these are "the present and future cadres of society, its experts, and administrators, and the candidates for those roles." Group II (slightly over or slightly underrepresented) includes those who work in the modernizing sector and visibly benefit from the system created by the Yugoslav revolution. Group III (heavily underrepresented) consists of peasants, private craftsmen, housewives, and the unemployed. In brief, some 59 percent of the population are still functioning in a primarily traditional society, outside the socialist and modern sectors of Yugoslav political/social life.

In twenty years, the Yugoslav political elite has evolved from an organization dominated numerically by peasants and ideologically by seasoned revolutionaries to a party of managers, administrators, technicians, and minor bureaucrats. Although Djilas's charge that the party has become a new class[21] is implicitly recognized by the sustained struggle against technocratism and the "red bourgeoisie," in all fairness, the LCY has served as a major channel for the upwardly mobile, while providing a political leadership possessing the skills needed to create and run a modern society. The steady rise of managers and professionals among parliamentary deputies was indicative of that trend; to what extent this has been reversed by the 1974 constitution remains unclear.

Yet the fundamental fact about the Yugoslav political elite is best captured in George Orwell's satiric phrase, "Some are more equal than others." The unifying reality/myth of partisan struggle has had major political consequences. Indeed, a core of revolutionary elites has dominated Yugoslav society from 1945 to the present. Legitimized by their role in the national liberation, these are the main figures on both the federal and republic levels. Despite the visible casualties at the top of the party (Djilas in 1954, Rankovic in 1966, and those such as Koca Popovic who resigned in protest with the fall of the Serbian party chairman Marko Nikezic in 1972), the "Club of 1941"* has held fast. It remains the infrastructure of the Yugoslav political leadership and elite, a source of underlying stability in times of apparent chaos and a potential future trouble spot.

Then there is what one might call a loyal opposition. These are the Marxist humanists associated with the intermittently banned journal *Praxis*, who support the general principles of self-management, while pointing to flaws in implementation. They are the critics, political gadflys whose questions point to some of the most painful problems of Yugoslav political and social life. Not surprisingly, they are frequently unpopular. Perhaps more important, their ties to the universities mean

*Those who joined the party at the beginning of the partisan struggle against German occupation.

a natural constituency, which from the regime's point of view is potentially dangerous.

As for changing elite patterns, perhaps the most notable shift in the 1970s was the skyrocketing power of the republic party elites vis-a-vis the federal center, its temporary forced decline, and the simultaneous rise of the military to positions of party prominence. One result of Tito's drive to recentralize the LCY, ridding the party of Communists who were "nationalist-minded," has been to strengthen the political significance of the army. At the Tenth LCY Party Congress in May 1974, twenty-one generals and other high ranking officers became members of top party bodies. This included a representative on the Executive Committee, fifteen members of the new Central Committee, six officers in the party and statutory commissions, plus another army general as public prosecutor. On the eve of the congress, General Franjo Hrljevic, an active duty army general, was appointed head of the UDBA, meaning that the civilian security apparatus which was removed from army control in 1946 is now back in the hands of the military. Not only did this level of participation hold firm at the Eleventh LCY Congress in 1978, but the armed forces' right to a regular seat both on the new Presidium and among the executive secretaries was recognized.

This is not to assume that there has been a fusion of party-army leadership roles at the highest level. Nonetheless, if one uses Huntington's index of interpenetration by the military of other social institutions[22]—in this case both the party and the security service—military influence on civilian power structures has become significantly greater than during the 1960s. Nor was the increased military participation limited to upper party echelons. Under the 1974 constitution army delegations officially sit in communal and republic assemblies, raising the question of whether it may become appropriate to think in terms of a party-army elite in Yugoslavia much as one would for many of the developing countries of the Third World.

SPECIFIC PROBLEM AREAS

Thus far the thrust of this chapter has been to provide a context within which one can understand fundamental problems facing Yugoslav policy makers, their perspectives, and the structure of the political environment. Here we will look briefly at the interaction of these problems before turning to their international dimension.

Yugoslavia is plagued with four major internal dilemmas:

1. A political/social need to deal with the deep-rooted, national (ethnic) antagonisms among its peoples.
2. Economic tensions created by differences in regional levels of development.
3. An ideological-organizational struggle over the nature of the Communist party.
4. Sociological/political difficulties due to the age homogeneity of the Yugoslav revolutionary elite.

The "Croatian events" of 1970–71 graphically demonstrated the degree to which historic Serb-Croat hostilities remain a running sore in the Yugoslav polity. At best, trust is paper-thin between the two major nations of Yugoslavia. Despite sensitivity to ethnic representation at the highest party levels evident at the Eleventh Congress in 1978, the manner in which the 1971 crisis was resolved has undoubtedly not been forgotten. If this were not enough for any political leadership to cope with, there are other ethnic trouble spots complicating attempts to come up with a workable national policy. The most sensitive of these is what to do about the Albanian "national minority."[23]

By 1971 there were 1.25 million ethnic Albanian citizens of Yugoslavia; that was double the number of Montenegrins and slightly more than the number of Macedonians. There were about half as many Albanians in Yugoslavia as in neighboring Albania. The majority of them (920,000) live in the Kosovo, an autonomous province within the republic of Serbia, making up roughly 74 percent of the province's population. Albanians also account for 17 percent of the republic of Macedonia, and 7 percent of the republic of Montenegro. The problem is not primarily with the Albanians living in Macedonia or Montenegro. Rather the key political question is whether or not the Kosovo with its large Albanian population should be granted republic status to become the seventh republic of Yugoslavia. Can the more than 900,000 Albanians be denied the local autonomy granted to fewer Montenegrins and Macedonians?

Numbers and time appear to be on the side of the Albanians. Today this minority is the fifth largest ethnic group in Yugoslavia, coming after Serbs, Croats, Slovenes, and Bosnian Moslems. Moreover, the Albanian birthrate is the highest in Yugoslavia, estimated by Yugoslav statistics at 3.7 percent. The Slovenes, now 1.7 million, have a significantly smaller birthrate, so that according to population projections, by 1981 the Albanian "national minority" will be the third largest ethnic group in Yugoslavia.

Yet this demographic logic is undermined by both historical and political considerations. From the Serbian viewpoint, the Kosovo is the heart of Serbia. Here the medieval Serbian kings were crowned. Here in the town of Prizren, Tsar Dusan established his empire in the fourteenth century. Here in 1389 Serbs fought Turks in the famous battle of Kosovo, a battle whose spirit still lives in the Serbian epic *Kosovo Polje.* Here in the dusty town of Pec, the Serbian patriarchate was founded in 1346 and the Serbian church became independent of Constantinople. In short, the Kosovo is historically sacred to the Serbs.

From the Serbian perspective, Albanians are interlopers forced on them by the Turks, who favored Muslim Albanians above Christian Serbs. Albanians came as "colonizers," forcing Serbs from the region in the seventeenth and eighteenth centuries. Albanians, in turn, date their claim back to the seventh century when the Kosovo was inhabited by the Illyrians, ancient ancestors of the Albanians. Here in 1878 the League of Prizren was established, marking the beginning of Albanian national consciousness. In short, as Peter Prifti has eloquently documented, both Serbs and Albanians claim title by virtue of (1) possession and (2) historic-symbolic significance.[24]

The decentralizing reforms of the late 1960s excited hopes of increased local autonomy throughout Yugoslavia. Open Albanian nationalism flared in the Kosovo. Rioting ensued, and there were demands that the province be granted republic status, use of the Albanian language at all levels, and a "national" university, and that Albanians living in the Macedonian republic should be protected. Soon violence spread to the Tetovo district of Macedonia.

Although the Kosovo has not received republican status, a number of concessions to Albanian nationalism were made. By 1970 Albanian was an actual rather than a token language in the Kosovo. Albanians had the right to fly the Albanian flag, an overwhelmingly sensitive issue, and they soon were to achieve the demand for a "national" university (one where the language of instruction was Albanian) at Pristina. There were economic improvements as well. As with Croat discontent in the 1970s, much of the smoldering resentment in the Kosovo hinged on economic issues.

In terms of the unresolved conflict between economic rationalizers and their opposition discussed earlier, the fact remains that although the standard of living in the Kosovo may have increased three times since the revolution, the gap between the life style available there and in Slovenia is larger than ever. It is not possible to achieve anything approaching equalization among the different republics and to simultaneously allow the northern, more developed areas of the country to

advance at the pace they feel capable of. For those in Ljubljana or Zagreb, just a finger-nail away from a West European standard of living
of which they are intensely aware, demands for "equalization" are seen
as economic exploitation.

In my view it would be fair to say that the most basic long-run
problem Yugoslavia faces is economic nationalism—a phenomenon
characterized by economic debates over resource allocation, within
which nationalism acts as an intensifier of differences and an obstacle
to compromise, whereas socialist economic rhetoric becomes a vehicle
for expressing national grievances otherwise repressed as illegitimate
within the Yugoslav system.

This brings us to the overlapping problems of the nature of the
Communist party and the tensions created by its aging political leadership. Given the nature of both "national" and economic dilemmas,
conflicts of interest between republic party leaders and central policy
makers can hardly be expected to disappear. In 1971 the republic elites
suffered a major setback. Yet the logic of self-managing socialism in
anything but name only supports them. In one sense such Croat leaders
as Tripalo and Savka Dapcevic-Kucar were captured by their political
constituency, not by a counterrevolutionary "mass movement." Whatever the temporary solutions, their replacements must live with similar political demands and pressures.

At the same time, the tendency for LCY membership to become
disproportionately white-collar swells administration at all levels, until those Yugoslavs who care fear that endemic bureaucratism is hard-
ening the arteries of any genuine revolution. The question of "who gets
the cookies" is just as acute in Communist as in noncommunist political
systems. And in Yugoslavia the symbolic discrepancy of workers' self-
management led by a party with fewer and fewer workers spells danger.[25]

In 1968 these pressures and apparent inconsistencies within Yugoslav society led to the challenge from the left in the form of the Belgrade student strike. Spontaneous, not initially political in content, the
strike came to include such highly touchy demands as elimination of
social inequality and unemployment and democratization of all sociopolitical organizations including the League of Communists. After several tense days, the strike was resolved peacefully, with Tito supporting
the majority of the student demands. He pledged to restore unity, and
appealed to the students to help him. It was a masterful cooptation of
the protest.

Nonetheless, the potential challenge from the left remains a continuing strain within the Yugoslav system. These are the children of the partisans who learned only too well the ideal of an "egalitarian socialist society." The sociological legacy of the revolution means that these politically sensitive future aspirants for power and responsibility within society are frustrated by the generational homogeneity of a Yugoslav leadership sanctioned by their role in the partisan struggle. Through no fault of their own, they do not belong to the "Club of 1941." Despite changes at the top of the party in 1974,[26] there is no contemporary substitute for that trial by fire. To attack from the left is the only legitimate challenge to a regime that the young claim both won and subsequently abandoned the revolution. Their anger supports the economic opposition to market socialism. The continuing struggle of the regime against the *Praxis* group of Marxist humanists, whom the party holds responsible for confusing and corrupting the students, shows the high priority the League gives to retaining control of ideological truth.

Nonetheless, it may be that after twenty-four years of stressing the party's "educational role" in society, it is no longer possible to return to the "commanding role" implicitly sought by the 1971–72 purges and reforms. Nor does the top party leadership appear united in support of such a commanding role. At least that seems to be the message of Kardelj's June 13, 1977, speech emphasizing the pluralism of self-managing interests and warning of the party's misuse of power.[27]

With the 1978 Party Congress Theses based essentially on Kardelj's new book, *The Roads of Development of the Socialist Self-Management Political System,* and on the historic Party Program of 1958, this institutional identity crisis so reminiscent of the late 1950s appears temporarily resolved in favor of "self-managing pluralism," i.e., a brake on party interference with self-managing organs.

Whether or not Tito has failed to create or recreate the revolutionary Yugoslav Communist Party that he appears to have in mind with his mini-cultural revolution of the early 1970s, the LCY faces an organizational crisis when this Godfather of Yugoslav communism leaves the political scene.

The craving for a total solution, a panacea that will somehow miraculously wipe out ethnic hatred, social inequalities, and economic conflicts at one blow, is a generic weakness of the Yugoslav revolution. First, it was to be the catharsis of partisan struggle, then self-management, then the economic reforms, then the constitutional amendments. What is needed is a mechanism, not a miracle or a new personality cult. For in the end, to the extent that self-managing socialism exists at all, it is basically incompatible with reliance on charismatic authority. The tensions created by trying to synthesize the norms of self-management with more than a quarter of a century of political dependence inherent in Tito's personality cult will be a major factor in determining future political outcomes.

The fact that Tito personally intervened to bring order in 1971 may prove extremely dysfunctional. As Huntington points out, charismatic leadership hinders the process of political institutionalization so vital for any party's survival. In 1971 Tito "saved" the country at the expense of reaffirming his position as an indispensable linchpin holding it together. The process of striving toward a participatory federalism in any multinational state experience implies civil disorder, even occasional severe dislocations. Somehow those who must deal with tomorrow's problems have to learn to work together. The irony of Tito's personality cult, an irony with more than a touch of pathos, is that in the early 1970s the giant of Yugoslav communism himself took a major step towards convincing the world that Yugoslavia is standing on glass legs that will shatter with his passing.

With such reservations about the impact of the coming succession crisis on the League of Communists, political observers have more and more fallen into the temptation to stress the army as a temporary or not so temporary substitute. To my mind, however, the army is not the answer. In view of perceived Serbian dominance in the military (attempts to change this ratio and move toward a proportional representation of other nationalities notwithstanding), major political influence of the armed forces has inevitable ethnic implications in the eyes of non-Serbian Yugoslavs. The question is not simply whether the army sees itself as neutral and as operating in a Yugoslav context rather than according to parochial ethnic interests, it is how such actions are seen by the constituency ostensibly served, and indeed how the army behaves.

Moreover, the Eleventh Party Congress spelled out explicitly the degree of army participation at the highest levels and more importantly established a process of selection that would make it extremely difficult for any one group to dominate. Thus one might hypothesize that, like the Mexican military, the Yugoslav armed forces has been politically involved in the orderly running of the country in such a manner as to reduce incentive for an ambitious military elite to intervene in the political process. But, rather than second-guessing the military mind in post-Tito Yugoslavia, let us consider the international factors that influence tomorrow's options.

THE FOREIGN POLICY COMPONENT

Nonalignment is a tricky concept.[28] Both East and West have seen it as a vague, primarily symbolic stance, each suspecting that to be nonaligned meant tilting toward "the other camp." From both sides of the ideological fence, it was viewed as a nonpolicy, a slightly immoral nonpolicy at that. By contrast, in the Yugoslav perception, nonalignment meant buying in, not opting out. Tito did not invent nonalignment. Yugoslavia joined in a process already existing in Asia and Africa, whereby newly independent states were attempting to change international priorities away from East-West ideological differences to the problems of what it is politically fashionable to call the North-South split, i.e., the differences between the "haves" and "have nots" on a continuum of modernization-development-industrialization. In this process ideology was only as relevant as its contribution towards these goals. To the developing countries, nonalignment meant more than their refusal to be surrogates in superpower conflicts marginally related to their national interests. It meant an active policy of influence-seeking whenever problems of special concern for their young, fragile societies were involved. This amounted to a policy of ad hoc, issue-oriented collaboration, pragmatically rooted despite the rhetoric surrounding efforts to find common platforms.

Yugoslavia moved toward nonalignment in answer to the isolation imposed by the Cominform break. That move came in part as a consequence of the Yugoslav election to the U.N. Security Council in 1949, when for the first time Belgrade experienced prolonged close contact with the newly emerging nations of Asia and Africa. Nonalignment maximized Tito's influence and options in an otherwise unpromising international environment. Nonalignment satisfied the psychological need to keep a window open for future contacts with the socialist East while simultaneously keeping open that essential door to economic relations with the West. Nonaligned allies had an additional advantage. They left Tito free to put forward the "Yugoslav model" within the international Communist movement, thereby potentially leaving room for the revolutionary expansionism that he had reluctantly abandoned with the Cominform split.

As the postwar bipolar international system moved beyond cold war into a "limited adversary relationship" between Moscow and Washington, in which East European countries came to be perceived less as satellites than as client states, and the nonaligned states of Asia and

Africa took to fighting among themselves, the concept of nonalignment became fuzzier than ever. The question persisted: nonaligned between whom? Nehru and Nasser died. Only Tito remained of the original architects. Yet even Yugoslav spokesmen who feel uncomfortable with "nonalignment" as a label cling to what they consider the positive content of that policy—demand for a democratization of the international system to allow small and medium-sized states to operate as independent political actors rather than as superpower clients. Moreover, nonalignment serves as the basis of a domestic compromise between those who prefer closer ties with the Soviet bloc and those who favor a more Western orientation. Given the strong position of both forces within the country, the nonalignment alternative helps to achieve an uneasy balance.

Throughout the 1970s the target of nonalignment shifted from the Third World to Europe, where the snail-like progress towards a European security conference provided a vehicle for Belgrade's efforts to achieve a common denominator of interests among small and medium European states.[29] Whatever it was not, the 1975 Helsinki Conference on European Security and Cooperation was at least a partial victory for Yugoslav foreign policy.

The nature of the Yugoslav party as well as its domestic political imperatives support the view that nonalignment will survive Tito. The advantages of that policy for maximizing Yugoslav influence within the increasingly autonomous Eurocommunist movement soured the 1972 honeymoon in Soviet-Yugoslav relations. Coolness returned to Belgrade's dealings with Moscow, Tito's Order of Lenin notwithstanding. Reportedly the credits promised during Soviet enthusiasm for his campaign to recentralize the Yugoslav party never arrived. Meanwhile trials of Cominformists (the euphemism for pro-Soviet forces within Yugoslavia) demonstrated Yugoslav opinion of Soviet pressure tactics. Yugoslav political leaders are anything but unsophisticated, nor do they lack experience in balancing between Moscow and other options. Certainly, Chinese leader Hua Kuo-feng's summer 1978 visit to Yugoslavia was most unwelcome from a Soviet perspective.[30]

Future policy will depend on the nature of such options, for realistically a clash of U.S.-Yugoslav interests can be expected in Europe with respect to both burgeoning Eurocommunism and the role of NATO. The Yugoslav attempt to retain its nonaligned status may lead to policy differences between Belgrade and Washington in regard to the Middle East as well. The manner in which U.S. policy makers respond to these situations will influence not only American-Yugoslav relations but, potentially, Yugoslav strategic choices. In turn, how such issues are resolved will have an impact upon the domestic ideological-organizational struggle—strengthening some contenders, weakening others.

Overall, Yugoslav foreign and domestic policy problems are hopelessly entangled. Indeed, there is a pattern of Yugoslav foreign-domestic policy interactions dating from the Soviet-Yugoslav split in 1948 whereby foreign policy imperatives first created, then consistently reinforced, Yugoslav commitment to expanded political participation, i.e., socialist pluralism. Had Tito and the top Yugoslav leadership not desperately needed an alternative to the Stalinist model, Yugoslav self-managing socialism would not exist. The drive to recentralize the LCY after the Djilas affair in the mid-1950s was cut short by the second Soviet-Yugoslav dispute when Khrushchev dumped Tito in favor of Chinese support for the Soviet "leading role" in the international Communist movement at the 1957 Moscow Conference of ruling Communist parties. To justify their continued defiance, the LCY came out with the party program of 1958, thereby strengthening the first tentative steps toward self-management. The 1958 program was pointedly reaffirmed at the June 1978 LCY Congress, a symbolic rehabilitation of the pluralistic ideas that had been consistently played down since the "Croatian events" in 1971.

This shift away from the party recentralization of the early 1970s was symbolically connected with Soviet-Yugoslav polemics over the nature of the Eurocommunist challenge to Moscow. The end result of contending with Soviet ideologies over whether Eurocommunism represented nonaligned politics or anti-Sovietism strengthened the position of Yugoslavs in and outside the party to whom socialist self-management meant increasing local autonomy, genuine market socialism, legitimation of interest aggregation, and the right to criticize without fear. Particularly throughout 1976–78, the fate of Yugoslav progressives became tied to that of the Western Eurocommunists, most especially the Italian party.

Nor are foreign-domestic linkages limited to the broad cycles of attempting to sort out the relationship of the LCY to self-managing political organs within Yugoslav society. The "national question" is made more difficult by the fear that foreign powers can and will exploit terrorist elements of emigre subcultures, while territorial, ethnic-based irredentist demands exacerbate Yugoslav relations with neighboring Balkan states. The economic debates are fueled by squabbles over foreign credits. At the same time, attempted economic solutions open the door to mass labor migration, which has major domestic and foreign policy consequences. As one Yugoslav graphically put it, to separate these issues is like trying to unravel a pig's intestines. It is beyond the scope of this chapter, which can at best identify them.

FUTURE PROSPECTS

Yugoslavia has a mixed hand. Ethnic conflicts, economic dilemmas, ideological-organizational struggle, and escalating expectations work toward paralyzing effective policy making or implementation. Yet political and economic self-interest is on the side of unity. There is a realistic understanding of the difficulties of surviving as a mini-nation in the Slovene capital of Ljubljana. The alternative of becoming the underdeveloped hinterland of a West European federation, say of Austria or Italy, does not particularly appeal to either Slovenes or Croats despite their resentment at being exploited by the less-developed republics of Yugoslavia. Even at the height of Croat bitterness in 1972, a solid moderate core felt continued attempts to work out national differences were feasible and desirable. Of course, Yugoslavia could slide into a civil war, but many intelligent Yugoslavs see that danger and are working frantically to prevent it. Witness the 1974 constitution's treatment of national considerations and the recognition of both regional and ethnic political reality evident at the 1978 LCY Congress.

Moreover, although this writer does not share the optimism of those who contend Yugoslavia has successfully created "a socialist political culture," self-management is a grand human experiment. Dedication to that ideal, for all the problems of making it work, has been at the heart of Yugoslav politics for more than twenty years.

Every year thousands and thousands of ordinary Yugoslavs have had to cope with trying to manage their own political and economic lives. Expanding the pool of those educated enough to bring needed skills to that process has been a priority. Indeed the nature of Yugoslav party membership indicates that most modern sectors of society have a real stake in their system and in continuing the experiment. As for foreign policy, Yugoslavia's most successful product has been its skillful, sophisticated diplomats. Thus even those who consider the Yugoslav system most fragile should take comfort in the fact that history does not repeat itself without the help of men and women who make policy. The process of trying to bring responsible participation out of the reality of Balkan apathy has given contemporary Yugoslav society strengths sadly lacking in the interwar Kingdom of Serbs, Croats, and Slovenes.

NOTES

This chapter benefited greatly from the research assistance of Rada Vlajinac of the Massachusetts Institute of Technology Center for International Studies.

1. Quoted by Vladimir Dedijer, *With Tito Through the War: Partisan Diary, 1941–1944* (London: A. Hamilton, 1951), p. 39.

2. See M. George Zaninovich, *The Development of Socialist Yugoslavia* (Baltimore: Johns Hopkins Press, 1968), pp. 44–50.

3. *The Constitution of the Socialist Federal Republic of Yugoslavia* (Belgrade, 1974), p. 307.

4. Bogdan Denis Denitch, *The Legitimation of a Revolution: The Yugoslav Case* (New Haven: Yale University Press, 1976), p. 34.

5. This was particularly true in Croatia and is a pattern that has continued. According to unofficial estimates in 1971, individuals who were ethnically Serbian living in the republic of Croatia accounted for roughly 35 percent of the Croatian Communist party as opposed to 17 percent of the republic population.

6. Reportedly the "national" composition of the top 205 party cadres after the 1974 Tenth LCY Congress included 60 Serbs and 27 Montenegrins as opposed to 29 Croats, 27 Slovenes, 15 Albanians, 13 Moslems, 5 Hungarians, etc. For analysis see Slobodan Stankovic, "Aftermath of the Yugoslav Party Congress," *RFE Research* 2074, June 5, 1974. The Veselin Djuranovic government, formed after premier Dzemal Bijedic died in an air crash in 1977, consisted of 10 Serbs, 5 Croats, 5 Montenegrins, 5 Macedonians, 4 Slovenes, 2 Albanians, 1 Moslem and 1 Hungarian. *Borba,* March 16, 1977

7. See Branko Horvat, "Yugoslav Economic Policy in the Post-War Period: Problems, Ideas, Institutional Developments," *The American Economic Review,* 61 (June 1971), supplement, p. 73.

8. See Robert Bass and Elizabeth Marbury, eds. *The Soviet-Yugoslav Controversy, 1948–1958: A Documentary Record* (New York: Prospect Books, 1954). For a subsequent Yugoslav version, see *White Book on Aggressive Activities by the Governments of the USSR, Poland, Czechoslovakia, Hungary, Rumania, Bulgaria and Albania towards Yugoslavia* (Belgrade: Ministry of Foreign Affairs, 1951).

9. Horvat, pp. 80–81.

10. Deborah D. Milenkovitch, *Plan and Market in Yugoslav Economic Thought* (New Haven: Yale University Press, 1971), pp. 54ff.

11. For an excellent analysis, see Dennison I. Rusinow, "Yugoslavia's Problems With Market Socialism," *American Universities Field Staff Reports (AUFS),* Southeast Europe Series, XI, 4 (May 1964).

12. Michael M. Milenkovitch, "Soviet-Yugoslav Relations and the Brezhnev Doctrine," *Studies for a New Central Europe,* No. 4 (1968–1969), pp. 112–121.

13. *Borba,* September 22, 1969.

14. Undoubtedly this solution reflected political struggle, for it in no way resembled the rumored streamlined seven-member executive committee that at least some party officials were talking about the summer before. *The Times* (London) June 2, 1977; for analysis see Slobodan Stankovic, "Top Party Hierarchy to be Reorganized," RFE Background Report 108, June 6, 1977.

242 Yugoslavia

15. As of May 1974, the state presidency had Serbs representing both Bosnia-Hercegovina and the Vojvodina as well as Serbia, although one may assume that these posts will rotate to Croat, Moslem, and Hungarian representatives.

16. See F. Stephen Larrabee, "Yugoslavia at the Crossroads," *Orbis* (summer 1972); Dennison I. Rusinow's four-part analysis, "Crisis in Croatia," *AUFS*, (June–September 1972); and Viktor Meier, "The Political Dynamics in the Balkans in 1974," in *The World and the Great Power Triangles*, edited by William E. Griffith (Cambridge, Mass.: MIT Press, 1975), pp. 61ff.

17. *Vjesnik,* February 11, 1977.

18. *NIN,* October 1972, and *Borba,* March 30, 1977.

19. Branko Horvat, *An Eassay on Yugoslav Society* (White Plains: International Arts and Sciences Press, 1969), p. 201.

20. Denitch, pp. 92–93.

21. Milovan Djilas, *The New Class: Analysis of the Communist System* (New York: Praeger, 1957).

22. Samuel P. Huntington, *The Soldier and the State: The Theory and Practice of Civil-Military Relations* (New York: Vintage Books, 1957).

23. Peter R. Prifti, "Minority Politics: The Albanians in Yugoslavia," *Balkanistica: Occasional Papers in Southeast European Studies, II* (1975), pp. 7–18.

24. Ibid., p. 10.

25. Recent figures indicate that although the number of white-collar workers declined to 41.8 percent in 1975, manual workers also continued to drop off slightly to 28.1 percent despite sustained efforts to recruit from that sector. *Vecernje Novosti,* June 12, 1976. Dolanc subsequently claimed that manual workers moved up to 28.9 percent. Ibid., June 7, 1977.

26. In one sense the 1974 Executive Committee of the Presidium can be seen as an attempt to make room at the top for the next generation of party leadership. In 1978 the average age of the Executive Committee (excluding Tito) was 53, roughly nine to thirteen years younger than the members of the collective state presidency. The problem was that the Executive Committee lacked independent authority and essentially operated as Tito's personal court, hence its abolition at the 1978 Party Congress. Yet that move marked the failure of one experiment, not of the attempt. Despite the inclusion of the majority of the members of the state presidency on the new Presidium, the average age of its membership minus Tito is 52. Eleven of the twenty-three members are under 55, two-thirds are under 60. Party secretary Stane Dolanc is 53; all of the new executive secretaries are in their forties or early fifties.

27. The best single discussion of these complex developments is Dennison Rusinow's "Yugoslavia's Domestic Developments," paper prepared for a conference on "Yugoslavia: Problems and Accomplishments," Woodrow Wilson Center, Washington, D.C., October 16, 1977.

28. Alvin Z. Rubinstein, *Yugoslavia and the Nonaligned World* (Princeton: Princeton University Press, 1970) and Leo Mates, *Nonalignment: Theory and Current Policy* (Dobbs Ferry, N.Y.: Ocean Publications, 1972).

29. See Radovan Vukadinovic, "Small States and the Policy of Nonalignment: The Yugoslav Position," *Southeastern Europe,* II, Part 2 (1974), pp. 202–212.

30. The Soviets were particularly bitter over the implications of including Macedonia on Hua Kuo-feng's itinerary. *Pravda,* August 24, 1978.

BIBLIOGRAPHY

Adizes, Ichak, and Mann Borgese, Elisabeth, eds. *Self-Management: New Dimensions to Democracy.* Santa Barbara, California: ABC-Clio Press, 1975.

Auty, Phyllis. *Tito: A Biography.* New York: McGraw-Hill, 1970.

Avakumovic, Ivan. *History of the Communist Party of Yugoslavia.* Aberdeen, Scotland: University Press of Aberdeen, 1964.

Bass, Robert, and Marbury, Elizabeth, eds. *The Soviet-Yugoslav Controversy, 1948-1958: A Documentary Record.* New York: Prospect Books, 1959.

Dedijer, Vladimir. *Tito.* New York: Simon and Schuster, 1953.

Denitch, Bogdan Denis. *The Legitimation of a Revolution: The Yugoslav Case.* New Haven and London: Yale University Press, 1976.

Djilas, Milovan. *Conversations with Stalin.* New York: Harcourt, Brace, 1962.

——. *The New Class: An Analysis of the Communist System.* New York: Praeger, 1957.

Fisher, Jack C. *Yugoslavia: A Multinational State, Regional Differences and Administrative Response.* San Francisco: Chandler, 1966.

Hoffman, George W., and Neal, Fred Warner. *Yugoslavia and the New Communism.* New York: Twentieth Century Fund, 1962.

Horvat, Branko. *An Essay on Yugoslav Society.* Translated by Henry F. Mins. White Plains, N.Y.: International Arts and Sciences Press, 1969.

Johnson, A. Ross. *The Transformation of Communist Ideology: The Yugoslav Case, 1945-1953.* Cambridge, Mass.: MIT Press, 1972.

Markovich, Mihailo. *From Affluence to Praxis: Philosophy and Social Criticism.* Ann Arbor: University of Michigan Press, 1974.

Mates, Leo. *Nonalignment: Theory and Current Policy.* Dobbs Ferry, N.Y.: Oceana Publications, 1974.

Milenkovitch, Deborah D. *Plan and Market in Yugoslav Economic Thought.* New Haven: Yale University Press, 1971.

Rubinstein, Alvin Z. *Yugoslavia and the Nonaligned World.* Princeton: Princeton University Press, 1970.

Rusinow, Dennison I. *The Yugoslav Experiment.* London and Berkeley, Calif.: Royal Institute of International Affairs and University of California Press, 1977.

Sher, Gerson S. *Praxis: Marxist Criticism and Dissent in Socialist Yugoslavia.* Bloomington: Indiana University Press, 1977.

Shoup, Paul. *Communism and the Yugoslav National Question.* New York: Columbia University Press, 1968.

Singleton, Fred. *Twentieth Century Yugoslavia.* New York: Columbia University Press, 1976.

Stojanovic, Svetozar. *Between Ideals and Reality: A Critique of Socialism and Its Future.* New York: Oxford University Press, 1973.

Ulam, Adam. *Titoism and the Cominform.* Cambridge, Mass.: Harvard University Press, 1962.

Zaninovich, M. George. *The Development of Socialist Yugoslavia.* Baltimore: Johns Hopkins Press, 1968.

Zukin, Sharon. *Beyond Marx and Tito: Theory and Practice in Yugoslav Socialism.* New York and London: Cambridge University Press, 1975.

10 East European Economies: Achievements, Problems, Prospects

Paul Marer

The aim of this chapter is to describe the most important trends and forces that have determined and will continue to shape the economic achievements, problems, and prospects of the countries of Eastern Europe. A basic theme is the fundamental diversity among the eight countries of this heterogeneous region. Eastern Europe includes the German Democratic Republic (GDR) and Albania, whose per capita income levels differ from each other at least tenfold. It includes an economic alliance system, the Council for Mutual Economic Assistance (CMEA), led by the Soviet Union, of which Bulgaria and Romania are both members even though each has a different kind of "special" relationship with the USSR. Eastern Europe embraces Yugoslavia (not a full member of the CMEA) with its unique, worker-oriented market socialism; Hungary with its New Economic Mechanism (NEM), under which enterprises are no longer assigned a compulsory plan; the GDR, Poland, and Czechoslovakia, whose economies depart in varying degrees from traditional, Soviet-type central planning; and Albania, whose economy today is more "Stalinist" than perhaps any East European economy ever was, including that of the Soviet Union during the 1930s. Perceiving the nature and extent of this diversity is the key to understanding the economy of Eastern Europe.[1]

The chapter will also treat the conceptual and practical problems of measuring economic performance. Since no single indicator of performance exists, five of the key economic indicators customarily relied upon by economists to evaluate a country's performance will be described and, where possible, quantified. Also to be discussed are the problems of obtaining standard statistical information for Eastern Europe and of interpreting both official data and statistics compiled in the West on Eastern Europe.

A third theme is Eastern Europe's economic relations with the USSR; a discussion of this subject will show how these relations have evolved during the postwar period and identify the critical issues of today and tomorrow.

A fourth theme is Eastern Europe's economic relations with the industrial West. In recent years, this relationship has become increasingly dominated by the surprisingly rapid and large accumulation of foreign debt by the CMEA—about $50 billion at the end of 1977. A section of the chapter will explain why and how this large increase in Eastern Europe's indebtedness occurred, identify which East European countries are particularly affected by it, discuss present efforts to deal with the problem, and suggest its implications for the future.

A further aim is to demonstrate, as specifically as possible, the particularly close linkage between economics and politics in Eastern Europe. With respect to external politics, the key, of course, is Soviet policy vis-a-vis Eastern Europe, which will be examined in some detail and from the perspective of Eastern Europe. Domestically, the political factor is particularly important in discussing such questions as whether and how each country's traditional, centrally planned economic system can be modified, and the nature of the forces both seeking and resisting economic reforms.

I. THE ECONOMIC "ENVIRONMENT" IN EASTERN EUROPE

The East European countries differ with respect to size, resource endowment, historical and cultural experience, nationality, language, level of economic development, direction and speed of changes in their economic systems, development strategy, economic performance, and political orientation. The variation is great even if the region is defined narrowly to include only the six core states of Bulgaria, Czechoslovakia, the German Democratic Republic, Hungary, Poland, and Romania; if Albania and Yugoslavia are included, the heterogeneity is even more pronounced.

To give the reader a flavor of the region's economic diversity, this section outlines, first, the different *initial conditions* under which central economic planning was introduced in the eight East European countries after World War II, and, second, the important *postwar events and circumstances which created or accentuated diversity* among these countries, even as they all introduced a somewhat similar "socialist" form of economic organization, which may loosely be called "central planning."

Initial Conditions After World War II

Size. Most striking is the difference in size between the relatively small, resource-poor countries that make up Eastern Europe and the continent-sized, resource-rich USSR, whose economic model was imposed upon the region after the war. In terms of population and land area, the East European economies ranged from tiny Albania to medium-sized countries like Poland, Romania, and the GDR.

Level of development. At the end of World War II, the region consisted of industrialized nations (the GDR and Czechoslovakia); countries at the beginning stage of industrialization, but already possessing a developed industrial sector (Hungary and Poland); and very poor, essentially agricultural societies (Romania, Bulgaria, Yugoslavia, and, the poorest country by far in all of Europe, Albania).

Statehood. In assessing initial environmental conditions, one must consider how long each nation-state had been in existence. A political unit with a history of territorial integrity and effectively functioning governments in a stable nation-state provided a more solid base for economic development than a unit where these conditions were largely absent. With respect to territorial integrity, only two East European countries, Bulgaria and Albania, have been located on essentially the same territory since before World War I. The nation-states corresponding to today's Hungary, Czechoslovakia, Yugoslavia, and Romania were formed only after World War I. By contrast, Poland was transformed after World War II with respect to its geography and the composition of its population; the GDR was formed as a nation-state in the late 1940s, and was subsequently diplomatically isolated from much of the Western world for about two decades.

Regional disparities and nationality problems. Many economic difficulties involved in the mobilization and allocation of resources can be avoided if a country does not suffer from sharp conflicts among different nationalities or other minorities within its borders or from serious regional inequalities. In both respects, Yugoslavia was (and still is) the most heterogeneous; significant ethnic and regional differences also existed (and still do) in Czechoslovakia. The other countries are more homogeneous in this respect, although in Romania, 13 percent of the population consists of minority nationalities (9 percent of whom are Hungarians). In Bulgaria, at least 10 percent of the population are Turks, Greeks, Romanians, Armenians, and others. The remaining East European countries, with the exception of the GDR, also have minority national groups and backward regions.

Resource endowment. The natural resource endowment of a country inevitably influences economic structure, industrial location, invest-ment policy, and foreign economic relations. The possession and exploi-tation of natural resources are important for the domestic economy and may provide significant export earnings. Ranking the countries from those with the best to those with the least adequate endowment, we find that the relatively well endowed are Poland (black and brown coal, copper, sulfur, lead, zinc, iron ore, aluminum, and natural gas); Ro-mania (oil and gas, coal, bauxite, and salt); Yugoslavia (iron ore, copper, timber, lead, coal, bauxite); and Albania (chromium, timber, bitumen, lignite, crude oil, gas, copper, and iron ore). By contrast, relatively poorly endowed with natural resources are the GDR (although it has brown coal, potash, iron ore); Czechoslovakia (coal, antimony, magne-site, pyrite, fluorspar, iron ore, copper, manganese); Hungary (bauxite, coal, natural gas, sulfur); and Bulgaria (low-grade coal, lead, zinc, cop-per, chromium, manganese ore, asbestos).

An important aspect of resource endowment is the suitability of the country's soil and climate for agriculture. Quite well endowed in this respect are Hungary, Romania, Bulgaria (reasonably self-sufficient in food and some possible net exports) and, to a lesser extent, Poland and Yugoslavia. However, the amount of resources devoted to agriculture and agricultural organization (especially with respect to insuring the stability of institutional arrangements and providing a good incentive system) are as important as, if not more important than, soil and cli-mate. East European countries differ from each other also in how they organize their agriculture; as a result, there is considerable diversity in agricultural performance.

Location and climate are also important for attracting tourists, who tend to seek sun and water. Yugoslavia, Bulgaria, Romania, and, to a lesser extent, Hungary have exploited this advantage since the mid-1960s by specializing in providing tourist services, while Albania has not taken advantage of its tourist potential. With respect to location, another significant factor is whether a country is landlocked, like Hun-gary and Czechoslovakia, or whether it has a long seashore and good seaports, like the GDR, Poland, and Yugoslavia.

War damage, reparations, and other unrequited transfers. The war had different effects on the countries of Eastern Europe in terms of the destruction of physical and human capital and of postwar reparations obligations. In terms of war-related destruction, the greatest damage was suffered by the territory that subsequently became the GDR and by Poland, whose capital and other large cities were largely destroyed. Reparations, which were made principally to the USSR, were accompanied by outright economic exploitation by the Soviets under Stalin. The GDR carried the largest burden by far, but substantial economic resources were also extracted from several other East European countries. A rough estimate, based on careful assessment but rather incomplete data, suggests that until Stalin's death in 1953, the size of the unrequited flow of resources from Eastern Europe to the Soviet Union was of the same order of magnitude as the flow of resources from the United States to Western Europe under the Marshall Plan, around $14 billion.[2]

Lack of regional cooperation. In addition to being isolated from much of the outside world after World War II, Eastern Europe lacked a strong historical tradition of regional economic or political cooperation. As noted by Aspaturian, historically, Eastern Europe has been comprised of small, relatively weak states, many divided from one another by ancient animosities; they have traditionally been manipulated and exploited by neighboring great powers for their own ends. In addition to the problems posed for these countries by Soviet domination after the war, lack of a tradition of regional cooperation made it all the more difficult to adjust to the new conditions. In addition, the Soviet Union under Stalin actively discouraged economic and political cooperation among the East European countries.

Further Differentiation During the Postwar Period

Ownership Patterns in Agriculture. There was a striking dissimilarity among the East European countries, first, in regard to the postwar implementation of land reforms and, second, after the initial collectivization drives had begun, in regard to the eventual decision to permit the private sector to remain dominant (Poland and Yugoslavia) or to transfer agriculture into predominantly socialized forms (all other countries). But even among the latter group, there are significant differences in the relative importance of the residual private sector.

The East European countries also differ in the form under which socialized agriculture functions. State farms are relatively the most important in Romania and Czechoslovakia (tilling approximately one-third of the arable land) and are least important in the GDR and Bulgaria. Moreover, "collective farms" vary with respect to size, organization, scope and extent of local initiative permitted, and the system of incentives and remuneration, to mention just a few of the relevant factors.

Defense burdens. East European countries vary in the size of the military expenditures that they decided, or were asked, to shoulder. During the 1950s Czechoslovakia carried a particularly onerous burden.

During much of its postwar history, Yugoslavia also allocated a relatively large slice of its resources to national defense. Even today, under conditions of relative peace, the burden of defense expenditures, including the role of the police force, border guards, and other control mechanisms, varies considerably from country to country.[3]

Critical events. Dramatic political events have served as important backdrops to economic policy. These have included the 1949–52 embargo of Yugoslavia by the Soviet Union and by the other East European countries; the embargo by the West (which was the direct consequence and manifestation of the cold war) aimed principally against the USSR but causing greater economic difficulties for the countries of Eastern Europe; the 1953 uprising in East Berlin; the 1956 riots in Poland and the revolution in Hungary in the same year; the Twentieth Congress of the Communist Party of the Soviet Union in 1956 where Khrushchev criticized Stalin and changed Soviet internal and external policies; the erection of the Berlin Wall in 1961 to stem the large outflow of professionals and skilled labor (between 1949 and 1961 more than two million residents—more than 10 percent of the population—emigrated to West Germany); the Soviet bloc's break with China during the early 1960s; the 1968 Soviet invasion of Czechoslovakia; the 1956 upheavals and the 1970 and 1976 resistance to retail price rises in Poland; the nearly complete political and economic realignment of Albania with China during the early 1960s and the severing of their links in 1978. There were also some dramatic natural disasters: the 1963 earthquake in Yugoslavia and the 1970 flood and 1977 earthquake in Romania.

Special links with particular countries. Among the environmental considerations that have brought significant economic benefits to one country but much smaller benefits or none at all to others are the following special political and economic links between particular countries.

Bulgaria and the USSR. The Soviets have granted substantial aid to Bulgaria in various forms; for example, several large, long-term, subsidized credits at an average interest charge of 2 percent—some in hard currency—totaled more than $0.5 billion by 1970. The bulk of the loans were or are to be repaid with products of industrial complexes newly established with the aid of these credits.

Albania and the rest of Eastern Europe and China. Until 1961, the Soviet Union and all East European countries gave large, subsidized credits and other forms of aid to Albania. According to one Western estimate, economic aid by the USSR totaled $156 million and technical and military assistance approximately $100 million, while

Eastern Europe (excluding Yugoslavia) provided $133 million in economic aid. (Yugoslavia aided Albania only during 1947–49, when a confederation between the two countries was planned.) In addition, hundreds of Albanians were sent to Eastern Europe for study or technical training, and the East European countries sent engineers and other experts to Albania. After 1959, the principal donor, of course, became China; according to one Western estimate, Albania had received $838 million in aid from its new ally by 1975. But China's abrupt change of policy, including its opening to the West and to Yugoslavia after the death of Mao, caused the two countries to sever their links. Today, Albania is isolated from all socialist countries and has only weak and tenuous commercial links with a few West European countries.

GDR and the Federal Republic of Germany. Under a protocol of the 1957 Rome treaty which established the European Economic Community (EEC), West Germany's trade with the GDR was classified as "intra-German" and was therefore exempt from the tariffs and levies which fall on trade with other non-EEC countries. A West German source that quantified the benefits which the GDR derives from this arrangement concluded that a conservative estimate of its total gain in 1970 was about $140 million, comprised of the following items:

Tariff exemption for GDR exports to West Germany;

Exemption from levies raised on agricultural imports from all other non-EEC countries;

Extra scope for price increases allowed by special arrangements for value-added tax;

Savings on interest payments owing to the interest-free swing credit provided by West Germany to finance trade between the two countries;

A fixed exchange rate between the two German currencies which leaves the GDR unaffected by the Deutschmark's repeated revaluations.

Since intra-German trade has been rising rapidly in recent years the GDR's gain from this special relationship is undeniably substantial.

II. CALCULATING AND INTERPRETING ECONOMIC PERFORMANCE INDICATORS

Data Availability and Measurement Concepts

For many years after World War II, few economic data were published by the East European countries. What was published tended to extol, often in a propagandistic fashion, the achievements of central planning under "socialism." Gradually, however, the volume of published economic statistics increased, and the quality and reliability of the data improved. This change was brought about principally by the need to base economic research and planning decisions on reasonably accurate data. At the same time, the pressure to show good performance tended to lead to exaggerations in reporting by the producing units (especially for those indicators on which bonuses are based) and sometimes also by the control organs, such as the ministries, as well as by the central compilers of the statistics. Notable differences remain among the countries in the details and quality of their official statistics, but the shortcomings—notably, the tendency to hide the economy's weak points—are still substantial, and the data disclosed still fall short of those commonly available for the Western industrial nations. In most countries there are no meaningful data on retail price increases and income distribution.

Accurate assessment of Eastern Europe's economic performance is further hindered by differences in the Eastern and Western concepts of national income accounting and growth-rate calculation, so that meaningful international comparisons require methodological adjustments of official East European data. These considerations, combined with the necessity of estimating missing data and making subjective choices and judgments regarding different statistical series, preclude the development of a fully defined, objective set of accounts on Eastern Europe's economic "performance."

A further difficulty is that "economic performance" is multidimensional, although this is so for any economy. The five indicators most often relied upon to measure performance are economic growth rates; production efficiency (i.e., how much input is needed to produce a unit of output, which, over time, is measured by the growth of productivity); improvements in the standard of living and the distribution of income among individuals, groups, and regions (a very important aspect of which is the rate and nature of inflation); the rate of unemployment; and the status of the balance of payments. Sometimes a comparatively good performance with respect to one indicator can be achieved only by a concurrent or postponed weaker performance in some other area of the economy. Discussed next are problems of calculation and interpretation of each of the five economic performance indicators, presented, when possible, with supporting data.

Economic Growth Rates

Meaning and interpretation. Perhaps the most important—certainly the most frequently cited—statistic is economic growth performance, i.e., how rapidly the aggregate output of goods and services produced by the economy is growing. A rapid growth in *real production* (in contrast to the money value of production, which may rise as a result of inflation) tends to make other economic targets easier to attain. These targets can be improving the standard of living; bettering the distribution of income by giving a larger slice of a growing pie to the poorest groups or regions; providing jobs to those willing and able to work; and increasing exports to pay for needed imports.

Generally, the higher the growth rate, the better the economy's performance, but sometimes that interpretation may not be accurate. One reason for this is that unusually high growth rates tend to create troublesome imbalances in the economy; a good example is Poland during the 1970s, to be discussed below. The nature of the imbalance depends on how a high growth rate was achieved: if it was financed from internal sources, through a high investment rate, then consumption (i.e., the standard of living) tends to suffer—as was typical of all East European countries during the 1950s; if the growth was financed mainly from external sources, i.e., by borrowing, then future growth rates may be impaired, as exports must go to service the foreign debt rather than to pay for current imports. Another typical problem with an unusually high industrial growth rate is that it pollutes the environment. This has been the case throughout Eastern Europe, as also in the West, most notably in Japan. The impact of industrial growth on environmental quality is not yet reflected in standard economic statistics collected and compared among nations.

Measurement problems. Growth rates depicting the output of an economy and its various sectors are published in greater or lesser detail by the central statistical offices of all East European countries. The growth rates officially claimed to have been achieved or planned show from moderate to spectacular results, depending on the country, economic sector, and period. Western experts consider the figures to be somewhat exaggerated because they are based on reports by enterprises subject, except in Hungary and Yugoslavia, to strong pressures to fulfill the plan. A further bias is caused by a reporting system which permits and encourages the pricing of "new" products so that the value of gross output is artificially increased. The exaggeration varies not only from country to country and sector to sector but also from year to year. The upward bias is believed to be the greatest in the official statistics of the less-developed countries, although the statistics of even the more-developed countries, especially those of the GDR, are not immune from this problem.

Western recomputations of East European growth rates employ definitions and methodologies and weight the component series in accord with standard Western approaches; but, of course, they must contend with the scarcity of published data.* Still, most Western experts believe that the recalculated series are better indicators than the official series of long-term economic growth trends.

Findings. A comparison of the officially published Net Material Product (NMP) and recalculated Western Gross National Product (GNP) output series is presented in Table 1 for each of the eight East European countries, as available, for sub-periods between 1965 and 1975 and annually for 1971–76. Available plan figures are also shown for 1977 and 1976–80. The tabulation includes data for Yugoslavia and scattered series for Albania.

The official NMP figures measure, in constant prices, gross output by sector less material costs, excluding the so-called nonmaterial service sectors. The recalculated GNP figures measure aggregate economic activity, including the service sectors, by summing indices of sectoral output in constant prices, using factor cost weights. Because NMP and GNP differ in coverage, methodology, and bases of valuation, the two series are not expected to present the same performance picture. The official NMP series, while biased upward, is believed to be one of the most important indicators used by the leadership in the East European countries to judge their own economic performance. The recalculated GNP series is the best Western estimate of how rapidly the East European economies are growing.[4]

Table 2 ranks the eight countries on the basis of their overall growth performance during 1970–75 according to official data. The ranking remains pretty much the same on the basis of GNP data (recalculated growth rates are not available for Yugoslavia and Albania), but would change slightly if 1965–75 growth rates were the criterion.

Based on 1970–75 performance, the eight countries can be divided into two groups: the three relatively fast-growing countries—Romania, Poland, and Bulgaria—and the other, less rapidly growing countries. Taking the 1975–76 actual and 1976–80 plan figures into account, Romania can probably claim the first place and Bulgaria the second.

The position of Yugoslavia and Albania is interesting to note. Yugo-

---

*Recalculated production indices by sector are based largely on officially published output series in physical units, an approach that may have a conservative bias because data in physical units do not reflect model changes and other quality improvements over time. This method also incorporates new products in the index with a certain lag after these products have been introduced.

Table 1 Average Annual Growth Rates of East European Countries' Net Material Product, Officially Reported (O) and Gross National Product, Recalculated (R), 1965–76 Actual and 1976–80 Plan

Period	Bulgaria		Czecho-slovakia		GDR		Hungary		Poland		Romania		Yugo-slavia		Albania	
	O	R	O	R	O	R	O	R	O	R	O	R	O	R	O	R
1965–70	8.7	4.8	6.8	3.5	5.2	3.2	6.8	3.1	6.0	3.8	7.7	4.5	6.1	n.a.	9.0	n.a.
1971	7.1	3.5	5.5	3.5	4.5	2.1	6.5	4.8	8.1	7.1	13.5	14.1	8.1	n.a.	n.a.	n.a.
1972	7.7	5.0	5.8	3.6	5.7	3.7	5.1	2.4	10.6	7.1	10.0	6.3	4.3	n.a.	n.a.	n.a.
1973	8.0	4.1	5.2	3.3	5.6	2.9	7.4	5.0	10.8	7.5	10.7	3.2	4.9	n.a.	n.a.	n.a.
1974	7.4	3.3	5.9	3.7	6.4	5.0	6.9	3.1	10.4	5.9	12.4	5.5	8.5	n.a.	n.a.	n.a.
1975	9.0	7.4	6.2	2.6	4.9	3.2	5.4	2.4	9.0	5.5	9.8	4.3	3.3	n.a.	n.a.	n.a.
1970–75	7.9	4.5	5.7	3.4	5.4	3.5	6.2	3.6	9.8	6.7	11.3	6.1	6.6	n.a.	6.3	n.a.
1976	6.6	4.6	2.6	1.9	3.7	2.4	3.5	1.2	6.6	5.7	10.5	7.1	4.0	n.a.	n.a.	
1977 plan	8.2		5.2		5.5		6.2		5.7		11.3		n.a.		n.a.	
1976–80 plan	7.7		5.0		5.0		5.5		7.1		10.5		7.0		6.3–7.0	

a Social product defined according to the material product approach.

Source: Paul Marer, "Economic Performance," except Bulgaria through Romania, official series for 1976, which is based on Jan Vanous, "The East European Recession," Table 11.

Table 2 Ranking of the East European Countries by Growth Performance, 1965–76 Actual and 1976–80 Plan (Average Annual Rate of Growth in Percent)

Country and Measure	1965–70	1970–75	1976	1977 Plan	1976–80 Plan
1. Romania:					
NMP	7.7	11.3	10.5	11.3	10.5
GNP	4.5	6.1	7.1	—	—
2. Poland:					
NMP	6.0	9.8	6.6	5.7	7.1
GNP	3.8	6.7	5.7	—	—
3. Bulgaria:					
NMP	8.7	7.9	6.6	8.2	7.7
GNP	4.8	4.5	4.6	—	—
4. Yugoslavia:					
Social product	6.1	6.6	4.0	*	7.0
5. Albania: NMP	9.0	6.3	*	*	6.3–7.0
6. Hungary:					
NMP	6.8	6.2	3.5	6.2	5.5
GNP	3.1	3.6	1.2	—	—
7. Czechoslovakia:					
NMP	6.8	5.7	2.6	5.2	5.0
GNP	3.5	3.4	1.9	—	—
8. GDR:					
NMP	5.2	5.4	3.7	5.5	5.0
GNP	3.2	3.5	2.4	—	—

*Not available.
Source: Table 1.

slavia ranks right in the middle, during 1965–76 performing about the same as Hungary. During 1965–70 Albania claims to have grown roughly on a par with Romania and Bulgaria, but its growth slowed during 1970–75 and its performance was roughly on a par with that of Hungary. To be sure, Albania's exceptionally poor and incomplete statistics and the absence of a Western recalculation undermine our confidence in the data and make it particularly difficult to compare its performance with those of other countries.

Population growth figures, needed to calculate the more meaningful per capita data, are presented in Table 3. The eight East European countries can be divided into four groups. At one end of the spectrum stands Albania, where the annual population increment is about 2.5 percent—an extremely high rate even by world standards—reducing Albania's growth rates on a per capita basis by at least 1.5 percent vis-a-vis every other East European country. At the other extreme is the GDR, whose population continues to decline by about one-quarter of one percent per annum, raising its per capita performance slightly.

Table 3 Index of Population Growth in the East European Countries, 1960–76
(Average Annual Percent Change)

Period	Bulgaria	Czecho-slovakia	GDR	Hungary	Poland	Romania	Yugo-slavia	Albania
1965–70	0.70	0.28	0.04	0.36	0.80	1.28	1.04	2.80
1970–75	0.56	0.65	−0.24	0.39	0.91	1.00	0.95	2.50[a]
1975–76	0.38	0.86	−0.30	0.48	0.92	1.00	0.95[c]	2.50[b]

[a] 1970–73.
[b] Assumed to be the same as 1970–74.
[c] Assumed to be the same as 1970–73.
Source: Paul Marer, "Economic Performance," Table 3.

Registering small population increases (in the one-third to two-thirds of one percent per annum range) are Bulgaria, Czechoslovakia, and Hungary. In the one percent per annum growth range are Romania, Poland, and Yugoslavia.

Comparing growth performance in the 1970s on a per capita basis and taking into account plan projections to 1980 would change the relative position of Albania, moving it down among the relatively slow-growing countries. The GDR would move slightly ahead of Czechoslovakia on the basis of NMP and also ahead of Hungary, on the basis of GNP.

The official NMP statistics presented in Table 1 reveal that in 1976 every East European country experienced a decline in the rate of growth of its output (no information was available for Albania) as compared with the average growth rates of 1970–75. For most countries, a decline in the growth rates can be noted in 1975. Because for some countries there are such large discrepancies between the officially reported and the recalculated growth rates, no particular significance should be attached to any single year's absolute growth rate number. Still, the trends indicate a general downturn in the growth rates in Eastern Europe, a phenomenon that may be called a growth recession (to distinguish it from "recession" proper, which normally indicates a stagnation or actual decline in the level of economic activity of a country). The reasons behind the decline in the growth rates and their future prospects will be discussed in Sections III, IV, and V.

Production Efficiency

The concept of efficiency is based on a comparison of output with costs. This indicator is especially difficult to measure in Eastern Europe, because the measurement of cost requires accurate information about prices and the allocation of inputs. In an economy in which most means of production, including the inputs, are centrally owned and allocated and in which prices are centrally and arbitrarily determined, the book-keeping on costs tends to be sloppy, since all transactions are, so to speak, "within the family," rather than at "arm's length," via the market. Consequently enterprises and planning units are often unaware of, or disregard, the real cost of production. This results in a double inefficiency: first, there is no real "market" test of whether or not something should be produced (except in the case of exports), and, second, relatively little effort is devoted to producing something as cheaply as possible by saving inputs or by substituting a cheaper input for a more expensive one. The typical American farmer's practice of frequently changing the composition of his animal feed in response to changing relative market prices of feed components is, for all practical purposes, unheard of in Eastern Europe. Without presenting any efficiency data, we can state that the consensus among specialists is that the East European centrally planned economies tend to perform comparatively poorly with regard to this particular performance indicator. To be sure, there are important differences among the countries in this regard. A key aim of contemplated or implemented economic reforms is to improve economic efficiency.

Standard of Living and the Distribution of Income

This indicator is the yardstick whereby a typical citizen, and tourist, measures and compares the performance of an economy. Two things matter: the demonstration effect of the higher living standard found in the industrial West—which is one of the most important factors pressing the decision-makers in Eastern Europe—and the rate of improvement from year to year.* One runs into serious difficulties in trying to measure, and especially to compare with Western figures, East European living standards, and changes thereof, on the basis of official data. One difficulty is that, typically, a much larger share of a family's consumption is comprised of "communal," i.e., public goods, such as education and the nominally "free" health care (although under-the-table payments to those delivering health care and other services have become the norm, not the exception). These countries also offer low-cost (i.e., subsidized) living accommodations and public transportation. This makes a comparison of wage, salary, and income tax *levels* as well as wage and salary *increases* across countries much less meaningful than in market-economy countries.

*The issue of comparative living standards is especially important in the GDR, whose population compares its standard of living with that of the people in West Germany, especially since both can watch West German TV. Generally, the more mobility across national frontiers, the more direct the comparisons between absolute living standards.

Still another difficulty in assessing living standards is the wide and growing differences among the East European countries in the availability of consumer goods. Thus, if one looked at the rapid increases in recent years of the average zloty wage paid to Polish workers and found also that the Polish consumer price index hardly changed during this period, one would be justified to conclude that the Polish standard of living had improved considerably in recent years. But when traveling in Poland, one finds that the queues in front of most food stores and other retail establishments are long; that regardless of the number of zlotys a family has in its pocket or in the bank, it typically has to wait eight to twelve years or longer for a decent apartment and four or five years to buy a car; and that certain highly prized consumer durables, including many Polish-produced ones, are available in the stores *only* for dollars or other Western currency—but not everyone has access to foreign currency and thus to these goods. As everyone, including the Poles, would admit, this situation has contributed to the potentially explosive tension that existed in Poland in 1978, a situation that certainly could not be deduced from standard performance statistics on the standard of living.

The availability of consumer goods is much better, for example, in Hungary than in Poland. This is noteworthy because aggregate data show that the two countries are at approximately the same level of per capita income. This difference in the availability of consumer goods in the two countries reflects in part a much larger allocation of the GNP pie to consumption in Hungary than in Poland, and in part the greater efficiency of Hungary's economic performance.

More fundamentally, however, the availability, quality, and choice of consumer goods is largely a function of a country's level of per capita income. Thus, we find the consumer in a much better situation in the GDR, in Czechoslovakia, and in the northern republics of Yugoslavia (especially in Slovenia) than in Romania, Bulgaria, the southern republics of Yugoslavia, and of course in that poorest of all European countries, Albania.

Another very important factor in comparisons of the standard of living is that in the East European countries a wide range of unpublicized economic and travel privileges are granted to the political, managerial, military, and scientific elite. This is an especially important consideration in those countries where the availability of consumer goods through the normal distribution channels is poor. These privileges are carefully differentiated by type of position, and are greater for those holding politically sensitive posts. The economic value of privileges, such as obtaining desirable apartments quickly and access to well-stocked special stores, can exceed the recipient's money wages. The power to grant and take away highly prized economic perquisites is one of the key levers in the hands of the party organization to secure loyalty to the regime from key people.

Unemployment

The number of workers without jobs is uniformly low, hovering near zero, in all East European countries except Yugoslavia, where unemployment is high, comparable to Western levels. The wiping out of unemployment (and the elimination of the most extreme forms of poverty) may well be the most significant economic and social achievement of the postwar regimes of Eastern Europe. However, this achievement is not without its costs and problems, mainly because practically all blue- and white-collar workers are guaranteed not only employment but the particular job which they hold at a given moment. Because the state does not allow inefficient enterprises to go bankrupt and because inefficient workers cannot (except in the most flagrant cases) be fired, there is less incentive for workers and limited opportunity for managers to improve labor efficiency than in a market economy.

Balance of Payments

This measure indicates in any given year whether a country is a debtor or a creditor vis-a-vis foreign countries. A sizable deficit is generally considered a "problem," especially if the deficit persists year after year, while a surplus is viewed as positive, a signal of the economy's fundamental strength, which makes it possible for the country to "earn" more than it "spends" abroad. But as with any simple assessment of a borrower-debtor relationship, the real situation is more complicated. Just as it is for an individual or a business, being a borrower country can be a wise decision if (1) the borrowed resources are put to a productive use, providing a rate of return in excess of the interest rate paid; and (2) the debt-service obligation (interest plus repayment of the principal falling due) does not exceed the borrower's capacity to pay it.

All East European countries have been heavy borrowers from the outside world since the early 1970s. But an assessment of the status of their balance of payments as an economic performance indicator is complicated by special factors. Their currencies are not "convertible" like the currencies of most Western countries. This means, on the one hand, that neither the citizens of the individual East European countries nor foreigners can exchange zlotys, levas, etc., for foreign currency, or convert foreign currency into zlotys, levas, and so on (with the exception of tourists under carefully controlled conditions or illegally on the black markets), and, on the other hand, that foreign holders of East European currencies (with the exception of tourists) cannot automatically command goods produced in these countries. Which goods can be imported from the East European countries is determined by their central plan (except in Yugoslavia and in Hungary), and not by the amount or type of currency a foreign buyer may hold.

Commerce among the socialist countries is arranged and settled, almost as if on a barter basis, bilaterally. The combined flows of trade and services (such as tourism and shipping) tend, in the aggregate, to be in balance; any imbalance that remains between two countries at the end of a period is normally settled by further shipment of goods from the deficit to the surplus country. (Certain interesting new deviations from this practice will be discussed in Section III.) Thus, East European balance of payments data should focus only on their transactions with the rest of the world, i.e., with the nonsocialist countries.

The situation in East-West commerce is as follows. All the East European countries have been borrowing principally from the industrial West, and in convertible, i.e., "hard" currencies, to import Western goods greatly in excess of their exports to the West. At the same time, the East European countries have been lending large sums—mainly to finance their own machinery exports—to Third World countries, which principally have nonconvertible "soft" currencies. These two kinds of debit and credit transactions (in hard and soft currencies) cannot be used to offset one another. The critical issue for these countries' balance of payments is their payment status with the hard-currency, principally the industrial Western, countries. Because their payment status is so intimately tied to the broader issues and problems of East-West commercial relations, East Europe's hard-currency payment figures will be presented and discussed in Section IV, which focuses on East-West commercial relations.

There is one other important difference in the approach and interpretation of balance-of-payments statistics for market economies with convertible currencies and East European (and other) economies with nonconvertible currencies. For a country with a nonconvertible currency, it is not enough to put the borrowed resources into productive use; it must also convert the increased production into convertible currencies, by increasing its exports only to countries that can pay in convertible currencies, i.e., principally to the industrial West. But the East European economies encounter problems in this respect, both in their own economies' inability to produce goods that are easily salable on Western markets and in the tariff and nontariff barriers their goods still face in Western countries. Thus, the East European countries find the "conversion" of their increased output into convertible currency a difficult task indeed, a problem that will be discussed in some detail in Section IV.

III. EAST EUROPE'S ECONOMIC RELATIONS WITH THE USSR

The most significant general factor in the relations between the Soviet Union and the countries of Eastern Europe is the large disparity between the population, territory, resource endowment, and military power of the USSR and those of the countries of Eastern Europe, individually and collectively. Given these differences, and given the objectives of Soviet policy, intrabloc relations involving the USSR are inevitably asymmetrical. They are, in the most general terms, marked by the dominance of a superpower and the dependence of six relatively small client states. Yugoslavia's relationship with the Soviet Union has differed in substance from that of the other six since the Stalin-Tito break in the early 1950s, when Yugoslavia first became politically and economically independent from the USSR; although relations were subsequently reestablished, Yugoslavia has carefully guarded its independence. The USSR and Albania severed practically all contact in the early 1960s.

Any relationship of asymmetrical interdependence offers opportunities for the strong to take advantage of the weak. In the political-military sphere the six East European nations have certainly been subordinated to the Soviet Union, although Romania has been able to achieve much greater elbow room to maneuver and is one of the two East European CMEA countries with no Soviet troops stationed on its soil (the other country is Bulgaria). An interesting question is, therefore, has the Soviet Union also asserted its power to dominate the East European countries economically? Has the Soviet Union exploited its political-military position for its own economic advantage? The historical logic of the situation would seem to support an affirmative answer, as do the well-documented cases of economic coercion by the Soviets under Stalin, and of Soviet military intervention in East Germany in 1953, in Hungary in 1956, and in Czechoslovakia in 1968.

Until after Stalin's death in 1953, the Soviet Union's political domination of Eastern Europe was accompanied by conventional types of economic extraction, such as reparations transfers (mainly from East Germany and also from Bulgaria, Hungary, Romania, and, indirectly, from Poland); by so-called joint stock companies in Eastern Europe, through which the Soviet Union took some of these countries' resources; and by the Soviet practice of paying unfairly low prices for East European exports (particularly well documented in the case of Poland).[5]

During the post-Stalin period, the economic relationship between the Soviet Union and Eastern Europe has changed substantially. Since the mid-1950s, the Soviet Union apparently has not obtained large unrequited resource transfers from Eastern Europe. In fact, some specialists argue that in recent years the USSR has actually been paying an economic price for the continued dependence of the East European countries on the Soviet Union. The essence of this argument is that a large share of Soviet exports to Eastern Europe consists of energy and raw materials that the Soviet Union could readily sell to the West for hard currency with which to buy urgently needed machinery and other commodities from Western countries, goods that the East European countries are unable to supply to the USSR.

Relations Under Stalin and the Adoption of the Soviet "Model"

Let us look at the question of Soviet-East European economic relations from the point of view of the East European countries. As is well known, after the postwar reconstruction had been completed, by 1948–49 (later in the GDR), the development strategy of all East European countries followed the Soviet model: the share of investment in national income was increased to very high levels, mostly at the expense of consumption; investment was concentrated in industry and, within industry, on machine building and metallurgy. As a result, these countries achieved good-to-spectacular growth rates, with fluctuations, but at the same time generated serious imbalances by building high-cost, quickly obsolete industries which left a legacy of serious economic problems.

Was the adoption of the extreme version of the "Soviet model" by national Communist leaders voluntary or imposed? We do not as yet have enough information to provide unqualified answers, yet the evidence points toward the latter. Countless eyewitness accounts testify to the decisive role Soviet advisers and shopping lists played in choosing development strategies in Eastern Europe during 1948–53, and perhaps beyond. Such Soviet actions can be explained in part by the USSR's desire to assure the dependency of these countries on the Soviet Union. In the case of Czechoslovakia and the GDR, Soviet industrial-strategic considerations also played a role. In these two countries in particular, there was a disproportionately large investment in machine building and in other industrial branches whose products were exported to the Soviet Union. In the GDR, war destruction and dismantling by the

Russians in metallurgy and in the chemical and engineering industries left the country's manufacturing capacity predominantly in the light and food industries and in light machine building. Yet while these latter industries were often operating below capacity because of supply shortages, and in 1958 were still producing far below 1939 levels, branches founded or expanded to produce for Soviet export (shipyards, railroad equipment plants, precision machinery, electrical machinery, and heavy industrial equipment) were operating above 1939 levels.[6] Available data are consistent with the hypothesis that at least in Czechoslovakia and the GDR, postwar development strategies were significantly influenced by Soviet strategic priorities.

A Hungarian economist arrived at a similar conclusion for Hungary:

> Decisions which shaped the economic structure of individual countries were based on bilateral economic relations, primarily the relations with the Soviet Union. This was so not only because the Soviet Union had a decisive share in each country's foreign trade but also because only Soviet industry was able to produce or to share the technical documentation of large metallurgical and machine-building projects and to supply the basic raw materials; and also because its prestige and experience served as an example to every socialist country. However, given the known distortions of Stalinist policy, this [approach] frequently resulted in one-sided decisions even in questions of detail.[7]

We tentatively conclude that during the first postwar decade the USSR was instrumental in forcing the development of high-cost industrial branches in some countries, possibly throughout Eastern Europe, probably for several interrelated reasons. First, Soviet leaders probably did believe that their own pattern of industrialization was ideologically correct and did have universal applicability for the new socialist states. Second, this model also had the beneficial political ramification of placing limits on the East European states' interaction with one another, and thereby heightened each state's dependence on the Soviet Union. Third, this dependence was beneficial to the Soviet Union as a means of supplementing its requirements for investment and strategic goods from the more advanced East European countries, and for other products from the less industrialized East European countries, during the Western embargo.

The Decade of Transition: 1956–65

During the second postwar decade (approximately 1956–65), the USSR must have realized that the political cost of economic extraction probably exceeded the economic benefits gained; hence extraction was discontinued in most cases. Also, as the embargo was relaxed and as the more developed East European trade partners gradually fell behind Western technological standards, the USSR probably considered imports from Eastern Europe less crucial. It is conceivable that during this period the USSR had no clear notions and no definite policy regarding what commodity composition could provide it maximum benefits from intrabloc trade. To be sure, large and very useful blocwide projects had been completed, such as an electricity grid and pipeline. But much discussion was also heard of the need for improved blocwide specialization and integration.

As a consequence of the development strategy followed in Eastern Europe, the region's poor endowment of natural resources, and the wasteful use of materials during the postwar years, net import needs of raw materials and energy grew rapidly during the 1960s. The smaller countries absorbed an increasing share of their total output of primary products domestically and redirected some raw material exports to the West. The USSR became a large supplier of their needs, to the extent of about $2.5 billion worth of raw materials and energy by 1970. Today, the Soviet Union imports mainly machinery and equipment, industrial consumer goods, and food products from Eastern Europe but often complains that many of the imports are not up to world standards.

Sometime during the late 1960s, the USSR had come to the conclusion, judging from its position in CMEA debates, that the exchange of raw materials for manufactures with Eastern Europe was disadvantageous because it limited the USSR's ability to import technology and other goods from the West, for which it had to pay predominantly with primary products, chiefly raw materials and fuels.

More than any other commodity, oil illustrates some of the key issues in Soviet-East European relations: both the Soviet Union's dilemma and the East European anxiety concerning the future source and cost of this vital commodity. But before discussing the critical issue of oil, let us consider briefly how prices for commodities to be traded are determined in intra-CMEA, and therefore also in East European-Soviet trade.

Prices in Intra-CMEA Trade

Intra-CMEA prices are based on those in effect on the world market in earlier years (averaged over a certain period), because such prices represent alternative opportunities to CMEA buyers and sellers and also because, given arbitrary domestic prices, CMEA countries have been unable to come up with an alternative to world prices acceptable to all members. There is no question, however, that considerable bargaining does take place on prices, if for no other reason than that "world market price" is an ambiguous concept. World prices are said to be adjusted to eliminate the influence of speculation and monopoly and to take into account CMEA demand and supply. Until 1975, intra-CMEA prices remained fixed for five years, and were based on average Western world prices of an agreed-upon earlier period. For example, an agreement was reached among CMEA countries in 1970 that intra-CMEA prices would remain fixed from 1971 through 1975 and would be based on the average world market prices of 1965–69.

In interpreting empirical studies of CMEA prices, it is important to note that individual commodity prices and quantities traded are determined not by single buyers and sellers in relative isolation from the prices of other commodities, as in the West, but by government agencies which bargain over a whole range of export and import prices at once. Bargaining power in such a situation may be exerted through prices (obtaining high prices for exports and paying low prices for imports) and also through quantities (supplying small or zero quantities of goods whose prices are disadvantageous and forcing the trade partner to supply specified kinds of goods in specified quantities, if prices are advantageous). Thus, if a Western observer finds the price of a particular commodity high or low relative to current world prices, this may be because the CMEA price has remained fixed while the world price has changed or, alternatively, because the price that is "out of line" may be compensated by offsetting deviations in the prices or quantities of other export and import items.

Gains from Trade

As to the benefits, or "gains," from trade, it is useful to distinguish between static and dynamic considerations. The issue with respect to the static gains from trade is whether or not CMEA countries trade according to their short-run comparative advantage. A substantial part of CMEA trade within the bloc is probably not according to this criterion, partly because Eastern Europe's capacity to export has been shaped decisively by its pattern of industrialization during the first postwar decade, and partly because opportunity costs are not fully known due to inadequacies in the system for determining domestic prices.

With respect to dynamic gains from trade, benefits are foregone if the preferential or "sheltered" CMEA market absorbs over a long time poor-quality goods and obsolete equipment, thereby reducing the incentive to innovate and produce "for the market," causing the exporter to fall more and more behind its competitors. This is the cost which appears to fall disproportionately heavily on the smaller and relatively more advanced CMEA countries like the GDR, Czechoslovakia, Hungary, and Poland. The importer of shoddy goods and equipment loses potential productivity gains, too; yet the importing country may not be able to resist buying such goods if its own producers are dependent upon the same CMEA suppliers for their export market. This is why in a bilateral, state trading framework, terms of trade considerations (i.e., changes in the export price index compared with changes in the import price index) cannot be divorced from the commodity composition of trade.

Commodity Composition and Bilateralism

This leads to the very important question of the commodity composition of trade within CMEA and especially in Soviet-East European commerce. As noted before, the goods traded are priced according to past world prices; these prices reflect neither cost of production nor demand/supply pressures within CMEA. Trade is balanced bilaterally. The transactions are denominated in so-called *transferable rubles* (Western world prices converted into transferable rubles at the official ruble/dollar rate) which play only an accounting role; export "earnings" do not represent real purchasing power within CMEA because they can be spent only on goods that the other country is willing to supply. This is an inflexible system which leaves open the question of how the kinds and quantities of goods to be imported and exported to the other CMEA countries are determined. This question can be approached only by bearing in mind that the real value of commodities traded within CMEA is judged by each country's planners, not primarily by what the commodity "costs" in CMEA but by how strongly it is in demand, either because it alleviates shortages and bottlenecks in the domestic economy or because it can be sold in the West for "hard" currency which in turn can be spent to purchase practically any good sold anywhere on the world market. Accordingly, goods produced in the CMEA countries are ranked according to the strength of demand for them. Goods in greatest demand are called "hard" goods; commodities in surplus that few countries would want are called "soft" goods. Different commodities have different degrees of hardness or softness and their ranking can change from time to time, as changing production and priorities alter the demand and supply picture. Speaking in terms of broad commodity categories, the ranking of goods from "hardest" to "softest" is generally as follows: (1) energy and raw materials that can be sold readily on the world market; (2) modern machinery, equipment, and spare parts that can be exported to or, alternatively, must be imported from Western countries; (3) standard machinery built in CMEA countries for which there is demand by the importing country; (4) products of the food and light industries needed in a CMEA country to alleviate domestic supply problems in the consumer sector; and (5) all other commodities.

Standard procedure within CMEA is for each country to try to balance not only total exports and imports with each trading partner, but also the sale and purchase of goods within each category of "hardness" or "softness." This is a very imperfect substitute mechanism used in the CMEA "market" where prices and money balances do not play the allocative role that prices and money usually play in a "real" market situation. We do not have enough information to calculate how successful this balancing between each pair of CMEA countries is, but our understanding is that bilateral balancing by types of commodities is pretty much the rule in all CMEA links *except* those between the USSR and the individual East European countries. This is evident from even a cursory glance at the trade data, which show that the Soviet Union is the principal supplier of energy and raw materials (ranked first in terms of hardness) to the East European countries while it mainly imports from them commodities that are ranked lower in terms of hardness (with the possible exception of Poland—a large exporter of coal to the USSR).

Toward a Balance Sheet of Eastern Europe's Commercial Relations with the USSR

It is sometimes claimed that trade with the USSR benefits the East European countries more than it does the USSR, almost irrespective of the prices at which commodities are exchanged. Or, as it is sometimes stated, the Soviet Union "subsidizes" the East European countries by its willingness to sell energy and raw materials for goods of lower "value."

Let's look at the situation from the point of view of a typical East European country that has no choice but to import a very large share of the energy and raw materials it needs, and for which exports must account, depending on the country, for 20 to 40 percent of its national income, about a third of them going to the Soviet market. First, a lot of exports that go to the Soviet Union incorporate energy and raw materials imported from that country. The embodied energy and raw material content of such exports is often much greater than one would suppose. Take textiles and clothing, which have large cotton, wool, or (in the case of synthetic fibers) crude oil content. Why should an exchange of, say, cotton imports from the Soviet Union for ready-made cotton clothes exports to the USSR be considered a Soviet "subsidy" to Eastern Europe, irrespective of the prices paid, opportunity costs of these two commodities on third markets, and domestic resource scarcities in the respective countries?

Then there is a further issue: what about the hard-currency import content of East European exports to the USSR as compared to the Soviet energy and raw material content of East European exports to hard-currency areas? Such comparisons are very important for this reason. In the final analysis, the critical *variable* which the ranking of commodities traded within CMEA measures by degrees of hardness is *the opportunity cost of hard currency:* would a country be able to obtain hard currency if it tried to sell this good to the West or would it have to spend hard currency if it could not purchase this or that commodity from a CMEA partner? Therefore, to the extent that East European exports to the USSR embody hard-currency imports, CMEA countries are selling to the USSR the hardest of all commodities, because they are *spending hard currency.* On the other hand, to the extent that East European exports to the West, where CMEA countries *earn hard currency,* embody Soviet energy and raw material imports, they are being "paid" for the Western goods they "transship" to the USSR. I am not aware that these types of calculations have been made in CMEA except in the case of Hungary, where a first approximation was made on the basis of Hungary's 1972 and 1974 input-output tables.[8] Focusing on raw material content only, the study found that the hard-currency energy and raw material content embodied in so-called ruble exports was 20 percent of the value of such exports, while the soft-currency energy and raw material content embodied in so-called dollar exports was 10 percent of such exports. Moreover, the most hard-currency-intensive branches in so-called ruble exports were chemicals and products of the light and food industries, commodities that are especially important in Hungary's exports to the USSR.

Furthermore, these calculations did not measure and compare the embodied content of imports and exports other than energy and raw materials; if imported intermediate products, machinery, as well as know-how, were also included, the discrepancy between the hard-currency content of ruble exports and the ruble-currency content of dollar exports would have been almost certainly much greater. This is because Hungary and the other East European countries import from the West a lot of the machinery and know-how that they use to manufacture ruble exports, whereas the machinery and know-how the USSR imports from the West are believed to be less concentrated in sectors providing exports to Eastern Europe.*

At this point the reader may well pause and conclude that it must be very difficult to draw up an accurate balance sheet showing who benefits and how much in Soviet trade with Eastern Europe. The reader may wonder also whether the CMEA countries themselves have a good idea of where these matters stand. This is, indeed, the case.

Several other issues are also very important in assessing economic relations between the Soviet Union and Eastern Europe.

One of these is the relatively recent development of East European participation in CMEA investment projects, the largest ones located in the USSR. East European investment in Soviet resource development is not new. But whereas during the late 1950s and 1960s these credits were typically small, bilateral, and designed mainly to increase the capacity of existing projects, since 1971 (the signing of the so-called Comprehensive Program of the CMEA), there has been a dramatic increase in the size and number of these projects, and in multilateral participation (but not ownership). The largest and by far the most important project is the $5 billion (that is the initial cost estimate— actual cost will probably be significantly higher) Orenburg natural gas pipeline, channeling gas from Soviet fields to Eastern Europe, scheduled to be completed in 1978. Each East European country except Romania agreed to build a section of the pipeline (Romania is providing only pipe and equipment), supplying labor and above-plan deliveries of equipment, technical services, and the hard currency with which to import the pipes and other machinery that must be purchased in the West. One form in which convertible currency is supplied by the East Europeans for this project is to assume their share of the convertible currency obligations of CMEA's International Investment Bank (IIB). Between 1976 and 1978, the IIB borrowed $2.05 billion, in four loans, on the Eurodollar market for the Orenburg project and provided these funds to the USSR, which made purchases, largely of pipe, for the entire project.[9] The East Europeans owe the IIB for their share of the Soviet hard-currency purchases and, according to IIB rules, must repay in hard currency at world market rates of interest.

Direct participation by Eastern Europe in construction projects in far-away Soviet territory has proved to be difficult and very expensive. Hungary, for example, is devoting 4 percent of its investment budget

---

*In any event, the large differences in the size of the Soviet and East European economies alone suggest that the hard-currency import content of Soviet exports should be much smaller than the hard-currency import content of East European exports.

to such joint ventures. Part of the money goes to sending workers to these projects. But to compensate for the hardship, and to provide incentive and special support facilities, the wages of a typical worker sent from Eastern Europe to these inhospitable regions of the USSR can be up to five times as much as what the worker would be paid at home, making direct labor participation increasingly difficult to justify economically. There are further problems in providing the needed technical services plus labor skilled in pipeline construction.

Because CMEA lacks a price and monetary system which would make possible more meaningful economic calculations (so that CMEA trade and specialization decisions could be made on a more rational basis), this has given rise, gradually, to a convertible currency financial subsystem within CMEA. One aspect of this subsystem is the hard-currency transactions of the two CMEA banks just mentioned. Another aspect is that today a certain portion of intra-CMEA trade is *valued* at current world market prices and is *settled* in convertible currencies. My own calculations, based on Hungarian statistics, show that in 1975 about 13 percent of Hungary's exports to socialist (CMEA plus other planned economy) countries and approximately 7 percent of its imports from the same group were settled in convertible currencies. Others estimated the share of convertible currency transactions within CMEA trade during the mid-1970s at between 5 and 10 percent in value terms.

The rise of a convertible currency subsystem since about 1970 reflects several developments. As the world market prices of certain commodities rose sharply after 1973 while intrabloc prices in CMEA remained unchanged for a time, it became uneconomical for the suppliers of such goods, mainly the USSR, to sell them to the CMEA countries, but they were obligated to do so under long-term agreements or contracts. Hence, so-called above-quota deliveries would often be made only against convertible currencies, at current world market prices. Another factor was the rising share of Western components—inputs, technology, and investment resources—acquired, mainly by the East European countries, for convertible currencies and incorporated into products supplied to the USSR and other CMEA countries, normally for transferable rubles. More and more, the East European countries are seeking to receive a certain percentage of the value of such exports in convertible currencies.

Looking Ahead

One of the key issues is the future availability and price of Soviet energy and raw materials to Eastern Europe. (Price is important because it determines the amount of resources the importer must give in exchange for Soviet goods.) The most important commodity by far is crude oil and other energy products.

The dramatic change in the world market price of oil during 1973–74 created a major disturbance in Eastern Europe, principally in the region's relations with the USSR. In 1975, crude-oil prices on the world market were about four times higher than they had been less than two years earlier. Since the Soviet Union was exporting large quantities of oil to five of the six European members of CMEA (none to Romania, which itself is a major producer, but significant quantities also to Yugoslavia, which is not a CMEA member), amounting to some 15 percent or more of total Soviet exports to these countries, adhering to the earlier fixed-price agreement within CMEA was costly to the USSR. This prompted the Soviet Union to insist on revising intra-CMEA prices as of the beginning of 1975 rather than one year later, as scheduled. Beginning in 1975, world prices were to be applied more flexibly, with intra-CMEA prices in any given year to be based on world prices for the immediately preceding five years (for some commodities, three years). The immediate effect was to worsen Eastern Europe's terms of trade with the USSR substantially (from a low of 4 percent for Poland to a high of 25 percent for the GDR) but still not by as much as would have been the case had current world prices been applied immediately. The deterioration of Eastern Europe's terms of trade vis-a-vis the USSR continued in 1976 and again in 1977, as expected, given the new price formula and the continued rise in the world price of oil after 1975.

The fundamental problem for the East European countries (including Romania, which is also a net importer of crude oil, from the Middle East) with respect to energy has three aspects. (1) How will they obtain the additional resources to pay the USSR for the rising price of oil? (2) Will they be able to obtain from the USSR the additional supplies of oil essential for their growing economies? (The East European countries prefer to buy from the USSR not only because prices are still somewhat cheaper than world prices, but mainly because they can more readily produce goods marketable in the USSR than goods suitable for sale in hard-currency markets.) (3) If sufficient oil cannot be obtained from the USSR, how will they find the hard currency to pay for the extra oil that must be purchased from the world market?

Perhaps the most critical question for Eastern Europe right now is the second one, which focuses on the Soviet Union's future ability and willingness to supply oil to Eastern Europe. To be sure, Russia's oil exports are continuing to grow—at 4.8 percent a year during 1976–80, compared with the 6.8 percent a year during 1971–75—but the question is: what will happen after 1980? The CIA has predicted that unless the

Soviet leadership takes some drastic policy action soon, Soviet oil output will peak by 1980 and decline thereafter, so that by the mid-1980s the Soviet Union itself may well be forced to import oil.[10] A leading expert on Soviet energy, Robert W. Campbell, believes that the CIA forecast to 1980 is likely to be proved correct and sees the Soviet Union as having three options: (1) continue to drift with respect to energy policy, in which case exports to the East Europeans will have to decline drastically during the early 1980s, and the USSR itself will have to spend billions of dollars to buy oil (probably an unacceptable option); (2) substantially reduce oil exports to the West (such exports account for almost 50 percent of Soviet hard-currency earnings), which would force the USSR to modify its current development strategy of relying on the importation of Western technology (probably also an unacceptable option); or (3) try to break the energy bottleneck by a massive importation of Western technology for oil exploration, production, refining, transport, and utilization, paying partly with other exports (the most probable option).[11]

It should be pointed out that each of the alternatives described is unfavorable for Eastern Europe; the effects will vary, depending on each East European country's energy and hard-currency situation.

Conclusions

The important points about the evolution of Eastern Europe's economic relations with the USSR can be summarized as follows:

(1) Soviet–East European economic relations underwent a fundamental change in the post-Stalin period: outright Soviet exploitation was discontinued by the mid-1950s, as economic relations were placed on a more equitable footing.

(2) Eastern Europe's postwar industrialization policies, copying—at Soviet insistence it seems—the Soviet model of the 1930s, did not follow these countries' comparative advantage, which would have been dictated by their resource endowment, i.e., lack of raw materials and relatively small size. It was not economical to build an extensive and often duplicative heavy industrial structure in each of the nations.

(3) One important consequence of postwar industrialization policies was that each East European country became locked in, to a greater or lesser extent, with the Soviet market, which was serving both as supplier of increasingly scarce energy and raw materials and as buyer of East European manufactures, a significant share of which had never reached, or had gradually fallen behind, world standards.

(4) The bottom line on the economic balance sheet of Soviet-East

European relations is difficult to calculate. The Soviets claim, and probably believe, that for some time they have been subsidizing Eastern Europe; a careful look at the facts and the issues suggests that this assertion is far from certain.

(5) Tangible advantages of membership in the CMEA trading bloc notwithstanding, the shortcomings and problems of too heavy reliance on each other's closed markets gradually became obvious to all CMEA members by the early 1960s. Foremost among these shortcomings are the general unavailability of advanced technology from CMEA suppliers; lack of stimulus to produce quality products; and serious obstacles—inadequate price and monetary relations foremost among them—standing in the way of intra-branch specialization agreements which could provide large and badly needed productivity gains to CMEA economies. One by one, these countries must increasingly depend on improved productivity as the backbone of their economic growth (in the so-called new, "intensive phase" of their stage of development) because they can rely less and less on rapid growth of industrial employment, and large additions to their stock of capital, financed by holding down consumption standards (which were the main sources of growth in the earlier, so-called "extensive phase" of their stage of development).

(6) One by one, each CMEA country, including the Soviet Union, adopted a new policy and program to reorient part of its trade from CMEA to Western countries. The timing, speed, and extent of this reorientation were geared to each country's own needs, perceptions, and possibilities. For the East European countries, critically important in this process of reorientation was the beginning of detente, first, because a Soviet rapprochement with the West automatically provided the green light for the East European countries to do likewise, and second, because it made the Western countries more receptive to trade, to lend money, and to enter into long-term industrial cooperation deals with the CMEA countries.

IV. EASTERN EUROPE'S ECONOMIC RELATIONS WITH THE INDUSTRIAL WEST

Expansion of Trade and Rising Indebtedness
All East European countries boosted sharply their imports from the industrial West during 1971–77 to help modernize their economies

with Western technology. They also required large increases of industrial materials purchases from the West to compensate for a slowdown in the growth of such imports from the USSR and from each other. Because the rate of growth of exports was considerably slower than the tempo of imports, all these countries undertook heavy borrowing from the West, pushing the total net hard-currency debt of the six East European countries from less than $5 billion at the end of 1970 to about $32 billion at the end of 1977. This huge increase in debt was partly planned—a deliberate policy of borrowing resources to modernize, which in turn was supposed to generate increased output with which to repay the funds—and partly unplanned. The unplanned increase in debt was the result of soaring world energy and commodity prices, the economic recession in the West (which made it more difficult for Eastern Europe to export to Western hard-currency markets), the extraordinary grain imports necessitated by repeated poor harvests throughout the bloc (which also reduced or eliminated Soviet grain exports to Eastern Europe), and the need to buy more materials and spare parts for the newly acquired Western technology than had been planned when the technology was first purchased.

Table 4 Eastern Europe and the USSR;
Net Hard Currency Debt, 1970–77 ($ Billions)

	1970	1974	1975	1976	1977
Bulgaria	.7	1.2	1.8	2.3	2.7
Czechoslovakia	.3	1.1	1.5	2.1	2.7
GDR	1.0	2.8	3.8	6.0	5.9
Hungary	.6	1.5	2.1	2.8	3.4
Poland	.8	3.9	6.9	10.2	13.0
Romania	1.2	2.6	3.0	3.3	4.0
Total EE Six	4.6	13.1	19.1	25.7	31.7
USSR	1.9	5.0	10.0	14.0	16.0
CMEA Banks[a]	0	.1	.5	1.1	1.7
Total European CMEA	6.5	18.2	29.6	40.8	49.4
Albania[b]	.3	n.a.	.8	n.a.	n.a.
Yugoslavia[c]	1.9	5.4	6.6	7.9	9.9

[a] The International Investment Bank, which at the end of 1977 had outstanding Eurocurrency loans of approximately $1.5 billion and the International Bank for Economic Cooperation, whose outstanding hard-currency obligation at the end of 1977 was under $.2 billion.
[b] Cumulative import surplus, as calculated by Michael Kaser in "Trade and Aid in the Albanian Economy," in *East European Economics Post Helsinki* (op. cit.).
[c] Gross debt, as reported by the World Bank. End–1977 net debt for Yugoslavia would be about $7.0 billion.
Source: Compiled from the reports of various Western banking and government institutions.

The growth of individual countries' hard-currency debt from 1970 to 1977 is presented in Table 4, which also includes the indebtedness of the two CMEA banks (remember, this debt is the shared responsibility of all CMEA members, in proportion to each country's equity in these institutions, which of course is the largest for the USSR) and, for comparison purposes, the debt of the Soviet Union as well as Yugoslavia. The figures presented are *net* (except Yugoslavia's), which means that each East European country's *gross* indebtedness is reduced by the amount of convertible-currency deposits it has in banks located in the West.

Between 1961 and 1977, Albania was also a large borrower—or grantee—from the People's Republic of China. Although Albania's borrowing had not been predominantly in hard currency, in one sense it was similar to the situation of the other East European countries because the resources it obtained came from outside the region. The fact that much of the credit Albania had received had been forgiven or simply will not be repaid, whereas the rest of Eastern Europe will have to repay what it has borrowed, is an important distinction when considering the *burden* of indebtedness, but not its *contribution* to growth, in the short run.

What is the meaning of these figures? That the debt of the East European countries is large, in fact extraordinarily large, cannot be disputed. If anyone had predicted ten years ago that by the end of 1977, the Communist countries would owe about $50 billion to the industrial West, that forecast would have been considered most unrealistic.

Several events in combination helped to bring about the present situation. First, detente made improved East-West economic relations possible. Second, the Communist countries changed their cautious credit policy and were willing to borrow large sums. Third, much of the huge trade surplus generated by the OPEC countries was deposited in Western banks, which were seeking opportunities to lend these funds profitably. Since borrowing by Western businesses was sluggish (due to the oil-price-rise-induced recession), East European borrowers were (and still are) courteously accommodated. Fourth, the recession in the West created excess capacity and large unemployment, which made Western governments eager to promote exports to willing buyers, and a crucially important means of promotion was providing government-backed (guaranteed and sometimes subsidized) credits. Fifth, strong competition among Western exporters and government credit agencies for Eastern orders practically eliminated earlier restraints on loans to Communist countries (although gradually stronger voices once again favoring credit restraint are now being raised in many Western countries). The United States stands alone among Western countries in restricting (via the Jackson-Vanik amendment to the Trade Act of 1974) government-backed loans to Communist countries (except to Yugoslavia, Poland, Romania, and, since 1978, Hungary).

Servicing the Debt

What is the meaning, and especially the implication for the future, of these large debt figures? One often hears contradictory views—ranging from extreme concern about the possibility of default, to no concern, on the grounds that these are centrally planned economies in full control of their balance of payments since they can commandeer goods to increase exports and, especially, restrict imports as needed.

What factors determine a country's ability to service its current and probable future level of debt (i.e., its ability to pay the interest charges and the principal due)? Six considerations are of importance: (1) the maturity and interest-rate structure of the existing debt; (2) the possibilities for commodity exports (on both the supply and demand sides); (3) the possibilities of generating net hard currency from sources other than commodity exports; (4) the possibilities for reducing imports; (5) world inflation rates and changes in the debtor's terms of trade; and (6) international credit market conditions and the country's standing in the international credit community.[12] A brief examination of how these considerations apply to the countries of Eastern Europe will help elucidate the forces that shape East-West commercial relations.

(1) *Maturity and interest-rate structure of the existing debt.* The larger the debt, the larger tend to be the interest payments; how large depends, of course, on the rate of interest charged. The maturity structure of the debt refers to the timing of the repayment obligations; the more the repayment is due in the *near* future (because the money was borrowed short-term or because long-term debt is coming due), the greater the current debt-service burden. Since most countries rely principally on their export earnings to generate money to service their debt, one way to standardize and compare the current burden of debt among countries is to calculate their debt-service ratios, i.e., the share of current exports that must be devoted to pay the interest and the principal falling due (which may, however, be refinanced, so that the actual burden in any given year can be less than the implied burden shown by these ratios). Table 5 shows the estimated 1970–77 debt-service ratios of the six East European countries and the USSR; only hard-currency (i.e., Western) exports, rather than total exports, are used in the denominator.

Table 5 Eastern Europe and the USSR:
Estimated Debt–Service Ratios (In Percent)

	1970	1973	1974	1975	1976	1977
Bulgaria	35	35	45	66	75	85
Czechoslovakia	8	15	17	22	30	31
GDR	20	25	24	27	33	40
Hungary	20	20	24	35	39	44
Poland	20	21	27	43	50	60
Romania	36	35	29	42	41	42
USSR	18	17	15	22	26	28

Source: Same as Table 4.

The debt-service ratios of two countries, Bulgaria and Poland, have risen especially dramatically in recent years. While no hard-and-fast rules can be laid down about levels that can be considered dangerously high, generally speaking, a ratio of over 25 percent is viewed as uncomfortable and over 50 percent as critical. Accordingly, in 1977, unless they were able to refinance, Bulgaria and Poland would have had to devote 85 percent and 60 percent, respectively, of their current hard-currency export earnings, not to pay for the current imports, but just to service their outstanding debt. The debt burden for these countries, and also for the rest of Eastern Europe, is thus considerable.

(2) *Possibilities for commodity exports to hard-currency countries.* This is perhaps the most critical variable in the short run, but especially in the medium-to-long run—over a three- to seven-year period. It is difficult to forecast this variable with reasonable accuracy because of the many factors involved in shaping a country's export performance.

In the first place, much depends on development and trends in the domestic economy of the country in question. The fundamental question is whether the debtor country can effectively transform borrowed resources into import substitutes or exports. This involves, in the first place, how large a share of borrowed resources is devoted to investment rather than to consumption: the larger the share that goes to investment, the more likely that productive capacity will be enlarged, which in the future should be able to generate exports; if money is borrowed to import consumer goods, this does not create additional capacity (unless these consumer goods are essential to motivate workers to produce, which tends to be the case in some East European countries, notably Poland).

The next important link is the rate of return on investment: has the money been used productively, or does it go into worthless show projects, unfinished construction, or unnecessary or unwanted inventories? Unfortunately, mistakes of planning make the East European countries susceptible to spending *some* of their resources in this manner.

The third step in transforming borrowed resources into hard currency is the ability to shift output into substitutes for hard-currency imports or into hard-currency exports. Can East European countries produce modern, high-quality semimanufactures and machinery as well as attractively packaged and marketed consumer goods for which there is demand in the West? Even in Poland, which has coal, sulfur, and copper, the *increase* in its Western exports must come largely from manufactures. This is also the case for all the other East European countries. (The USSR, by contrast, is richly endowed with energy and raw materials, if it can extract and transport them, but this is a difficult task without more Western participation.) The East European countries' record in producing such manufactures is mixed; a strict supply-, rather than a demand-, oriented central planning system is not very conducive to the production and marketing of modern, high-quality manufactured goods. How much improvement there will be in this regard by individual East European countries during the next three to seven years depends chiefly on two developments: the extent and success of economic reforms within each country (discussed in Section V) and the extent and success of their so-called industrial cooperation programs with Western firms.

With respect to the external environment, the crucial question is the absorptive capability of the Western market for potential East European exports. Assuming that the East European countries can overcome all the domestic hurdles to their exports mentioned above, will the West be willing and able to buy increased quantities of East European manufactures? The degree of Western willingness is influenced by the status of East-West political relations: the greater the difficulties, the greater the legislative and psychological resistance to imports from Communist countries. And Western ability to buy East European goods is largely the function of Western economic performance: the more rapidly these economies grow, the greater the demand—the more room—for Eastern imports.

(3) *Possibilities of generating hard currency from sources other than commodity exports.* There are several such other sources. One is *exporting armaments* to certain Third World countries (armaments exports are not included in published commodity export data; it is believed that these are of importance for Czechoslovakia and the GDR and of course for the USSR). Another source is *exporting tourist ser-*

vices, which is of considerable significance first and foremost to Yugoslavia, but also to all countries, with the exception of Czechoslovakia which has not tried to attract Western tourists, for political reasons, since 1969, and Albania, which has been openly xenophobic.[13] A third source is *exporting shipping services* (of great importance to Poland and the USSR and also to Bulgaria), and a fourth, *remittances* from migrant workers (to Yugoslavia) or from relatives (mainly to Poland).

Finally, mention should be made of the so-called *internal exports.* This latter revenue source is a complex institution that is growing in importance and often requires the authorities to close their eyes to, and in some countries actively to encourage, black-market currency operations. The basic idea is to sell certain goods and services within the country for hard currency only, but the variations on this theme can be almost infinite. Initially, so-called hard-currency shops were set up to sell imported Western goods, such as liquor, to Western tourists, for hard currency. Subsequently, certain high-quality domestically manufactured and handcraft goods were also made available in these shops to Western tourists or to citizens earning or receiving (e.g. from relatives in the West) hard currency. In some countries, as in the USSR, the elites are rewarded with special coupons to enable them also to shop in these stores for goods unavailable for local currency.

The new twist in some countries is that a growing number of the scarcest goods and services desired by the population—such as automobiles and apartments, for which the waiting can be several years—are offered by the state against immediate delivery for hard currency, with no questions asked as to the source of the foreign money. This policy is the most notable in Poland, where private owners of apartments in Warsaw frequently rent only to those who can pay in hard currency, and where a large segment of the population devotes considerable effort to acquire, nominally illegally, dollars and other convertible currencies from tourists and other sources.* Poland's $13 billion debt and a debt-service ratio of 60 percent are clearly responsible for this policy, which seems expeditious from the point of view of the pressing debt problem it intends to mitigate. But from a different point of view, this policy appears to be rather short-sighted, with many undesirable longer-term

*The availability of many scarce goods only for dollars or other Western currency is the principal reason why the black-market rate for the dollar in Poland in 1978 was five times more favorable for the seller than the official tourist exchange rate. One may note, further, that the official rates were not unrealistic in comparison with the purchasing power of the zloty, at least for those few goods and services (such as restaurant meals) that a Western tourist would be interested in and able to buy in Poland, with local currency.

economic and social consequences, including a growing lack of respect for a government that discriminates against the holders of its own currency, not to speak of the arbitrary nature of the income distribution that results, because many citizens are unable or unwilling to acquire hard currency illegally.

(4) *Possibilities of reducing imports.* Conventional wisdom holds that this is the ultimate weapon whereby the planners in a centrally planned economy can control their balance of payments. While this statement has truth in it, the flexibility of the planners to control imports is limited. To what extent it is limited depends on the composition of imports (the more it consists of such essential commodities as energy, raw materials, and basic consumer goods such as grain, the less flexibility there is), and on the politically acceptable reduction in the rate of economic growth and in the availability of consumer goods which a reduction of imports tends to bring about. The individual East European countries differ greatly from one another in these respects. The leadership in Poland in 1978 appeared to be the most constrained by a combination of domestic economic and political considerations: if imports were reduced significantly (especially if cut all across the board rather than selectively, because every organization clamors for more Western imports), economic efficiency and long-term growth would suffer. Consumer dissatisfaction might suddenly erupt again, as in 1970 and in 1976—a constant threat the Polish leadership must contend with. On the other hand, if imports are not reduced, there is a possibility of not being able to meet the country's debt-service obligations on time; this would have its own unpleasant ramifications for Poland.

(5) *World inflation rates and changes in the terms of trade.* Other things being equal, a high rate of world inflation should make it easier for the East European countries, as for all other debtors, to service their debt. But high rates of inflation tend to be reflected in high rates of interest charged on newly acquired debts, so if East European countries need additional loans or refinancing (which is likely), this could also hurt them. Most important to any country are changes in its terms of trade, i.e., changes in the price level of its exports as compared with the price level of imports. A significant improvement makes things easier; a deterioration creates additional difficulties. Changes in the terms of trade are difficult to predict for any country.

(6) *International credit conditions and the debtor's credit-worthiness.* Another extremely complex set of factors to evaluate, this variable, like the stock market, can change rapidly from one year to the next. As long

as Western governments are willing to lend to promote exports, as long as Western commercial banks are flush with money which they must lend out to make money, international credit conditions will continue to be supportive of the East European countries' desire to run a trade deficit and to refinance portions of debt that are due. But the situation might change, especially if Poland or Bulgaria or another country were forced to reschedule its debt or to seek some other form of debt relief.

What overall conclusions can be drawn with respect to the economic relations of Eastern Europe with the industrial West? Unsatisfied East European and Soviet needs for Western technology, manufactures of all kinds, industrial raw materials, and grain remain large, holding the prospect for increased imports in the years ahead. But unmet needs are not the sole determinant of trade. Over the short run, say, for the next two to four years, it seems almost inevitable that these countries' indebtedness to the West will continue to rise. But over the medium to long run, the continued growth of East-West trade must rely on the ability of the East European countries to expand their hard-currency exports.

In addition to the determining factors already mentioned, two further aspects may be considered: industrial cooperation and economic reforms.

Many East European countries hope that they can overcome some of the traditional barriers to an expansion of East-West trade, especially of Eastern exports, by entering into larger and more complex forms of industrial cooperation with Western firms, mainly with multinational corporations. There is no internationally accepted standard definition of industrial cooperation beyond the convention that it must encompass more than simple, arm's-length, commerce; it includes such transactions as subcontracting, licensing, coproduction, and joint ventures. In many cases, the East European countries and the Soviet Union do not want simply to become customers for Western products, but prefer to obtain modern technology as well as managerial and marketing know-how under industrial cooperation agreements. This approach is prompted in part by these countries' development strategy, a key aspect of which is a narrowing of the East-West technological gap, and in part by their acute shortage of hard currency, which they hope can be alleviated by industrial cooperation agreements with the West. The record up to now with regard to such agreements is somewhat mixed but promising, provided that the political, institutional, and systemic problems can be identified and cooperatively solved.[14]

V. ECONOMIC REFORMS

One of the most important issues affecting East-West trade and industrial cooperation in particular and the future economic performance of the East European countries in general concerns the prospects for economic reform. To explain why the reform of the economic mechanism in Eastern Europe is so important, it is necessary to describe briefly the nature and consequences of the traditional centrally planned economy that was introduced in all East European countries after the war.

The Traditional Centrally Planned Economic Model

The economic institutions and policies adopted by the Soviet Union under Stalin in the early 1930s were transplanted to each East European country after World War II. The main features of a traditional centrally planned "command economy" are the following:[15]

1. All significant means of production are nationalized or collectivized, with the agricultural sector being a partial or near-full exception in several countries.
2. Economic decision making is hierarchical so that inter-enterprise relationships are vertical, i.e., determined through the respective administrative hierarchies, rather than horizontally, through the market.
3. Planning is pervasive and is mainly in physical units rather than in value terms; it involves the administrative rationing of inputs and outputs.
4. Managerial and worker incentives stress fulfillment and over-fulfillment of quantitative production targets.
5. Prices are set administratively, tend to remain unchanged for long periods, and, as a rule, do not fully reflect costs and demand-supply pressures.
6. Money plays a passive role in the producing sectors of the economy, except with respect to wages and the retailing of consumer goods. The exception is necessary because the total wage bill, less personal savings, must approximately equal the volume of consumer goods and services made available to the population, multiplied by the price tags placed on these goods and services by central authorities. Thus, there is consumer choice but no consumer sovereignty; that is, consumers can choose among the goods already produced, but their choice will have little influence on what will be produced.
7. Foreign trade is a monopoly of the state; its principal function is to secure goods that cannot be produced domestically at all, or only

in inadequate quantities. Foreign trade is conducted by specialized foreign trade enterprises (FTEs), and there is little direct contact between producers of exports and users of imports and foreign suppliers and buyers. The official exchange rates are arbitrary and play no role in deciding the pattern and direction of trade.

The Feasibility and Consequences of the Traditional Model

The effective functioning of the traditional model is predicated upon —and makes possible for a time—a rapid growth of inputs: capital, labor, energy and raw materials, and technical knowledge. Initially, a rapid growth of inputs is made possible by a mobilization of unemployed or underemployed resources (including bringing women into the labor force and transferring people and resources from the usually less productive agricultural sector into the more productive industrial sectors); by the decline, stagnation, or very slow rise of living standards; and by borrowing from abroad easy-to-adopt, standard industrial technology.

In simplified terms, there are two basic sources of economic growth: increasing inputs and increasing productivity. Inputs (capital, labor, energy and raw materials, and knowledge) can grow rapidly and yield good growth rates. But in a traditional centrally planned economy, the rate of growth of inputs must, inevitably, decline over time, as reserves are used up, as resources become increasingly scarce, as increases in consumption can no longer be postponed, and for several other reasons.

If the rate of growth of some or all inputs decreases, the rate of growth of output will also decrease, unless the tempo of productivity improvements can be accelerated. But this precisely is the Achilles heel of a traditional centrally planned economic system.

Under traditional central planning, many decisions in an increasingly complex economy continue to be made at the top of the hierarchy. But because these big, unwieldy bureaucracies have inadequate information and too many contradictory pressures and goals, they make many mistakes. Subordinated units have little incentive to correct the mistakes because they must fulfill the plan. So inefficiency results, continues, and compounds. Product mix and product characteristics should respond to demand, especially in the case of exports, but the isolation of producing enterprises makes them unaware of, and generally uninterested in responding to, demand pressures. The consequence is that quality goods become harder to produce. This, in turn, leads to increasing difficulty in exporting manufactured goods to hard-currency markets. For these reasons, all traditional centrally planned economies began some time ago to ask, and now are asking with increasing ur-

gency, how to motivate enterprises to pay attention to costs, to improve
the efficiency of their operations, and to take the initiative in producing
better quality, improved, or new products. The answer, sooner or later,
will be that the economic system must be "reformed."

Reform Concepts

Modification of the centrally planned economic system entails a
redistribution of decision-making authority from the top of the hierarchy to lower units.[16] The crucial questions are: for which decisions, and
how far should the devolution of decision authority be permitted to go,
and on what basis will the lower units make the decisions? A key aspect
of these questions is how enterprise performance is to be evaluated: on
the basis of producing more and more of the same standard goods, or
on the basis of making "profit"? If the latter, will the desire to generate
profits lead to economically sound decisions? A prerequisite for sound
decisions is that the calculations that go into determining what actions
will lead to profits should be soundly based, i.e., that the prices of inputs
(direct and indirect) and outputs should reflect the costs of production,
the alternatives on which the same goods can be bought or sold on the
world market, as well as the preferences of the system's directors.

There are two basic concepts of decentralization: administrative and
economic.[17] Administrative decentralization means a partial devolution of authority over selected decisions from higher to lower tiers
within the administrative hierarchy; economic decentralization means
giving a considerable role to domestic and foreign market forces. Economic decentralization is by no means the same as "capitalism" as we
know it, because all the important means of production remain, as
before, under state ownership. A more accurate term is "market socialism." Most of us in the West and many economists also in Eastern
Europe believe that, in the long run, economic decentralization is the
only truly effective way of combining the basic features of a socialized
economic system with effective economic performance.

Resistance to Reforms and Problems of Implementation

The implementation of economic reforms means changing the status
quo. Such changes always disturb vested interests, which can routinely
be expected to resist. More fundamentally, there are three types of
"reasoned" resistance to economic decentralization: ideological, political, and economic. *Ideological* resistance is based on the view that
reliance on the market is incompatible with socialism. *Political* resistance is based on the fear that a devolution of central authority in

general, and to "market forces" in particular, would mean loss of central (party) control. *Economic* resistance is based on fear of serious adverse consequences for the economy during the transition period. Typically, a centrally planned economy operates under conditions of repressed inflation: there are serious shortages, as for example in the consumer goods sector in Poland. (There are shortages also in the producer sectors, but they are not as obvious because there are no queues, like those in front of the retail stores.) One well-justified fear is that if market forces were allowed to operate, they would quickly result in inflation. But if prices remain fixed, how can market forces operate? Furthermore, many large enterprises have potential monopoly power and could take advantage of market freedoms by raising prices and limiting output. Allowing the market to function would also release the considerable pent-up pressures for more Western imports, whereas increasing hard-currency exports would not be easy, at least not in the short run. But if a country's economy owes $13 billion and has a debt-service ratio of 60 percent, its economic policy *must* be focused on the short run! There are many other questions and concerns, including how to make a market-oriented system compatible with fulfilling the fixed and long-term trade agreements among the CMEA countries, especially those with the USSR.

These are real problems but they are not insoluble. At the same time, this discussion underscores an important point: systemic reforms of the economic decentralization type are most difficult to introduce at a time when the economy is operating under great pressures and tight constraints, such as the potentially explosive consumer-goods shortages, and large foreign debts. Such a situation is current reality for many East European countries. Hence the paradox: the greater are the economic pressures, the greater is the political inclination to introduce comprehensive economic reforms but the more severe are the economic constraints and difficulties in their implementation.

Economic Reforms Already Undertaken

Since the early 1950s, all countries in the region, including the Soviet Union, have experimented at one time or another with reforms of various kinds, but only three countries have made a genuine commitment to comprehensive economic decentralization: Yugoslavia in the early 1950s, Czechoslovakia in 1967, and Hungary in 1968.

Yugoslavia was able to introduce successfully a unique, worker-oriented economic system for a combination of reasons, not the least important of which was the political imperative to make a firm commitment to a distinctly Yugoslav system of economic organization as a way of marshalling support for Tito's independent stand vis-a-vis the Soviet Union and the rest of Eastern Europe.

In *Czechoslovakia*, the introduction of comprehensive reforms in 1967 was accompanied by political changes which were unacceptable to the Soviet Union. That experiment was ended by the August 1968 Soviet intervention.

Hungary is the one CMEA country that has successfully introduced such a reform—called the New Economic Mechanism (NEM). It is the only CMEA country today whose economic system is significantly different from those of the other members. To be sure, the formal and informal intervention by central authorities in the economy is still considerable, and is certainly greater than was intended when NEM was introduced in 1968. Still, the NEM is a noteworthy, and possibly permanent, experiment in the history of economic systems, conceived and carried out rather adroitly under remarkably difficult circumstances.

VI. CONCLUSIONS

It is essential to remember that there are all-important differences among the East European countries and that it is difficult to make accurate generalizations about "Eastern Europe," a region of diverse cultures, resources, stages of economic development, and forms of economic organization.

One defensible generalization is that compared with most Western and Third World countries, the East European economies have performed well in terms of growth rates, created or enlarged a skilled and increasingly well-educated work force, solved the problem of unemployment, and provided at least a minimum standard of living to most of their citizens. At the same time, however, economic pressures today are accelerating in all East European countries. Four of the most important pressure points, felt to a greater or lesser extent by the leadership in all the countries, are:

1. The rate of growth of domestic inputs has been slowing down in most countries for some time. The East European countries are experiencing increased difficulty in transferring resources from the less productive agricultural-rural sectors into the more productive industrial-urban sectors, as agricultural production is becoming one of the bottleneck sectors. To maintain their tempo of growth, improved productivity of resource utilization is strongly desired by all countries.

2. The East European countries are facing a growing shortage and increasing cost of energy and other raw materials. Critical in this regard are the future ability and willingness of the Soviet Union to supply oil and gas to its East European trading partners. For this reason also, the East European countries want to restructure their industries away from energy- and material-intensive sectors toward labor- and skill-intensive branches. But in the absence of clear signals regarding the profitability of enterprises and industrial branches, and in the face of lobbying pressure from the industrial groups that would be adversely affected, central planners are reluctant to close down enterprises, a factor that makes industrial transformation difficult. Moreover, a restructuring of industry requires large resources that are not easy to obtain either from domestic or from foreign sources.

3. A critically important domestic constraint on resource allocation is the growing pressure of consumerism: consumers want more and better goods and want them within their lifetime, preferably *now.* This increases the need and urgency for improved economic efficiency but at the same time reduces the maneuverability of central planners to solve economic problems.

4. An increasingly important external constraint is the growing indebtedness of all East European countries (with Albania a possible exception) to the industrial West. These pressures are particularly severe for Poland and Bulgaria. Adding to the domestic constraints to enlarge the production of goods marketable in the West for hard currency is the problem of increased Western protectionism facing Eastern Europe's manufactured and agricultural products. Especially important in this regard is the increased protectionism the East European countries are encountering in the European Economic Community: first, its Common Agricultural Policy is hurting especially badly some of the East European countries; second, new members of the enlarged Community are replacing third-party suppliers; and third, as the Community grants special trade preferences to the less developed, nonmember, West European and Third World countries, the East European countries *de facto* are increasingly discriminated against.

In addition to the economic pressures facing the East European countries, they must contend also with increased uncertainties in the international political environment. Future Soviet policies are one of the great unknowns that must concern leaders and peoples in Eastern Europe. A change of leadership in the Soviet Union is expected soon. If a strong ruler emerges who is able to consolidate power quickly and decisively, then the key question for Eastern Europe is: will Soviet policy change, maybe in the direction of a new economic isolationism, possibly even increased confrontation with the West? If so, this would almost certainly reduce the maneuverability of the East European states, at least those that are members of CMEA, because such new Soviet policies would tend to enforce increased "bloc discipline." This analysis suggests that the interest of the East European countries, and that of the United States, lies in a policy of continuing East-West detente, dialogue, and economic cooperation.

On the other hand, if after Brezhnev there were a long period of transition and uncertainty with regard to Soviet policies, this would create problems as well as opportunities for Eastern Europe. The leadership in some countries might become, or remain, extremely cautious, taking a wait-and-see attitude regarding important policy issues. The leadership in some other countries might, however, move decisively to solve problems, and possibly strike out on some new course. In the realm of trade, and economic policy more generally, such a new course might entail decisions to attract foreign direct investment on a substantial scale, a move that must be preceded by domestic reforms; to join or take a more active role in international economic organizations, such as the IMF, the World Bank, and GATT; and perhaps most significant of all, to implement comprehensive economic reforms. (Of course, should the new Soviet leadership itself move decisively in these directions, most East European countries would follow along.)

With respect to economic reforms, a strong case can be made, as mentioned earlier, that experimenting with partial or administrative reforms does not make much of a difference, that only carefully prepared and comprehensive reforms involving economic decentralization would have a significant impact. Within CMEA, only Hungary has successfully introduced, nurtured, and protected such reforms, while avoiding the political "excesses" that doomed the reform experiment in Czechoslovakia. Thus, under favorable international political conditions, Hungary's economic reforms may well point toward the possible future evolution of the East European, and perhaps even the Soviet Union's, economic system.

NOTES

The author acknowledges with thanks the valuable comments of John P. Hardt and Jacek Kochanowicz; however, he remains solely responsible for content.

1. The most recent, authoritative, and comprehensive compilation of studies on the economies of Eastern Europe, including studies on each of the eight countries, is the 1427-page *East European Economies Post-Helsinki* (A Compendium of Papers Submitted to the Joint Economic Committee, Congress of the United States) (Washington, D.C.: US GPO, August 24, 1977). Sections I and II of this chapter make extensive use of the author's contribution to that volume, "Economic Performance, Strategy, and Prospects in Eastern Europe."

2. Paul Marer, "Soviet Economic Policy in Eastern Europe," in *Reorientation and Commercial Relations of the Countries of Eastern Europe* (A Compendium of Papers Submitted to the Joint Economic Committee, U.S. Congress) (Washington, D.C.: US GPO, 1974).

3. See T. P. Alton, et al., "Defense Expenditures in Eastern Europe, 1965–1976," in *East European Economies Post-Helsinki*.

4. Methods of calculating the indices, the definitions used, as well as the many problems and pitfalls of making intertemporal and international comparisons are found in Thad P. Alton, "Comparative Structure and Growth of Economic Activity in Eastern Europe," in *East European Economies Post-Helsinki*.

5. For details, see Paul Marer, "Soviet Economic Policy in Eastern Europe."

6. Edwin Snell and Marilyn Harper, "Postwar Economic Growth in East Germany: A Comparison with West Germany," in *Economic Developments in the Countries of Eastern Europe* (A Compendium of Papers Submitted to the Subcommittee on Foreign Economic Policy of the Joint Economic Committee, U.S. Congress) (Washington, D.C.: US GPO, 1970), pp. 567, 570.

7. Sandor Ausch, *A KGST-egyuttmukodes helyzete, mechanizmusa, tavlatai* [CMEA Cooperation, Situation, Mechanism and Perspectives] (Budapest: Kozgazdasagi es Jogi Konyvkiado, 1969).

8. K. Beke and L. Hunyadi, "A Magyar export importanyagtartalma" [The Import Content of Hungarian Exports], *Kulgazdasag* (Budapest), July, 1977.

9. *East-West Markets,* August 7, 1978, p. 8.

10. Central Intelligence Agency, *The International Energy Situation: Outlook to 1985* (Washington, D.C.: April 1977).

11. Robert W. Campbell, "Implications for the Soviet Economy of Soviet Energy Prospects," *The ACES Bulletin,* vol. XX, no. 1 (spring 1978): 23–52.

12. For a more detailed discussion of these issues and the political context of Eastern Europe's debt, see the thoughtful and provocative article by Richard Portes, "East Europe's Debt to the West: Interdependence is a Two-Way Street," *Foreign Affairs,* vol. 55, no. 4 (April 1977).

13. For an approach to the estimation of Eastern Europe's tourist revenue, see Paul Marer and John Tilley, "Tourism," in *Reorientation and Commercial Relations.*

14. For a discussion of achievements and problems, see Paul Marer and Joseph C. Miller, "U.S. Participation in East-West Industrial Cooperation Agreements," *Journal of International Business Studies* (fall-winter 1977).

15. This section is based on the excellent study by Morris Bornstein, "Economic Reforms in Eastern Europe," in *East European Economies Post-Helsinki*.

16. Ibid.

17. Ibid.

11 Eurocommunism in Eastern Europe: Promise or Threat?

Jiri Valenta

A Czechoslovak government minister recently quoted the opening words of Marx's *Communist Manifesto:* "A spectre is haunting Europe—the spectre of communism." Then he added: "But today it is the other way around—a spectre is haunting communism—the spectre of Europe!"

Eurocommunism is an ambiguous and perhaps even an improper term. Yet in spite of its geographic and historical imprecision, it is being used and accepted by some political observers as a convenient designator for the partially converging evolution of the autonomous, pluralistic type of socialism now evolving in several West European Communist parties, particularly the Italian Communist party (PCI) and the Spanish Communist party (PCE).

The vitriolic Soviet attack on the secretary general of the PCE, Santiago Carrillo, in June 1977, convinced even the most skeptical policy makers and political observers that the phenomenon of Eurocommunism has been taken seriously in the East. Thus, one of the earlier skeptics, Austrian Chancellor Bruno Kreisky, referred to the "genuine" character[1] of the dispute between the USSR and the Eurocommunists. Other observers go even further, believing with Yugoslav thinker and philosopher Milovan Djilas that with the emergence of Eurocommunism "the church has to split."[2] Although there are some, like Henry Kissinger, who question the sincerity of the Eurocommunists themselves, no one seems able to deny that Eurocommunism, whatever it means, is a cause of great concern in Eastern Europe and in the USSR.

The importance of Eurocommunism became particularly apparent after the famous Madrid meeting in March 1977. There, three West European Communist party leaders—Enrico Berlinguer, Carrillo, and

Georges Marchais—recognized the appealing quality of this term and with initial hesitation and varying degrees of ambivalence began to employ it. The term, as they use it, is not meant to define a concept or a coherent doctrine, but rather to describe the trend towards independence and the adaptation of communist tenets to the conditions of their own countries, which would be free of the lack of democracy noted in the USSR and East European countries.[3] When asked to define Eurocommunism briefly, the leader of the recently legalized Spanish party, Carrillo, described it as a dialectical synthesis of two aspects: "socialism running parallel to democracy, freedom with universal suffrage, and alternation of parties in the government" and "independence ... without obeying orders from Moscow."[4] Similarly, Italian Communist leader Berlinguer described Eurocommunism as "the joint evaluation of the problems of democracy and socialism which the Communist parties of Italy, France, and Spain arrived at in an autonomous manner."[5]

In spite of differences among the Eurocommunists on a number of issues, the two-dimensional definitions of Carrillo and Berlinguer adequately reflect the complexity of the Eurocommunist phenomenon; as such, they serve as an appropriate starting point for our inquiry into the effects of Eurocommunism upon Eastern Europe. To help determine this influence, several crucial questions must be asked: What are the historical origins and turning points in the development of Eurocommunism? What past and present linkages exist between Eurocommunism and autonomous and reformist trends in Eastern Europe? Is Eurocommunism likely to encourage a trend toward reformism and liberalism in Eastern Europe, or instead a trend toward cold-war-like isolationism?

THE ORIGINS OF EUROCOMMUNISM

Eurocommunism is not the product of a sudden shift in the tactics of West European Communist parties, but rather of a long historical evolution in the European Communist movement. In my opinion, it is misleading to think of Eurocommunism as limited exclusively to Western Europe; it is, instead, a phenomenon whose development is characterized by a constant flow of ideas, influences, and experiences between Eastern and Western Europe.

The political origins of Eurocommunism go back to the experience of the Communist parties in the Comintern, the Spanish Civil War, and the Cominform, and to the dramatic suffering of non-Russian Communist leaders under Stalin. Some of the characteristic ideas of Eurocommunism originated in Eastern Europe. In the sense that Eurocommunism signifies independence from the USSR, it had its beginnings in 1948 and 1949 in Tito's Yugoslavia. This brand of Eurocommunism was practiced with different degrees of success in Poland under Gomulka and in Hungary under Nagy, both in 1956, and under Hoxha in Albania and Ceausescu in Romania since the 1960s.

Insofar as Eurocommunism stands for a type of socialism that is democratic and pluralistic in nature, it can be traced back to Marx's earlier philosophical works, particularly his *Economic-Philosophic Manuscripts,* and to the writings of many subsequent Marxist thinkers, the most important being Gramsci, Lukacs, Sartre, Fisher, and Garaudy. The political applications of some of the elements of this type of socialism were introduced in an ill-fated historical experiment in Czechoslovakia between 1945 and 1948, to some degree in Yugoslavia after 1952, in Hungary for a short time in 1956, and more significantly for a brief period in Czechoslovakia in 1968 under Dubcek.

Moreover, it should be stressed that the West European Communist parties had their own Stalinist past, as did most of the East European parties. All of them followed the Soviet lead in condemning Tito in 1948 and 1949, not a single one daring to raise its voice in Yugoslavia's defense.

Although a strong case can be made that the theoretical underpinnings of certain elements of pluralistic socialism were developed in West European parties (mainly Gramsci's) before they were considered in Yugoslavia, these parties, on the whole, seem rather to slowly *follow* the example given by Yugoslavia. For example, in the 1950s the Yugoslavs exercised a strong influence on Palmiro Togliatti, the engineer of the PCI's "road toward socialism," and were altogether very supportive of the Italian party in its search for an evolutionary path to socialism.[6] The PCI, inspired by Khrushchev's 1956 secret speech denouncing Stalin and by his subsequent program of de-Stalinization, established ties with the Yugoslav Communist party (LCY) after Togliatti's visit there in 1956. In contrast, the more orthodox French Communist party was at the same time very slow in pursuing the Soviet-Yugoslav rapprochement that had been initiated by the PCI. Meanwhile, the latter, encouraged by the process of de-Stalinization in the USSR and in Eastern Europe and by the Yugoslav experience, began, after 1956, to take an increasingly critical view of the Soviet style of socialism and its application in Eastern Europe, and to forge its own model of socialism. It was in this spirit that Gramsci's disciple Togliatti, in a famous interview published by the Italian journal *Nuovi Argomenti* in 1956, rejected the notion of the USSR as being the "single guide" of the Communist movement. Togliatti stated that the "Soviet model is no longer obligatory," thus inaugurating his renowned thesis of "polycentrism."[7] Even more importantly, Togliatti posed the significant question of whether Soviet society had not already reached "a certain form of degeneration." It is worth noting that the Soviet leaders immediately recognized, even at this early date, the potentially damaging effects of this West European judgment and subjected Togliatti to severe criticism.[8]

In 1956, however, West European criticism of the USSR was still in its infant stage. The PCI, as well as the other West European Communist parties, basically supported the Soviet intervention in Hungary in November 1956, even though such a position was detrimental to their electoral chances at that time. Nevertheless, the lesson afforded by the 1956 revolts in Hungary and Poland was not ignored by the West European Communists; they began to move, some slowly, some quickly, into a more independent and critical posture with regard to the USSR. The PCI under Togliatti's guidance took the lead in this process and at the same time began to seek a better understanding of and to support reformist and liberal trends in Eastern Europe. Thus, even at this early date, the process of reinforcement of Eurocommunist trends in Eastern and Western Europe had begun.

The PCI was influenced by, at the same time that it supported, the Yugoslav reforms in 1958 and the "system of market socialism" in 1963, both of which were based on reformist economic thought of early Polish origin. As in 1956, the PCI was criticized in 1958 for its support of the Yugoslavs. Khrushchev's second effort toward de-Stalinization, which came after the Twenty-second Party Congress in 1961, further encouraged the PCI's search, under the leadership of Togliatti, for a "new model" of socialism—one that would be relevant to the countries of the West and different from the "undemocratic tendencies" of East European socialism. Suddenly at this point, in the early 1960s, the PCI was joined in its endeavor by the exiled Spanish Communist party, led by Carrillo. In 1965, after the death of the French pro-Soviet leader Maurice Thorez, the French Communist party, by then under the leadership of Waldeck Rochet, also joined in to some extent. Several other West European Communist parties, such as the Swedish, went through a similar evolution. The process of de-Stalinization and Europeanization in the West European Communist parties had been launched at the regional level.

Those who advocated the Europeanization of West European Communist parties began to favor a policy of broad coalition with various political and social forces, including the religions at home and support for human rights. In this vein, they were critical of the cultural orthodoxy of Walter Ulbricht's regime in East Germany, the anti-Semitic literature in the Ukraine, and the trial of Siniavsky and Daniel in Moscow.

In addition, reform-minded intellectuals of West European Communist parties—Garaudy, Radice, Luport, Fisher, and Marek—had established, beginning in 1963, a promising transnational dialogue, whereby ideas and experiences could be exchanged with leading East European reformist theoreticians at various symposiums and meetings.

Here began the process of differentiation between conservative and reformist elements in the European Communist movement, which led eventually to the Prague Spring experiment and the 1968 invasion of Czechoslovakia by five Warsaw Pact countries. East German leader Ulbricht and his ideologists dated the origins of the "Czechoslovak counterrevolution" back to the famous conference in Liblice in Czechoslovakia in 1962, where Marxist theoreticians from the East and the West rehabilitated Franz Kafka. Indeed, the leading theoreticians of the West European Communist parties began, after 1963, to perceive the parallel process of de-Stalinization in Czechoslovakia as a significant development of relevance to West European communism.

Nevertheless, before 1968 the conflicts between the Eurocommunists and the conservative establishment in Eastern Europe and in the USSR, although of a very definite nature, were muted and restrained owing to the generally shared belief in solidarity with the ruling parties. The invasion of Czechoslovakia in 1968 dramatically altered this relationship.

PRAGUE SPRING, 1968:
EUROCOMMUNISM IN ACTION

The Prague Spring of 1968 was a product not only of the process of de-Stalinization as it was being carried out in Czechoslovakia but also of various reformist trends in European communism (both East and West). In terms of pluralism and human rights, the scope of Dubcek's "socialism with a human face" was much broader than that of Nagy and Gomulka in 1956, and went even further than any phase of the Yugoslav experiment.

Thus, it is not surprising that the Prague Spring was seen not only by the PCI and the PCE, but also by the PCF and other West European

Communist parties, as well as by reformist elements in Eastern Europe (in Yugoslavia, Poland, East Germany, Hungary, and even the USSR), as a relevant example of democratic socialism in a Western-type country such as Czechoslovakia, which was characterized by a well-developed and essentially democratic cultural and political tradition. After his visit to Czechoslovakia in May 1968, the secretary general of the PCI, Luigi Longo, declared that the Czechoslovak experiment not only "helps the parties of certain socialist countries" but also assists "the Communist parties of the capitalist countries in their struggle to create a new socialist society—young, open, and modern."[9] In April of the same year, the secretary of the French Communist party, Waldeck Rochet, also praised Dubcek and pledged support for his program, which he saw as contributing to the "expansion of socialism."[10]

In simpler terms, the Prague Spring can be considered the forerunner of Eurocommunism, and the Czechoslovak reformists can be considered its forefathers in their attempt to forge a model of socialism that, rooted in the Western tradition, differs from that of the USSR. As Carrillo, another enthusiastic supporter of Dubcek's reformist program, stated: "If the term 'Eurocommunism' had been invented in 1968, Dubcek would have been a Eurocommunist."[11]

Fearing that the conservative bureaucracies in the USSR and in Eastern Europe would attempt to crush Prague reformism, the PCI, PCE, and PCF mobilized seventeen West European Communist parties on behalf of the embattled country. During the crisis, this coalition of West European Communist parties used considerable pressure to discourage the intervention. Among other tactics, they threatened to convene in a separate conference to condemn the USSR. The French Communist leader Rochet even served at one point as mediator between the Czechoslovak and Soviet leaderships. Although Eurocommunist pressure did not deter the invasion, it caused much confusion and procrastination, and was a factor which contributed to the moderation of Soviet behavior during and after the intervention.

More importantly, the invasion, which Ernest Fisher, reformist leader of the Austrian Communist party, christened a manifestation of *Panzerkommunism,* served as a warning as to the Soviet version of "proletarian internationalism." In Carrillo's words, "the Soviet invasion of Czechoslovakia in 1968 was the last straw." After that, "any idea of internationalism ended for us."[12]

After Czechoslovakia the Leninist model of socialism in the USSR and in Eastern Europe became an even greater liability and embarrassment to the parties in Western Europe, which were competing for electoral votes. This was particularly true for the PCF, for which the invasion was a crucial turning point. The PCF had never openly opposed the USSR on a major policy issue. The support for Dubcek was the first joint anti-Soviet venture of the French, Italian, and Spanish Communist parties, their first joint action as Eurocommunists.

On the whole, the invasion has encouraged a worldwide trend toward greater autonomy for most Western Communist parties, particularly the European ones. As Spanish Communist leader Manuel Azcarate pointed out, "It posed for Communist parties the need to assert their independence with renewed vigor."[13] More importantly, the invasion encouraged a new trend toward "socialism with a human face," even surpassing what occurred in Czechoslovakia. Although the autonomy of the individual parties was not a new idea, democratic socialism as a relevant model for the West *was* new, at least for some West European Communist parties. Thus Czechoslovakia's "socialism with a human face" served, if not as a model, perhaps, as Azcarate has observed, as "the most specific point of reference" for the rejection of the "Soviet model" of socialism and "for pointing out the rise of the new trend in the Communist movement which has become known as Eurocommunism."[14]

THE RISE OF EUROCOMMUNISM

The post-invasion climate in Czechoslovakia exacerbated the long conflict still in process between the reformist and conservative forces in the European Communist movement. It brought about an increasing willingness on the part of many West European Communist parties to challenge Soviet authority and to adopt a critical attitude toward the authoritarian regimes in Eastern Europe.

Conservative elements in East and West European Communist parties were able to slow down the momentous rise of Eurocommunism in some of the parties only by expelling, in 1969 and 1970, the most outspoken critics of the invasion, such as French leader and philosopher Roger Garaudy and Austrian thinkers and leaders Fisher and Franz Marek. Nevertheless, even the reformist elements in the PCF, under the new leadership of Marchais (the invasion is believed to have crushed the health of Rochet), began slowly to accept most of Garaudy's critique and to strive for a Eurocommunist alliance with the PCI. In this process some of the exiled East European Marxist theoreticians and politicians, who considered themselves close to the Eurocommunists, exercised considerable influence on reformist circles in the West European Communist parties, particularly the PCI. One of the major indictments of East European political systems was written by the exiled Polish Eurocommunist theoretician Wlodzimierz Brus and printed by the PCI publishing house: *Sistema Politico e Proprieta Sociale nel Socialismo.*[15] Furthermore, PCI reformist circles had developed a close relationship with the exiled Czechoslovak Eurocommunist-minded politicians and publicists Jiri Pelikan and Zdenek Mlynar. Moreover, in the 1970s periodicals close to the PCI were able to publish some major political testimonies and documents that had been smuggled out of Czechoslovakia. The most significant of these—a letter from Dubcek, an interview with Josef Smrkovsky, and the latter's memoirs—appeared in the journal *Giorni Vie Nuove,* whose editor-in-chief, David Lajola, is a Central Committee member of the PCI. It is easy to see, then, that the flow of Eurocommunist ideas from Czechoslovakia, as well as from Poland, in an East to West direction after 1968 was an important factor in the rise of Eurocommunism.

Also significant in the rise of Eurocommunism was the international climate of detente that evolved in Europe as a result of the protracted process leading to the Helsinki Conference of 1975, and which encouraged the West European Communist parties to demonstrate their increasing concern about the issue of human rights in Eastern Europe and in the USSR.

Criticism by the West European Communist parties became especially strong in 1969 and 1970 during the final destruction of Czechoslovak socialism and the subsequent process of so-called "normalization" in that country. The French and Italian Communist parties exerted substantial pressure on Husak's leadership in the early 1970s in the hope of preventing the trials that were being prepared for the reformists who had supported Dubcek in 1968.

The emergence in the 1970s of the French Communist party, once one of the most pro-Soviet parties, as a new champion of personal liberties and human rights in Eastern Europe was remarkable. When a spokesman for hard-line elements in the Czechoslovak party, Presidium member Vasil Bilak, failed to mention the PCF among the Communist parties "guilty" of assaulting the process of "normalization," the Marchais leadership was said to have sent a protest, demanding to be included among the heretics.[16] This and other actions of the PCF reflected its efforts to follow the PCI in the defense of political pluralism and civil liberties in Eastern Europe. The PCI and PCF rapprochement of November 1975 and the requirements of French internal politics (alliance with the Socialist party) hastened the efforts of the PCF to overtake the PCI in its criticism of the internal policies of the East European regimes and the USSR. Thus the PCF criticized the banishment of Solzhenitsyn from the USSR, and when a BBC film on Soviet labor camps appeared on French television in late 1975, the PCF joined the PCI in an unequivocal and open condemnation of the oppressive policies of the USSR.

About the same time, during the preparatory meetings for the East Berlin Conference of European Communist and Workers' Parties, the PCF also began supporting the coalition of autonomous parties in Eastern Europe (Romanian and Yugoslav), and the PCI and PCE in Western Europe. In the final stages of preparation for the conference, the Soviet party, supported only by some of the loyalist East European Communist parties along with a few parties in Western Europe (among which the only significant entity was the Portuguese party),[17] reached an uneasy *modus vivendi*. The conference took place in East Berlin in June 1976, and the concessions made there by the CPSU and the loyalist parties with respect to the notion of proletarian internationalism were interpreted by the autonomous parties as an ideological justification for the independence of European Communist parties. The results of the conference brought a kind of institutionalization of the type of Eurocommunism that began after the Czechoslovak invasion of 1968. In the reformist circles also, the results of the East Berlin Conference were seen, to paraphrase the East German dissident Wolf Biermann (who subsequently joined the Spanish Communist party), as a "remarkable and gratifying change" and "a clear step toward socialist democracy," which would also have a positive effect on Eastern Europe. According to Biermann, "the Eurocommunists have encouraged dissidents to become more courageous and more clear-sighted."[18]

THE CHALLENGE OF EUROCOMMUNISM

Indeed, after the East Berlin Conference, the rise of Eurocommunism became a significant challenge to East European conservative establishments and to the USSR itself. The relationship between the Eurocommunists in Western Europe and the reformist and dissident circles in Eastern Europe became mutually more reinforcing. The latter, some of them considered Eurocommunists themselves, were encouraged by the results of the conference and intensified their efforts to appeal to the Eurocommunists in the West for moral and political support. The former stepped up their selective, but nevertheless effective, intervention on behalf of the dissidents and reformists in Eastern Europe, hoping that Eurocommunism would serve as a "reference point" for Eastern

Europe and would aid in its "democratization."[19] After East Berlin, the Eurocommunists rejected even more forcibly the prevailing Leninist model in Eastern Europe, seeing it as irrelevant to Western Europe, and willingly became the most outspoken allies of human rights groups in Eastern Europe and the USSR. Said Lucio Lombardo Radice, a leading theoretician of the PCI, "There must be complete freedom in socialism, or else it cannot call itself socialism."[20]

Claiming that intolerant actions on the part of the regimes in Eastern Europe and the USSR violate the final documents of the Helsinki Conference and, even more importantly, the final documents of the East Berlin Conference, Eurocommunist officials began to participate in rallies where they demanded the release of political prisoners in Czechoslovakia and in the USSR, to protest against the oppression of Catholic priests in Czechoslovakia and Jewish dissidents such as Shcharansky in the USSR, and to intervene increasingly on behalf of dissidents in Eastern Europe. Eurocommunists supported both the signatories of "Charter 77" in Czechoslovakia (some of them of Eurocommunist persuasion, some of them noncommunists) and workers in Poland jailed during violent food riots and strikes (in June 1976), as well as the Workers' Defense Committee (KOR) of Polish intellectuals who took up the cause of the jailed workers. They also protested against the expulsion of East German dissident Biermann and supported his persecuted friend, the philosopher Robert Havemann—both of whom consider themselves Eurocommunists. In all three issues, Eurocommunist pressure was one of the factors which perhaps helped to moderate, at least for a time, the behavior of the regimes in Czechoslovakia, Poland, and East Germany. Most of the signatories of "Charter 77" were not tried, the Polish workers were not punished severely, and thus far Havemann has not been forced to leave East Germany. Presumably, if there had not been fears about the reactions of the Eurocommunists, the repression would have been much harsher. Eurocommunist pressure and the Soviets' fear that dissident issues might damage relations with the West in general, and with the Eurocommunists in particular, were two of the most important factors in somewhat moderating the behavior of officials in those three East European countries.[21]

The East European reaction to increasing interventionism on the part of the Eurocommunists was twofold. On the one hand, among the reformist circles and dissidents it reinforced the hope that Eurocommunism might aid the process of democratization and reform in Eastern Europe. Eurocommunist intervention, as Polish dissident historian Adam Michnik put it, "helped to free many Polish workers from prison," but it also reinforced the people's hope that "it is possible to create socialism with a human face"[22] in Eastern Europe. On the other hand, Eurocommunist interventionism led to growing hostility on the part of several East European regimes, particularly those of Czechoslovakia and East Germany. Their fear of Eurocommunism was reflected by the paradox that the Italian and French Communist newspapers *L'Unita* and *L'Humanite* were no longer permitted to be sold in some East European capitals, even though some West European noncommunist newspapers were still available. This situation goes hand in hand with the attitude expressed by the Czechoslovak newspaper *Rude Pravo*, which complained that the Prague regime would get better treatment from "many bourgeois journals" than from "the editors of *L'Unita.*"[23]

Indeed, the continuing debate among the East European elites and the USSR and the pressures from some East European leaders for expulsion from the Communist movement of these parties are unmistakable signs of growing apprehension about the effects of Eurocommunism in Eastern Europe. The available evidence suggests that these pressures may have triggered the frontal, public attack on Eurocommunism by the Czechoslovak hard-liner Vasil Bilak, who accused the Eurocommunists of pursuing "unprincipled and treacherous policies,"[24] and the *New Times* attack on Eurocommunism and the Spanish leader Carrillo in June 1977.[25]

THE LIMITS OF THE CHALLENGE

Eurocommunism, particularly after the East Berlin Conference of 1976, imposed itself upon Eastern Europe as a potentially serious challenge to certain of the regimes and to the USSR's interests in the region. Having established this, however, one cannot fail to point out the limits of the Eurocommunist "cancer" in Eastern Europe. To say that Eurocommunism may have destabilizing effects on Eastern Europe is not saying very much. It is important to see where in Eastern Europe this influence exists and to what degree. It should be remembered that Eastern Europe is a region in which historical, cultural, economic, and political levels of development vary considerably from country to country. Perhaps Eurocommunism could find a fertile ground for growth in such countries as Czechoslovakia, Poland, East Germany, and Hungary, where Western traditions have penetrated to a considerable degree. It is toward some of these countries that the concern of the Eurocommunists is directed, and when they do exert influence in Eastern Europe it is, consequently, with great selectivity. For example, with regard to policies in support of the dissidents in Eastern Europe and in support of human rights, their attitude toward Yugoslavia and Romania contrasts sharply with their attitude toward Czechoslovakia and East Germany—thereby manifesting the same sort of selectivity with respect to human rights that the Carter administration has exhibited in the United States.

Although this double standard of the Eurocommunists regarding East European dissidents weakens their claim to unwavering principles, they cannot be considered to be mere opportunists. Elements of political opportunism are involved here, to be sure, but political realism plays a much greater part in determining the Eurocommunists' selectivity. Also the growth of the dissident movement in Czechoslovakia, East Germany, and Poland is somewhat more noticeable at the present time than in other East European countries. In response, two of these regimes—those of Czechoslovakia and East Germany—have shown considerable hostility in their attitudes and policies toward Eurocommunism. The Czechoslovak regime in particular has become a major advocate of the anti-Eurocommunist campaign in Eastern Europe.

Conversely, the more tolerant Kadar regime in Hungary, with its relatively good record on human rights, has managed to maintain friendly relations with the Eurocommunists, as indicated by Kadar's visit to Italy in 1977 and his talks with Berlinguer. Kadar himself is believed to see Eurocommunism as supportive of his program of domestic reformism and his liberal policies.

The same cannot be said about the Romanian regime, one of the most authoritarian in Eastern Europe. This is also partly true of the Yugoslav regime, which, since 1971, has clamped down on domestic dissidents in an effort to reinstate centralized political control. According to Milovan Djilas, Yugoslavia has jailed proportionately as many political prisoners as has the USSR.[26] Yet, in spite of Djilas's call for support of the Eurocommunists on questions pertaining to human rights, the Eurocommunists do not wish to meddle in Yugoslav affairs. The Eurocommunists seem to have their best relations with Yugoslavia and Romania, doubtless because of the autonomous, independent foreign policies of both countries. As noted, independence and autonomy are important factors in the phenomenon of Eurocommunism. Both of these countries, unlike Czechoslovakia and East Germany, have certain characteristics typical of underdeveloped states (particularly Romania and southern Yugoslavia). And since the Eurocommunists hold that the right of a Communist party to adapt its policies to the prevailing conditions of the country is crucial to the country's independence, they probably view the highly centralized and authoritarian political system of Romania as more relevant and applicable there than the Eurocommunist model of pluralistic socialism.

Probably a more important determinant of the Eurocommunists' attitudes and policies toward Yugoslavia and Romania are old historical ties and common interests. The special relationship between the PCI and the Yugoslavs has already been mentioned. Similarly, Romania has cultivated close relations with the PCE since the mid-1950s. Radio Espana Independiente (Radio Independent Spain)—the PCE's clandestine radio station (traced initially to the USSR)—had been broadcasting from Romania seven times daily via eleven separate radio frequencies from the mid-1950s until 1977, when the PCE was legalized in Spain. (One of the transmitters was believed to have been located in Hungary.) In the late 1960s and the 1970s, both Romania and Yugoslavia became important allies of the Eurocommunists, who were struggling to become truly autonomous political forces in their respective countries. This development was clearly demonstrated during and after the Czechoslovak crisis and during preparations for the East Berlin Conference. The push for human rights in Romania and Yugoslavia, then, is not in the interests of the Eurocommunists, since it might force these two regimes to move closer to the USSR.

In sum, the Eurocommunists apparently do not wish to carry to an extreme their interventionism in Eastern Europe. An unselective, overly aggressive human rights crusade in that region could lead very possibly to the imposition of more rigid controls by hard-line elements, causing the deterioration of Soviet relations with the Eurocommunists and with the West as a whole. The motives of the Eurocommunists become clearer when viewed in the light of the broader challenge associated with detente. The Eurocommunists are not interested in a total break with the USSR and the East European regimes, for this could force both elements into a more hostile attitude and even precipitate a return to the Cold War in Europe.

Finally, the intrusions of the Eurocommunists on behalf of the dissidents in Eastern Europe have until now been limited to cases where human rights were severely violated. The critiques of East European regimes are circumscribed by the lack of thoroughgoing analyses of their failings. A broad analysis has been urged by several Marxist thinkers and publicists from Eastern Europe, such as Wlodzimierz Brus, Zdenek Mlynar, and Jiri Pelikan. Perhaps if the Eurocommunists had carried out a thorough examination of Czechoslovakia's ill-fated attempts from 1945 to 1948 and in 1968, they would have found that some of the elements of their domestic programs, such as the insistence on excessive nationalization on the part of the PCF, were unrealistic and self-defeating. A critique of this sort has been attempted by PCE leader Santiago Carrillo in his study *Eurocommunism and the State.* The underlying thesis of Carrillo's controversial study is that Eurocommunism should be the very antithesis of the models of socialism now prevailing in Eastern Europe and in the USSR. This thesis brought him into serious collision with the Soviet leadership. There are indications that other Eurocommunist parties (thus far the PCI and the PCF) do not wish to follow the example of their Spanish comrades, fearing that this would inevitably precipitate an open break with Moscow.

In fact, the Eurocommunists, including the PCE, although definitely interested in promoting reformism and human rights on a selective basis, have no intention of severing relations with the ruling parties. That would be counterproductive and dangerous, as argued earlier. The Eurocommunist parties and the USSR still share important foreign policy interests, such as the weakening of U.S. influence in Europe, the prevention of a strong West Germany, and support for the national liberation movements in Third World countries. Important elements in some of the Eurocommunist parties, particularly the PCF, resist the process of estrangement from Moscow in foreign affairs.

EUROCOMMUNISM:
A PROMISE OR A THREAT?

The term Eurocommunism, despite its ambiguities, accurately describes the thrust of the European Communist movement toward autonomy and independence, and the development of a pluralistic model of socialism. Eurocommunism did not make its appearance overnight and can hardly be considered a tactical move on the part of several West European Communist parties. In a broad sense, the rise of Eurocommunism may be seen as the outcome of a previous tendency toward polycentrism and diversity, which in part originated in Eastern Europe in the late 1940s and the 1950s. Since then, sustained linkages and a two-way traffic, from East to West and from West to East, have developed between autonomous and reformist trends in both parts of Europe. As noted, the Soviet-led occupation of Czechoslovakia was the great catalyst in bringing about the rise of Eurocommunism. The Eurocommunists' stand on behalf of Dubcek's regime is also of great significance, since it represented the first joint, multilateral action on behalf of their fellow Eurocommunists in Eastern Europe. The post-invasion climate and the process of detente leading to the Helsinki Conference in 1975 provided a framework for the rapid rise of Eurocommunism in the 1970s.

But it was the 1976 East Berlin Conference that institutionalized diversity and Eurocommunist independence. After this conference, the issue of civil liberties, particularly in Eastern Europe, became a touchstone for the Eurocommunists. Since then there has been a growing concern in Eastern Europe and in the USSR with the "infection" of Eurocommunism and its containment. Needless to say, the support of increasing numbers of Eurocommunists for reformists and dissidents after East Berlin has become a very disconcerting issue, especially when one considers that Eurocommunism may be seen as an alternative model of socialism to that offered by and prevailing in Eastern Europe. Undoubtedly, the successful participation of the PCI in the Italian government in the foreseeable future would make this challenge even more dramatic.

On the other hand, it would, in my view, be premature to conclude that the effects of Eurocommunism and the Soviet and East European responses to it are foreclosed. Eurocommunism may become an explosive issue, but we do not know how, or when, or even if this is going to happen. Eurocommunism has its limits, and the Eurocommunists themselves, being political realists, remain cautious and selective in their support of human rights and personal liberties in Eastern Europe.

In addition, the Eurocommunist influence differs from one East European country to another, for a variety of reasons. So do attitudes and policies in several East European countries. The conflicting and contradictory reactions of East European and Soviet leaders toward Eurocommunism after the East Berlin Conference, reminiscent of the debate on Czechoslovakia in 1968, demonstrate the lack of consensus concerning the issue.

Yet, in some East European countries, the challenge of Eurocommunism is probably being taken seriously by party officials. So far, the most consistent and visible manifestations of the seriousness of the challenge have occurred in Poland and in Czechoslovakia. In Poland, which shares with Italy a Catholic heritage and with France an intellectual and cultural affinity, the Eurocommunists served in 1976 and 1977 as one of the supportive factors in developing an alliance between the workers' opposition and the nonconformist intellectuals of the Workers' Defense Committee.

In Czechoslovakia, a country close to both Italy and France in its political, economic, spiritual, and cultural heritage, the Eurocommunists gave their support to and prevented harsh punishment of the signatories of "Charter 77"—a Magna Charta of broad coalitions of Eurocommunist-minded and noncommunist intellectuals, politicians, and workers (including several members of Dubcek's leadership). Both "Charter 77" and the Madrid declaration of the same year sounded like the U.S. Bill of Rights in their defense of the civil liberties and political rights of citizens. "Charter 77" demonstrated that the happenings of 1968 were not accidental. Czechoslovakia, which is less immune to the ideas of Eurocommunism than any other country in Eastern Europe, still shows no signs of accepting "normalization." Not only is it a country with problems of great relevance to Western Europe, but it is also one in which thousands of Dubcek's former supporters from "the party of the expelled" see themselves as sharing the ideals and goals of the Eurocommunist movement, to which they look with hope and expectation.

This is not to say that Eurocommunism is viewed exclusively with a messianic hope. Many spokesmen for dissidents in Czechoslovakia and Poland neither believe in Eurocommunism nor are concerned as to whether Eurocommunism represents a fundamental or a tactical change: their main goal is to force the ruling elites into a defensive position, and indeed they have been relatively successful in both countries from 1976 to 1978. The indecisiveness and vacillations of both regimes, Czechoslovak and Polish, reflect their internal strife. It is possible, then, that Eurocommunism in Eastern Europe did not die with the Prague Spring of 1968, and that it may reappear in one form or another in Czechoslovakia, or in Poland. Even East Germany is not totally immune to the "infection" of Eurocommunism. In the summer of 1977, Rudolf Bahro, a Eurocommunist-minded East German official and the executive of an East Berlin factory, in his book *The Alternative,* called for the spread of Eurocommunism in Eastern Europe and for the formation of a new league of Eurocommunists, deriving its inspiration from Karl Marx's original group of supporters in London in the 1850s. Similarly, a manifesto, allegedly drawn up in secret by an East German Communist opposition group, called, just as Bahro had, for the "Eurocommunization" of East Germany. Also, some Czechoslovak leaders have exhibited a curious interest in a mythological interpretation of Czechoslovak history. According to this interpretation, the eighth year of each decade assumes a symbolic importance. Vasil Bilak, a member of the "healthy forces" who asked for "fraternal assistance" in 1968, views Eurocommunism as a mortal threat. In 1977 he expressed his fears that the "counterrevolutionary" domestic forces uncovered by the Eurocommunists, along with other "anticommunist centers," would indeed attempt to launch various campaigns in connection with the tenth anniversary of the Prague Spring in 1978.[27] Furthermore, in 1977 the Czechoslovak press also revealed that the danger of a Prague Spring movement was real, not only in Czechoslovakia but also in certain other East European countries.[28] Such apocalyptic prophesies, however, were not fulfilled.

A definitive statement about the future effects of Eurocommunism on Eastern Europe would be premature at this point. However, it can be said that Eurocommunism exists and causes concern, at least in the eyes of conservative elements in the East. It would hardly be fair to blame the Eurocommunists for not taking stronger public stands in favor of human rights and for not directly attacking the USSR and East European regimes—policies that are not pursued by any West European governments. It is in the interests of both East European dissidents and reformists and the Eurocommunists themselves that they avoid a cold-war-like rupture with the USSR.

As long as the Eurocommunists are not excommunicated from the Communist fold and their present idea of Eurocommunism is tolerated, they may be able to influence the East European regimes toward moderation and prevent some of the extreme repressive measures witnessed in Poland and Czechoslovakia in 1976 and 1977. As long as the Eurocommunists stay within the Communist movement, it is more difficult for the hard-liners in Eastern Europe and the USSR to screen the two-way traffic of reformist impulses and ideas between Eastern and Western Europe, and to label them political heresy. As long as the Eurocommunists continue to work from within, they are able to provide not only support for the limited but gradual expansion of individual liberties in at least some East European countries, but also backing to the autonomous policies of other East European countries (Yugoslavia and Romania), as well as a measure of hope for the future democratization of socialist countries in Eastern Europe and eventually in the USSR itself.

NOTES

An earlier version of this chapter appeared in *Problems of Communism,* March–April 1978.

1. *Arbeiter Zeitung* (Vienna), July 6, 1977.
2. *El Pais* (Madrid), May 10, 1977.

3. Radio Espana Independiente (Radio Independent Spain), March 3, 1977, and Radio Paris, March 3, 1977. Both are in Foreign Broadcast Information Service, *Daily Report: Western Europe* (Washington, D.C.—hereafter FBIS-WEU), March 4, 1977.

4. Radio Munich, July 18, 1977.

5. Radio Roma, September 19, 1977, in FBIS-WEU, September 19, 1977.

6. Wolfgang Leonhard, *The Three Faces of Marxism* (New York: Holt, Reinhart & Winston, 1977), p. 300.

7. *Nuovi Argomenti* (Rome), June 19, 1956.

8. *Pravda,* July 2, 1956.

9. *L'Unita* (Rome), May 8, 1968.

10. *L'Humanite* (Paris), April 20, 1968.

11. *L'Unita,* July 14, 1977.

12. Santiago Carrillo, *"Eurocommunismo" y Estado* (Barcelona: Editorial Critica, 1977), pp. 166–67.

13. Manuel Azcarate, "Europe and Eurocommunism," *El Pais,* July 30, 1977.

14. Ibid. Also see a similar evaluation in "Nine Years from Czechoslovak Events," *L'Unita,* August 21, 1977.

15. Wlodzimierz Brus, *Sistema Politico e Proprieta Sociale nel Socialismo* (Rome: Riuniti, 1974).

16. See Bilak's speech and editorial comment, *Listy* (Rome), III, 2 (March 1972), pp. 11–14.

17. Incidentally, most of these parties supported the invasion of Czechoslovakia (Luxemburg, West Berlin, West Germany, Portugal).

18. See interviews with Biermann, *Der Spiegel* (Hamburg), November 22, 1976, p. 38, and *Le Monde,* November 21–22, 1976.

19. Carrillo, in *L'Unita,* November 1, 1976.

20. See George Urban's interview with Radice, *Encounter,* no. 5 (1977), pp. 8–22.

21. See an interview with a signatory of "Charter 77," Zdenek Mlynar, *Arbeiter Zeitung,* June 18, 1977; also an interview with Polish dissident Adam Michnik in *L'Expresso* (Rome), December 5, 1975.

22. Interview with Michnik, *L'Expresso.*

23. *Rude Pravo* (Prague), November 23, 1976.

24. *Le Monde,* April 1, 1977.

25. "Contrary to the Interests of Peace and Socialism in Europe," *New Times* (Moscow), no. 26 (June 1977), pp. 9–13.

26. *New York Times,* February 2, 1971.

27. *Rude Pravo,* April 29, 1977.

28. *Tribuna* (Prague), September 14, 1977.

12 Nationalism and Integration in Eastern Europe: The Dynamics of Change

Teresa Rakowska-Harmstone

The dynamics of political life in post-1945 Eastern Europe have been shaped by the interplay of two key sets of political forces: the presence and policies of the Soviet Union as the superpower dominant in the region, and social forces for change within East European states emergent from the national traditions and political culture of each. Among countries discussed in this book, only Yugoslavia and Albania have escaped direct Soviet tutelage—in 1948 and in 1960, respectively. But even these two countries cannot avoid the effects of Soviet influence as it radiates through the region; for the other countries, it has been, and ultimately still is, even now, a determining variable. The two sets of forces work at cross-purposes more often than they complement each other, an incongruity that has found its reflection in the region's endemic instability. In the 1960s and 1970s this instability has been augmented by the impact—within the Communist fraternity—of the dispute between the USSR and China, and, in social relations generally, by the opening up to the West, started by Nikita Khrushchev's "peaceful coexistence" policy and continued under Leonid Brezhnev's "detente."

The Soviet presence in Eastern Europe has been responsible for the establishment and maintenance of a Communist political system in each of the countries concerned,[1] and has largely determined the form, if not necessarily the substance, of each regime's policies, particularly with respect to the promotion of economic and social transformation aimed at the establishment of "socialism," and "internationalist" foreign policies. Also, it has imposed limits to change for the states within the reach of the Soviet armed might. Indigenous political forces, on the other hand, caused the initial deviations from the Soviet model, and have shaped national attitudes to the system, as well as social responses to the Communist policies and demands that confront each national regime. Outside influences encourage the deviant patterns. Western influence reinforces traditional Western elements in the political culture of most East Europeans, while the challenge to Soviet leadership and to the universality of the Soviet model within the Communist movement strengthens the drive for national self-determination of all East European parties. In the latter context Eurocommunism in particular tempts not only with a model of sovereignty but also with a promise of accommodation to political pluralism.

As Eastern Europe entered the 1970s, it seemed that the ability—and will—of the Soviet Union to enforce strict conformity were in decline, despite the 1968 intervention in Czechoslovakia. The patterns of change developed in the sixties implied further differentiation, as East European systems were responding broadly to each country's specific demands in three areas: the search for domestic legitimacy in the wake of the "loss of faith" crisis that followed de-Stalinization; the search for an economic management formula that would break through the barrier between an extensive and an intensive growth pattern; and the assertion of national *raison d'etat* in domestic and foreign policies. As I wrote in 1972:

> The resurgent nationalism and the pressures demanding the freedom to pursue one's "own thing," including political liberalization and economic rationality, all point to particularistic solutions. Moreover, and despite appearances, these tendencies operate in an increasingly favorable environment, characterized by an overall decline in Soviet influence, effectiveness, and credibility, and by the corresponding need of local elites to establish their credibility and legitimacy in local, national terms. This in the general framework of competing universalist claims of the two communist superpowers, which negate the old claim to one ultimate truth, and open new alternatives for the smaller states. . . . In addition there . . . is the change in the style of Soviet leadership, its frequent lack of resolution and consensus, and the consequent absence of the "will to act."[2]

But as the seventies unfolded and the trends toward change continued, a new countervailing force emerged in the form of a Soviet policy to consolidate the "world socialist system," namely to integrate Eastern Europe with the Soviet Union, aiming over the long range at the establishment of an organic relationship that would incorporate East Europeans into the Soviet body politic beyond the point of return. The formulation by the Soviet Union of a coherent new theory of integration (in the early seventies) does not necessarily mean that the policies implementing it will or can be successful. But it has produced a new and powerful element that stands to hinder the further emancipation of the East European states.

The dynamics of interaction between national forces for change and the new Soviet thrust for integration will shape conditions in Eastern Europe in the eighties, the effects of which will also be felt in the international arena. On the face of it, the two forces are on a collision course. The direction of East European change patterns is rooted in national self-assertion and seeks modifications in the Soviet-imposed political model that would respond better to national political cultures and developing social demands. The policy of bloc integration, on the other hand, reasserts the Soviet leading role and aims at an eventual total submergence of East European variants into the Soviet model. The room for maneuver left to East European leaders within the new blue-print remains to be tested, as does their ability successfully to negotiate national demands within it. So does the Soviet leaders' perception of a permissible mix of differentiation and conformity that would be con-gruous with their policies in Eastern Europe, in Europe in general, and in a global context.

SOVIET PRESENCE

The Soviet Union's presence in Eastern Europe is the result of the Allied victory over Nazi Germany in World War II and of the subse-quent polarization of political and military strength between the two superpowers—the USSR and the USA—which left the former domi-nant in Eastern Europe. A "secure" Eastern Europe has been a Soviet strategic target of first priority since 1943–45, dictated by the perception of the importance of the region both as a defensive buffer zone in case of another attack from the West, and as the staging area for the exten-sion of influence westward into Europe, the dual perception that has had strong roots in Russian and Soviet history. The basic asymmetry of power between the Soviet Union and the East European states, and a consistently low priority assigned to the region in Western strategic considerations, were key factors that allowed for the establishment of undisputed Soviet hegemony there.

The three initial postwar years (1945–48) served to consolidate Soviet power in the region, a task that was enormously facilitated by the Red Army's occupation of most of the area. By 1948 Communist parties were firmly in control, and Eastern Europe entered a period of enforced conformity known as the "Stalinist" period, which ended with the dictator's death in 1953. Under Stalinism, and led by the "Muscovites" within each East European party,[3] each country was transformed into a mini-copy of the Soviet system. Each was run directly by Soviet "advisers" located strategically within party, policy, and military bureaucracies. Each followed identical economic and social policies (minor variations were allowed reflecting specific conditions), and spoke with a Soviet voice in foreign policy. Each was tied to the Soviet Union by bilateral ties and was economically exploited, as, for example, in the case of the notorious joint companies. The Yugoslav party's successful resistance to these arrangements, possible only because it had an independent power base at home, resulted in that country's expulsion in 1948 from the Cominform. The expulsion, a shock to the Yugoslav Communists at the time, proved to be a blessing in disguise. It launched Yugoslavia on its "own road to socialism" that survives to this day, and released it (along with geographically isolated Albania which, nonetheless, remained faithful to Stalinism) from direct Soviet tutelage. In the captive states, the "nationalist deviation" of Tito served as an excuse to purge, in 1949–50, his alleged would-be imitators in the "native" factions of the East European parties: Traicho Kostov in Bulgaria, Laszlo Rajk in Hungary, and Wladyslaw Gomulka in Poland as well as their "accomplices." All the key victims were executed except Gomulka, who was spared because of his popularity among the Polish party's rank and file. In Czechoslovakia, Gustav Husak and Josef Smrkovsky were tried and imprisoned on charges of Slovak and Czech nationalism, respectively, Smrkovsky in 1953 and Husak in 1954. The turn of some of the "Muscovites" came with Stalin's last purges in 1951–53: Rudolf Slansky and eleven co-defendants were tried in Prague, and Ana Pauker, Vasile Luca, and Emil Bodnaras, in Bucharest. In Romania the purge paved the way for the strengthening of the "native" faction in support of Gheorge Gheorgiu-Dej even before Stalin's death. In the other parties "Muscovites" were gradually replaced when Moscow's control slackened at the time of the struggle for Stalin's succession, and in the subsequent era of Khrushchev's ascendancy.

A new phase of Soviet policy, one of relative relaxation, emerged in 1953. The sudden decompression in Eastern Europe, which accompanied the jockeying for power within the leadership of the Communist Party of the Soviet Union (CPSU) between 1953 and 1956, released the suppressed nationalist elements in Hungary and Poland. These forces erupted in 1956 in the Hungarian revolution (which attempted to remove Hungary from the Soviet orbit altogether), and in a workers' revolt in Poland that brought Gomulka back to power. Notwithstanding the armed suppression of the Hungarian revolution, Khrushchev confirmed the new autonomy gained by the East European parties in the chaotic period of succession to Stalin. Soviet "advisers" were withdrawn, and East European Communists were allowed to develop policies that would respond to their countries' needs, provided that none of the basic Soviet policies and requirements were undermined. This new Soviet emphasis on "viability"[4] resulted in the strikingly differentiated evolution of the East European states.

Far-reaching innovations were introduced. Poland de-collectivized and is now the only country within the bloc (except for Yugoslavia outside) with agriculture largely based in peasant-owned holdings. The autonomy of Poland's Roman Catholic church has been reasserted, a price the Polish United Workers' Party (PUWP) has had to pay for the episcopate's cooperation in preventing political explosions; the price has included concessions to Polish national culture, of which the church has traditionally been a guardian. Even so, another round of workers' riots—in December 1970—resulted in a change in the Polish leadership, with Gomulka replaced by Edward Gierek. Economic reforms took the form, on the one hand, of a decentralized command planning model of the New Economic System (NES) adopted in the GDR, and on the other, of a socialist market model of Hungary's New Economic Mechanism (NEM). Nationalism became enshrined in Romania's official communist orthodoxy under Nicolae Ceausescu, and in Romanian foreign policy. In Czechoslovakia, Aleksander Dubcek and his collaborators established "socialism with a human face." The latter, however, proved to be too much for the post-Khrushchev CPSU leadership of Leonid Brezhnev and Alexei Kosygin. The Czechoslovak party's permissive attitude to political pluralism and freedom of expression, and above all its claim to have found a new model to fit developed communist societies,[5] triggered another military intervention in August 1968. This time it was a collective endeavor by members of the Warsaw Treaty Organization. It also served as the background for the enunciation of the "Brezhnev doctrine" of limited sovereignty.

Thus the "relaxation" phase in Soviet policy ended in 1968; a new policy of integration began to be articulated in 1969, and it emerged as a fully developed blueprint for action in the early 1970s.[6] The policy envisages simultaneous steps toward integration in three basic areas: political, economic, and cultural. The Communist systems' party-state dichotomy is reflected in the dual character of the bloc's *political integration:* in parallel and mutually reinforcing efforts at interparty and interstate integration. The interparty integration, most important by far, if less visible, proceeds on the basis of the multiplication and institutionalization of contacts between leaders as well as between lower-level functionaries of the ruling parties, in order to coordinate policies and to synchronize technical aspects of the parties' multifaceted activities. The contacts are multilateral and bilateral, and take place at the international, national, and sub-national levels. The leaders meet formally once a year, usually in the Crimea, in addition to numerous other contacts. Functionaries meet frequently in various locations throughout the region to coordinate specific activities or campaigns; a recent example has been a blocwide campaign of political socialization. The Warsaw Treaty Organization is the instrument of political integration at the state-to-state level, particulary in military matters and in foreign policy. Formal sovereignty of member states is strongly emphasized at this level in recognition of the national sensibilities of all the states, but particularly Romania, the one openly recalcitrant member. The degree of compliance varies widely, but progress in political integration has been reflected in the synchronization, throughout the bloc, of constitutional instruments to formally enshrine the "leading role" of the Communist party in society, as well as a constitutional, or treaty, commitment to a common, Soviet-directed, foreign policy. In Poland (one of the last to comply), the action, in the form of constitutional amendments adopted in January 1976, generated political protests that forced modifications in wording to make the amendments more palatable.

CMEA is the instrument of *economic integration*, envisaging a "socialist division of labor" as well as joint planning, technological integration, and joint projects, some of them of supranational character. Objective economic forces strongly favor integration: the necessary economies of scale are feasible only on an integrated basis. Moreover, East Europeans depend heavily on imports of Soviet fuels and raw materials and on Soviet markets for their manufactured goods, the quality of which is inadequate for Western markets. Economically, Eastern Europe is increasingly a burden to the Soviet Union, but the political trade-offs involved are obviously considered to be worth the costs. At the same time some economic compensations for the Soviet Union have also been introduced, such as annual renegotiations of prices paid for Soviet products by CMEA partners, and East European investments in the development of Soviet natural resources.

Cultural integration, which envisages the development of "internationalist" and "socialist" attitudes, depends on the growth of contacts and is the least developed as well as the least likely to succeed, because it envisages basically an imposition and dissemination of Soviet (Russian) culture and cultural models regarded by most East Europeans as inferior to their own. Cultural integration is nevertheless vigorously promoted by the Soviet Union, particularly in its efforts to coordinate and dominate social science research and historiography. An attempt to "internationalize" history has been visible in more than one East European country, as has been an emphasis on the study of the Russian language. Voices from Moscow have been heard discussing future integration of the bloc's educational systems, but so far little genuine response has been noted throughout Eastern Europe. In the late seventies the emphasis has been on a coordination of work in the broad area of political socialization.

Mindful of lessons of the past, the regional integration policy that has emerged in the seventies is more subtle and more rational than either Stalin's *Gleichschaltung* or Khrushchev's integration "from above," pursued in the early sixties. It aims at a gradual long-term integration from below, that will accrue piecemeal in selected areas, and thus will not trigger East European defense mechanisms. It relies on persuasion and incentives rather than on force. The incentives are designed to operate within the considerable range of autonomy left to East European regimes but in the context—to be sure—of overwhelming Soviet political, economic, and military preponderance. A promise of economic benefits and international contacts and status secured under the Soviet umbrella balances gradual erosion of national sovereignty implied in common arrangements; the erosion is further obscured by the principles that adherence to each of the multiple types of joint endeavors is strictly voluntary. Finally, as a trend outwardly parallel to that currently pursued in Western Europe, the policy of regional integration is internationally highly respectable, particularly in its economic aspects.

The existence of an elaborate Soviet blueprint for integration of the region into the Soviet state system carries no assurance that it will or even that it can be successfully implemented. Forces of nationalism in Eastern Europe, socioeconomic pressures for democratization, particularly in the northern tier, and the prevalent Russophobia are formidable obstacles. Moreover, the East European regimes' enthusiasm for and participation in joint arrangements varies with their perception of how these would affect their countries' national interest, and progress made towards real integration has been minimal. Nevertheless, the policy is a good indicator of the current and future thrust of Soviet policy. Economic pressures for integration and their long-range impact should not be underestimated. Neither should the quality of relentless pressure generated by the "senior partner" in conditions of basic asymmetry of power in the region, especially if one keeps in mind that Soviet support is the ultimate guarantor of the survival of most, if not all, East European Communist regimes.

DOMESTIC PATTERNS

The Soviet presence guarantees the survival of Communist systems in the bloc countries (the two independent Communist states, Yugoslavia and Albania, also benefit here indirectly), but the guarantee is a liability in most parties' relations with their own societies, because with few exceptions the Russians have traditionally been hated and communism distrusted through the region. Consequently, in the seventies, as much as in the sixties, each party has been preoccupied with efforts to generate legitimacy of its own based on a national consensus. In doing so, the East European parties have had to acknowledge and to make an attempt to respond to three basic types of pressures that have been in the forefront of social demands in their societies: the pressure for national sovereignty; the pressure for political democratization and pluralism; and the pressure for an improvement in the standards of living.

But, given the international situation and the characteristics of Communist political systems, none of these demands can actually be met. Soviet power and Soviet pretensions to regional and global leadership preclude genuine sovereignty for any state within the bloc, and place enormous pressure on the two mavericks—Yugoslavia and Albania, the first of which also faces critical ethnic nationalism at home. Leninist characteristics of Communist political systems (inclusive of Yugoslavia and Albania)—the monopoly of power appropriated by each Communist party on the strength of its ideologically legitimated role as the vanguard of the working class and exercised on the operational principle of democratic centralism—are incompatible with either pluralism or democratization. The command planning system, typical of Leninist systems, is highly dysfunctional to the development of the technological-intensive stage of economic growth that is required for a meaningful improvement in the living standards.

Within these limits, nevertheless, some dialogue at least has developed between Communist regimes and their societies, to find accommodation in one or more areas of these demands. Patterns of change and adaptation have taken different forms depending on each country's political culture, its level of development, the abilities and perceptions of its leaders, and the magnitude of outside stimuli. Superficially, it has been easy to accommodate nationalism in most countries, and economic experimentation has taken place, if not always effectively. Concessions in the political sphere have proven to be the most difficult, however, because of the threat that pluralism carries to the systems' survival.

Historically Russophobia affected most of the East Europeans, with the exception of the Bulgarians, the Yugoslavs (mainly Serbs), and the Czechs. The Soviets' entry into the region and their subsequent behavior in 1948, 1956, and 1968 only served to aggravate anti-Russian hatreds and lost them the few friends they had had. Also, only a few states in East-Central Europe between the wars had strong indigenous Communist movements and, as is well remembered throughout the region, the postwar Communist systems there were imposed from the outside, with Yugoslavia and Albania as the two exceptions. (Czechoslovakia was a partial exception, since the Czechoslovak Communist party gained 38 percent of the popular vote in the free elections of 1946, thus emerging as the major party. The full Communist takeover in Czechoslovakia came with the coup of 1948.) For all of these reasons it has been imperative for East European Communist regimes to "nationalize" themselves as much as possible, a policy that became not only possible but also indicated when "native" factions came into power; nationalism has grown to be progressively more important for regime maintenance with the passage of time.

Appeals to national traditions and invocations of national interest find an immediate response among the populace as much as among the parties' rank and file, and nationalism affects not a few of the leaders despite their avowed loyalty to "internationalism." In ethnically homogenous states such as Poland, Hungary, or Albania, or in the states with small but troublesome national minorities such as Romania, nationalism has been vital in generating popular support for foreign and domestic policies. The value of national symbols is readily recognized: the royal palace in Warsaw, virtually destroyed during World War II, was reconstructed, and the return of the Crown of St. Stephen to Budapest by the United States in 1978 was accorded all the pomp and circumstance deemed essential for a national treasure. National symbols are also important in multi-ethnic societies, such as Yugoslavia or Czechoslovakia, as signs of national unity, but particular ethnic nationalism there (as in the Soviet Union), has been a major stumbling block on the road to national integration: it has been a destabilizing political force and a vehicle for decentralization, inclusive of separatism, for example on the part of the Croats and the Slovaks.

The image of an outside "enemy"—basically the Soviet Union in the local context, although a traditionally hostile neighbor also serves—has been particularly functional to the cause of national unity, as in the case of Yugoslavia. But for the bloc parties the stress on nationalism carries an ever-present danger of bringing to the surface latent anti-Russian feelings. A policy or a statement that implies "standing-off" to the Russians carries an immediate pay-off in popular approval, although very few East European leaders have felt secure enough openly to pull the bears' whiskers; Romania's Ceausescu has been an outstanding exception. The Romanian party has openly legitimized its rule in nationalism, a decision that has been reflected in unique (within the bloc), ideological formulae (national communism as a supreme value as well as the denial of the leading role to the CPSU), in an independent foreign policy, and in assimilationist policies towards national minorities. The GDR is a special case, because it represents only a part of the German nation; the SED therefore found it both difficult and frustrating to manipulate nationalist symbols. In the seventies the stress has been on the emergence of a socialist German nation, as an entity distinct from and superior to the bourgeois German nation represented by the Federal Republic of Germany; the future of the GDR is "indissolubly" connected with that of the other socialist nations.

Invocations to national unity have frequently and not incidentally tapped sources of national chauvinism and have emphasized intolerant and undemocratic features of traditional nationalism. This trend is superbly summarized by a Polish dissident writer; his emphasis on an "outside" approval for the revival of this type of nationalism and, obliquely, on the dangers of being swallowed up by Russia are worth noting:

> Nation, fatherland, patriotism are the words uttered frequently and willingly in the press and on television. Today in Poland the needs of national consciousness are satisfied mostly by visual methods. Films are made of the Piast [the first Polish dynasty, 8th-14th century] period, or else the novels of Sienkiewicz [famous 19th century patriotic writer] are remade for the screen. For three hours a viewer can watch a Polish hero wearing a breastplate bearing the image of the Virgin Mary and bearing a sword whom neither the Tatars nor the Swedes can conquer. He is thus confirmed in his "Polishness" and is strengthened by historical traditions. After leaving the theater he may read a review of the movie that will further perk up his self-esteem: a review permeated by the Old Polish spirit, sentimentally patriotic. But a viewer will not find in any newspaper a review that would tell him that

there is no contemporary patriotism without a consciousness of human rights, and that freedom of the nation depends on the realization of these rights. The show has been successful. Sons of workers, peasants, and working intelligentsia sit in rows gaping at a shadow—in sound and color—of a mounted knight, wearing a breastplate. Really, this is weird. Especially if one considers when and where the spectacle is taking place: in Poland, thirty years after the reform camp took over. . . . For a foreigner it is too complex to comprehend new conditions and manipulations as a result of which the filming of the defense of Czestochowa [a 17th-century siege by Swedes of a cloister] has become a patriotic alibi for the power structure. . . . What bothers me most is that today in Poland *sarmatyzm* [the nobility's code of martial virtues] has been licenced, that it is obviously needed by someone, for some reasons, and that *it has been approved from outside.* It is not only the sword and the breastplate, but also the new military paraphernalia: September (1939) battles, helmets of the revolts, and forest camps . . . and anti-Semitism. Sometimes I am very much afraid that very soon all of this would become a *Polish folklore,* an equivalent of a *lezginka* [Caucasian dance]: and our virile nationalists will catch on too late and without batting an eyelash, when they, and the rest of us, will be swallowed up together with all this folklore; then our traditions of national struggle will be good-naturedly tolerated, as was the coat of the nobility [*kontusz*] in royal-imperial Galicia, or as the Cherkess ensembles are now tolerated in Russia. Because possibly all of this has been agreed upon, and somewhere some bureaucratic heads have known for a long time that it will be necessary to include in the accounts also this small, *internal,* nationalism, one more to be added.[7]

The uses of nationalism for a Communist regime and its manipulative value emerge from the quotation, illuminating one side of the issue. What does not emerge is that the strength of nationalist feelings makes them difficult to manipulate. There is more to the nationalism of East European Communist elites than just cynicism and subservience to Moscow. East European national communism—pioneered by the Yugoslavs—has contributed to polycentrism in the past and to Eurocommunism now. In bloc relations it has been a major force behind the post-Stalinist autonomization and a source of conflict between bloc members; it poses constant challenge to the Soviet leadership and a major roadblock to integration. One dimension of nationalism, however, remains unexplored: would Communist elites continue to espouse the nationalist cause if by doing so they created a threat to their survival as the ruling group?

Pressures for democratization and pluralism are generated as much by elements of traditional political culture as they are stimulated by economic development and modernization. The latter inevitably results in a higher degree of social politicization, and the demands for political participation increase in proportion to improvements in economic standards and in access to social services. It appears, however, that the intensity of political demands is directly related to the type of political culture: the more authoritarian it is, the fewer demands there are for basic political changes and the easier it is to accommodate the pressures under the party's umbrella. But if democratic or anti-authoritarian elements exist in a political culture, they reinforce the impetus towards democratization fostered by modernization to form an explosive political mix. It is no accident therefore that growing social pluralism has been more readily controlled by the party in the countries where the political culture is more congruous with the system, as in the case of the GDR, Romania, or Bulgaria, and that pressures for democratization have repeatedly led to explosive political situations in the countries with political cultures incompatible with Leninism, as in the case of Czech democratic traditions or the Polish and Hungarian individualistic and aristocratic political heritage.[8]

As pointed out above, the leading role of the party (i.e., the party's monopoly of power, which cannot be shared with other social groups) creates an insurmountable obstacle to democratization. Inevitable corollaries of the leading role of the party, i.e., its monopoly to aggregate social interests as well as to assign social priorities, are the denial of the very existence of social conflict and sub-system autonomy, and consequently the absence of any machinery for conflict resolution; the application of the principle of democratic centralism to the total range of social relations; and the maintenance of the monopoly of communications. None of the ruling elites has been able to compromise on the party's leadership principle (and that includes the League of Communists of Yugoslavia) because of their need to retain power. The range of accommodations, however, has been very broad—the most far-reaching changes took place in Yugoslavia, where additional constraints imposed by the CPSU's vigilance have not been enforceable.

The key question of how to deal with the problem of interest articulation and conflict resolution has been in the forefront of the attention of the party elites as well as of the revisionists; the spectrum of approaches to the problem on the basis of Marxist-Leninist positions has ranged from neo-Stalinism, through the "reactionary left," "Marxist-humanism" (a moral stance), and "socialist pluralism," to "efficient authoritarianism."[9] In practice the latter model has been preferred, and a range of techniques have been developed to substitute for institutionalized pluralism, all of them under the party umbrella: bureaucratization of major interests ("institutional" pressure groups); partial transformation of the "transmission belts" (party-directed social organizations such as the trade unions) into interest articulators but not quite into Western-type "associational" groups (in Yugoslavia and to a limited extent also in Hungary); the technique of cooptation and consultation of professional and technical elites (pioneered in the GDR but adopted throughout the bloc), and party-run mass "participation" techniques, practiced by all.

The two most centralized systems, Romania and Bulgaria, have made the least accommodation to social interests; the GDR has successfully practiced bureaucratization, cooptation, and participation techniques; the Hungarian variant, which also included limited transformation of transmission belts into interest-access channels, is the most far-reaching in the bloc, and has also been the most successful. In the devolution of power, however, it lags far behind the Yugoslav experiment in self-management and decentralization. The Czechoslovak venture into socialist pluralism was cut short by Soviet intervention, and Czechoslovakia has returned to the ranks of neo-Stalinists. In Poland, all the orthodox techniques have been tried but none of them work, and a stand-off conflict between the regime and society has come out into the open in the mid-seventies.

In general, there are four major variants in the practical approach to the articulation of social interests:

1. Interest articulation is allowed only within the party through bureaucratization and cooptation; this approach has been pioneered by the GDR and is utilized by most of the others;

2. Interest articulation is permitted within a somewhat broader circle of social organizations; this has meant some, but not substantial, diminution in the scope of the party's leading role (Hungary);

3. Interest articulation is permitted within a wide spectrum of social organizations; this has resulted in a substantial erosion in the exercise by the party of its leading role (Yugoslavia and "Prague Spring" Czechoslovakia);

4. Interest articulation emerges totally outside institutional channels and is not controlled by the party. This has taken the form of spontaneous riots and unrest ("anomic" pressure groups," e.g., GDR, 1953; Poland, 1956, 1968, 1970 and 1976; Hungary 1956; Romania's workers' strike, 1978), and of organized opposition groups, existing illegally outside the system, that have emerged in Poland in the aftermath of the 1976 summer riots. These groups are a unique phenomenon in Communist systems. They operate openly, basing themselves on a countrywide network, inclusive of regular publications. While the extent of their

mass support cannot be determined, it is obviously sufficient to prevent suppression by the authorities, for fear of a popular explosion. The groups are therefore tolerated, although individual leaders are periodically harassed by the police.

Because of the basic incompatibility between the Leninist political system and political pluralism there are no prospects for democratization going beyond the current Hungarian model within the bloc (to wit, the experience of Czechoslovakia), or beyond the Yugoslav model outside the bloc. Whether or not any of the "Eurocommunist" parties eventually comes up with a viable solution to the contradiction remains to be seen. Experience so far indicates that it is doubtful, as long as the parties maintain their Leninist characteristics.

Attempts at economic reform—to keep up a high rate of growth and to satisfy consumerism—have produced two variants: a market-type reform with indicative rather than command planning and decentralized economic management (Yugoslavia, Czechoslovakia prior to 1968, and in a more modest version, Hungary); and a decentralized command planning system, pioneered by the GDR. The latter variant is preferred by the Soviet Union for the bloc, but it has failed, by and large, to deal with the problems of transition from an extensive to an intensive growth pattern. In early 1978 there were signs that most East European regimes were embarking on a new round of economic reforms; and there were some indications that the effectiveness of the Hungarian variant may have made that pattern more acceptable to the others.[10]

The Soviet party has been the most cautious and the least pressed to provide channels for interest articulation, and the Soviet perception still enforces the limits for the East Europeans. For the CPSU the acceptability of innovations is directly proportionate to the perception of the threat of "infection" they carry, thus the minimization of the probable impact of any innovation affecting the party's leading role is in the interest of the innovators.[11] The techniques used by the Soviet Union to deal with various types of innovations range from direct suppression to assimilation. In cases when, for whatever reason, suppression appears to be inconvenient or infeasible, an isolation technique has been used—a given phenomenon is judged to be a peculiarity of a given country, and is allowed to continue, provided it will not spread to "fraternal countries." An example has been the tolerance of the position of the church and the aberrant agricultural pattern—as well as the current open opposition—in Poland; also the tolerance of Romanian shenanigans in foreign policy, and of the Hungarian market-type New Economic Mechanism.

INTERNATIONAL PATTERNS AND
IMPLICATIONS

The Soviet presence in Eastern Europe has always been officially justified in terms of defense and security requirements. The memory of the World War II German invasion helped to create an image of a revanchist Bonn in league with American "imperialists" within NATO, nurturing aggressive designs. Initially, the image served well to cement common Soviet and East European foreign policy, but it began to wear out over time; by the late seventies the defensive justification for the Soviet presence in Eastern Europe was no longer credibly tenable. The West's repeated hands-off attitude there has meant the recognition that the region belongs in the Soviet sphere of influence; moreover, the Soviet Union's nuclear parity with the United States has effectively precluded any such interference. At the same time, the new German *Ostpolitik* signaled the acceptance by the Federal Republic of Germany of the postwar territorial settlement, the validity of which has been legitimized further by all the European states, the United States, and Canada at the 1975 Helsinki Conference on Security and Cooperation in Europe. The danger of an invasion from the West has never been more remote. Nevertheless there has been no parallel Soviet disengagement in Eastern Europe. On the contrary, the seventies have seen both a major build-up of conventional military power by the Warsaw Treaty Organization (far in excess of NATO's conventional capabilities as well as of "policeing" needs in the bloc) and the launching of a new effort at integration between Eastern Europe and the Soviet Union. Logic suggests that it is the region's *offensive* value that may now be of greater importance. The two aspects of Soviet–East European policy in the seventies—the massive build-up of conventional military strength and the emphasis on integration—would seem to combine at the basis of a new European and global "outreach": a quest by the Soviet Union for strategic, political, economic, and last but not least, "ecumenical" influence as the leader of the world "progressive forces." In other words one interpretation may be that the strategy has shifted, from securing the region for its own value, to transforming it into a staging area for further expansion, with East Europeans playing a role of junior partners in the endeavor.

The Soviet shadow looms large in Western Europe and in the Balkans, as anyone can testify who has counted the comparative strength of the WTO and NATO divisions and hardware, and who has tried to escape Radio Moscow signals on European airwaves. Increasingly,

Western observers point to a growing vulnerability of West European states, particularly those of peripheral importance in the NATO system, and to Soviet pressures that fall short of open threats but that impose constraints on the pursuit of policies displeasing to the Soviet Union.[12] A none-too-subtle glimpse of Soviet military capabilities on terrain resembling their own was conveyed to representatives of Greece, Turkey, and Yugoslavia invited to Soviet military exercises in the Caucasus (Operation Kavkaz), and to Scandinavians in a similar invitation to exercises on the Finnish border (Operation Sever). Speculation as to whether or not the Soviet Union will advance into Yugoslavia after President Tito's death—to bring back the prodigal son as well as to gain direct access to the Adriatic—feeds daily European rumor mills. By all indications the military strengthening of WTO forces is designed to provide the build-up for a strategy of political blackmail rather than for direct military action. And it has already created preconditions for a "Finlandization" of Western Europe, should the United States withdraw its strategic umbrella, for whatever reasons.

A strategy of economic integration of socialist states within the CMEA system is generally assumed to be incompatible with their developing strong bilateral economic ties with the West, an assumption that has provided some of the impetus in the West for the development of trade with the socialist countries. Although a multiplication of East-West trade exchanges carries the potential for a differentiation in the bloc's pattern of trade, there are also aspects of these exchanges that actually facilitate the bloc's integration.[13] Western technology transfer can be applied most efficiently on an integrated basis, taking advantage of economies of scale, and thus it promotes the "socialist division of labor"; also trade flows can be coordinated (as joint planning develops), fostering the same aim. The greater the success of the East Europeans in developing economic reciprocity with the West, the less of an economic burden they are to the Soviet Union without any significant decline in their ties to the bloc. But, if their vulnerability to Western price fluctuations, combined with high indebtedness to the West, results in a crisis (as in the case of Poland), the regime's dependence on Soviet support—economic and political—increases, thus blending it even more closely into the Communist state system.

Economic contacts are a channel for the penetration into Eastern Europe of unwelcome Western ideas, but they also facilitate transmission of "socialist" models westward. The East Europeans' old ties with Western Europe, and the image they project of "straining at the leash" of Soviet dependence, make them preferred partners for West Europeans and far more sympathetic and believable than the dour and "primitive" Russians—an ideal "Trojan horse" from the Soviet point of view. Overall, vigorous East-West commercial exchanges, particularly when combined with Western credits and other such initiatives as joint projects, tend to promote interdependence between the economies of socialist and capitalist Europe, opening up new avenues of political influence. In a "mirror image" perception, the Soviet leaders see the process as a means for extending "socialist" influence westward, just as Western politicians view the development of economic relations as an opportunity for the transmission of Western ideas eastward. The Soviet conviction, rooted in Marxist-Leninist ideology, that history marches towards "socialism" makes such a risk of Western "infection" supportable. The Soviet Union also seeks a regional dialogue between CMEA and the EEC.[14] If successfully developed, cooperation between the two regional organizations would not only promote interdependence but would also further enhance the socialist bloc's cohesion and the Soviet leading role within it.

In the seventies CMEA's economic role has also acquired new dimensions in promoting relations with Third World countries, a significant if little noted development. The 1971 Comprehensive Program included a stipulation, directed specifically at the less-developed countries (LDCs), that nonmembers could join the organization, offering participation in the "international division of labor" as a new avenue to economic development (inclusive of scientific and technological cooperation, credits, and preferential status). A change in the CMEA charter in 1974 gave it a legal authority to enter international agreements as an organization. Thus CMEA may now conclude agreements with nonmembers (individual states or international organizations), enabling them to participate in the organization's economic system.

Among full members of CMEA[15] three are non-European: Mongolia, which joined in 1962; Cuba, which joined in 1972; and Vietnam, which joined in 1978. All are Communist states. Because of their geographic remoteness, however, they are outside the mainstream of CMEA activities; their main link with the organization is their dependence on and support by the Soviet Union.[16] Yugoslavia, North Korea, Laos, and Angola have observer status. Yugoslavia was the first (1965) and was reported to have participated in the work of 20 CMEA bodies in 1976. Nonsocialist countries that have special cooperation agreements with CMEA are Finland (since 1973) and Iraq and Mexico (since 1975). Colombia and Guyana applied to sign similar agreements, and interest was expressed by others, including Afghanistan, Argentina, India, Iran, Jamaica, and the Republic of Yemen.

Economic partnership between CMEA members and the LDCs offers apparent advantages to both sides: it involves barter trade based in bilateral (or multilateral) clearing arrangements, guaranteeing market, supply, and price for a specific period of time (mostly one year). It assures a market and a supply of manufactured goods for the LDCs. For CMEA members, it provides an outlet for products that are nonmarketable in the West because of poor quality. Neither side has to use scarce hard currency. The arrangements are advertised by CMEA members as a developmental alternative to the dependence on capitalist countries and are therefore attractive to the LDCs, economically and ideologically. Some contracts, and in growing numbers, have stipulated payments in convertible currencies, however; moreover, CMEA members have shown consistent surpluses in their trade with the LDCs so far, thus rendering the image of economic advantage to the latter somewhat problematical. For the Soviet Union economic transactions under the CMEA label facilitate also a "political outreach," by developing long-range economic dependency ties with specific groups of developing countries. It should be noted that most Third World countries that have been attracted to a partnership with CMEA consider themselves to be socialist. Some, such as Vietnam and Angola, already had strong political and economic dependency ties with the Soviet Union and/or Cuba.[17]

Eastern Europe has also been vitally important to the Soviet Union in political-ideological terms. The existence of a cluster of "socialist" states where Soviet hegemony is acknowledged validates the CPSU's claim to the universality of its model as *the* model for a future socialist world, in the face of competing Chinese claims and models of "national roads to socialism" developed by other autonomist parties. In Vernon Aspaturian's phrase, socialist Eastern Europe serves as a "fig leaf of communist internationalism"[18] for the Soviet Union, and is therefore indispensable for the exercise of its "ecumenical" role. In the Soviet interpretation the "world socialist system" (the WTO-CMEA complex led by the Soviet Union) constitutes the leading element of the three contemporary "world progressive forces"; the other two are the "international workers' movement" and the "national liberation movement." All three are seen as evolving towards world socialism, the world's ultimate fulfillment and destiny.

Currently it seems that the international role assigned to the East Europeans under the new policy will virtually insure for them a degree of flexibility in dealing with internal problems, notwithstanding the simultaneous emphasis on greater bloc cohesion. If the trends continue, a success in the extension of Soviet influence beyond the bloc may carry a price tag of still greater autonomization in intrabloc relations. In the final analysis it is doubtful, however, that the CPSU will ever willingly give up its claim to a hegemonial position within the bloc, or the movement, or its identification of the Soviet state's *raison d'etat* with the goals of world revolution. In the general context of Moscow's foreign policy the obvious liabilities that the control of Eastern Europe implies for the Soviet Union—endemic political instability and the "infection" value for domestic Soviet politics as well as the economic burden—appear to be outweighed by the advantages derived from integrating the region into the Soviet international system.

NOTES

1. Within a broader context this applies also to Yugoslavia and Albania. Soviet support for the development of the Partisan movement there was of significant, if not decisive, importance.

2. Teresa Rakowska-Harmstone, "Patterns of Political Change," in Adam Bromke and Teresa Rakowska-Harmstone, eds., *The Communist States in Disarray: 1965–1971* (Minneapolis: University of Minnesota Press, 1972), p. 346.

3. The leadership of each party was generally divided into three factions: the "Muscovites" (who spent the war years in Russia and frequently were long-term functionaries of the Comintern); the "natives" (who spent the war years in their own countries and participated in anti-German resistance movements), and "foreigners" (who spent the war years in the West).

4. J. F. Brown refers to the "Stalinist" period as the period of "cohesion," and to 1953–68 as the period of "viability." See "The Interaction Between Party and Society in Hungary and Bulgaria,"· A. C. Janos, ed., *Authoritarian Politics in Communist Europe* (Berkeley: Institute of International Studies and University of California Press, 1976), pp. 109–114.

5. For an analysis of the "rules of the game" that apply here, see Zvi Y. Gitelman, *The Diffusion of Political Innovation from Eastern Europe to the Soviet Union* (Beverly Hills and London: Sage Publications, 1972).

6. For a discussion of the Soviet theory behind the integration policy see Teresa Rakowska-Harmstone, " 'Socialist Internationalism' and Eastern Europe —A New Stage," *Survey*, no. 1 (98), winter 1976.

7. Kazimierz Brandys, "Nierzeczywistosc (fragmenty)" [Unreality—fragments], *ZAPIS I* (London: Index on Censorship, first Polish edition, January 1977), pp. 33–34. Translation and bracketed explanations are by this author. Italics are in the original.

8. For the development of these themes, see Teresa Rakowska-Harmstone, "Aspects of Political Change," Teresa Rakowska-Harmstone, ed., *Perspectives for Change in Communist Societies* (Boulder: Westview Press, 1978).

9. For a discussion of these concepts, see Zvi Y. Gitelman, *Beyond Leninism: Political Development in Eastern Europe* (Pittsburgh University Center for International Studies. University of Pittsburgh October 1971), pp. 23–28.

10. In early 1978 there was a vigorous discussion of impending economic reforms in Poland and in Hungary (reported by oral contacts); see also the *Manchester Guardian Weekly,* March 5, 1978 (Lucbert in *Le Monde* on Czechoslovakia); and *The Washington Post,* April 19, 1978 (report on Romania).

11. For further discussion, see Gitelman, *The Diffusion of Political Innovation.*

12. See Walter Laqueur, "Perils of Detente," *The New York Times Magazine,* February 27, 1977.

13. See Carl H. McMillan, "Some Thoughts on the Relationship Between Regional Integration in Eastern Europe and East-West Economic Relations," to be published in F. Levcik, ed., *Internationale Wirtschaft: Vergleich und Inderdependenz,* Festschrift fur Franz Nemschak (Vienna).

14. J. Pinder, "Community and Comecon: What Could Negotiations Achieve?" *World Today,* 33, 5 (1977), 176–188.

15. China was originally an observer, but withdrew after the break with the Soviet Union. Albania, one of the founding members, has been inactive since 1961.

16. Cuba's trade with the Soviet Union is heavily subsidized: both of its key export commodities, sugar and nickel, are purchased by the Soviet Union at prices above world prices; oil is sold to Cuba in transferable rubles. The Cubans political "proxy" role in Africa appears to provide the necessary *quid pro quo.* Cuba's membership in CMEA has also been an asset in making the organization attractive to other Latin American countries.

17. For research in the section on CMEA relations with the Third World, I am indebted to Mr. Stephen Millar, of the Institute of Soviet and East European Studies, Carleton University.

18. Vernon V. Aspaturian, "The Political-Ideological Aspects," Charles Gati, ed., *International Politics of Eastern Europe* (New York: Praeger Publishers, 1976), p. 22.

CONTRIBUTORS

VERNON V. ASPATURIAN is Evan Pugh Professor of Political Science and Director of the Slavic and Soviet Area Studies Center at Pennsylvania State University. He is the author of *Process and Power in Soviet Foreign Policy, The Soviet Union in the World Communist System, The Union Republics in Soviet Diplomacy,* and coauthor of *Foreign Policy in World Politics* and *Modern Political Systems: Europe.*

ANDREW GYORGY is Professor of International Affairs and Political Science at the Institute for Sino-Soviet Studies of George Washington University. He has written and edited several books, most recently *Nationalism in Eastern Europe* and (with Peter Toma and Robert Jordan) *Basic Issues in International Relations,* and has contributed to scholarly books and periodicals.

ARTHUR M. HANHARDT, Jr. is Professor of Political Science at the University of Oregon and the author of several book-length studies on the politics of the German Democratic Republic. He is also the coauthor of several volumes dealing with East European politics.

TERESA RAKOWSKA-HARMSTONE is Professor of Political Science at Carleton University, Ottawa, Canada. She is the author of several volumes dealing with Soviet nationalities, Soviet politics, and the governments of Eastern Europe. She is coeditor of *The Communist States in Disarray* and editor as well as coauthor of *Perspectives of Change in Eastern Europe.*

ROBERT R. KING is a White House Fellow currently assigned to the National Security Council of the U.S. government, while on leave from Radio Free Europe in Munich. He is the author of a major study dealing with minority problems in the Balkans and of numerous articles focusing on Bulgarian and Romanian politics.

ANDRZEJ KORBONSKI is Professor of Political Science at the University of California at Los Angeles. He is the author of *The Politics of Socialist Agriculture in Poland, 1945–1960,* and has written on various aspects of East European politics and economics, problems of East European integration, and East-West trade for scholarly books and periodicals.

BENNETT KOVRIG is Professor of Political Economy at the University of Toronto, the author of several books dealing with Hungarian politics and of *The Myth of Liberation: East-Central Europe in U.S. Diplomacy and Politics since 1941.*

PAUL MARER is Associate Professor of International Business and Director of the East Europe Program of the International Development Institute at Indiana University. A specialist on Soviet, Eastern European, and East-West trade, his publications include *Soviet and East European Foreign Trade, 1946–1969: Statistical Compendium and Guide; Postwar Pricing and Price Patterns in Socialist Foreign Trade;* and *US Financing of East-West Trade.*

NICHOLAS C. PANO is Professor of History at Western Illinois University. He is the author of several studies on Albania and has specialized in articles and essays dealing with various aspects of Albanian politics.

ROBIN ALISON REMINGTON is Associate Professor of Political Science at the University of Missouri and a research affiliate of the Massachusetts Institute of Technology Center for International Studies. Her publications include *Winter in Prague: Documents on Czechoslovak Communism in Crisis* and *The Warsaw Pact: Case Studies in Communist Conflict Resolution.*

OTTO ULC is Professor of Political Science at the State University of New York at Binghamton, the author of *The Politics of Czechoslovakia* and of several publications dealing with legal and political problems in Eastern Europe, particularly with Czechoslovakia.

JIRI VALENTA is Assistant Professor of Political Science at the U.S. Naval Postgraduate School in Monterey, California, where he serves also as Coordinator of Soviet and East European studies. He is the author of a forthcoming book on the 1968 events in Czechoslovakia and has contributed articles to learned journals on Eurocommunism, Angolan politics, and Eastern Europe with special emphasis on his native Czechoslovakia.

Index

Shehu, Mehmet, 202, 204, 211
Siberia, 94, 115
Silesia, 4, 8, 43, 61
Siniavsky, Andrei, 294
Siroky, Viliam, 106, 111
Sistema Politico e Proprieta Sociale nel Socialismo, 297
Skanderbeg, 189
Slansky, Rudolf, 103, 105, 111, 151, 311
Slavs, 2, 4, 91, 185, 189
Slovakia, 8, 74, 99; and Czechoslovakia, 104, 106, 107, 111–113, 116, 118–119
Slovaks, 1, 6, 7, 214, 311, 317
Slovenes, 1, 17, 214–215, 228, 232, 240
Slovenia, 221, 223, 258
Smrkovsky, Josef, 117, 297, 311
Sofia, 171, 182, 184, 186
Solzhenitsyn, Aleksandr, 298
Soviet Military Administration in Germany (SMAD), 124–127, 136
Spahiu, Bedri, 194
Spain, 291
Spanish Civil War, 291
Spanish Communist Party (PCE), 290, 293–296, 298, 301, 303
Stalin, Joseph, 129, 151, 153, 173, 292, 311; and Bulgaria, 172; and Czechoslovakia, 100–101, 105; and Eastern Europe, 7, 9–10, 248, 261, 282, 314; and Hungary, 75–77; and Yugoslavia, 217
Stalinism, 67, 72, 151, 292, 319; in Albania, 189, 195, 201, 244; in Bulgaria, 171, 175; in Czechoslovakia, 103–104, 112, 119; in Eastern Europe, 11, 310–311; in Poland, 48, 50–51, 57, 61, 62; in Romania, 150, 153
Stalinization, 40–41, 46–47. *See also* De-Stalinization
State and Revolution, 218
St. Stephen, 95
Stoica, Chivu, 158
Sublime Porte, 169
Sudeten crisis, 2, 7, 101
Svoboda, Ludvik, 114
Sweden, 222, 293
Szalasi, Ferenc, 72
Szeklers, 2

Tetovo, 233
Third World, 95, 231, 238; and CMEA, 324, 325; and Eastern Europe, 2, 16, 17, 20, 27–29, 260, 277, 286, 287, 303
Thorez, Maurice, 293
Thrace, 4
Tildy, Zoltan, 74
Tirana, 190, 193–195, 202, 208
Tito, Josip Broz, 41, 204, 213, 234–239, 292; and Hungary, 78–79; leadership of, 216–218, 223, 226–227; post-Tito, 165,

182, 210, 225, 231, 323; Titoism, 15–16; and USSR, 76, 173, 311
Todorov, Stanko, 179–180
Togliatti, Palmiro, 292–293
Toscs, 1
Trade Act of 1974, 276
Transylvania, 7, 8, 74, 94, 147, 152
Treaty of Trianon, 6, 72
Trieste, 217
Tripalo, Miko, 222, 227–228, 234
Truman Administration, 10
Tsankov, Georgi, 175
Tsolov, Tano, 179–180
Turkey, 2, 4, 7, 31, 146, 168; and Albania, 189; and Bulgaria, 169, 246; and Serbia, 233; and USSR, 323; and Yugoslavia, 214–216

Ukraine, 158, 294
Ukrainians, 1, 146
Ulbricht, Walter, 123–124, 128–137, 139, 142, 294
Uniate Catholics, 1, 4
Union of Soviet Socialist Republics (USSR), 249, 278, 290; and Albania, 34, 189–190, 193–195, 204, 207–210, 261; and Czechoslovakia, 41, 49, 100–119, 316; and GDR, 121–131, 133–137, 139–142; and Eastern Europe, 2–4, 7–17, 20–28, 31–35, 244–248, 261–275, 287, 308–326; and Eurocommunism, 290–306; and Hungary, 72–75, 81, 85, 91–96; and Poland, 39–40, 44, 49–50, 62, 64–68; and Romania, 145–151, 153, 161–166; and West, 277, 279, 281; and Yugoslavia, 216–220, 222, 224, 225, 228, 238–239, 249. *See also* Communist Party of the Soviet Union; Stalin; Khrushchev; Brezhnev
Unita, L', 300
United Nations (UN), 2, 70, 122; and Eastern Europe, 3–4, 11–12; Security Council, 4, 237
United States of America (USA), 44, 111, 170, 248, 276; and Albania, 193, 194, 208–210; and Eastern Europe, 6, 8–10, 17, 22, 34; and GDR, 122, 139, 142; and Hungary, 74, 92, 95, 316; and NATO, 168, 322–323; and Romania, 149, 164; and USSR, 13, 33, 310; and Yugoslavia, 238

Vaculik, Ludvik, 107, 117
Vas, Zoltan, 73
Vatican, 58, 91
Vienna, 72, 74, 92, 94
Vietnam, 12, 15, 35, 210, 324–325
Vishinsky, Andrei, 148

091970